"Several years in the making through a Working Group of the Society of Christian Ethics, this rich and innovative volume is the first major scholarly contribution to the emerging field of Asian American Christian ethics. Grace Y. Kao and Ilsup Ahn's work helps define a field of thought and will be the benchmark for future contributions to Asian American Christian ethics. I highly recommend this volume for anyone interested in cutting-edge work in ethics."

—**William Schweiker**, *The University of Chicago, President of the Society of Christian Ethics*

"This book has deeply informed and challenged my thinking. Kao and Ahn invite us on a crucial exploration of the development and application of a new subfield called Asian American Christian ethics. No one who claims to be interested in the field of ethics can ever consider themselves fully informed if they fail to interact with this first, and hopefully not last, major contribution to the academic discourse from the Asian American experience relegated to the margins."

—**Miguel A. De La Torre**, *Professor of Social Ethics and Latino/a Studies, Iliff School of Theology*

"This significant work is sure to transform the field of Christian ethics. *Asian American Christian Ethics* challenges us to think theologically, to think ethically, and to delve into the very conditions of our existence with one another in order to understand the past, present, and future that is still to come. This volume is a must for students and scholars who want to know what happens when Christian ethics and Asian American critique intersect."

—**Wonhee Anne Joh**, *Associate Professor of Systematic Theology, Garrett-Evangelical Theological Seminary*

D1431338

Asian American Christian Ethics

Asian American Christian Ethics
Voices, Methods, Issues

GRACE Y. KAO
ILSUP AHN
Editors

BAYLOR UNIVERSITY PRESS

© 2015 by Baylor University Press
Waco, Texas 76798

All Rights Reserved. No part of this publication may be reproduced, stored in a retrieval system, or transmitted, in any form or by any means, electronic, mechanical,
photocopying, recording or otherwise, without the prior permission in writing of
Baylor University Press.

Unless otherwise stated, scripture quotations are from the New Revised Standard
Version Bible, copyright 1989, Division of Christian Education of the National
Council of the Churches of Christ in the United States of America. Used by
permission. All rights reserved.

Cover Design by AJB Design, Inc.

Library of Congress Cataloging-In-Publication Data

Asian American Christian ethics : voices, methods, issues / Grace Y. Kao and Ilsup
Ahn, editors.
365 pages cm
Includes bibliographical references and index.
ISBN 978-1-4813-0175-6 (pbk. : alk. paper)
1. Christian ethics. 2. Asian Americans--Religion. I. Kao, Grace (Grace Y.),
joint editor.
BJ1251.A85 2015
241.089'95073--dc23

2015006699

Printed in the United States of America on acid-free paper with a minimum of
30% post-consumer waste recycled content.

Contents

Preface

The origins of this book can be traced to the inaugural meeting of the Asian and Asian American Working Group of the Society of Christian Ethics. Founded by Ilsup Ahn in 2008 for the purposes of promoting the scholarly and professional development of members of Asian heritage, approximately one dozen of us gathered in Atlanta out of a desire to support one another's work in Christian ethics and to increase the visibility of Asian and Asian American perspectives in theology and ethics within the guild.

After introducing ourselves to one another, we quickly noticed something curious about ourselves. Only a very small minority of us was currently engaged in scholarship that either had special relevance for Asian American communities or that seriously theorized our identities and experiences as Asian Americans. Since we found this collective observation about us odd (i.e., a random sampling of women at the SCE would surely have more than a tiny fraction pursuing feminist/womanist/mujerista scholarship, a random sampling of African American SCE members would surely have more than one or two members working on issues of perennial concern for the black church), we not only began to float hypotheses about why this was the case but also committed then and there to change the situation. As nearly all members present at that inaugural meeting were graduate students or junior scholars, we also realized that if we judged Asian American Christian ethics worthy of scholarly pursuit, it would be *we* who would have to give birth to the subfield.[1]

This anthology, the first book-length study of Asian American Christian ethics, would not have been possible without the space and financial support provided by the SCE to rethink the enterprise of Christian ethics from our particular racial–ethnic perspectives.[2] In successive years a steady stream of new members has joined our Working Group, and those original graduate students and junior scholars have moved through the ranks through faculty appointments, tenure, and promotion. Our initial experimental explorations of Asian American Christian ethics have likewise matured through discussions over successive meetings and shared meals as well as through the many ways we have learned from other colleagues through cosponsored sessions with the Latino/a Working Group and the African and African American Working Group. We have since grown in our confidence in identifying ourselves as Asian American Christian ethicists. It is now with great joy that we are able to present to a wider audience a sampling of the kind of conversations and questions we have collectively pursued at these conferences.

This book marks the first major scholarly contribution of the nascent but emerging subfield of Asian American Christian ethics. As coeditors and contributors who are all active members of that SCE Asian and Asian American Working Group, our aim in this book is to show how and why Christian ethics self-consciously pursued through the lens of Asian American perspectives is distinctive: it remains conversant with the scholarly literature in Christian ethics without being reducible to either the dominant ways of doing Christian ethics or to other explicitly contextualist approaches. It is thus worthy of consideration not only by students and scholars of Christian ethics alike, but also by Asian American and other Christian communities to which we hold ourselves accountable.

We wish to acknowledge the many people who have made this book possible. We thank first our contributors for their pioneering labors and willingness to work collaboratively and conscientiously—in several cases under a very tight schedule—during the design, editing, and production processes.[3]

As scholars, we all stand in the debt of several professional associations who have nurtured our professional development along the way. Beyond the Society of Christian Ethics mentioned above, these associations include, but are not limited to, the Asian, North American Religion, Culture, and Society Group (ANARCS) of the American Academy of Religion (AAR); the Asian Pacific American Religious Research Initiative (APARRI); the Pacific, Asian, and North American Asian Women in Theology and Ministry (PANAAWTM); the Institute for the Study of Asian American Christianity (ISAAC); the Wabash Center for Teaching and Learning in Theology and Religion (for hosting professional development and pedagogy workshops for Asian/North American Asian American Religion and Theology faculty); and the institutions at which we work, Claremont School of Theology and North Park University.

Special thanks must also be given to Baylor University Press: to Carey Newman, our editor, for believing in this project from the start and to the entire production team for their care and professionalism.

As coeditors, we thank one another for friendship and support throughout this book project, from conception to the published volume you see here. In true collaborative fashion, we have pursued a shared vision, pushed and refined each other's thinking, and taken turns in doing the heavy lifting in ways that played to each of our strengths.

We remain grateful to our spouses, Nathaniel B. Walker and Jaeyeon Lucy Chung, for their loving-kindness, encouragement, and willingness to take on additional household responsibilities when we needed the time to bring this project to completion.

We dedicate this book to our children, Preston (P. J.) Walker, Keenan (K. C.) Walker, Daniel Ahn, and Joshua Ahn—third-generation Taiwanese American "hapas" and second-generation Korean Americans, respectively—whose lives warmly enrich our own and who continue to negotiate their way in the world as Asian Americans. It is for them and future generations that we do this work.

Introduction

What Is Asian American Christian Ethics?

GRACE Y. KAO AND ILSUP AHN

With this first-ever anthology on Asian American Christian ethics, we Christian ethicists of Asian descent in the United States think through selected topics and issues in Christian ethics from diverse Asian American Christian perspectives. In so doing we join our Asian American colleagues in related fields, such as theology, Bible, sociology, and ministry, in bringing insights from our communities and scholarship from Asian American studies to bear on our respective disciplines. As the literature to date in this subfield of Christian ethics only exists in journal-article and book-chapter form, this volume marks the first major scholarly contribution of Asian American Christian ethics to the larger community of Christian theologians, ethicists, and church members as well as to pan–Asian American networks across the country.[1]

Since we are attempting to introduce a new subfield called Asian American Christian ethics, it is appropriate that we provide some answers at the outset to the following three questions: Why do we need Asian American Christian ethics? Who are Asian Americans for the purpose of Asian American Christian ethics? What exactly is Asian American Christian ethics—how is work in this subfield to be done?

The Rationale: *Why* Asian American Christian Ethics?

Since the civil rights, second-wave feminist, and postcolonial movements of the latter half of the twentieth century, theorists are increasingly attending to the significance of their own social location in their research. Scholarly self-reflection in explicitly contextualist approaches (viz., Latin American, black, minjung, feminist/womanist/mujerista) now abound in liberation theologies, biblical hermeneutics, sociology, pastoral ministry, and other fields of study. Ethicists have likewise

1

"spoken" from their particular and historically specific standpoints as opposed to from a purportedly impartial "view from nowhere" and have accordingly rooted their ethical analyses in ways that situate their claims to knowledge or normativity.

Consider the following example to illustrate the importance that taking cultural particularity seriously can make in ethics. In light of the anthropological finding that the experience and expression of human emotions is largely culturally determined, some ethicists have challenged the cross-cultural applicability of and working assumptions about emotions in several Western accounts of normative ethics or virtue ethics. Religious ethicist Paul Lauritzen cites anthropologist Michelle Rosaldo's findings to show how the experience of anger in Western society differs markedly from that of the Ilongot people of the Philippines. Put succinctly, while Westerners generally understand anger as a "sort of psychic force" that must be carefully guarded lest it spiral out of control, the Ilongot apparently do not experience anger as an explosive force. Since, for the Ilongot, the distinction between an interior, private sphere of personal emotions and a public realm in which private emotions can be expressed simply does not exist, "it makes perfect sense [for the Ilongot] to 'pay' someone for his or her anger, at which the anger is simply given up, not repressed."[2] If we were to incorporate this anthropological discovery as a source of ethical reflection, we would be led to conclude that most of the moral norms governing anger in the West would fail to be relevant to—and thus helpful for—the Ilongot. This example reveals that a contextual approach to ethical studies may be not only justifiable but also required if the resultant analysis is to be of any practical use.[3]

When we turn specifically to the question of the contributions that Asian American Christian ethics can make (and thus, this subfield's rationale), we must first consider the place of Christianity in Asian America. Christianity is the largest religious group with which Asian Americans identify (42 percent), with the second largest group being "unaffiliated" (26 percent) and the third largest group being Buddhist (14 percent). Asian American Christians also exhibit high levels of religious commitment according to commonly used measures of analysis.[4] Studies that take into consideration how Christian beliefs and practices figure into the lives of Asian Americans would thus help to shape our understanding of a large percentage of this demography.

In turn, even though Asian Americans currently represent less than 6 percent of the entire U.S. population,[5] we contend that greater awareness about this minoritized group could facilitate a better understanding of the full range of the American experience. Asian Americans are the "best-educated, highest-income, and fastest-growing race group in the country [surpassing Hispanics]" according to a recent comprehensive nationwide survey, and they are also the most likely of any major racial or ethnic group in the United States to live in racially diverse neighborhoods and to marry interracially.[6] These and other findings not only disclose the current realities and changing landscape of America but also—and more importantly for our purposes—cry out for theo-ethical examination, as several of our contributors have begun to do in this volume.

Beyond expanding our sociological or historical understanding of current social realities in the United States, we submit that the development of Asian American Christian ethics could prove fruitful for the field of Christian social ethics as a whole. Asian American Christian ethics begins by recalling that "experience" has long been recognized as one of the four traditional sources of Christian theological and ethical reflection, along with Scripture, tradition, and reason.[7] The subfield accordingly mines the experiences and perspectives of Asian Americans as a vital source of moral wisdom.[8] In so doing, not only do we Asian American Christian ethicists empower ourselves to speak from our distinctive social location, most notably from our placement in the racial hierarchy in the United States, but also we are able to "correct" for the ways that Asian Americans are not uncommonly ignored, misunderstood, caricatured, or otherwise marginalized in both academe and the broader society.

Most importantly, the emerging subfield of Christian ethics can contribute to the field as a whole by allowing for less visible and previously undertheorized dimensions of social phenomena to surface. For example, that Asian Americans have been on America's shores since the eighteenth century *and* still remain a largely immigrant group—in fact the largest group of new immigrants according to the 2010 U.S. Census in part due to massive changes in immigration patterns stemming from the 1965 Immigration and Nationality Act—can affect our understanding of immigration as a social issue if we are willing to think through and with Asian American experiences on this topic. Moreover, that many Asian Americans' ancestral countries of origin have been—and still remain—deeply affected by the legacy of Western imperialism and U.S. military power provides many Asian American scholars with a type of postcolonial investment not reducible to those emerging from other regions (viz., Latin America, Africa, the Middle East). Finally, that Asian Americans are more likely than the general public to live in multigenerational family households,[9] to be married as adults, to have lower rates of birth outside of marriage, and to raise children in a household with two married parents all likely affect many Asian Americans' understanding of what a "normal" family looks like. Asian American Christian ethicists can subsequently draw upon their experiences, in addition to other sources of theo-ethical insight, to affirm in parts and interrogate in others this sense of normalcy as *normative* for Christians. These examples, to be sure, do not exhaust all that can be marshaled to explain the exciting potential that incorporating Asian American memories and lived experiences holds for work in Christian ethics.

The Question of Identity: *Who* Are Asian Americans for the Purposes of Asian American Christian Ethics?

Just as those who presented their work or activism as "feminist" in the early years of the first and second waves of the movement had to provide some indication of the meaning of the term, so the explorations of Asian American Christian ethics advanced in this volume raise comparable questions of the meaning of the qualifier "Asian American." Though the answer may seem obvious to some, the term has been used for multiple purposes—legal, racial, political, cultural—and thus can denote a variety of meanings.

Historically, the term Asian American originated in the late 1960s by activists who sought to provide a new identity for Asians in America—one as self-determining subjects rather than as "oriental" objects. Their idea was to "claim America" and to unite different Asian ethnicities together in an imagined community for the political purposes of mobilizing collective resistance against racial inequality and oppression.[10] As Asian American studies scholar Mark Chiang recounts, however, the constituencies that originally comprised the extension of Asian American soon changed in three notable ways given major shifts in immigration patterns beginning in the mid-1960s with reforms in U.S. immigration policy and the rise of Japan and the "four Asian tigers" (Hong Kong, Singapore, South Korea, Taiwan). First, the dramatic increase of new immigrants from Asia meant that the first generation now outnumbered the second generation and later (n.b., previously, new immigration from Asian countries had been severely restricted from the time of the 1882

Chinese Exclusion Act). Second, the expansion of new ethnic groups altered the Asian American population of mostly Chinese, Japanese, and Filipinos to one of a "heterogeneous grouping of East Asians, South Asians, and Southeast Asians."[11] Third, U.S. immigration policy preferences for skilled workers, coupled with the gains of civil rights legislation, created a new middle class among Asian Americans and thereby widened class divisions. In light of these changes, Chiang is right to conclude that it has become increasingly difficult to generalize about "who Asian Americans are in any singular way," including geographically or politically.[12]

The heterogeneity today of all those who fit under the Asian American nomenclature bears highlighting, given the tendency (even among some Asian Americans themselves) to elide significant internal differences within, between, and among different ethnicities or essentialize in other ways what it means to be a person of Asian descent. An instructive description of the diversity that we scholars who work under the category Asian American have been tasked to hold together can be found in the preface of Mary F. Foskett's and Jeffrey Kah-Jin Kuan's groundbreaking anthology on Asian American biblical interpretation:

> As Asian Americans, we are scholars working in the United States and Canada with ethnic and racial identities that tie us to the cultures and histories of East, Southeast, and South Asia; and the Pacific Islands. Sometimes the ties are quite direct, as in the case of persons born, raised and educated in Asia who come to North America to study or teach; sometimes such ties are experienced and negotiated in the context of second-, third-, or fourth-generation Asian communities in North America; sometimes the ties are partially obscured or even more difficult to negotiate, as in the case of the increasing population of adoptees born in Asia and raised in North America by non-Asian (mostly white) families, or the growing numbers of bi- or multi-racial ("hapa") persons in North America. With such multiplicity assumed, the designation "Asian American" refers not to a single culture, history, or experience.[13]

It is indeed difficult to generalize about community members given the ways in which we differ from one another in our ethnic ancestry, facility in Asian languages, class and socioeconomic background, and levels of acculturation and assimilation, among other factors. Some of us trace our origins to the sugar plantation or railroad laborers of the nineteenth century; others have arrived more recently as high-skilled workers on H-1B visas; still others are the children and successive generations of those who fled war-torn countries in the second half of the twentieth century, and even those possibilities do not exhaust all migration paths. There is no singular historical event that binds us all together (e.g., the internment of Japanese Americans does not play the same role for Asian Americans as the legacy of slavery does for African Americans); no common language to reference other than English (akin to the role that Spanish plays for Hispanics or Latinas/os, whether or not individuals are fluent); and no across-the-board common Asian cultural, philosophical, or religious tradition upon which to draw (n.b., "Hindu culture in South Asia is radically different from the Confucian heritage in East Asia, the Muslim traditions in Indonesia and other Southeast Asian countries, and ethnic subgroups such as the Hmong").[14] As our Asian American colleagues in Bible conclude, and as we shall affirm below, the term Asian American is accordingly "more a social and political designation than a cultural identifier" in signaling the "experience of living in North America as a member of a constellation of racial/ethnic minority communities."[15]

Given the aforementioned considerations, we now provide a two-pronged answer to the question of how we are conceptualizing Asian American for the purposes of Asian American Christian ethics. The first part is racial or genealogical and corresponds with the definitions of the U.S. Census Bureau and U.S. Office of Management and Budget (OMB) as well as with popular usage: the "Asian" part of Asian American refers to "a person having origins in any of the original peoples of the Far East, Southeast Asia, or the Indian subcontinent, including, for example, Cambodia, China, India, Japan, Korea, Malaysia, Pakistan, the Philippine Islands, Thailand, and Vietnam."[16] Take note that our working definition encompasses neither persons with genealogies from other parts of the Asian continent (e.g., Central Asia, Western Asia or the Middle East, Russia) nor Native Hawaiians and Other Pacific Islanders.

While the exclusion of, say, Afghanis from counting as Asian American generally goes uncontested, the omission of Native Hawaiians and Other Pacific Islanders arguably warrants some explanation, since the latter are not uncommonly lumped together with Asian Americans.[17] We do not, however, follow suit out of our appreciation that the incorporation of Native Hawaiians and other Pacific Islanders under the Asian American umbrella has been marked with controversy, which is why growing numbers of Pacific Islanders are "contesting their involuntary representation by Asian Americans."[18] Indeed, it was Native Hawaiian/Pacific Islander (NHPI) activists who successfully lobbied for their populations to be tracked separately from Asians, which can be seen in publications of the OMB since 1997 and the Census Bureau since the 2000 Census, out of a belief that "statistics would reveal NHPIs as an underclass, a community that still faces barriers to participating fully in American society."[19] Our decision not to fold NHPIs under the Asian American banner thus corresponds with current OMB and U.S. Census definitions. It also, and more importantly, discloses our desire not to profess to "represent" the concerns of a group (out of any sincere but misguided notion of inclusion) when none of our book's contributors could credibly do so.

Having established the racial and genealogical portion of our understanding of who Asian Americans are for the purposes of Asian American Christian ethics, we turn now to the more subjective part of our two-pronged definition. We stipulate that not all work in Christian ethics produced by Asian American scholars should qualify as Asian American Christian ethics.[20] Just as scholarship authored by women is not ipso facto feminist, so we invoke the social activist origins of the term Asian American in our characterization of Asian American Christian ethics as work in Christian ethics written by those who specifically adopt a pan-ethnic Asian American consciousness, identity, or set of concerns therein.

Here, it is important to highlight that the ability for any scholar of Asian descent to inhabit a pan-ethnic Asian American mindset or focus should not be taken for granted but instead understood as a moral accomplishment. Historian K. Scott Wong has documented how "pan-Asian solidarity . . . [has] not [been] the norm": for example, during World War II, Chinese Americans with a few exceptions were "knowingly or not, complicit in the persecution of Japanese Americans" as they sought ways to present themselves as "good Asians" and loyal Americans over and against America's wartime enemy (e.g., they wore "I am Chinese" buttons and took advantage of the internment by moving into the properties previously occupied by Japanese Americans).[21] While the activist movements of the 1960s and 1970s did much to mobilize Asian Americans as a collectivity with shared aims, and while Asian Americans today can draw upon a host of existing pan-Asian organizations, churches, and other resources to assist them in the strengthening of pan-Asian community, Asian Americans may still have to contend with issues of language barriers, cultural differences, and distrust between members of discrete groups due to lingering historical animosities and unresolved conflicts in their countries of origin (e.g., as between Japan and Korea, Taiwan and China, India and Pakistan, and so forth).

Today, whether Asian Americans are initially drawn together due to geographical proximity, assumptions of cultural affinity,[22] or pursuit of common ministerial or other professional aims, pan–Asian solidarity can deepen from a recognition that Asian Americans as a group are likely to be subjected to similar experiences of ignorance, prejudice, racial discrimination, or stereotyping by members of either the majority or other minoritized cultures. What is more, as it is not uncommon for persons of Asian descent in the United States to experience (non-Asian) others either mistaking the true nature of their ethnic origins or dismissing the fact of the matter as irrelevant, this pervasive but mistaken "all Asians look [or act] alike" perception can lead Asians of any ethnicity to be vulnerable to insults intended for others (e.g., Vietnamese Americans being called "chinks"), or, in the worst cases, even hate crime violence (e.g., Chinese American Vincent Chin being killed by disgruntled white autoworkers out of a belief that he was a "dirty Jap"). These racialized experiences, in turn, can be used to shape pan–Asian American empathy and thus communal identity for the purposes of advocating for the full humanity and restoration of all.

So understood, what we wish to signal politically in a nonessentialist fashion by "Asian American" in Asian American Christian ethics can be compared to what some feminist theologians have described as the meaning of "Asian" in Asian theology. With full knowledge of the ways in which the "categorical and representational term 'Asian'" has been put to racist, nationalist, and colonialist uses, Nami Kim still affirms the "strategic use" of the term Asian to signal the "political denominator that binds a group of people together based on the common history of oppression and struggle in the United States as well as struggle against American imperialism in Asia."[23] Kim's admission of the danger *and* continued usefulness of the term Asian is evocative of feminist postcolonial theologian Kwok Pui-lan's account of the "naming of theology as 'Asian' . . . [as] a discursive and political construct, arising out of the particular historical moment of the recovery of political and cultural autonomy in the 1960s."[24] More specifically, Kwok explains that it is not that "most Asian male or female theologians consciously or unconsciously construct an 'essentialized' notion of 'Asia' and proceed to write and articulate an 'Asian' theology," it is that they retain their diverse understandings of what constitutes being Asian while deploying the term to "signif[y] a collective consciousness against the theological hegemony of the West and . . . [to] affir[m] that God's revelations and actions could be discerned through the histories and cultures of Asian peoples."[25]

Following Kwok and Kim's reflections on the strategic use of the term Asian in Asian theology, we, too, reject the notion that use of the descriptor Asian requires us ethicists to distill some abstract, sine qua non essence of "Asianness" upon which to base subsequent findings. We nonetheless follow our Asian American colleagues in Bible, as well as our other Asian American colleagues in theology, in seeking to develop particularly Asian *American* (not simply Asian) theo-ethical reflections.[26] Though we fully acknowledge the many similarities we may share with fellow Asians in Asia and elsewhere, our particular histories and embodied racialized experiences in the North American context shape our perspectives on various topics of Christian ethical analysis, thereby prompting us to reflect on the concerns and struggles that persons of Asian descent face, particularly in the United States.[27] Thus in developing Asian *American* Christian ethics, rather than Asian Christian ethics, we recognize our present groundedness and do not presume that what may be true of or helpful for Asians in the United States would likewise be true of or helpful for Asians the world over.

In drawing attention to the strategic use of the term Asian American for Asian American Christian ethics, we must say a final word about what we do not intend by our nomenclature. Deploying a pan–Asian American perspective or consciousness for the purposes of Asian American Christian ethics neither requires any given scholar to prioritize her identity as an Asian American above all others, for we fully acknowledge that many Asian Americans, including the majority of our book contributors, identify more readily with their ethnicity (alongside of other important signifiers like sex) than with their race.[28] Nor should our Asian American descriptor compel scholars who use it either to have to "claim America" against Asia in any binary fashion or position themselves over and against their Asian counterparts.[29] While the United States has been the only home that some Asian Americans have ever had (and thus it would never occur to them to claim anything other than an American nationality, identity, or citizenship), the lives of others with strong and ongoing transnational ties to their homeland render any hard and fast categorical distinction between Asians in America and Asians in Asia difficult to maintain.[30]

The Methodology: *What* Is Asian American Christian Ethics?

Having unpacked the "why" and "who" of Asian American Christian ethics, one question remains: how might scholars pursue work in this subfield of study? Might we simply understand Asian American Christian ethics as Christian ethics "done by Asian-raced persons from the United States, and/or . . . done with the explicitly political goal of helping to address issues confronting Asian American communities"?[31] If so, our methodology would be comparable to the manner in which the majority of scholars in the related field of Asian American biblical hermeneutics have described their enterprise.

In his groundbreaking book *What Is Asian American Biblical Hermeneutics?*, Tat-siong Benny Liew aligns himself with Derridean radical hermeneutics when laying out a different and innovative methodology. Liew begins by positioning Asian American biblical hermeneutics as a convergence between Asian American studies and biblical studies and then situating the subfield within postcolonial studies and in alliance with other minority communities. He then proceeds not only to deflect any essentialist (mis)understandings of Asian American identity or culture, but also to deconstruct exclusionary (it-takes-one-to-know-one), ethnographic, or colonial assumptions of referentiality when answering the "who" and "what" questions of method. Due to the instability of identity and his rejection of the "colonial" desire for "authentic" representation in "identity based" approaches, Liew proposes that Asian American biblical hermeneutics take an "identity inventive" route instead. His "citational invention of tradition . . . [or] reference without referentiality" proposal thereby puts the identity question on the back, not front, burner in stipulating that "what is [ultimately] 'Asian American' about Asian American biblical hermeneutics hinges on its references to contemporary Asian American scholarship."[32] Liew's ultimate purpose is not to offer "prescriptive" propositions but to present "prefigurative" remarks so as to open up other options and opportunities to level the "playing field" (i.e., the concern being that the white-dominated and more established field of biblical hermeneutics does not carry a racial-ethnic label and thus is presumed legitimate, while the younger subfield of Asian American biblical hermeneutics is commonly coded as "multicultural" or "racial-ethnic" and thus constantly pressed to provide a rationale).[33]

We find much to commend in Liew's proposed methodology. Many Asian American Christian ethicists will similarly find themselves drawing upon postcolonial studies and standing in solidarity with other racial-ethnic minority groups for several reasons: the origins of the formation of Asian American studies in the multiracial third world strike of the civil rights era, the struggles of Asian peoples with colonialism of all kinds (e.g., American, British, Japanese, Chinese) and its lingering effects, and our common understanding of white supremacism as something all people (including whites) need to resist, among others. In line with Liew's critique of identity based approaches, Asian American Christian ethicists will also share in his suspicions about essentialist or colonialist understandings of identity or representation for the reasons discussed in the previous section. Finally, we find in Liew's "prefigurative" versus "prescriptive" remarks a helpful distinction, for we, too, are more interested in presenting this first book on Asian American Christian ethics as something that provides a "group of people recognition, rights, privileges, responsibilities, and obligations" within the field of Christian ethics than in demanding prescriptively that our readers concur with the normative ethical judgments we reach here or in subsequent chapters.[34] We do not, however, seek to appropriate Liew's "citational invention of tradition" methodology for the purposes of Asian American Christian ethics and thus will propose a different way forward.[35]

We now suggest two different, though by no means mutually exclusive, ways of conceptualizing work in Asian American Christian ethics. The first might be described as agency- or advocacy-centered; the second as an approach especially interested in bringing Western and Asian philosophical, theological, and cultural traditions together in critical dialogue and for selective retrieval for Asian American Christian ethics. In presenting these two ways of thinking methodologically in Asian American Christian ethics without insisting on conformity to both or even to either model, we leave room for diversity, flexibility, and originality for further articulations by scholars who have other ideas to contribute to this nascent subfield.

The first approach recalls the criteria that Grace Y. Kao initially proposed in her "Prospects for Developing Asian American Christian Ethics"—an article that emerged from the first collective exploration of these methodological questions by the Asian and Asian American Working Group of the Society of Christian Ethics (SCE) in 2010. Beyond drawing upon theologian Jonathan Y. Tan's description of Asian American theology as contextual, inductive, and "genuinely nourished . . . [and] guided by the 'external criteria' of the Gospel," Kao adapted Bible scholar Gale Yee's selective retrieval of W. E. B. Du Bois' four-part criteria for authentic black theater: that it (Asian American biblical hermeneutics for Yee, Asian American Christian ethics for Kao) be "about us," "by us," "for us," and "near us."[36]

Asian American Christian ethics might be said to incorporate work "about us" in one of two ways. The first would be through scholarly attempts to document and account for the manner in which Christian ethics are understood in various Asian American communities (e.g., the ways in which the biblical command to honor one's parents is commonly fused with Confucian understandings of filial piety in East Asian contexts, the complex reasons why conservative Protestant Asian immigrant subcultures are likely to interpret material success as manifestations of divine blessing). The second would be through a scholarly emphasis on the development of moral agency, so as to produce "mature, responsible, and self-actualized moral agents" through the process of "uncovering, challenging, and transforming the . . . structures" that stifle such growth and maturation.[37] In this second case, sometimes Asian American Christian ethicists will discover that powerful systems of injustice are what block the healthy development of moral agency; in other cases the "fault," so to say, will be interpersonal and thus arguably more within our direct power to change.

In conceptualizing Asian American Christian ethics as additionally "for us," we must make a number of important clarifications. Sometimes Asian American Christian ethicists will affirm members of the Asian American community by offering empowering and liberating insights when attending to specific areas of vulnerability that Asian Americans are wont to face.[38] That is, insofar as Asian American Christian ethicists interrogate that which demeans our full humanity or robs us of our sense of worth (e.g., pressures to conform to white standards of physical attractiveness or communication styles, meet gendered expectations of masculinity or femininity, "prove" one's loyalty or sense of belonging to America to offset "perpetual foreigner" suspicions), they can be said to be operating in this mode. In other cases, it may be more appropriate for Asian American Christian ethicists to deliver prophetic critique and admonishment than validation of the status quo, such as when certain "culturally particular or dominant patterns of sin" (e.g., authoritarianism, [hetero]sexism, overconsumption in ways that despoil the environment, and ways of relating to others that do not serve the commonweal) need to be named and rebuked.[39]

To be sure, work "for us" should not be read in any purely insular way in either intent or reach, as the subfield of Asian American Christian ethics is premised on the idea that more than Asian Americans (just as more than Christians) stand to gain from our findings.[40] To use a common example, when many of us Asian American scholars disrupt the stereotypical public image of us as the "model minority," we attempt to do a minimum of two separate things: (1) advocate for the interests of fellow members of our communities (in surfacing the real needs and struggles of ethnic subgroups who are neither high-achieving nor financially stable but in fact are struggling in poverty and exposing the real harm to young people caused by extreme parental or communal pressures to excel), and (2) stand in solidarity—not competition—with other racial-ethnic minoritized communities in refusing to allow our racial group's stereotypical success to be used as evidence for their apparent underperformance.[41] This is to say that work ostensibly done "for us" can and should produce analyses in Christian ethics for the benefit of all.

Kao's final "near us" guideline is intended to encourage Asian American Christian ethicists to remain connected to real flesh-and-blood Asian Americans so as to be able to "explore the effects of either our normative conclusions on our particular communities, or our experiences as Asian Americans on those normative conclusions themselves."[42] In other words, Asian American Christian ethicists need not draw solely from their personal fund of insights and anecdotes, but should ideally hold themselves accountable to the broader Asian American community—to their "histories, cultures, traditions, struggles, concerns, dreams, and aspirations."[43] The aim, in short, would be not only to increase their pan-ethnic understanding by staying in relationship with others, but also to "test" the adequacy of their judgments on members of the community in a continuous feedback loop. In so doing, Asian American Christian ethicists could embody what Michael Walzer has described as a "connected critic" as opposed to a wholly "neutral" or dispassionate one, as it would be difficult to understand why "if [the critic] were a stranger, really disinterested . . . he would involve himself in their affairs" to begin with.[44]

This final "near us" criterion originally proposed by Grace Y. Kao serves as a bridge to the newly proposed one developed by Ilsup Ahn in his solo-authored chapter in this volume on virtue ethics. In now unpacking this second methodological suggestion for doing Asian American Christian ethics, we shift our emphasis from moral agency and advocacy to the range of sources that Asian American Christian ethicists should understand are at their disposal. In a method he calls "cocritical appropriation," Ahn envisions a critical excavation and appropriation of rich and diverse sources of Asian and Asian American history, culture, and tradition alongside of a similar process of critical appraisal and selective retrieval of more mainstream and other contextualized ways of doing ethics.

This methodological approach in Asian American Christian ethics requires scholars to engage in double critical efforts in a two-step process. The first would involve a critical exploration of how non–Asian American Christian thinkers (predominantly non-Asians from the West) have critically deployed their historical, cultural, and social traditions while analyzing various ethical issues or problems. In this step, scholars could draw upon selected moments within the historical development of Christian ethics in the West, from early church thinkers reflecting upon biblical themes to contemporary defenses, appropriations, and interrogations of such scholarship (e.g., the continued use in Christian virtue ethics of the writings of Aristotle and Aquinas, successive refinements on Christian ethical thinking about the "just war" from the time of Augustine onwards, contemporary criticisms of the work of Reinhold Niebuhr from the margins).

The second step would involve inviting Asian American Christian ethicists to turn to Asian American histories, cultures, and traditions as sources also ripe for critical discussion and retrieval. In so doing, scholars would go beyond assessing what others have said or done in their comparative engagement of Western and Asian American traditions so as to provide a constructive integration of the dual critical appropriations. The point would be neither to use the West as a foil to the East nor vice versa in recalling the details of one tradition only to show the superiority of the other, nor to succumb to the charge of essentialism in mining Asian and Asian American philosophical, religious, and cultural traditions as potential sources of moral wisdom. More specifically, if Asian American Christian ethicists were to draw upon Confucian, Taoist, Buddhist, or other popular religious or cultural practices originating from their ancestral countries of origin, their doing so should not be automatically interpreted as automatically more compatible with or representational of Asian Americans. Instead, readers should understand the critical appropriation of Asian traditions as part of a creative attempt to construct work in a new subfield of Asian American

Christian ethics—not to return nostalgically to some "purer" Asian past undefiled by Western contact. The method of cocritical appropriation, then, intends to make possible a new and creative "traditioning"—one that does not simply or uncritically reinscribe the past.[45]

To reiterate, both Kao's "near us" guideline and Ahn's method of cocritical appropriation would require scholars to remain rooted to Asian American traditions, communities, experiences, and histories. It would not, however, additionally require them to balance their so-called Asianness with their Americanness in any mathematical way so as to pass any explicit or implicit test of authenticity. To be clear, while Ahn's proposed methodology might lead some Asian American Christian ethicists to emulate the approach taken by some Asian American theologians who explicitly draw from Asian philosophies and religions either to illustrate the Asian portion of their work or to offer paradigms they believe would be more receptive to Asian or Asian American audiences,[46] the subfield of Asian American Christian ethics need not necessarily privilege the selective retrieval of Eastern traditions or practices over Western ones. Because individual Asian American Christian ethicists will vary in the hermeneutical stance they take to either sets of traditions (some scholars more generous, others more suspicious), the subfield of Asian American Christian ethics should not be understood as in principle preferring the conceptual use of, say, *jeong* (the untranslatable Korean concept of deep connection or attachment) over the theory of moral sentiments of David Hume, the Taoist understanding of *yin* and *yang* over Hegelian dialectics, the critical analysis of Chandra Talpade Mohanty over Michel Foucault, and so forth, simply because the first of the aforementioned pairs is judged to be more "Asian" and thus more appropriate for Asian Americans than the other.

The conceptual road map that we have suggested for Asian American Christian ethics has been of two kinds: one criteria-driven and focused more on questions of developing moral agency, the latter more focused on the sources that Asian American Christian ethicists should feel free to use and engage critically. Though we did not impose either methodological approach on our contributors, as editors we nonetheless find in the following chapters elements of both: every author identifies for the purpose of this work as Asian American Christians ("by us"), draws from personal knowledge of Asian American experiences and from those of others in the community ("near us"), and affirms and admonishes Asian Americans where appropriate ("about us") both for their own good and for the benefit of all ("for us"). In turn, every author spends time canvassing the rich tradition of Christian ethical reflection on his or her topic as well as the manner in which Asian Americans are already invested in it—experientially, historically, culturally, and so forth—so as to provide a constructive way forward in the articulation of Asian American ethical response to the topic at hand (cocritical appropriation).[47] We hope, in closing, that these two ways of thinking can help our readers and future scholars of Asian American Christian ethics to grasp the diverse ways of understanding this new subfield of study and its potential.

The Structure of Our Book and an Invitation to Readers

We invite you once again to explore with us our development and application of Asian American Christian ethics to a selection of topics and concerns. You will encounter in these pages theo-ethical reflections on some perennial issues in Christian ethics (peace and war, family/marriage/parenting, gender and sexuality, economics and wealth, virtue ethics), some pressing social maters (race relations, immigration, health care, the environment) and some special interests of Asian Americans (education, plastic surgery). You will learn from contributors who inhabit ethnic, generational, and denominational diversity and who are almost equally divided in terms of gender (with slightly more female than male authors). But you may also perceptively notice the absence of authors from certain demographics among us (e.g., South Asians, those who explicitly identify as queer) as well as the dominance of some voices over others (e.g., East Asians over the rest, mainline Protestants over evangelicals or Catholics). We regret this feature of our book, as our composition of contributors reflects not only the current makeup of members in the Asian and Asian American Working Group of the SCE, but also the more limited range of voices that are typically found among those doing research in Asian American theology, Bible, and ministry. It is our hope, however, that as the literature in Asian American Christian ethics grows and matures, it will attract a broader range of scholars who are eager to join in our work.

To facilitate ease of understanding among our readers, all chapters will follow a similar format. To be more specific, each contributor will begin by describing the range of Christian responses to the matter at hand, then show how Asian Americans are particularly invested in the topic, and then conclude with a constructive proposal for an Asian American

Christian ethical response. A few discussion questions will close each chapter, thus making this book ideal for use in classroom settings.

To recall our use of Liew's "prefigurative" versus "prescriptive" distinction, rest assured that we do not understand ourselves as presenting a definitive statement on what Asian American Christians should think about the topics explored herein. Rather, we invite everyone who reads the following pages to engage critically with *Asian American Christian Ethics* to see for her/himself the relevance and plausibility of the analyses we provide and the pronouncements we make. To repeat, where our readers find themselves wanting more clarification or disagreeing with our findings, we welcome them to continue the conversation by making their own contributions to this nascent but emerging new subfield of study.

Gender and Sexuality

HOON CHOI

In general, a common assumption in Christianity, Western society, and many other ancient religious texts from non-Western cultures is that humans are naturally divided into two sexes. This bifurcation has traditionally determined gender identity, attitudes, behaviors, reproductive roles, and social roles.[1] However, many feminist and queer studies scholars have argued against such a binary construction of gender, identifying it as a way for heteropatriarchy (the dominance of heterosexual males in society) to maintain established patterns of power.[2] Furthermore, scholars of various ethnic backgrounds have argued that this perpetuation of power is revealed when one closely examines how race is gendered by dominant racial groups; for example, the well-documented feminization of Asians and Asian Americans has prevented them from being seen as equals to their more politically powerful counterparts (e.g., Western imperialists or members of mainstream white society).

In this chapter I promote an Asian American Christian ethical approach to gender and sexuality as a response to Western heteropatriarchal hegemony. To that end I make evident both the heteropatriarchal pattern of power within the spectrum of Christian beliefs and practices in general as well as the dominant groups' hegemonic approaches to maintaining the status quo. I then point to the particular ways in which Asian Americans are often perceived: Asian American women as commonly sexualized and submissive, and Asian American men as effeminate and weak by the standards of mainstream American society. Additionally, within some Asian American communities, individuals may further experience discrimination as a consequence of Asian-Confucian patriarchal norms that may still be operative. For example, women may be treated as second-class citizens in church, men may feel inadequate for not living up to the normative expectations of "real" men, and gender-queer and LGBTIQ individuals may experience other ways of being silenced. I will conclude this piece by suggesting a possible approach to a more authentic understanding of gender and sexuality from an Asian American Christian ethical perspective. This approach will refer to Jesus of Nazareth as a model to explore common experiences of oppression among the sexual diversity of Asian identities and how those experiences can move Asian American Christians to social action. Solidarity through that shared experience may result in the creation of media watchdog groups, civil rights groups, or blog sites through social media that inform and empower Christian communities to fight the violations committed against them. However, solidarity will also force Asian American Christian communities to reflect on the ways in which they perpetuate the very injustices that they criticize. The hope is that such a process will help Asian American Christians and those outside of their boundaries to acknowledge and respect the full dignity and rights of human beings bestowed on us from God.

Christian Thinking about Gender and Sexuality

Early Christian Responses to Sexuality: A Theology of Sexuality

Throughout Christian history, views on sexuality have been one directional in that theological thinking mainly determined one's understanding of sexuality. Traditional religious sources (tradition and Scripture), in addition to reason and experience, were the starting points by which theologians made sense of reality. Of course scholars did not interpret these religious sources out of a vacuum but drew upon current thinking within their sociohistorical contexts. For example, Christian theories on the duality of the body and the soul were often grounded upon the dualistic thinking of the Greek and Roman philosophical tradition.[3] More specifically, Aristotle believed that the woman, with her female organs, was somehow lesser in being compared to man; Aristotle also taught that the body is female and the soul male.[4] Among others, Stoic philosophers broadened dualistic thinking by presuming that anything belonging to the bodily/female realm, including bodily or sexual desires and emotions such as fear and anger, was irrational and therefore necessitated control because of its disruptive potential and liability to excess. The human will, in contrast, which was commonly identified with the male realm of the mind/soul, was to regulate and have mastery over the body.[5]

These early Greek influences can be seen in many early and medieval Christian expressions of dualism that characterized sexuality by making accusations—against themselves and others—about unchaste desires. People are characterized as lustful and impure because "they are tempted by 'the flesh,' and they wrestle with a Satan who is master over it."[6] St. Augustine's *Confessions* is the example par excellence of this tendency. He accused himself of having an irrepressible, uncontrollable sexual concupiscence. His adolescence was marked by a fight between two forces: on the one hand, "the mists of slimy lust of flesh . . . the dark mist of lust . . . the tribulation of the flesh . . . the violence of [his] flooding passions," which was "controlled by the madness of sensuality," and on the other, the spirit, or "the moderate relation of mind to mind," or "a light touch of Your [God's] hands . . . Your voice."[7] As a result, he believed that sexual relations within marriage "make something good out of the evil of lust."[8] While St. Augustine believed that our bodies, sex, and marriage were ultimately good, he was nevertheless deeply suspicious of their propensity to cause evil.[9] Since women were by nature more associated with bodiliness and (original) sin and thus contrary to salvation, they were permanently marked as "a source of temptation to men . . . symbolically identified with evil," and therefore had to be controlled.[10] Men dodged this fatal culpability thanks to the view that women influenced their disordered actions—a view that then justified male dominance over women. Along this same line of reasoning, however, even Augustine could not deny the possibility of a woman's salvation as long as she overcame her corporeal nature and lived according to the spirit. According to Augustine, there were many ways to do this. One of the ways for women to obtain salvation was through virginity.[11] Within this pessimistic view of human nature and sexuality, men and women remained redeemable, but their postlapsarian state made it difficult for women in particular to break free of the bondage of disordered sexual desires without virginity or celibacy.

The legacy of St. Augustine's theology of human sexuality is indisputable. Many Catholic thinkers upheld St. Augustine's view on sexuality, albeit with significant modifications. St. Thomas Aquinas, for example, argued that sexual desire, which is *not* intrinsically evil, nevertheless lost something in the order of nature as a result of original sin. Hence, St. Thomas concluded that procreation resulting from natural unimpeded processes justified sexual desire.[12] However slight, this acknowledgment of the goodness of human (physical and emotional) inclinations would later have a significant historical effect.

The most influential Protestant Reformers, Martin Luther and John Calvin, promoted the perspective of a dominating hierarchal structure, with man (husband) at the top, and sustained a suspicious attitude toward sexual activity by identifying it a result of our sinfulness.[13] Both Luther and Calvin upheld marriage as a remedy for sexual sin so as to minimize human sin as much as possible. However, compared to medieval theology, they possessed a more optimistic view on sex within marriage and marriage itself and did not believe that celibacy vows were a feasible solution for most Christians. In *On Marriage Matters*, Luther wrote that "God has created man and woman so that they should come together with pleasure (lust) and love, willingly and gladly with all their hearts. And bridal love or the will to marry is a natural thing, implanted and bestowed by God."[14] While acknowledging celibacy as a "high, rare," or "special" gift, Calvin and Luther further presented celibacy as a much rarer phenomenon than as portrayed in medieval theology.[15] Thus, while acknowledging the legitimacy of marriage, married sex, and celibacy, they sharply criticized the "vow" of celibacy and believed that it was taken on by too many.[16] Still, the Protestant Reformers contended that human sexuality, including sexual activities within marriage, could never be seen outside of the context of sin. Not even the fruits of marital sex, be it procreation or love, could justify sexual desire, and sexual activity could only be forgiven.[17]

The traditions of regulating sexual activity, sexual renunciation, and heterosexual, married, procreative sex—all within a framework of skepticism regarding sexuality—owe their existence to these and other seminal Christian thinkers. One common thread among them is a theoanthropological assumption of dimorphic gender.[18] Karl Barth wrote, "In the whole reach of human life, there is no abstract human, but only concretely masculine or feminine being, feeling, willing, thinking, speaking, conduct and action, and only concretely masculine and feminine co-existence and cooperation in all these things."[19] Similarly, Pope John Paul II has argued that "[i]n the 'unity of the two,' man and woman are called from the beginning not only to exist 'side by side,' or 'together,' but they are also called to exist mutually 'one for the other.'"[20] In both cases there is a supposition that men and women exist in complementary relations with each other. Even if they provide more positive views of marital relations, their dualistic attributions for men and women as given by earlier Christian thinkers remained essentially unchanged: men and women continued to be seen dichotomously as either rational or emotional, strong or weak, independent or dependent, vigorous or frail, hard or soft, aggressive or passive, public or domestic/ private, abstract or concrete, activating or receiving, and conquering or nurturing, respectively.[21]

Later Christian Responses: Sexual Theology

Developments in medicine, biology, and social sciences have led to challenges of dimorphic explanations of gender differences. Scientific discoveries of the nineteenth and twentieth centuries, for example, show that even at the bodily structural level, women's bodies are not simply "receptacles for sperm." Ovum and sperm meet "together in order to form a new reality," which therefore rules out the analogy of the womb passively receiving a seed given the active role the ovum plays in aiding the passage of the sperm.[22] Concomitantly, philosophical paradigms shifted from medieval to Enlightenment perspectives and eventually included postmodern world views. As such, the unidirectional trend, namely from religious beliefs to sexual experience (theology of sexuality), started to move in the other direction, from bodily/sexual experience to religious meaning (sexual theology).[23] The rationale for this reversal is the theological supposition that a proper understanding of the human body and bodily experiences will disclose God's action and intentions.[24] This new paradigm results from the recognition that an objective understanding of human sexuality and gender can lead to rigidly rationalistic understandings of body/sexuality.[25] Christian scholars began to acknowledge that their normative definitions of gender and sexuality only reflected the reality of a limited number of people, often to the benefit of Western hegemony. In order to disrupt this one-sided view to see reality more clearly and accurately, scholars began to consider viewpoints not just from the traditional "center" but also from oppressed, marginalized, and "minority" groups. In America two of the earliest and most notable groups of interest were African American slaves and women. The abolition and suffrage movements revealed the unjust structures of American society. They also served as the impetus for acknowledging that slaves and women are not naturally less rational or more fragile and passive respectively, but instead lacked equal or even adequate access to opportunities. These constructed distinctions of race, gender, and sexuality, however, had served to maintain the status quo by upholding the white, Western, and male hegemonic power structure in America. By differentiating and depicting slaves as naturally animalistic and skilled at physical labor, or women as naturally more emotional, nurturing, and irrational (compared to men), dominant groups sought to prevent those oppressed groups from encroaching into educational and sociopolitical realms that could lead them to positions of power.[26] This resultant preservation of hegemonic masculinity and patriarchal norms of femininity not only applied to issues of sexuality and gender but also could be seen across other binary constructed relationships (e.g., white/black, Western/Far Eastern, upper class/lower class, etc.).

From a theological perspective, then, one must at least be suspicious of echoes or repetitions of these assumptions and rhetoric on race, gender, and sexuality in theological power structures. Gender role assignments resulting from a theology of gender complementarity, for example, usually mean in practice assignments toward which sex is purportedly "naturally" inclined (domestic childbearing and child care for women and public civic engagement, material productivity, and even warfare for men).[27] Historically, attempts to restrict social roles by this basis inevitably led to inequities that hinder growth in human and Christian life.[28] The virtue of agapic self-sacrifice, for example, continues to be more specifically expected of women because they are traditionally associated with receptivity, passivity, and submission. While some women may possess some of these qualities, feminist scholars have increasingly noted the harm in regarding these traits as essential or inherent to women.[29] In the first case, an inflexible insistence upon these norms in this gender complementarity model can lead a battered woman to believe it is her Christian duty to remain submissive or subject to her husband.[30] Bracketing these extreme and tragic cases of domestic violence, one can easily come up with numerous situations where different manifestations of abuse and violence can more easily appear acceptable within this schema of self-sacrificial love.[31] As a result, many feminists have found the agapic model unsatisfactory since the situations coming out of it too often lead women toward destructive self-abnegation and even more asymmetrical sacrifice of women on behalf of men, whether in the family, workplace, or elsewhere.[32]

Secondly, a focus solely on these dualistic gendered qualities undermines the multifaceted natures of women and men alike. That is, the current Roman Catholic and comparable evangelical complementarity model downplays men's domestic capabilities and capacities along with women's potential and competence for participating in active public roles.[33] This model simply ignores or dismisses as relevant all the ways in which men receive, encircle, and embrace *as well as* all the ways in which women are proactive and leading.[34] The destructive result is that these rigid gender roles can become obstacles to the creation of mutual, loving, and Christian relationships.[35] By focusing on some aspects of human sexuality as if they were the whole of a person, an individual is not able to entirely express her/himself in relation to her/his spouse, family, and ultimately God.

Thirdly, related to this limitation of self-expression to another, Christian thinkers (especially those from the Roman Catholic tradition) have often deemed compulsory childbearing and procreativity as not only natural but also one of the two essential ends for sexual intercourse in a marriage.[36] The underlying idea is that women, unlike men, are naturally (reproductively) vectored toward childbearing and therefore men and women are made for each other with fecundity as their ultimate goal. Before Vatican II, while many sought to *allow* sexual relations within a marriage even when conception could not occur (i.e., infertility, rhythm method),[37] these instances were inevitably seen as either a lesser, abnormal, or deficient expression of the love between the two. These cases raised some serious questions about persons who chose to live as single, separated, divorced, or widowed; those who were married but without offspring (whether or not due to infertility); gays and lesbians; and even celibates (religious or not).[38] Also, such attitudes forced one to focus on a relationship between physical body parts or sexual organs and biological functions, not between the two full human beings with interpersonal, moral dimensions.[39]

By disrupting these normative definitions, then, scholars began to consider one's gender and sexuality not as normative, unchanging, singular, and "given," but as fragmented, fluid, diverse, and constructed. In addition to the aforementioned scientific discoveries, postmodern scholars identified the socially constructed aspects of gendered norms, noting that what was considered given or "natural" was inextricably connected to historical, socioeconomic, religious, and cultural contexts.[40] When one examines the differences in gender and sexual norms in non-Western cultures, the diversity of gender identities and expressions within American culture alone, and the existence of intersexual persons all over the world, one can conclude that Christian scholars who challenged gender and sexual dimorphism were right to do so.[41]

While Western, feminist academics correctly acknowledged the need to take biological and social experiences seriously and recognized that sexual and gender norms had been formulated in ways that privileged male experience, what many lacked was a deep understanding of their own privilege and location. The next generation of scholars of color drew attention to the ways in which this scholarship drew mostly from white, middle-class, educated, North/Euro-American privileged academics, thus excluding the perspectives and experiences of other oppressed groups. Christian scholars subsequently included more marginalized, oppressed, and minority voices in an attempt to better understand what it means to be human and how that helps us seek fulfillment in all of us and in God.[42] Kwok Pui-lan captures this sentiment well: "The lifting up of every voice, the celebration of diversity, the affirmation of plurality, helps us to see glimpses of the amazing grace of God in all cultures and all people."[43] Toward that end, I now present Asian American perspectives on sexuality and gender.

Asian American Reflections on Sexuality and Gender

The singular term "Asian American" is inherently inadequate, as found *passim* in this volume.[44] As such, I proceed with some caution about using the term Asian American. However, it is still useful to bring to light some structural sins perpetuated by dominant groups.[45] Also, through the complex intertwining of races, ethnicities, genders, sexualities, religions, and generations, marginalized groups are able to create a strategic solidarity of the socially disinherited that may lead to moral action for social justice.

Over the years Asian Americans (AAs) have been portrayed disadvantageously. Generally, postmodern secular and religious scholars have maintained the notion that AAs (more specifically, their sexuality) are "socially shaped in ways that maintain social and political dominance for whites, particularly men."[46] In our "post-racial" or "color-blind" society, these racist constructions have shifted from being overtly racist to covertly racist.[47] In the infamous case of *People v. Hall*, 4 Cal. 399 (1854), Chinese immigrants were declared to be different in "language, customs, color, and physical conformation; between whom and ourselves nature has placed an impossible difference."[48] More recently, contemporary notions of AAs as a "model minority," which depicts AAs as "hardworking, law-abiding, and self-sufficient people," may suggest racial valorization rather than discrimination, but in reality still works to segregate Asian Americans as foreign and position them below the glass ceiling somewhere in the middle of the racial hierarchy as the "middle-man minority."[49] More specifically, the detrimental constructions of AA sexuality have reinforced racial hierarchy, giving AAs the message that they will continue to not be fully accepted. However, gender characterizations of AA women and men have been neither monolithic nor consistent through time.

In the period before World War II, for example, AA men's work was often associated with virility and strength; some, although certainly not all, AA groups of men were portrayed as hypersexed, violent, filthy, shifty, and dangerous "Yellow Perils" with a "strong appetite for white women."[50] Indeed, many AA immigrant men were working in industries that would be considered "men's work" (agricultural farming, construction [railroad] work).[51] Yet these characterizations are not what many would associate with AA men today. Gradually AA men began to be portrayed as impotent, asexual, and/or feminine, especially after World War II.[52] AA men (and boys) began to work in "feminizing" jobs or "women's occupations," such as in laundries, restaurants, and domestic businesses, including being "houseboys." Those who were able to break out of the margins were kept in check through model and middleman minority status. Such hegemonic constructions of masculinity would be harmful to *any* men inasmuch as it does not allow men an outlet for unmet expectations of manliness.[53] More particularly, however, AA men have been uniquely isolated, ostracized, and "castrated" *as* AA men.[54] Thus AA men's characterizations of being asexualized distinctively reinforce disadvantageous racial structures in relation to their white counterparts.

AA women have not only been associated with familiar patriarchal characterizations of women (e.g., submissive, domestic, and passive), they have also been stereotyped racially.[55] This "double bind" prevents AA women from escaping their inferior status. That is, even if one takes away the complex web of disadvantages felt and experienced *racially* by AA women, they nevertheless remain subjected to sexist stereotypes as women. If one does not treat their gender as a disadvantage, however, they must still contend with racism as Asians. Thus, they may be stuck in a double bind as double minorities.[56]

It is inaccurate, however, to assume that they are stereotyped uniformly. Eastern and Southeastern Asian and Asian American women are often simultaneously constructed as hypersexualized and submissive vixens. South Asian and Asian American women, on the other hand, are often constructed simultaneously as sexually available objects or as desexualized persons.[57] Their desires, including sexual desires, are secondary to those of their family and community; they are thereby "denied full access to the power of their own desire by silencing their sexual longings."[58] Thus, whatever situation, status, talents, or gender, there is an assumed deficiency on the part of AAs and they are pejoratively characterized in ways that may not reflect their own self-perceptions and that may hold them back from advancing fully in American society.[59]

The Effects of Asian American Agency

Aside from my discussion above about disadvantages for women, I have written elsewhere of some of the dangers of these socializations and pointed to some possible outcomes when men's socialized identities are threatened.[60] Particularly, I have discussed the fact that many men chose to live in the streets or commit suicide during the economic crisis in South Korea. Rather than sacrificing one's "manliness" as a result of losing their jobs (as economic performance is one masculine indicator), many chose to hide the fact.[61] Even when men found a way to keep their jobs, the pressure to keep their productivity and performance high, the stress from the prospect of losing their jobs, the demands from their superiors to meet the minimum bottom line, and their loneliness from not being involved with their familial duties contributed to an identity time bomb. Many resorted to alcohol, cigarettes, and sexual services to relieve those anxieties, to no avail, particularly since they had been socialized to suppress communication about their feelings.[62]

The picture is not dissimilar in the United States, of course. Christine E. Gudorf finds that most men do not, in fact, have the perceived power that they either claim or want. Similar to some Korean male experiences, men in the Western world become isolated and feel lonely, anxious, and emotionally repressed when they cannot live up to expectations and feel inadequate as men. These conditions have potential effects, including a lack of relational skills in nurturing children, friendship, and relationships with spouses or partners, often with lethal consequences.[63]

Hegemonic sexist and gendered ideologies affect AAs more particularly. While women are certainly disadvantaged in Western societies, white women as a whole have access to resources and privileges that AA women do not. Even when women are objectified by the media, for example, "the template for the feminine beauty standard is a *white woman.*"[64] Thus, while the image of rail-thin models and actresses may have a correlation with eating disorders in general,[65] there is at least a greater diversity of white images in the media "offering alternative body types, and whites are at the center of the size acceptance movement."[66] Images of Asian American women are a singular representation, one that is defined by both white American and East Asian standards.[67] Molded into this monolithic idealization, women are sometimes victimized as a result. As a casualty of exotification and fetishism, there are cases across the United States that document Asian American women being specifically sought out as the targets of kidnapping, rape, and torture. After media bombardment of certain stereotypical images, society gazes upon AA women (and sometimes physically responds to them) as objects of their fantasy. With experiences of everyday racism, it would almost seem psychologically sensible to many AA women to desire to be white as to internalize racism and struggle with self-hatred.[68] Of course one can claim that they simply should not go with the social flow. According to Rosalind S. Chou, however, "as a social being, it takes exceptional strength to define oneself without regards to externally imposed definition."[69] Anyone ever exposed to such exploitation and intimidation knows how difficult it is to stay true to oneself.

Similarly, while many men deal with stress caused by expectations to wield the perceived power that many of them do not actually possess, AA men deal with additional levels of stress. To be a perfect male in the United States, one must suppress all "female tendencies" and dispositions. Within such a construct, AA men—feminized in representations of hegemonic white Western masculinity—can never achieve perfect male status.[70] Some AA men attempt to access this masculine power by "whitening" as a strategy to avoid racism, to cope with the power they lack, or to reap the benefits of white masculinity.[71] The strategy for gaining power via whitening, for example, took a variety of forms in my young-adult life: befriending or dating exclusively white people, listening to and talking about classic rock, siding with the dominant culture against Asian minorities on political issues, etc. However, according to David Eng, there is a long history of exclusion of the AA man from power and normative masculinity.[72] Nevertheless, as a result of fears of appearing weak, effeminate, or gay, AA men sometimes resort to "bad boy" posturing or looking or acting "tough."[73] Such posturing may have some momentary benefits[74] but it can certainly lead to violence and it very often has: both violence from AA men and violence done to them.

Sometimes AA men are the perpetuators of violence when bad posturing is not enough. Hence, to prove their manliness, the posturing at times becomes actualized. When there is no outlet for the rage from their experience of racism, it shows itself violently. As a case in point, there has been some discussion of Asian American men's fraternities in American universities being even more over-the-top with hazing rituals in part because of anxieties about their masculinity.[75] More often, however, AA men are the recipients of physical, emotional, and symbolic violence at the hands of other men. Such violence manifests itself in many forms, including bullying, street violence, profiled and targeted violence, and "symbolic castration" through disinterest from women.[76]

Chou suggests that the long assault of racism has taken its toll on Asian Americans. Recent findings confirm that these experiences of racism, accumulated over time, are related to negative health outcomes, psychologically, emotionally, and physically. We have known for a long time that in general, "emotionally abused or battered [individuals] are depressed, drained, scared, ashamed, and confused."[77] However, recent studies suggest that the effects of a more systematic racist oppression psychologically damage people living within it.[78] There are also correlations between such psychological damage and everyday racism, resulting in worse health outcomes. The infant mortality rate (about 10.2 per 1,000 births), for example, among African American women is higher than white women (3.7 per 1,000 births) with a similar socioeconomic background (all with college degrees or higher). In fact white mothers have better health outcomes than the same bracket of African American mothers, even when compared with white American mothers without a high school education (9.9 per 1,000).[79] More studies are on the way to look at the effects of damage done over a life cycle. There are also a number of research organizations that look at the health outcomes of Asian Americans and their relation to racism.[80]

Asian American Double Bind Extended: Sexism Within

The harm does not all come from without. Because AAs live in a "liminal world," they find themselves in hybrid situations that may be characterized by transethnic, cross generational, transcultural, interlinguistic, and possibly even interreligious beliefs. That is, AAs can be multiply influenced by a diversity of experiences and backgrounds. As such, AAs and some aspects of their Asian heritage can also contribute to their ongoing struggles. This phenomenon can be demonstrated through the stories of multiple AA communities. For the purposes of this chapter, I will focus on their "extended binds" in AA Christian communities.

I refer to the extended bind to point not only to sexism and racism experienced by AAs in a Western hegemonic society but also to sexism within their *own* communities. There are several factors at play; one major factor is the legacy of neo-Confucian patriarchal ideologies, especially among those with an East Asian background. Although much of the discussion regarding the harm from this form of Confucianism revolves around the exclusion of women from holding certain ecclesial positions, I will highlight the negative results for both women and men.

A Confucian system defines a person in terms of one's relationship within familial, social and, in fact, cosmic order. This order is harmonious insofar as it maintains certain roles according to one's age, class, and gender. In this system motherhood is women's "avenue to security, respect, and power," not participation in public activities.[81] Because many AA churches tend to maintain this ideological stance even when in the United States, women face many struggles within their Christian communities. These struggles range from women not being able to advance to (or even imagine being in) leadership roles (including the priesthood or other clergy roles) to being ordained but not being able to properly carry out their ministry because of the limitations set by their own racial-ethnic communities. For some, their alternative is to serve in non–Asian American communities to transcend these limitations, while others choose non-Asian churches simply as their calling and because they want to be there. Even if the community allows for women to hold certain positions, they are often either put in service to more senior ministers or priests (as "assistants" or deaconesses in Protestant denominations and as "sisters" or nuns in Roman Catholic and Anglican denominations) or "relegated to the nursery or children's classes."[82] In short, certain AA *cultural norms* and Christian *churches* often justify AA women's second-class status with the Confucian and Christian beliefs that men should be in charge and women's sacrifices will be rewarded. Their Confucian cultural heritage tells them that their sacrificial efforts will deeply "move the heart" of the heavens, which in turn induces a transformation in their husband to make a "big sacrifice" to be family-oriented despite their public duties.[83] Simultaneously, the churches also invoke certain passages (e.g., Eph 5:22-28) to stress similar notions of male headship and women's heavenly rewards and the transformation of their husbands as a result of the sacrifices.[84] Such an uneven application of the Christian notion of sacrifice against women is what Sang Hyun Lee and Andrew Sung Park cite as a sin of sexism that is particular to Asian (especially Korean) American Churches.[85] Lee cites domestic abuse, women working double days, and women being put in secondary roles in the churches as cases in point.[86]

Unsurprisingly, the benefits from this patriarchal structure are allocated among AA men. However, they are not unilateral allocations. Many AA men become victimized as a result of the very system that was meant to covertly give them an advantage. To start, there are only so many positions of power within a church community that are occupied by a selected number of (mostly) men. The remaining AA male population is left to feel and be deemed as inadequate, incompetent, or powerless.[87] AA men attempt to escape this bind at least in their religious communities since they are already labeled as weak, passive, and effeminate outside of the church. It has been my experience that the struggle among men for these limited positions of power or the simple recognition of power plays a major role in much of the conflict within AA Christian congregations, including over visible financial conflicts. Because of all this, many Korean American Protestant Churches, with which I am familiar, have myriad positions for deacons and elders to accommodate its members' demand for titles. Perhaps due to the downward social mobility many immigrants experience, the church becomes the place where many immigrants hope to reclaim their lost social standing and status.[88]

Heterosexism: Triple Bind

In their Christian communities, some AA women and men suffer from a different version of the bind: a triple bind. Gender-queer and LGBTIQ AAs have not only experienced racism and sexism from Western society but have also been discriminated against for being LGBTIQ—and more so for being LGBTIQ *and* Asian. They are often ostracized by the two groups that they frequently consider their own. Gay Asian men particularly suffer discriminations from their religious and racial-ethnic communities *and* from other (gay) men, given their norms of masculinity. Large segments of the gay community have ruled them out, for example, as undatable (i.e., "no Asians" on dating sites),[89] and AA churches exclude them from many of their Christian communities.[90] Influenced by the teachings of their Christians churches, even their family members do not support their coming out, "accusing the devil of infiltrating" their minds.[91] To come out in these communities would be, "quite literally, the ultimate failure—moral, social, and personal all at once."[92]

In fact the hotly contested issue surrounding the LGBTIQ community was an arena in which many first-generation and second-generation AA churches came together politically. According to Sharon Kim, despite the fact that the first wave of Korean immigrants in the early 1900s had a very public, political face, Korean Americans stayed away from being involved in political action since the L.A. riots.[93] Since then, only one issue galvanized theses churches to take political action, Proposition 22 on the 2000 ballot to defend the "traditional" definition of marriage against same-sex marriages. Many first- and second-generation pastors aligned themselves with the anti-LGBTIQ stance by purchasing advertisements in ethnic newspapers, preaching from the pulpit, and distributing petitions at Sunday services.[94] Even though the senior pastors eventually resigned from their various positions within these various groups that were protesting gay marriages, prompting a rift between the two generations of AA churches, their consensus stands against gay marriages stayed intact.[95]

It becomes quite evident that there is a shared culpability, albeit in differing degrees. The categorizing and oppressing of AA men and women by Western, white male hegemony crosses the lines of sexuality and certainly plays a major role in the unjust treatment of AAs. However, AAs and AA Christians churches in particular cannot be exonerated because they too participate in the perpetuation of the discriminatory treatment based on gender or because of heterosexism.[96] A critical self-reflection tied to the ongoing efforts to resist sexist and racist structures in the United States is in order.

An Asian American Christian Ethical Approach to Gender and Sexuality

An AA Christian ethical approach to sexuality and gender must begin, therefore, from both within and without. It must ensure that Asian Americans are outspoken about the harm inflicted upon them by the dominant power structures. Simultaneously, it must reflect on and criticize instances and patterns of injustice and oppression within AA Christian churches. In order to become neither oppressors themselves nor complacent about their status as second-class citizens, AA Christians must take on an active approach that seriously considers both the objective goodness (and dangers) of their inherited Asian and Christian traditions and subjective experiences (and shortcomings) that enhance those traditions. As a starting point, the wisdom of Jesus of Nazareth can serve as an impetus for AA Christians to fight *against* gender and racial socialization of their brothers and sisters and *for* the victims within their own communities. Such an impetus can lead to practical actions and sound strategy.

Christ against Western Hegemony

Much like the caricature through which AA men and women are seen, Jesus may be seen as a "wimp" or too "feminine" by today's Christian churches and society's standards.[97] Yet according to the Gospels, Jesus ministered with assertiveness *and* "in tears, in pity and tenderness, in eschewing the privileges of authority," and by being in solidarity with the outcasts of society.[98] That is, Jesus not only stood by the marginalized but he also embodied diversity in his very being. If one wants to emulate Jesus, James B. Nelson suggests that one must realize that the central issue is that Jesus was not only a man but also the epitome and fullness of humanity![99] Thus, AA Christian men *and* women can relate to and imitate Jesus by standing with the people who are marginalized as imperfect women, inadequate men, hypersexual AA women, weak AA men, or asexual beings. To be complacent about our gender socialization that victimizes women and men in many ways (AA or otherwise), then, is not to be Christian.

Through evoking such motivation and vision, one may be able to envision some practical ways to first recognize and then combat the structural and attitudinal sins committed against them. Many AA scholars have already recognized these sins in the following ways. Asian Americans' racial identity is "institutionally reinforced, self-defined, and regularly practiced."[100] As such, this identity is not always an identity of choice. Rather, based largely on this racial identity, AAs have been lumped together and racialized as both model minorities and "perpetual foreigners" by the dominant power structures.[101] Russell Jeung argues, therefore, that the racial group boundaries are symbolic and permeable so that AA's racial identity can "establish a racialized sense of self and community that constitutes a meaningful identity, and not just a racial category that is ascribed from the outside."[102] These boundaries, then, can be articulated by using symbolic narratives of common, representative experiences. Such an insight provides these racially differentiated AAs to mobilize and form a "reactive solidarity."[103]

AA Christian churches can offer up, then, their uniquely "differing organizing logics for panethnic self-understanding."[104] One of these common, representative experiences of AA Christian communities is the aforementioned marginalization and oppression. Many AA Christian theologians find the roots of solidarity in this commonly shared experience of suffering from marginalization as it becomes part and parcel of their shaping of an Asian American identity.[105] More specific and practical to the subject matter, AA Christian communities can form Asian media watchdog groups, civil rights groups, or social media groups that can report on the perpetuation of the dominant society's unjust racial socializations.[106] Moreover, these groups can provide gender and racial analyses so that ethnic caucus groups within AA Christian churches can be empowered and equipped with appropriate tools to combat racism and sexism specific to their communities. Such groups, in solidarity with other AA Christian groups, can share information and experiences to brainstorm better ways to fight the structural hegemony that suppresses their potential in this country and beyond.

As AA Christian scholars work to improve hegemonic structures, however, it is vital that they use an effective approach. Thus, I suggest that AA Christian scholars develop language that is more relatable and less threatening. Terms such as white guilt, white racist supremacy, white/male privilege and perpetrators, and so forth are indeed necessary and must be explained with care and thoroughness. However, it has been my experience that when I explain these concepts to a group in a position of power, it is more effective when I employ familiar language to which the group feels it can relate. Whether it is simply putting the blame on men or white people for the structural sins of patriarchy or white supremacy, I believe direct confrontation and blame is "neither therapeutic . . . nor helpful."[107] Without denying the truth of white guilt or male privilege, my goal is to use words that my target audience would be more willing to hear so as to enable those in positions of power to be receptive to what I have to say and to start to acknowledge the unjust racial, ethnic, and gender structures of society.[108]

One of the ways that I find helpful is to have the dominant group reflect on their experiences. One can suggest to the group times when they were oppressed, when their rights and dignity were compromised (e.g., when their superior or boss treated them in dehumanizing ways, when they were ostracized by a group of people or by family members, when they may have traveled abroad and were caricatured by members of the host country as ignorant or crass Americans, etc.). One can invite the group to imagine what that experience was like and how it would be if they had to relive those experiences every day. Only by having them walk along this path can one gently start the conversation about structural sin. This strategy may foster better dialogue and understanding because they may feel less defensive and guilty about the structural problems of the society that favors them over the marginalized. This way, without sugarcoating the reality of structural sin, one has a better chance at accomplishing the lesson without an accompanying defensive reaction.[109] An AA Christian Ethical (AACE) approach to gender and sexuality, then, does not simply render abstract norms and conclusions about how to think about the issue but sees the issue in the context of fostering real, flesh-and-blood Asian American communities and developing their moral agencies.

Christ against Eastern Sexism

When do the oppressed become oppressors? Sarah, who was considered the property of her husband, Abraham, became an oppressor herself when she "obtained" her own property, Hagar, the resident alien.[110] When do AA Christians, who are marginalized and oppressed, become oppressors? The context of AA Christian communities, where men in positions of power perpetuate the double, or heterosexist triple, bind is one area where oppressed AAs (heterosexual men) gain their power back and become oppressors.

Here, Jesus can be a model once again to evoke a sense of necessity for action. Not only can Jesus be seen as too womanly and feminine by today's church and society's standards, he would also have been considered a kind of person that would be labeled "queer" in our modern day terms. Mary Douglas, Robert Goss, and others see Jesus as a queer Christ and question the rigid, binary understanding of gender and the understanding of Jesus' sexuality as a result of such dimorphism.[111] Similarly, Kwok Pui-lan claims that one can arrive at a more authentic picture of Jesus if one is to remove a viewpoint of erotophobic, celibate, dominating men that function to perpetuate the social values of elite men.[112] Putting Jesus in his historical context, then, one can plausibly claim that Jesus was himself queer in the sense that he did not marry and remained celibate, which was not normative for his time. This reimagining of the fullness of Jesus, then, calls not only for the emancipation of the "racial and ethnic other" but also of "multiple others," certainly including the "religious other" and the "sexual other."[113]

As a consequence, the AA Christian community can reflect on multiple questions aimed at recognizing its participation in the unchristian practice of marginalizing its own members. Again, by strategically drawing upon examples that are more relatable and less threatening, communities can reflect on and relate their experiences of being racially, ethically, and culturally excluded in America to draw similarities to the exclusions of their own members based on their gender or sexuality. For example, explaining the concept of male privilege and gender injustice within the church to a conservative Korean Christian group of mostly men, I found that the audience was much more willing to listen when I drew parallels to their experiences of racism in America. From there I encouraged the participants to apply Jesus' message, which is foundational to all calling themselves followers of Christ, to fellow Christians within the walls of our churches and houses first. That way we are more credible and qualified to make claims of structural sin beyond those walls. Because most individuals are not solely either victims or perpetrators, we need to make a concerted effort to enable them to reflect on the times when they were hurt, when they were the victims, when their dignity was taken away, *and* when they may have done the same to others. Only when empathy arises from this process can anyone even begin to talk about reconciliation and forgiveness.

Conclusion

Heteropatriarchal, hegemonic femininity and masculinity hurt men and women across the board. Hegemonic femininity must exist to serve, uphold, and support the maintenance of hegemonic masculinity. Hegemonic masculinity hurts men because most men do not (cannot) live up to male expectations, causing anxiety for men to produce and prove their manliness. Race complicates this socialization as Asian Americans are often disadvantaged in Western society. Culture, ethnicity, and religion further complicate the picture as many Asian Americans, rather than finding solace in their homes and churches, are treated as second-class citizens. To begin the process of reconciliation, healing, and social change for Asian American Christians, Jesus must serve as the example par excellence both as a model to evoke action and to emulate his ministry and strategy to be in solidarity with the disadvantaged. Taking his cue, Asian Americans must be actively involved in recognizing, pointing out, and working to ameliorate the situations of structural and attitudinal sin. However, this process must recognize that Asian American Christian communities are not simply exonerated from their sins. The effort must also be made within their own churches to acknowledge and improve on places where they are also perpetuating inaccurate and perhaps discriminatory notions of gender and sexuality. However, particularity of this AACE approach is such that, rather than just telling the community what to think/believe and what is right and wrong, one must provide compassionate and congenial conversational spaces as a precondition for any efforts of fostering Christian communities and developing moral agency. By bringing all human communities closer to the full realization of humanity by mirroring the fullness of Jesus' humanity, Asian American Christians can participate in Jesus' mission and continue to "go and do likewise."

DISCUSSION QUESTIONS

1. Choi describes the ways in which racial stereotypes of Asian Americans can differ for men and women: men are desexualized and feminized, while women are portrayed as docile, submissive, and perhaps sexually available. How did these stereotypes emerge and why, in your opinion, do they persist?

2. Choi gives several examples of the ways in which the pressures of conforming to societal or cultural standards of masculinity lead Asian and Asian American men to assert their social standing and power in the church, to performances of hypermasculinity, and in the most tragic of cases, to suicides. What can be done about this? How might Christianity be a source of healing?

3. Choi's Jesus is one he describes as expressive of the fullness of humanity (not just maleness). He is also "womanly" and "feminine" by today's standards and also arguably "queer." Have you ever thought of Jesus this way? What might seeing Jesus through the eyes of contemporary norms of gender and sexuality do for our thoughts on those topics?

4. Choi has suggested that concepts like "white guilt," "white racist supremacy," and "white/male privilege" should be taught to

conservative Christian audiences with care. He also narrates that he has been most successful in explaining to Korean American Christian men the concepts of gender justice when he has analogized the oppression of gender to that of race. What do you think about Choi's emphasis on rhetoric and tactics of persuasion? Is he right?

Marriage, Family, and Parenting

SHARON M. TAN

This chapter explores the issues Asian Americans face in their marital and familial relationships, and the interaction of these issues with the Christian theological tradition on marriage and family. As Asian American Christians create family life in the North American context, they must take into account the deeply imbedded family values and systems that they as Asians may have inherited, their notions of what Christianity contributes to the subject, and the interplay of both in the North American context in which these must now be lived out. They must create a way of living that is attentive to their experiences and to their Christian traditions (including their reverence for Scripture), while giving due respect to their extra-Christian or even non-Christian traditions and beliefs. This balance helps them live in wholeness in the context and society in which they live.

A widely accepted method of Christian ethics is to draw from four sources: Scripture, reason, experience, and tradition.[1] In the "Christian Theologies" section of this chapter, I will canvass the range of theo-ethical reflections on marriage, parenting, and family. As I will show in the "Family Values" section, Asian Americans bring a variety of distinctive concerns to these topics. Furthermore, the diversity of Asian American experiences means that there is no single Asian American approach to marriage, parenting, and family life. In the "Constructing" section, I propose that a consistent theme in the Christian Scriptures is that God calls God's people out of their surrounding culture to live in a new way and to relate to each other and to God in new ways. Drawing from my own experiences as an Asian immigrant to the United States who is raising Asian American and biracial children, I suggest that the task for Asian Americans is to reinterpret these Christian and Asian traditions in light of their experiences and thus create new ways of relating in marriage, family, and parenting that are congruent with their call to be Christians living in God's new order. This will often entail a bicultural approach to life and creative new ways of relating and retelling their stories and imagining their futures.

Christian Theologies of Marriage, Parenting, and Family

Christian theologies of marriage, parenting, and family are both numerous and disparate. In this section I will briefly describe some of the theologies that have been profoundly influential in Christianity: the biblical norm of love as traditionally conceived and which has influenced the theologies of Augustine of Hippo, which have in turn significantly influenced the Roman Catholic Church; the theology of Martin Luther that has so influenced the Protestant Church; feminist critiques of the traditional concept of love; and, finally, a contemporary theology by influential American theologian Stanley Hauerwas.

Theological reflections on marriage or family almost universally acknowledge love as the foundational element in Christian relationships. Traditional formulations of God's love envision agape love as selfless and sacrificial. Agape love is thus formulated as disinterested and even impersonal, and one who so loves does not prioritize oneself or one's own family above others. One is to love and to sacrifice for all equally just as God does. A long tradition of Christian thought and practice following the examples of Jesus and the apostle Paul has accordingly valorized abstinence and celibacy. Paul privileged singlehood over marriage and celibacy over family life (1 Cor 7:32-34, 38). The writers of the Epistles accepted the institutions of marriage and family and articulated an approach that, although patriarchal, was less rigid and authoritarian than the prevailing Greek and Roman cultures. In the concern for order in the household (see Eph 5:21, 6:14; Col 3:20-21; 1 Tim 3:4), the husband is to love his wife like Christ loves the church and the father should not frustrate his children.[2]

Augustine of Hippo has been very influential in the development of the Christian theology of marriage, in particular the Roman Catholic tradition. Augustine saw marriage as a divine sacrament and therefore indissoluble. Reflecting on the Adam and Eve story in Genesis 2, he was inspired by the natural bond and friendship between Adam and Eve before the fall. While sin inaugurated humanity's condition of birth and death, the union of man and woman has always been, and will always be, a permanent good for three primary reasons: it promotes fidelity, procreates children, and cultivates friendship. In fact Augustine argued that the bond of friendship underlying marriage takes precedent over the importance of procreation. The bond of friendship preserves and sustains the validity of all marriages, including marriages between elderly persons (who are beyond their reproductive years) and those who are sterile. The union of marriage is always good, but it is strengthened through procreation.[3] As theologian Willemien Otten explains, "Augustine shows us a view of society united at its inception. Sin may have conditioned the way in which humans produce offspring . . . but it cannot fundamentally undermine their bond of friendship."[4]

Despite these strong views in support of marriage, Augustine is best remembered for condemning sexual pleasure: the Christian ideal remains chastity because sexual intercourse is still the vehicle for transmitting original sin and thus only reserved for procreative purposes.[5]

The theology of Martin Luther founded the Protestant Reformation and has significantly influenced Protestant Christian views of marriage and family. While acknowledging that both Jesus and the apostle Paul counseled celibacy (Matt 19:10-12, 1 Cor 7:8-10), Luther saw that it would be impossible for most people. Most people need marriage so that the sin of lust, "which flows beneath the surface, is counteracted and ceases to be a cause of damnation."[6] Luther drew heavily upon the Old Testament, particularly from Genesis and Proverbs, to inform his understanding of marriage and family. For Luther the creation story offered in Genesis 2 is God's unchanging word and is thus understandable and applicable to one's own life and marriage. "These words teach us where man and woman come from, how they were given to one another, for what purpose a wife was created, and what kind of love there should be in the estate of marriage."[7]

A wife is God's gift. God "created for [Adam] a unique, special kind of wife out of his own flesh. [God] brings her to him, [God] gives her to him, and Adam agrees to accept her. Therefore, that is what marriage is."[8] This is reiterated in Proverbs 19:14: "House and wealth are inherited from parents, but a prudent wife is from the LORD." The husband is to love his wife as Christ does, in commitment and sacrifice and in responsibility and care.[9] In this, however, the husband still retains the authority and power in the relationship. Thus, the family system was patriarchal, but in what Don Browning called a "love paternalism" or "chastened patriarchy."[10]

Of particular interest is Luther's expansion of the estate of marriage into the realm of family and raising children. For Luther the point of marriage is not just to produce offspring and control one's lust but also to raise children to serve God. He stresses this point of proper child care so heavily in his sermon on the estate of marriage that he seems to speak against his own understanding of *sola gratia*: "If you really want to atone for all your sins, if you want to obtain the fullest remission . . . bring up your children properly."[11] In fact bringing up children properly is the most direct route to heaven (with the contrapositive holding true as well).[12] This is more difficult than it first appears because parents naturally worry more about their children's bodies than their souls. Therefore, parents must be willing to discipline their children both spiritually and corporally (Prov 13:24, 22:15, 23:14). If one does this, one's children will "lighten you in your hour of death, and to your journey's end."[13]

Both Augustine and Luther continued the patriarchal view of marriage and family assumed in the New Testament. Elizabeth Schüssler Fiorenza has noted that despite the New Testament household codes (*haustafeln*) appearing relatively tolerant compared to Greek and Roman norms at the time, many of the Epistles' injunctions on the topics of marriage and household still reinforce a "cultural-patriarchal pattern, insofar as the relationship between Christ and the church clearly is not a relationship between equals."[14] Other feminists have noted that the injunction toward sacrificial love in patriarchal cultures has often been used to keep women in submissive roles, as men in authority have used it to sanctify and legitimize unilateral sacrifice by women without acknowledging its applicability first to themselves. They insist that sacrifice, to give oneself for another without gain, only has meaning if it is freely given without coercion or manipulation. Feminist theology has accordingly expanded the notion of agape love and has looked to the mutual and egalitarian relationships *within* the Trinity to guide its notion of love between husband and wife: as the three persons of the Trinity are equal and in mutual relationship, so the love between husband and wife is to be mutual and egalitarian.[15]

Stanley Hauerwas proposes a contemporary interpretation of marriage and family that has incorporated feminist critique. Hauerwas asserts that marriage takes place in the context of the church. First and foremost, Christian marriage is not about fulfillment. Fulfillment is a possibility, but it is not the purpose. Marriage is a vocation, as is being single. Both marriage and singlehood are vocations where one partici-pates in the "upbuilding of that community called the church."[16]

While the explicit purpose of marriage is ecclesial, Hauerwas asserts there is also a personal dimension of marriage. Marriage is a venue for God to teach us patience and faithfulness. To emphasize this point, he offers a thought-provoking statement: you always marry the wrong per-son.[17] This statement is intended to highlight the absurdity of the promise of lifelong fidelity in marriage grounded on affections. Affections will always wax and wane. It is often the case that a spouse may no longer seem to be the correct choice or even the same person one once chose to marry. The primary challenge of marriage is learning how to love and care for the stranger to whom one finds oneself married. This can only be accomplished through fidelity and patience and within the context of the church.[18] If the vow of marriage is not to be absurd, it must be grounded in something other than our affections. Marriage should be grounded in God, "whose love is as true and firm as the ancient earth and whose faithfulness is as fixed as the heavens."[19] Thus, it is correct to assert that for Hauerwas marriage is not where one learns about love. It is where one learns fidelity and patience. There is no difference between human and divine love. The clear implication here is that love, care, fidelity, and patience are to be developed in both partners to the mar-riage, thus marriage is mutual and egalitarian as well as self-sacrificing.

Expanding the discussion to parenting and children, Hauerwas asserts that Christians who are married have a duty to have children.[20] Having children is the ultimate expression of hope that God will con-tinue to care for the world and the church.[21] Hauerwas understands the role of "parent" to be an officer of the church. Children are not our pos-sessions but gifts from God.[22] A family itself is a school of virtue where we learn to love our neighbors. This is because family makes one learn that we have obligations that we do not choose. "If we are to learn to care for others, we must first learn to care for those we find ourselves joined to by accident."[23] Thus it is appropriate to characterize Hauerwas' understanding of family as more historical than biological.[24] The family is not a fact, but a story about relationships that are to be formed and nurtured in love.

Asian American "Family Values" in Marriage and Parenting

While the term "Asian American" implies that there is a pan-Asian iden-tity in North America, there is considerable diversity in the population as discussed in the introduction and elsewhere in this volume. Any reflection on marriage and family life among Asian Americans must recognize that the term "Asian American" covers a culturally and ethnically diverse population of refugees, first-generation immigrants, families who have been in the United States for multiple generations, adoptees, transnationals, and persons of multiracial heritage, among others.[25]

Despite the diversity evident in Asian American culture, a number of scholars have identified some pan-Asian family values. These values are heavily, though not exclusively, influenced by Confucianism and are also found in non-Confucian cultures such as the Philippines and India.[26] The primary values reflected in this heritage include respect for authority, parents, and elders as sources of wisdom; ancestor veneration; consensus decision-making; the priority of the collective (e.g., family and society) over the individual; orientation toward educational success; delayed gratification through emotional and material self-discipline; and the importance of saving face,[27] or the avoidance of bringing shame to both oneself and to others since one's actions and reputation reflect upon that of the entire family. Also much discussed in the literature, including that by U.S. Roman Catholic Bishops,[28] is a deep desire Asian communities have shown for the value of harmony and a preference for indirect, rather than direct, communication.[29]

Among these values, the sense of familial obligation and filial piety are most pertinent to the focus of this essay. The extended family is viewed as more important than the individual; one's self-image is intrinsically related to the concept of an integrated family. One analogy that has been employed to capture the difference between typical Western and Confucian conceptions of the relation between individual and family is that the West tends to conceive of the self as a slice of pie—a part of a whole that retains its own individuality. Within Confucianism the relationship is more like a soup, where one's identity is established only within the context of the whole.[30]

The Asian extended family system has typically been patriarchal, patrilinear, and patrilocal.[31] In the traditional Confucian authoritarian system, the legal power of male over female family members was nearly total. The relationships that comprised a patriarchal family were described as complementary or mutually dependent: husbands or fathers were to provide financially and maintain authority and emotional distance but depend on their wives to provide them moral and emotional support; wives were to be subordinate to their husbands, but mothers were dominant in child rearing; and children were expected to be loyal and obedient to their parents and to take care of their parents in their old age. The extended family unit served as the social and economic safety net for all of its members.[32] In line with its patriarchal orientation, family resources were traditionally concentrated on educating the boys or sons (not "wasted" on the girls or daughters who would eventually leave the family to join their future husbands), for it was the adult sons who would have the primary responsibility of looking after their parents in their old age. Stories of filial piety that are centuries old have taken on mythic qualities and are still being repeated.[33] Jeffrey Meyer notes that while many of these stories can read as exaggerated or even ridiculous, their "powerful influence still supports Asian Americans and has enabled them to succeed as immigrants."[34]

In comparison, Filipino family systems have traditionally been more egalitarian than Confucian family systems, and Filipina women have always had a greater amount of gender equity relative to family systems in other parts of Southeast Asia.[35] Precolonial Filipino culture was less patriarchal than Confucian cultures. Before their subjugation under Spanish colonization, Filipina women participated in both communal and familial decision making and had equal opportunities for receiving education, and female children were equally respected and valued within the greater family unit and enjoyed rights of inheritance. These rights, among others, were mostly, if not totally, mitigated by the patriarchal (Christian) and economic (colonial, feudal, and capitalist) interests of Spanish colonization.[36] Today, Filipino gender roles bear the influence of Spanish culture, with distinct complementary gender roles where men are "macho" and women are the caretakers.[37]

Whether one lives by the model of Confucianism, precolonial Filipino society, or another Asian culture, Asian Americans who live in both mainstream white and "traditional" Asian worlds often struggle with the expectations of both cultures. While the dominant North American culture praises assertiveness, independence, direct communication, and spontaneity—all manifestations of autonomy and individuality—Asian Americans who subscribe to Confucian or other similar norms are commonly perceived by their (non-Asian) peers as comparatively reserved, quiet, obedient to authority figures (including parents), and self-effacing. In addition, their preferred communication style, in contrast to their non-Asian peers, still tends to be indirect and nonverbal (to allow oneself and others to "save face").

This is changing. Because of their exposure to North American culture, Asian American households are becoming (or can become) more egalitarian and less hierarchical than traditional Asian families.[38] As women have entered the workforce and their economic power has increased, their claim to the family resources has also increased, and wives have wielded more power in the family. The family's preference for boys has also somewhat lessened, and girls now have more, if not equal, claims to the family's resources.[39] Rather than between mothers and sons, as in traditional Asian families, the strongest relationships in Asian American families are becoming those between husband and wife and between mothers and children.

Mothers nurture their infants, holding them and attending to them, thus leading to the formation of close ties between mother and child. Emotional self-control and maturity is expected of children when they reach the age of six or seven. However, adolescents reportedly develop socially later than those of North American culture, and this is reflected in their courting relationships. Parents in Asian American families play a larger role in approving or disapproving their potential partners.[40] Many adult children also still remain at home until they marry, regardless of economic climate.[41]

In what follows, I will unpack some of these patterns of family life among Asian Americans further and introduce some distinctive concerns that have arisen among Asian Americans.[42]

Cohesive Family Relationships

According to Pew Research studies in 2013, Asian Americans have the lowest percentage of single families (one in six) in America when compared both to other minorities and the general population (one in three). Twenty-eight percent of Asian American families live with at least two adult generations in the same household.[43] Vietnamese and Filipino families are most likely to have a multigenerational household, followed by Chinese, Indian, Korean, and Japanese. Fifty-four percent of Asian Americans say that a successful marriage is one of the most important things in life; the general public reflects this disposition at only 34 percent. Sixty-seven percent of Asian Americans say that being a good parent is one of the most important things in life, while only 50 percent of the general American public reflects this.[44]

If we disaggregate the heterogeneous group "Asian Americans" and look at Filipino Americans in particular, we will see Filipino family relationships as likewise interdependent and close-knit. They are characterized by the following values: *utang ng loob* (reciprocal obligation), *hiya* (shame), *amor proprio* (self-esteem), and *pakikisama* (getting along). They prioritize the virtues of harmony, reciprocity, and mutual obligation in family life. They respect elders for their wisdom, not inherent authority due to age.[45] *Pakikisama* as a dominant value means that family members must get along harmoniously with others, even at the sacrifice of one's individual interests.[46]

Cohesiveness and intact family unity are strengths in Asian American families, but these strengths can also limit new possibilities. The pressure to conform to "family values" can discourage growth, creativity, and innovation of new forms of social life. The strong family structure in Asian American families works to solve problems within families, but it can also result in a closed problem-solving loop.[47] The reason for this is moral and social: when one transgresses filial piety, gender roles, family obligations, or other social norms, the act of transgression brings shame upon the household.[48] Thus the success of any member of the family, including a child, in fulfilling family expectations continues the family's good standing and inclusion into the community. In contrast, failure brings shame. For example, divorce is perceived as failure because it disrupts the harmony of the household as well as the obligations of family members to one another. It is a cause of shame as it exposes the rifts and disloyalties within a family, thereby causing that family to lose face in the community.[49] Finally, since family cohesiveness is commonly expressed as filial piety and in the children's loyalty to the parents, once the parents of adult children die, it is not uncommon for the family to drift apart.[50]

Involved Parenting

Asian American parenting styles vary considerably. In a study of Filipino American and Chinese American families, the researchers found subtle differences in cultural value and meanings of parent-child relationships. In both Filipino and Chinese American families, daughters described a good mother-daughter relationship in terms of communication, trust, and knowing that the mother cares. In addition, reflecting the more egalitarian nature of a Filipino family compared to a traditional Chinese or Confucian one, Filipina girls hoped for the possibility of a mother-daughter friendship. Girls described good father-daughter relationships in terms of communication and closeness, but this did not develop as often as good mother-daughter relationships did.[51] In turn, Filipino American and Chinese American boys valued communication and their mothers' sacrifice on their behalf. In addition, Filipino sons articulated trust as a description of a good relationship; they also valued communication and friendship with their fathers and admired their fathers' strength. On the other hand, Chinese sons valued communication, guidance, and respect for their fathers.[52]

Reflecting its Confucian influence, there are two terms for parenting in the Chinese language and culture: *guan* and *chiao shun. Guan* means to govern, but this does not mean to control but to care and be concerned through support.[53] *Chiao shun* means the moral training or development of the self.[54] Chinese parents govern their children by training them to be obedient so as to live in harmony with the social network the child is in.[55] It is the duty of Chinese parents to teach their children how to live respectfully of their elders and in harmony with society, and to restrain their emotions by controlling their tempers.[56]

As alluded to earlier, Confucian-influenced Asian parents are stereotypically more formal and less emotionally expressive than their Caucasian counterparts.[57] They are more authoritative and expect children to obey them.[58] Since they believe that it is discipline and hard work—not innate ability or talent—that lead to success, parents simply expect children to work hard to succeed in school. Parents support their children instrumentally rather than emotionally, that is, by providing educational opportunities and material support, even at a sacrifice.[59] There is more emphasis on education, discipline, and hard work, and less emphasis on verbal and physical affection.

The Western literature on parenting promotes a style of parenting that involves high expectations of children alongside high support for children in the form of physical and emotional affection. This is termed "authoritative parenting." "Authoritarian parenting," on the other hand, involves high expectations of children and low emotional support and physical affection. Asian families have been seen as authoritarian because Asian parents do not traditionally support their children through verbal affirmation or physical touch (e.g., hugs and kisses). However, Asian parents have high expectations of their children and give them the high instrumental support for education necessary to achieve the high expectations. Often termed "training," this parenting style raises the self-esteem and adaptiveness of Asian American children by enabling educational success. Additionally, when Asian parents acculturate to

Western culture, they also adopt more verbal and emotional supportive roles, which in turn support greater success.[60] Studies have shown that integrated and assimilated families who raise children with both training and authoritative parenting styles produce more successful children.[61]

"Tiger Mothers"

Because parents are responsible for training their children, and success is attributed to discipline and hard work rather than innate ability, the success or failure of children is a source of pride or shame to the family. The familial pressure on Asian American children to achieve in ways that augment social status thus takes on moral implications. The most visible face of this style of parenting in America is the "tiger mother."[62] For example, Yale Law School professor Amy Chua describes herself compelling her children to achieve through tactics considered draconian by Western standards, like prohibiting television and playdates, requiring hours of daily piano or violin practice, and accepting nothing less than straight As on her children's report cards.

While there are numerous problems with "tiger mom" parenting, I will focus here on four. First, the temptation to characterize all Asian Americans who are successful as having been parented by tiger moms implies that it is extreme parenting that accounts for their achievements and discounts what the children themselves have accomplished. That is, the location of the success of children in the tactics of their tiger moms who force them to excel undercuts the value of attaining educational success or cultivating musical talent through discipline and hard work.

Second, there is a downside to the high expectations of achievement set by those Asian American parents who do adopt Chua-like tiger mom tactics. Because failure would bring shame, children can be deterred from taking risks and exploring.[63] Also, there are stresses associated with maintaining a high expectation of achievement, and these anxieties can lead to rebellious behavior, withdrawal from school,[64] and a higher than average suicide rate for teenage girls and older women.[65] Because many Asian American parents are first-generation immigrants, and often both work, they have little time to help children with their homework or to go to school conferences. Thus, even though education is highly valued, specific needs may be overlooked.[66] Also, children who are pressured by their parents to succeed often experience conflict between the values of the home for high achievement and the values of the dominant culture, for example, for material consumption or athletic prowess. Children who bear the brunt of this conflict might find themselves withdrawing from the family and find parents losing communication with them.[67]

Third, because the tiger mom caricature conforms well to the "model minority" stereotype (of Asian Americans as exceptionally smart and hardworking), it facilitates overlooking the subgroups that are in fact struggling (not excelling) according to standard social, behavioral, academic, or economic measures.[68] For example, Chinese and Korean Americans have significantly higher annual incomes and levels of education than Hmong and Cambodian Americans (sometimes drastically so).[69]

Finally, in addition to the fact that not all Asian American subgroups meet tiger mom or model minority expectations, other non-Asian groups also display high rates of success, thus showing that there is not a necessary causal link between tiger mom tactics, Asian American cultures, and successful children. In *The Triple Package*, Amy Chua examines both Asian (Chinese and Indian) and non-Asian (including Lebanese, Nigerian, Cuban, and Mormon) immigrant cultures that have been more successful (defined in terms of income and educational and professional achievement) than others in North American society. Chua locates the economic and career success of these groups in three characteristics: (1) a superiority complex, (2) a sense of insecurity despite the superiority complex, and (3) the ability to control impulses and delay gratification.[70]

Multigenerational Households

In multigenerational households under the traditional Confucian model ("three generations under one roof"), parents live with their adult children (typically the eldest son) with the paternal grandfather as the final authority. Husbands have authority over wives, and mothers-in-law exert considerable authority over their daughters-in-law. Mothers run the household and grandparents may do some housework and care for grandchildren.[71] In the North America context, however, usually it is the adult children that head Asian American multigenerational households.[72] There is often a cultural gap between the less acculturated grandparents and the more acculturated grandchildren, correlated with the recency of immigration or the immigration status of the grandparents. The similarity of the immigrant culture to the dominant culture is also a factor in the cultural gap. Chinese, Korean, and Vietnamese cultures, all of which have stronger Confucian influence, are more dissimilar to North American culture.[73] There appears to be a lesser cultural gap in Japanese households, perhaps because Japanese American immigration is more established in America compared to other Asian immigration, and, ironically, because the anti-Japanese sentiment and internment of World War II increased pressure on Japanese Americans to conform to the dominant culture. Although Chinese immigration occurred at the same time as Japanese immigration (and in some cases earlier), acculturation of the Chinese immigrants was delayed in the exclusion era (1882–1943) because Chinese workers were restricted to men who were not allowed to marry local women. Filipino and Indian immigrants also experience less of a culture gap: Filipino immigrants come already influenced by Spanish and American colonialism, and the Asian Indian immigrants by British colonialism.[74]

Grandparents are the source of familial history and the transmitters of traditional culture, and Asian American children defer to their Asian grandparents in the same household. However, this intergenerational communication may be limited by language and culture.[75] There may be conflict between grandparents and parents over raising the children or cultural conflict between grandparents and grandchildren over the extent of grandparent authority. This creates a crucible in the home for many Asian American grandchildren to navigate the expectations of different cultures—they learn to be "Asian" from their families and to be "American" from influences outside the home.[76]

The Special Case of Refugees

A high proportion of Asian American adults—74 percent—are first-generation immigrants who were born abroad, and Asians represent 36 percent of new immigrants (430,000 people) each year in the United States.[77] Refugees represent only 10 percent of the immigrant population for any given year in the United States. From 1983–2004 three of the top five countries of origin for refugees to the United States were from Southeast Asia: Vietnam, Cambodia, and Laos.[78] In 2011 a total of 80,000 refugees, divided into regional allocations, were allowed into the United States. Allocations for refugees from Southeast Asia represented just over 68 percent of the 80,000 at 54,500.[79]

Refugee families experience difficulties particular to their circumstances. Refugees are involuntary immigrants who come displaced from their homes, perhaps many times over (i.e., successive displacements) and perhaps over the course of many years. They have experienced physical, cultural, and emotional homelessness and a continued sense of alienation. Acculturation occurs at different rates, if at all.

There are several family issues both voluntary and involuntary that recent immigrants face in common. First, there is the disruption of traditional family roles and expectations as previously discussed (i.e., wives enter the workforce and gain economic power, parents work long hours and are unable to supervise children closely). With the exception of those who have come on H-1B visas, poverty is common. Children generally learn English faster than their parents (in cases where the parents did not emigrate from English-speaking parts of Asia such as Hong Kong or India) and are the translators and the cultural mediators of the dominant culture. This shifts power dynamics in the family. Parents can also feel like they have lost their children to modernization, the dominant culture, or even the gang culture.[80]

Transnational Families

Transnationalism is a strategy for families to maximize their resources and opportunities in a world of uneven development, unequal relations, and legal barriers to mobility. In the global capitalist economy, labor from a country with scant resources moves to another country with more abundant resources to earn money to send back to families in the first country. However, the second country enacts legal barriers to movement and immigration, preventing families from joining the workers. The workers are also restricted from full participation in the host country and culture, leading to a subclass of workers with few resources and rights. Although this has happened in history (e.g., the Chinese in the nineteenth century), it is exacerbated by heightened capitalism[81] and recent immigration.[82]

Transnationalism is common in Filipino families. However, it is considered a breakdown in the fabric of the family as it reverses gender roles. Women are more easily employed overseas as domestic workers and so become the breadwinners of the family. In addition to role reversal, the geographical separation imposed on transnational families also changes traditional expectations of labor and of marriage, family cohesiveness, and social life.[83]

Constructing Asian American Christian Ethics for the Asian American Christian Family

In the previous sections, we have considered Western Christian traditions, some Asian traditions, and the experiences of Asian Americans. This section suggests that an ethical life for Asian Americans is enabled when Asian Americans are able to navigate the intersections of the Asian values and the North American values and world that they live in; in other words, when they can live biculturally and partake of the best of the multiple contexts in which they find themselves.[84] Since Asian Americans are a relatively recently defined social group who are so internally diverse, there is no one widely acknowledged pathway through these intersections. Asian Americans must be given the freedom to experiment and innovate while creating new ways of conceptualizing marriage, family, and parenting that lead to their ethical living and flourishing in North America.

Biculturality and Adaptation

The Hebrew Scriptures contain stories of the families that founded and lived in the early years of the tradition. They describe a particular immigrant family—that of Abraham, Isaac, and Jacob—and the God who called them out of their native land into a new land, culture, and particular relationship with God. These stories show the struggle of the ancient Hebrews to break free of their surrounding cultures and religions and to formulate a new understanding of their God and God's requirements of them.

Especially of relevance for Asian American purposes are the instructions to the followers of God to relativize their family traditions and cultures in order to live the life to which God has called them. In a type of refugee experience, the Hebrew people went into exile in Babylon. However, the Scriptures indicate that God encouraged them to settle, marry, have children, and build their lives and homes in the land where they were exiled (Jer 39:4-7). They were to create a new way of living and continue in their faith but also adapt again (and again) to their new surroundings.

Similarly, in the New Testament, the theme that God calls God's people out of the surrounding culture into a new one continues. Jesus also began life as a refugee (Matt 2). His call to his disciples to reject their families and follow him (Matt 19:29, Luke 14:26) was an instruction to immigrants into the new "kingdom of God" to leave their traditional ways of family and family culture in order to build a new way of living in the new order, and a new way of understanding marriage and family.

I suggest that an ability to leave one tradition and adapt to a new way of living is also the mark of Asian American identity and ethics.

Granted that North American culture is not to be equated with the promised land, nor to Babylon, nor to God's new order as proclaimed by Jesus, Asian Americans can identify with the experiences of migration, exile, strangeness, and search for refuge, and with the accompanying need to leave traditional cultures as they forge new ones in new settings. And because North American culture is not the new order of God, Asian Americans should retain the best of their Asian cultures and preserve ethnic identity while adopting the best of North American culture.[85]

Marriage

Marriage in the Hebrew Bible existed within a confluence of religious, social, and legal arrangements, which included a wide spectrum of recognized relationships.[86] Marriage in biblical times was also polygamous, reflecting the social and legal milieu of the time. The patriarchs and kings had several wives and concubines each, and King Solomon had a thousand. However, in contrast to the surrounding culture and practice, the story in the Hebrew Scriptures of the first human beings contains instructions about marriage to the contrary. One reads in Genesis 2 that Adam was lonely, so God made Eve for him. Adam and Eve are part of each other, and both are created by God and animated by God's spirit. The Hebrew Scriptures then describe the institution of marriage as when the man leaves his parents to join with his wife (Gen 2:42). Thus, the very first instruction on marriage in the Scriptures, predating the fall, is to the *husband* to leave his family and join with his wife when they marry (Gen 2:24). In traditional patriarchal settings, both in biblical times as well as more recent times, this particular instruction has in fact been interpreted in the reverse to legitimize the incorporation of the wife into the husband's culture and family. In patriarchal societies the wife leaves her family and culture to join the husband's.

Instead, this instruction should be interpreted as a reversal or counterpoint to the patriarchal atmosphere in which the Scriptures were written and continue to be lived. It is an instruction to the husband to yield his social and cultural dominance in order to develop a relationship of mutuality with his wife, and, by implication, to develop biculturality in the marriage and family. The wife naturally learns the husband's culture in a society that is traditionally patriarchal. However, the instruction to the *husband* to leave his parents to join with his wife is an instruction to the husband to honor his wife's culture and to learn to navigate both his and his wife's ways of living. Interpreted as an instruction to the traditionally socially and culturally dominant partner to adjust to the socially or culturally subordinate or less powerful partner, the Genesis passage is then an instruction to one to learn multiple and new ways of living and adapting to one's surroundings.

This reading of the Genesis passage supports the feminist critique of patriarchy in favor of the notion that marriage should be an egalitarian and mutual relationship, as described in the "Christian Theologies" section of this chapter.

There are implications of this for Asian American marriages. Marriage is the crucible where Asian Americans, presumably like other members of minority ethnic groups, learn to live in ways other than how they were first enculturated. However, even families from the same ethnicity have cultural variations that lead to differences. Any egalitarian and mutual marriage, with its normal give-and-take, is a practice in biculturality.

I suggest that those who view the Hebrew and Christian Scriptures as authoritative in any way should take seriously the antipatriarchal and proegalitarian implications of the words of the text, especially considering its place in the story of Adam and Eve before the fall. In other words, this proegalitarian instruction about marriage is one from the very beginning, one that does not yield to circumstances occasioned by human frailty. It is an instruction to the socially and culturally dominant partner to yield that dominance to the socially or culturally subordinate or less powerful partner in the marriage.

Recognizing both that power dynamics between males and females are more complex today and that each spouse in a marriage may be more powerful in different ways (e.g., socially, economically, culturally), I suggest that the general instruction is that in the different ways where a spouse is dominant, he or she is to relinquish that dominance and consciously adapt to the other in marriage. Furthermore, since the Genesis instruction assumes that the husband moves from his family, this applies within a multigenerational household as well. The dominant marriage partner (typically the husband) in the multigenerational household yields to the needs of the subordinate partner (typically the wife). In this way the marriage becomes a blend of both cultures and can create the community of God that Stanley Hauerwas imagines, as described in the "Christian Theologies" section.

Parenting

Parenthood reflects the relationship God has with God's people. God is described as a loving Father who cares for his children, the Israelites (Deut 32:6; Isa 43:6; Ps 68:5, 89:26). In turn, children are gifts from God to their parents. Parents are to teach their children about God through the stories and commandments (Deut 6:4-9)—in other words, to represent God to their children—and children must honor their parents as they honor God (Exod 20:12).

As in the case of marriage, biblical stories of parenthood can be seen to portray God's order in contrast to prevailing culture. While the ancient Hebrews practiced primogeniture, or the inheritance rights of the firstborn son, the Hebrew Scriptures tell stories that show that neither primogeniture nor paternal favoritism automatically imputed divine favor. For example, Cain was the firstborn and Abel, the second born, yet the Scriptures describe God as favoring Abel and Abel's gifts. Although Isaac favored his firstborn son Esau, it was Jacob, the younger twin, who inherited the Abrahamic blessing. Although Jesse favored his older sons, it was David, the youngest, whom God chose to be king of Israel.

The New Testament also reinterpreted many of the family ties established in the Jewish culture of the time. First, the boy Jesus prioritized God, his "Father," over his natural parents in his visit to the temple (Luke 2:41-52). Contrary to expected patterns of those times, Jesus was not married and had neither family nor home. In fact he called his disciples to reject their family in order to follow him (Luke 14:26). Over the course of his lifetime, he reinterpreted the family unit in light of God's new order: those who followed him were his family instead of his mother and brothers. In his final moments, he gave his mother to his disciple John to care for, calling them mother and son (John 19:26-29).[87]

Primogeniture is no longer a common practice, but Asian Americans are to reinterpret other cultural practices in light of God's new order. If the Christian Scriptures show that God disregards the family order of the culture of the time, then we should ask if Asian American families should also disregard the cultural preference for boys over girls. Also, as the authors in the New Testament challenged the absolute authority of parents over children (children are to obey their parents "in the Lord"), and as Jesus prioritized relationships according to God's order over that in the natural family, we should call the absolute priority of family order in Confucian-influenced cultures into question. Without the need to adhere to traditional cultural preferences or family order, families can be free to allocate resources where they are most needed or can be most effectively maximized.

Asian Americans draw from multiple cultures and must reconcile the need to adapt to Western culture and the need for continuity in their own culture. Children need to survive in both (or more) cultures, and parents are uniquely positioned to help them.[88] For example, the use of shame[89] as a tool to control behavior, while adaptive in a society and culture with high emphasis on conformity and which prioritizes society and family over individual health and needs, is in conflict with North American values of independence, individuality, and risk taking. Family conflict and high contrast in culture produces youth and children that are highly anxious because they cannot reconcile the two different value systems.[90] I suggest that parents who feel "shamed" by their children's behavior recognize that this shame is located in cultural expectations that are not dominant in North America. To shame their children instead of dealing with the behavior in other more culturally adaptive ways will not produce the desired results but instead have negative consequences on the children, leading to more shame.

Because children and youth adapt faster to the dominant culture than do their parents,[91] Asian parents must intentionally and proactively remain in communication with their children and their children's social needs. This can happen when Asian parents allow their way of thinking to be challenged.[92] For them to lead the way in helping their children achieve biculturality and navigate the external world and culture, the parents must be willing to explore possibilities along with their children and be open to discussing values and meanings in the different cultures, and to create with them a future that is unique to their circumstances, honoring of their family values, and open to communication about their desires and aspirations in the discernment about what they will do in life. Parents may even have to exercise agape in the traditional sense of self-sacrifice as they help their children navigate the world in a way that is best for the children, and not necessarily for their own traditional ideas of family.

Asian American parents must also deal with their and their children's experience of the racialization of ethnicity. Asian American children, while growing up in American culture and adopting American norms, perhaps even for several generations, may never simply be seen as fully American. Parents of these children will need to teach their children about how to deal with racism.[93] This may be particularly pertinent in biracial families. Biracial children may feel excluded from the cultural and racial identities of either parent—either not being Asian enough or not being white/black/Latino/a enough. This is a lonely place, especially in teenage years and early adulthood, when cultural identities are being forged. While monoracial parents may identify with their children's predicaments, they must yet guide their children through them. They can approach this as a creative time, when new possibilities in culture and identity can be imagined and family stories can be continued in new ways and new chapters.

Telling the Story

As the stories in Scripture of the Hebrew people and early church have guided and nourished Christians, the stories of Asian American (and other) immigrants and refugees can also guide and nourish their families and succeeding generations. It is the telling and retelling of one's story that gives one identity and personhood; it is the telling and retelling of family stories that carry the family's existence and meaning into the future. It is the telling and retelling of personal and family stories in light of God's new order that shapes one's relationship to the divine.

All Christians are sojourners (Phil 3:20; 1 Pet 1:1, 3), but refugees and immigrants arrive with particular stories of overcoming or surviving great adversity. When they encounter the vastly contrasting cultures in North America, they experience adjustment difficulties that are understandable in light of their experiences. Extending their family stories to include the experience of migration would enable them to constitute a narrative to give sense and coherence to their lives.[94] The friends of refugees and recent immigrants need to pay attention to the losses the refugees have had of former friends, neighbors, culture, and way of life.[95] The family and its friends may need to understand that the culture clash between old and new lead to real struggle, and they may need to honor the family's search for ways to incorporate both old and new cultures.[96] Paradoxically, stories steeped in pain or shame may need to be told and retold in safety for healing and understanding to happen. This may be a place of real help and healing that the friends of the family can contribute, in their willingness to listen, interpret and reinterpret, and understand in nonshaming ways the meanings of these stories.

Since extended family is the repository of the fuller family narrative, Asian Americans who maintain family cohesiveness and interdependence are better able to transmit their stories to the next generations. The transnational family is in a unique position to live and create meaning from the impact of globalization and heightened capitalization on human lives and relationships. As described above, *pakikisama*, the Filipino idea that there is mutual cooperation, responsibility, and mutual aid in extended families, is the value that maintains the transnational family.[97] Thus, while in the midst of the economic, cultural, and legal chaos of transnationalism, families can tell and retell stories of the love and responsibility families are capable of. Telling those stories would help people understand how alienation can be navigated or perhaps even transformed by the forging of new relationships, and that new sources of strength and community may be found.

In the telling and retelling of the individual or family narrative, meaning and purpose can be developed. As immigrants and their subsequent generations maintain their narrative, they interpret and reinterpret their circumstances and create new ways of understanding the life that they have. This not only gives an understanding of the past, it also provides a possible vision for the future. As noted above, Hauerwas implies that true family is more historical than biological;[98] the family is more about stories than about blood. One might even suggest that stories are thicker than blood.

Stories of my own family's Christian faith in China have undoubtedly influenced my own journey in both faith and vocation in North America. To not pass these stories on to my children—along with the stories they inherit from their father's side of the family, as well as the stories that have shaped North American culture—would be to deny them a source of strength and identity that is part of their heritage. It is the children's task to weave these stories together into an ongoing narrative of where and how they belong in community, and it is the task of their parents to guide them through it, offering their experience and wisdom while all the while recognizing that ultimately, the task is theirs.

As Asian Americans retell their particular stories in light of their larger family story, respecting their Christian traditions and non-Christian influences, they will be able to imagine a future that responds to their past but is also capable of creating a new way of living. Stories of courage and risk in the past encourage bolder actions in the future. Stories of survival and hope in the past sustain hope and faith for the future. This is the way forward.

DISCUSSION QUESTIONS

1. What are important Asian American "family values" that are adaptable to North American culture? What Asian American family values should be maintained, in spite of whether they are adaptable to North American culture? Why?

2. Do you agree with the author of this chapter that biculturality is a desirable quality? Is there moral value in biculturality? What are some bicultural ways of organizing family life? Use your imagination! Why shouldn't Asian American families completely assimilate or completely separate from the dominant culture?

3. A visible segment of Asian Americans emphasize educational success, and as described in this chapter, success has moral implications in the Confucian culture. Are there parallels in Christianity to this? If not, what does this mean to Asian American Christians?

4. Has your story resonated with any others in this chapter? How is the family narrative sustained in your family?

✦ 4 ✦

Virtue Ethics

ILSUP AHN

Should we develop an idea that can be called "Asian American Christian virtue ethics"? If so, why do we need the qualifier "Asian American" before "Christian virtue ethics"? I attempt to answer this question by demonstrating how an Asian American Christian virtue ethics can be possible through a critical reflection and an in-depth reading of various related texts. Before beginning, let me first emphasize that there have been few systematic or theoretical efforts to construct the concept of Asian American Christian virtue ethics by Asian American Christian ethicists. The lack of critical discourse on Christian virtue ethics in Asian American Christian communities, however, should not be interpreted to mean that Asian American Christians are not interested in Christian virtue ethics. With that said, I consider this essay only as an initial theological-ethical attempt to construct the concept of Asian American Christian virtue ethics.

This essay is comprised of three parts. While the first part explores how Western Christian thinkers have developed Christian virtue ethics in the long history of appropriating the Western philosophical tradition, especially the Aristotelian model, the second and the third parts respectively deal with how Asian American Christians may be invested in this topic and what Asian American Christian virtue ethics might look like. In doing so I introduce a method of "cocritical appropriation." The essence of cocritical appropriation lies in the hermeneutical synthesis of Asian American Christians' critical efforts, which are comprised of two steps. The first step is a critical exploration, in which Asian American Christians examine how other Christians (predominantly European American) critically appropriate their cultural and social ethos. For example, the main explorative question for this step is the following: How have Western Christian thinkers critically appropri-ated their philosophical and cultural traditions in establishing Christian virtue ethics? The second step is to critically appropriate the ethical construction of Western Christian thinkers in light of Asian American Christians' theological reflection as well as their ethical critique of their own cultural ethos and historical traditions. In the second step, Asian American Christian ethicists attempt to answer the following question: How can we critically engage Western views on Christian virtue ethics in regard to their theological appropriation of Asian cultural and social ethos? It is inevitable that the construction of Asian American Chris-tian virtue ethics is in need of more in-depth and complex internal and external theological engagements. Let us first investigate how Christian virtue ethics has been developed in Western philosophical and religious traditions.

Western Christian Perspectives on Virtue: Virtues in Western Philosophical and Religious Traditions

In the Western philosophical tradition, one of the most fundamental questions to ask in ethics concerns moral motivation: What motivates moral action or why be moral? Foundational thinkers of Western phi-losophy such as Plato and Aristotle attempted to answer these questions by arguing that all human beings strive after the attainment of the moral ideal or the good. By observing human behaviors using their philosoph-ical insights, they came to conclude that humans are born with a certain moral nature to seek after good and order rather than evil and disorder. They differed, however, on defining what the moral good actually is. For example, while Plato defines the moral good in accordance with the realization of ideal order (natural or social), Aristotle is more interested in the actualization of any given rational capacity and potentiality in terms of attaining goals. Aristotle's explanation seems to be more pow-erful because he perceives correctly that human behaviors are motivated by desire, and all human desires have a single goal: the satisfaction of desire. He then points out the need to shape and modify these desires. Unless we shape and modify our varied desires by a certain rational prin-ciple or discipline, our behaviors will not be anything better than those of animals and beasts. In a nutshell, this rational principle or discipline is what he means by virtue, and virtue is a necessary component for living a good life. To be human means to live a good life, and in order to live a good life, we need to nurture and attain virtue. Aristotle explains virtue by exemplifying such concepts as temperance, courage, fortitude, and justice (the four cardinal virtues). Ultimately, a good life is a virtuous life, and a virtuous life is possible by nurturing and training our given capacities to be fully blossomed (especially a rational capacity). Aristotle explains that virtue has several characteristics. As a trait of one's character of intellect, a virtue is not only desirable and praiseworthy but also relatively stable and consistent. At the end of the day, a virtuous person is known by his or her patterned behaviors. As Aristotle perceives, these patterned behaviors are possible through habituation. For him a courageous person is one who tends to behave courageously in situations that call for courageous action.

Greek philosophy's influence and contribution to later Western philosophical, cultural, and religious tradition have been enormous, and two key aspects are especially important to recognize. First, reason (particularly practical reason) is widely recognized as the primary moral faculty for the realization of individual and social virtues. For Plato the concept of civil order is to be governed by reason, not by desire, passion, or selfish interests; likewise, for Aristotle, since the moral life aims at choosing the mean between excess and deficiency in correspondent emotions and actions, and the role of practical reason is essential in making the choice of the mean, practical reason is regarded as the primary moral faculty. The other aspect is that, as Aristotle argues in his *Nicomachean Ethics* and *Politics*, human beings are by nature social and political. Plato's and Aristotle's philosophical discourses on moral virtue(s) also have several controversial aspects, such as the exclusion of women, foreigners, and children from the realm of moral and political virtues; they also regard slavery as something of a natural condition, politicizing nature or the natural.[1]

Above, we have briefly reviewed how Greek philosophy has set the tone in terms of establishing Western perspectives on moral virtue(s). The method of cocritical appropriation requires us to start with the critical review of Greek philosophy, because as Jean Porter argues, along with the biblical sources, the ideals and theories of virtue that emerged in Greek philosophy and were further elaborated in the Hellenistic Roman empire comprise two formative sources for Christian reflection on the virtues.[2] Considering that Asian American Christians' historical and social context is North America, which is predominantly influenced by the Western cultural and social tradition, it is appropriate for us to start by investigating how Western Christian thinkers critically appropriate their philosophical, cultural, and historical traditions.

Among the earliest Christian theologians, Augustine of Hippo (354–430) is the most conspicuous in terms of the extent and depth of theological reflections on Christian virtues. In his book *City of God*, Augustine critically appropriates Greek philosophy from a theological standpoint. He points out that although it appears that the soul rules the body and reason governs the vicious elements, unless the soul and reason do not serve God the way God commands to us, we do not in any way exercise the right kind of rule over the body and the vicious propensities.[3] According to Augustine, without having the knowledge of the true God and the perfect love of God, one cannot attain true virtue. All other kinds of virtue would ultimately turn out to be vices, because although the virtues may be regarded by some people to be genuine and honorable, they would inevitably be "puffed up and proud," so these seeming virtues can only be accounted vices rather than virtues.[4] In order to attain true virtue, then, the knowledge and love of God are indispensable. From this theological vantage point of the centrality of the knowledge of the true God and the perfect love of God, he reinterprets and appropriates the popular Greco-Roman views on virtue. To be more specific, Augustine holds that although the fourfold divisions of virtue (temperance, fortitude, justice, and prudence) are right, they ought to be redefined according to the centrality of the knowledge and love of God. He summarizes his point as follows:

> I hold virtue to be nothing else than perfect love of God. For the fourfold division of virtue I regard as taken from four forms of love. For these four virtues . . . I should have no hesitation in defining them: that temperance is love giving itself entirely to that which is loved; fortitude is love readily bearing all things for the sake of the loved object; justice is love serving only the loved object, and therefore ruling rightly; prudence is love distinguishing with sagacity between what hinders it and what helps it. . . . So we may express the definition thus: that temperance is love keeping itself entire and incorrupt for God; fortitude is love bearing everything readily for the sake of God; justice is love serving God only, and therefore ruling well all else, as subject to man; prudence is love making a right distinction between what helps it towards God and what hinders it.[5]

Augustine's theological account of Christian virtue ethics is a classical showcase of how we could critically reevaluate and theologically appropriate the given philosophical or cultural traditions from the vantage point of theology. As Jean Porter correctly points out, Augustine follows both Plato and the Stoics in claiming that the virtues are all fundamentally expressions of one quality, but he critically redefines and reconceives that quality with the idea of Christian love.[6]

Thomas Aquinas (1225–1274) is a great theological synthesizer who offers the most influential scholastic theory of virtues. By critically appropriating Aristotelian philosophical ethics as well as Augustine's theological virtue ethics, Aquinas develops his influential account of Christian virtue ethics. Following Peter Lombard, Thomas first defines virtue in his *Summa Theologiae* as "good qualities of soul disposing us to live rightly, which we cannot misuse, and which God works in us without our help."[7] Following Aristotle, Aquinas understands virtue as a habit that leads us to a good end. A virtue is, as J. Philip Wogaman writes, "a disposition of the will to choose means that are appropriate to that ultimate end."[8]

Perhaps the most distinctive aspect of Aquinas' virtue ethics is his integration of two types of virtues: the four Aristotelian cardinal virtues (temperance, fortitude, justice, and prudence) and the three theological virtues (faith, hope, and love [*caritas*]). According to Aquinas, while the former can be "acquired" through mindful habituation, the latter can only be possible through the supernatural "infusion" or "instilling" of God.[9] In developing two-tiered sets of virtues, Aquinas makes it clear that with the acquired virtue only, one cannot attain the ultimate human *telos* (end), which is eternal happiness through the union with God. Since eternal and ultimate happiness lies beyond the limits of human nature and capacity, the infusion of God's grace is necessary for the life of supernatural happiness. We can see how Aquinas' delineation of four cardinal virtues is largely Aristotelian. For example, temperance is the virtue of controlling one's passions and desires; fortitude is the virtue of resisting various impulses inculcated and caused by such fears as toil or danger; justice is the virtue of a right ordering of relationships and distribution; and prudence is the practical virtue that orders the will according to rational principle. Aquinas reasons that the four cardinal virtues could be pursued and attained by any reasonable persons who strive after "natural happiness."

According to Aquinas, unlike the four cardinal virtues, there is an order of generation among the three theological virtues of faith, hope, and love (*caritas*). Since by faith the intellect apprehends what it hopes for and loves, he holds that faith must precede hope and charity. Yet he soon quickly adds that although faith precedes hope, and hope charity (as activities), as dispositions they are all infused or instilled together. Aquinas also holds that there is a different kind of order—the order of perfection—among the three infused virtues, and love precedes faith and hope in that both faith and hope are quickened by charity. Both faith and hope receive from charity their full complement as virtues. He writes, "For thus charity is the mother and the root of all the virtues, inasmuch as it is the form of them all."[10]

Aquinas' critical appropriation of Greek philosophy (particularly Aristotle's) differs from that of Augustine. In Richard Niebuhr's typological terms, Augustine's appropriation typifies the "Christ the transformer of culture," according to which culture is under God's sovereign rule, and Christians must carry on cultural work in obedience to the Lord. Aquinas' appropriation represents a different paradigm, "Christ above culture," which attempts to synthesize Christianity and culture into a hierarchical structure.[11] In some sense Aquinas' critical approach appears to be more appealing and effective in terms of integrating two heterogeneous lists of moral virtues, because in Augustine we can only discover a sweeping negation of the non-Christian moral virtues. According to Augustine, without being anchored in knowledge and love of God, the four cardinal virtues would ultimately turn out to be "splendid vices." Aquinas' theological appropriation of Aristotelian virtue ethics also entails some critical problems. For example, as Reinhold Niebuhr discusses in his *The Nature and Destiny of Man*, the theological virtues of faith, hope, and love have nothing to do with the exigencies of human freedom, thus rendering the dialectical relation between "love" and "justice" untenable in regard to Christian social ethics.[12]

With the dawning of the modern period, although virtues were not entirely ignored either by moral philosophers or by theologians, theological interest in moral virtues was largely eclipsed by other theological concerns such as justification by faith (Martin Luther) or modern natural law (Hugo Grotius). According to Jean Porter, although there were some exceptions (e.g., Jonathan Edwards[13] and Friedrich Schleiermacher), throughout the twentieth century there were a number of Catholic and Protestant theologians who attempted to rediscover traditions of virtues and virtue ethics as a resource for theological ethics.[14] Some of the most influential philosophers and theologians include Elizabeth Anscombe, Philippa Foot, Iris Murdoch, and Alasdair MacIntyre. Among these, MacIntyre's *After Virtue* seems to be most prominent. In this contemporary classic, MacIntyre indicts the philosophical failure of the Enlightenment project that strives to construct a new system of ethics based on some premises concerning human nature. MacIntyre traces the reason of modernity's ethical failure to the loss and ignorance of the ancient approach to ethics, particularly the teleological scheme of Aristotle's philosophy and ethics. MacIntyre's main thesis, therefore, is to revive Aristotelian virtue ethics by making a crucial distinction between what any particular individual at any particular time takes to be good for him and what is really good for him as a person. MacIntyre emphasizes, "It is for the sake of achieving this latter good that we practice the virtues."[15] Thanks to MacIntyre's work, a growing number of philosophers and theologians (from Martha Nussbaum to Stanley Hauerwas) have turned their attention to the virtues and related topics such as the moral significance of the emotions, particular communities, and traditions.[16]

Stanley Hauerwas is the most influential Protestant theological ethicist to promote virtue ethics as the most vital approach to Christian ethics. Among his many books, *The Peaceable Kingdom* and *A Community of Character* are crucial. According to Hauerwas, the modern ethical situation is in a bleak situation due to the symptomatic reductionism characterized by an excessive concern with ethical dilemmas or quandaries. The excessive focus on present ethical dilemmas such as abortion without exploring and investigating the historical background surrounding the moment of decision typically characterizes our modern ethical situation. As a result of this modern ethical reductionism, which only concentrates on choice and decision, more important aspects such as the character, community, and history are largely ignored in moral discourse. Hauerwas' point is not that ethics is unconcerned with decisions or moral principles; rather, he addresses ethics as being primarily about who we are, not what we should do. Christians are to come to a certain ethical decision not through their decisionist preference but out of deep consideration of the historical and communal context out of which a person's character is formed and matured. Hauerwas thus develops a new type of Christian virtue ethics, according to which the narratives of the Christian community play an essential role in helping Christians form characters and virtues. As he writes, "We Christians are not called on to be 'moral' but faithful to the true story, the story that we are creatures under the Lordship of God who wants nothing more than our faithful service."[17]

Hauerwas' critical integration of virtues and narratives shows us that belongingness to a certain community is an essential element of forming virtues because a community is the primary carrier of narratives.

Christian stories not only constitute a tradition but also form a community. Although Hauerwas' Christian virtue ethics is distinguished by its emphasis on Christian narratives and the belongingness to a certain Christian community, the basic method of embodying Christian virtues is largely Aristotelian. Hauerwas stresses the importance of continuous practice; like a skill, one can only develop a virtue through continuous practices and performances. Virtue is also learned from the recognized model, as Aristotle typified in his *Nicomachean Ethics*. Just as the Greeks' young people were to embody the virtue of courage by following after the model of Greek heroes, Christians are to adopt the godly virtues by following the models of God's people in Scripture.

Thus, Hauerwas' narrative approach to Christian virtue ethics has both pros and cons. On the one hand, as Jennifer A. Herdt points out, "his writings have done a great deal to shift the attention of the discipline away from quandaries and principles to the formation of Christian convictions and assumptions in the context of living social practices."[18] On the other hand, however, his rhetoric of Christian particularism ("the church does not have a social ethic; the church is a social ethic"[19]) may jeopardize civic friendship and Christian churches' responsible solidarity with the world. "Practices and vocabularies that are deemed non-Christian or secular may be seen as sources of temptation or of contamination from which one must separate oneself, thus jeopardizing civic friendship."[20]

Hauerwas is also criticized by non-European Christian ethicists such as Miguel A. De La Torre, who faults Hauerwas for not adequately considering the social location of oppressed people. De La Torre writes that "death is also caused by economic, social, and political structures, and Hauerwas' refusal to make Martin Luther King's story his own, or to seriously consider the plight of the disenfranchised, negates his advocacy for pacifism."[21] De La Torre also interrogates Hauerwas' innocent but uncritical appropriation of Christian churches as the ethical community for fostering Christian virtue and character: "But how can communities of color trust a church or the social ethics that the church advocates from a Eurocentric church that historically has been anti-Semitic, racist, sexist, and colonialist, and in many cases continues to be so?"[22] Not all non-European Christian ethicists, however, may necessarily agree with De La Torre on this particular criticism. For example, Jonathan Tran writes that Hauerwas' "strange silence" on issues of race exhibits why in his case silence has been the "better course." According to Tran, "Not every white guy in a position of influence, ecclesial or otherwise, needs to publicly address the issue of race."[23]

Despite the criticisms brought against Hauerwas' narrative theology and virtue ethics, we should not forget that Hauerwas' original intention to develop a narrative theology and his Christian communitarian virtue ethics was not to promote Christian sectarianism. His consistent theological nemeses have been spurious civil religions, political liberalism, and soulless capitalism. One of his theological–ethical strategies to fight these cultural and social challenges was to foster Christian virtues by grounding them in the substantive sources of Christian community.

Racialized America, Asian American History, and Asian Cultural Heritage

Above, we have reviewed how Western Christian virtue ethicists from Augustine to Hauerwas have critically reevaluated and appropriated the philosophical, cultural, and social ethoi according to their distinctive theological orientations. Despite their differences in terms of their critical methodology (e.g., reflective for Augustine and narrative for Hauerwas), there seems to be a predominant consensus among Western Christian theologians that the primary moral faculty of embodying various virtues is what Aristotle calls practical reason. No matter how differently they are construed, the roles and functions of practical reason are widely recognized to be crucial because they are deeply involved with the evaluation of various goods and the pursuit of a morally excellent life. Thus, without proper exercise and operation of practical reason, one cannot live a good and virtuous life.

How might an Asian American Christian perspective differ from these Western views on Christian virtue ethics? If there is any distinction, what would be the defining difference? It is my contention that the heart, rather than the mind, becomes the most important moral faculty for many Asian American Christians in forming Christian moral character and virtue. This, of course, does not mean that Asian American Christian virtue ethics is quintessentially noncognitive, antirational, or emotive. Nor should it mean that the virtues of heart have nothing to do with the virtues of mind. There are different layers of moral faculties in the human soul, and the conflict between these layers is not necessary or structural. In fact the unconscious harmony and unity between these layers (e.g., between practical reason and the heart) may be possible and even desirable. Before exploring the possibility of Asian American

Christian virtue ethics, let me emphasize first that the concept of moral faculty should be separated from the concept of moral virtue. Moral faculty differs from moral virtue in that while the former is held accountable for one's moral act and functioning, the latter denotes one's moral characters and qualities. What I am trying to do in the following is not to deconstruct the Western Christian moral virtue ethics per se, but to reformulate it by critically unearthing a more innermost moral faculty (i.e., one's heart).

Why would Asian American Christian virtue ethics regard the heart as the key moral faculty in construing and embodying Christian virtues? In what sense does the heart become the primary moral faculty of leading a virtuous Christian life for Asian American Christians? There are two reasons why the heart becomes the primary concern with regard to the construction of Asian American Christian virtue ethics. While the first refers to the distinctive historical experiences of many Asian Americans who have endured various racial and social discriminations as the smallest racial minority group in the United States, the second addresses the distinctive philosophical and cultural traditions they inherit from their ancestral countries of origin. We need to investigate these two factors more extensively.

As is well documented, many Asian immigrants and U.S.-born citizens have historically suffered from various racial discriminations. Since the enactment of the Chinese Exclusion Act of 1882, which became the most vivid racist immigration policy against nonwhites, Asians were systematically discriminated against until the Immigration and Nationality Act of 1965, which finally eliminated racial/nationality-based discrimination in immigration quotas. During this period, many Asians were subjected to racial abjection. On this topic Julia Kristeva, a Bulgarian-born French philosopher, develops the concept of "abjection" by investigating a certain form of life that is based on exclusion. According to Kristeva, this form of life is "clearly distinguishable from those understood as neurotic or psychotic, articulated by *negation* and its modalities, *transgression, denial, and repudiation.*"[24] Kristeva theorizes that abjection is coextensive with social and symbolic order both on the individual and the collective level. She goes further by saying that "abjection assumes specific shapes and different codings according to the various 'symbolic systems.'"[25] Social psychologists such as Derek Hook regard racism as one example of these symbolic systems. He writes, "Kristeva's notion of abjection has much to recommend it as the basis for a tentative analytics of racism to be able to understand racism's extremities of affect, its visceral, pre-discursive and bodily forms."[26]

Perhaps the most dramatic demonstration of the racial abjection against Asian Americans was the internment of Japanese Americans during World War II. In 1942, in the wake of Japan's attack on Pearl Harbor, the U.S. government rounded up 120,000 Japanese Americans on the West Coast and relocated them to "concentration camps" or "war relocation camps." President Franklin D. Roosevelt authorized this measure by issuing Executive Order 9066. Even the Supreme Court upheld the constitutionality of the exclusion order (*Toyosaburo Korematsu v. United States*: December 18, 1944). Several witnesses of camp survivors reported how they were *abjected* while they had to endure humiliation, feelings of despair, and physical hardships.[27]

Korean American theologian Wonhee Anne Joh analyzes the negative psychical economy of racial abjection by critically reflecting on her own discriminatory experiences. According to Joh, abject peoples often internalize their status as abjected and thus see themselves as "garbage." "Not only are we severed and expelled by the oppressing other (the dominant/normative self) but we sever and expel ourselves in order to become a subject."[28] The most problematic effect of racial abjection is its negative infusion of self-hatred, and it continues to bleed into all relations, "projecting onto others whose parts of ourselves we find to be garbage."[29]

The questions remain: What relationship do Asian Americans' historical experiences of racial abjection have to do with the conceptualization of the heart as the primary moral faculty with regard to the establishment and embodiment of Christian virtues? How might the historical experience of racial abjection affect Asian American Christians in constructing their distinctive virtue ethics?

In the first case, the historical, and in some cases ongoing, experience of racial abjection has rendered Asian American communities skeptical about the reliability, strength, and authority of the Western moral ideals as well as the legal system of justice. Being racially abjected, Asian Americans have developed a distinctive awareness that society as a whole can be easily mobilized in such a way that irrationality becomes a new norm while rationality is rejected by those who are supposed to protect and maintain common goods and universal values. Because of the historical experiences of racial abjection, Asian Americans began to see the alleged Western moral virtues with a suspicious eye.[30] This moral suspicion has become a moral wake-up call for many Asian Americans, which has subsequently led them to realize that Western moral ideals and virtues may not turn out to be as truthful or trustworthy as they first appeared to be. Unfortunately, Western Christianity does not seem to be exempt from this suspicion. What did Western Christianity do during the widespread colonial exploitation of people and environment on a global scale? This suspicion is further ratified by the "self-centeredness objection" to virtue ethics in general. According to Huang Yong, there is a legitimate concern toward virtue ethics; "since virtue ethics recommends that we be concerned with our own virtues or virtuous characters, it is self-centered."[31] In agreeing with David Solomon's self-centeredness objection, then, Yong emphasizes that "such a morality [Western virtue ethics] is, therefore, self-centered, since it takes one's own happiness as the motivation to be moral."[32] Asian Americans also realize that Western virtue ethics from Aristotle to MacIntyre has been traditionally developed by those socially and morally privileged rather than by the socially and morally underprivileged (slaves, women, foreigners, minors, the colored, the disabled, the outcast, etc.). This realization has provided Asian American ethicists with a critical standpoint in developing Asian American Christian virtue ethics. For Asian American virtue ethics, the following query becomes the foundational question: How would socially and morally underprivileged people have understood what it means to live a life of virtue?

Sadly, all too often the virtues of those who hold social privileges and hegemonies, as well as political powers and dominance, turn out to be dubious and hypocritical, if not inherently false or wrong. The overall suspicion toward the Western moral virtue is then linked to a perspectival suspicion toward the most important and foundational moral faculty of the Western moral tradition: practical reason.[33] Therefore, Asian American Christians begin to look for an alternative moral faculty that is more deeply seated in our soul. For Asian American Christians, virtue is no longer understood as the subject matter of practical reason and its functioning; instead they would focus on the innermost character of the people's heart. Unlike those who hold social privileges and political hegemonies, the socially marginalized and disenfranchised tend to judge people's moral character by looking into the people's heart rather than by checking on their practical reasoning. For them the excellence of the soul in the sense of the full realization of one's practical moral reasoning is no longer regarded as the primary criterion that measures one's moral virtue; instead of the excellence of practical moral reasoning, the deep-rooted moral characteristic of the heart becomes the new moral criterion. As we will discuss shortly, the moral characteristic of the heart is comprised of the three qualities of the heart: strength (firmness), transparence (purity), and orientation (directivity).

There is another factor that leads Asian American Christians to look for an alternative moral faculty: that is, their Asian roots. As many Asian American immigrants and their children have established their lives in America, many of them actually inherit and transmit their cultural and social traditions consciously as well as unconsciously. In other words, although they may acquire a new cultural or political identity as residents or citizens in American society, their social identity as Asian American remains deeply characterized by their Asian roots. One specific philosophical and cultural root that explains why the heart becomes the primary moral faculty with regard to the construction of Asian American Christian virtue ethics is especially important to unpack, and can be best explained by exploring the ancient philosophical school of Confucianism. Before discussing Confucianism, let me first emphasize that what I am trying to do in the following is to critically appropriate a particular element in Confucian philosophical tradition rather than to integrate Confucian moral theory and Christian virtue ethics. As Korean feminist scholars argue, Confucianism is often blamed as the source of the patriarchal society.[34] According to Namsoon Kang, for example, Confucian values "force women to stay in private sectors, for there is a strict distinction between women's and men's places, between women's work and men's work."[35] This is the reason why we need to appropriate a particular element from a critical perspective.

According to Wai-ying Wong, as early as the time of the late Western Zhou (1046–771 B.C.E.), virtues were emphasized and used to evaluate a person's behavior, particularly among the nobles. Some of these virtues include filial piety (*xiao*), fraternal duty (*ti*), kindness (*ci*), generosity (*hui*), loyalty (*zhong*), and empathy (*shu*).[36] Chinese virtue ethics, however, were greatly enhanced by two Confucian thinkers: Confucius himself and Mencius. The contributions made by Confucius to virtue ethics were manifold, among which the shift of the emphases from the external social norms or criteria of behavior to the internal qualities of one's character is particularly conspicuous. With regard to the importance of the heart as the primary faculty of moral virtue, we should investigate the word *xin* (心), which is translated as heart, or mind, or heart/mind. For example, James Legge translates *xin* as mind in his translation of Mencius, while D. C. Lau translates it as heart. Kwong-loi Shun, however, translates it as the heart/mind. What, then, is *xin*, or the heart/mind?

The origin of the term *xin* goes back to ancient China. *Xin* is found in some of the earliest classical texts, such as the *Book of Poetry* and *I Ching*, and it became a significant philosophical concept among the various schools of the Warring States period, although it often referred to the physical organ or repository for the human being, as does the English word "heart." According to Kwong-loi Shun, *xin* as the capacities of the heart/mind is described as follows:

> "*Xin*," a term often translated as "heart" or "mind," can have desires (*yu*) and emotions (*quing*) and can take pleasure in or feel displeasure at certain things. It can also deliberate (*lu*) about a situation, direct attention to and ponder about (*si*) certain things and keep certain things in mind (*nian*).[37]

Xin is identified to have three functional aspects: emotion, volition, and cognition. As we will see shortly, this understanding has a striking similarity to the biblical understanding of the heart. According to John Berthrong, the heart/mind is distinguished by the combination of two qualities: the intellectual qualities of rationality and deliberation alongside an emotional response. Even in the earliest Chinese philosophical literature, *xin* is regarded to be the mind as the agent of reason and the heart as the organ of the emotions.[38] The seminal concept of *xin* is well exemplified in Confucian texts. For example, as Berthrong notes, the anecdotes of *Analects* 6, sec. 5 and 2, sec. 4 demonstrate that *xin* is the "reservoir of human desire as well as virtue."[39] *Xin* as the source or reservoir of the moral virtue is most clearly delineated by Mencius. As Dennis Arjo argues, the defining moment of Mencius's moral thought is accounted for by his description of the four *duan* (端), the "sprouts" or "germs" or "stirrings" of moral virtues, in *Mencius* 2A:6. Identified as the basic features of our moral psychology, the incipient moral sentiments called *duan* refer to the four hearts (*xin*) of compassion, shame, courtesy, and modesty, and our sense of right and wrong. When these basic moral natures of the heart are properly developed, they become moral virtues that reflect a more conscious and deliberate awareness of how we ought to behave and relate with others.[40] As a primary moral faculty, the Confucian concept of *xin* can perhaps be compared to the Aristotelian notion of practical reason in the Western philosophical tradition.[41]

Above, we have examined the cultural and historical background of how Asian American Christian virtue ethics can come to regard the heart as a primary moral faculty of virtue and virtue ethics. The historical experience of having been subjected to systemic racial abjection and the discovery of the Asian philosophical root regarding *xin* as the primary moral faculty become reasons why Asian American Christians should engage in the cocritical reevaluation and appropriation of the moral significance of the heart. It is my contention that the uniqueness of Asian American Christian virtue ethics lies in this critical awareness that the true virtue is revealed by the moral qualities of the heart. How can we, then, determine the moral qualities of the heart? What are the possible moral criteria by which we can evaluate the distinctive features of Christian virtue? In the following I answer these questions by constructively suggesting the tripartite criteria that can determine the moral qualities of the heart. In doing so I will critically explore and investigate the Scriptures from the vantage point of an Asian American Christian hermeneutics.

Virtue as the Restoration of the Heart: Beyond the Excellence of One's Soul

There are some similarities and differences between the Confucian and the biblical understandings of the heart (Heb. *lēḇ, lēḇāḇ*; Gk. *kardía*). First, the similarities. Both the ancient Chinese and the ancient Hebrews regarded the heart as the vital physical organ, and they also shared the common understanding that the heart can refer to psychological functioning beyond the physical level. Just as the ancient Chinese believed that *xin* (the heart/mind) is comprised of three aspects (emotion, volition, and cognition), the Hebrews also acknowledged that the heart is the seat of three psychic spheres (emotion, volition, and intellect). This view is reaffirmed in the New Testament. Various passages of the Scriptures, for example, testify that the heart can be glad (Prov 27:11; Acts 14:17), sad (Neh 2:2), troubled (2 Kgs 6:11), courageous (2 Sam 17:10), discouraged (Num 32:7), fearful (Isa 35:4), and moved by hatred (Lev 19:17) or love (Deut 13:3). The heart is also described as the seat of the appetites and desires (Ps 37:4), including both bad (Rom 1:24) and good (Rom 10:1). As in the Hebrew Bible, the heart is regarded as the seat of the volition and will. The heart can plan wicked deeds (Prov 6:18) and may become perverted (Prov 11:20). The heart can also be lifted up with pride (Deut 8:14), while it also may become hardened (Zech 7:12). One can also renew the heart by setting one's heart to seeking God (2 Chr 12:14) or the law (Ezra 7:10). Last but not the least, the heart (*kardía*) in the New Testament is the seat of intellectual life. The process of cogitation takes place in the heart (Judg 5:16, Mark 2:6). The heart harbors intellectual thought (1 Chr 29:18), and one meditates on the deep things of life in the heart (Ps 4:4, Luke 2:19). The intellectual aspect of the heart is further exemplified in Proverbs 16:9 (one makes his plans with the heart) and Ecclesiastes 8:16 (one seeks knowledge and understanding with the heart). The heart is understood as the storehouse of memory (Prov 3:3, Luke 1:66). Wisdom in the broader sense is also known for the quality of the heart (1 Kgs 10:24, KJV).

Despite the conceptual similarities between the Chinese and biblical views on the heart, there is one critical difference between the two. The biblical understanding of the heart is distinguished by its critical understanding that the heart is the innermost spring of the human personality, which becomes the contact point with God as it is directly open to God and subject to God's influence. For example, the heart speaks to God with trust (Ps 27:8, Ps 28:7), and the word of God can dwell in the heart (Deut 30:14), which becomes the birthplace of faith. God not only looks upon the heart (1 Sam 16:7) but also knows its secrets (Ps 44:21). God not only can test its moral quality (Ps 17:3) but also can give the human being an understanding heart (1 Kgs 3:9, KJV) or take away all understanding (Job 12:24). God is also said to have poured forth God's love in people's hearts (Rom 5:5), in which Christ could dwell (Eph 3:17) so that the peace of Christ may reign (Col 3:15). An equally distinctive aspect of the biblical understanding of the heart is that the heart can be easily defiled and contaminated by evil thoughts and desires. The heart is also understood to have a major defect: its natural inability to act in accordance with the torah. Jeremiah 31:31-34 and Ezekiel 11:19 and 36:26-27 describe this natural defect of the heart in human beings in regard to the necessity of God's salvific engagement to renew people's defective, imperfect, incomplete, and wicked hearts.

From the vantage point of the method of cocritical appropriation, the Asian philosophical and moral insight (the Asian root)—identifying the heart as the key faculty of virtue—is critically appropriated in light of Asian American Christians' historical consciousness and their biblical hermeneutics. To be more specific, Asian American Christians can draw upon the philosophical concept of Confucian *xin* by constructively comparing it with the biblical understanding of the heart as well as by critically reinterpreting their distinctive historical experiences, particularly the experiences of racial abjection. As a result of this cocritical approach, Asian American Christians can develop a new conceptual paradigm to understand virtue and virtue ethics.

This new conceptual paradigm is identified as "restorative" as opposed to the traditional "teleological" paradigm. More specifically, the virtue of the heart is conceived in terms of the moral restoration of the broken, damaged, and defective aspects of the heart; this understanding can be differentiated from the teleological paradigm, according to which virtue is conceived of "from potentiality to actuality." According to more teleological ways of thinking, virtue is paradigmatically conceived as excellence in the sense of the best actualization of one's given capacities, potentialities, or Mencian *duan*. Distinguished from this approach, Asian American Christian virtue ethics intentionally thematizes the brokenness of our world and the defects of our heart. As demonstrated above, for many Asian American Christians, the brokenness of our world and the defects of our hearts are not merely an ideological issue; they are, rather, historical and existential realities that constantly affect our lives and psyches. The historical experience of racial abjection clearly shows that one's true moral virtue is more than a matter of choosing the mean between two extremities or vices. It is also more than the nurturing of one's given capacities, potentiality, or Mencian *duan* through education and habituation. Thanks to their historical experience of being the target of racial abjection, Asian Americans have begun to develop a different moral sensibility that looks deeper into a person's innermost self rather than a person's achievements, skills, or reputation. According to this new moral sensibility, a person's innermost virtue is determined not so much by the degree of one's achievement, skill, or reputation, which is largely contingent on the historical or social circumstances and the availability of opportunities, as by the moral qualities of the person's innermost self, that is, the heart.

According to this new paradigm of virtue, those who were socially or structurally abjected and thus divested of any chances to demonstrate their excellence (at least in the public realm) may still realize that the life of virtue is possible for them in the sense of restoring and reinstalling the integrity of their heart. Though abjected, they begin to peruse the innermost feelings, thoughts, and volitions of their heart in relation to the Christian virtues of faith, love, and hope. Although they realize that their innermost feelings, thoughts, and volitions are deeply affected

...just, irrational, and broken realities of this world, they strive to maintain and restore the integrity of their hearts by continuing to hold on to the Christian virtues of faith, love, and hope instead of losing their hearts to distrust, hatred, or despair. We can find an exemplary case in the story of Joseph in the book of Genesis. As we can imagine, due to his ethnic background and social status, Joseph must have been subjected to ethnic/racial/class abjection in a foreign land. For all the circumstantial injustices and social irrationality, Joseph's story demonstrates that he somehow restored and kept the integrity of his heart without being colonized by despair, hatred, and vengeance. His dramatic reconciliation with his betraying brothers exemplifies the extraordinary aspect of the virtue of the forgiving heart.

Above, we have discussed the conceptual paradigm of Asian American Christian virtue ethics as a restorative kind rather than a teleological type. According to the restorative model, the Christian virtue of the heart is conceived in the qualities called for that display and exemplify Christian ideals such as faith, hope, and love. Without these qualities, a life of faith, hope, and love is thus not possible. Analogically speaking, these qualities can be compared to the qualities of the "good soil" in the parable of the sower (Mark 4:1-9). The soil as such does not produce any grain without being sown with the seed. The seed must be provided from an external source, and Christians may regard the seed as the word of God—God's covenantal promise. The Christian virtue of the heart is deeply committed; it is not self-oriented. It is not established, either, for the sake of displaying its own excellence or glory; rather, the heart displays the qualities of what Jesus calls the kingdom of God. Every Christian, however, is still responsible for restoring and keeping one's heart. What does it mean, then, to restore and keep one's heart? What qualities are called for in order to restore and keep one's heart? By what criterion do we know the virtue of the heart? I answer these questions by critically conceptualizing the tripartite moral criteria: the strength, purity, and directivity of the heart. As we will see shortly, each criterion is respectively matched with the Christian moral ideals of faith, love, and hope.

The first moral criterion that qualifies the virtue of the heart is strength. Strength may be identified as firmness of the heart, which is qualitatively distinguished from hardness of the heart. Without this firmness one may not maintain faithfulness in carrying out the mission or fulfilling the law and commandment. Firmness of the heart is distinguished from its hardness in that the former is deeply characterized by the trait of resilience while the latter is not. We have two contrasting examples in the Bible: Saul and Paul. According to 1 Samuel 13:8-15, Saul performed unlawful sacrifice by offering the burnt offering to God by himself (9). He knew that he was not authorized to perform the offering ceremony. In response to Samuel, who sternly rebuked his unlawful sacrificial ceremony, Saul justified himself by saying, "When I saw that the people were slipping away from me, and that you did not come within the days appointed, and that the Philistines were mustering at Michmash . . . I forced myself, and offered the burnt offering" (11-12). To this Samuel responded, "You have done foolishly; you have not kept the commandment of the Lord your God, which he commanded you. The Lord would have established your kingdom over Israel forever, but now your kingdom will not continue; the Lord has sought out a man after his own heart; and the Lord has appointed him to be ruler over his people, because you have not kept what the Lord commanded you" (13-14). Saul's heart was not firm enough to wait another minute at the sight of impending attack from his enemies.

The Scriptures also illustrate opposite examples, among which the leaders in the book of Judges and many prophets are particularly conspicuous. In the New Testament, Paul paradigmatically exemplifies the strength of the heart in his life as well as through his letters. In an apparently vindictive manner in his struggle against his adversaries, he describes the sufferings he went through as follows: "Five times I have received from the Jews the forty lashes minus one. Three times I was beaten with rods. Once I received a stoning . . . danger from Gentiles, danger in the city, danger in the wilderness, danger at sea, danger from false brothers and sisters" (2 Cor 11:24-26). The strength of the heart is indispensable for believers to carry out their calls as well as God's commandments. Without this quality one may not fulfill one's faithfulness to the end. One needs to be reminded here that the strength of the heart as such is not faith; the firmness itself is like the quality of the vessel, which contains the faith. This quality, however, characterizes the faith.

The second qualifying criterion for the virtue of the heart is purity, or wholeness of the heart. Purity here does not mean innocence or naïveté; it rather means the undividedness of one's heart by different pursuits of interest. Purity means the state of the heart's full commitment to a single purpose or goal. Søren Kierkegaard is right when he defines the purity of the heart as "to will one thing."[42] The lack of this quality leads many into the state of dividedness of one's heart. In various places the Scriptures negatively describe the state of dividedness. For example, James 4:8 narrates that sinners can be identified as those who are "double-minded," and it is imperative for them to cleanse their hands and "purify" their hearts in order to draw near to God. In the same manner, Psalm 12:2 also writes that the ungodly are characterized as those who utter lies to each other with flattering lips and a "double heart." In Matthew 6:24 Jesus warns his followers that one cannot serve two masters: "No one can serve two masters; for a slave will either hate the one and love the other, or be devoted to the one and despise the other. You cannot serve God and wealth." The case of Ananias and Sapphira in Acts 5:1-11 illustrates that double-minded people may be liable to pay high prices for their lack of purity in their heart. As a qualifying criterion, the purity of the heart is paired with love, just as the strength of the heart is matched with faith. When the Christian virtue of love is displayed and demonstrated through the purity of the heart, the kingdom of God becomes a reality in relations. The purity of the heart is indeed an indispensable quality that renders the Christian virtue of love genuine and truthful; without it the Christian virtue of love is untenable.

The last qualifying criterion of the heart is its directivity. In Acts 7 Stephen delivers his last speech to the council (Sanhedrin), which brings charge against him with a false accusation (blaspheme). In his speech, while he was summarizing the history of Moses' exodus, he points out the wrong directivity of the heart of the Jewish ancestors as follows: "Our ancestors were unwilling to obey him; instead, they pushed him aside, and in their hearts they turned back to Egypt" (39). The book of Daniel 6:10 illustrates a different example, in which Daniel demonstrates an opposite directivity of the heart distinguishing himself from Jewish ancestors: "Although Daniel knew that the document had been signed, he continued to go to his house, which had windows in its upper room open toward Jerusalem, and to get down on his knees three times a day to pray to his God and praise him, just as he had done previously." These two cases show us that along with strength and purity, the heart is deeply characterized by its direction. Whether we realize it or not, our heart is set to a certain direction, and with direction our moral identity is determined. The directivity of the heart also represents the heart's innermost desire and hunger, and this becomes the reason why the quality of directivity is coupled with the Christian virtue of hope. As Jürgen Moltmann notes in his *Theology of Hope*, hope strengthens faith and motivates a believer to lead the life of love. Hope also creates a "passion for the possible" that is centered around the hope of the resurrected and the returning Christ. "[I]n the medium of hope our theological concepts become not judgments which nail reality down to what it is, but anticipations which show reality its prospects and its future possibilities."[43] The heart's directivity saddled by the passion of hope becomes the driving source of change that believers are to make on the world.

We have now reviewed how the three moral criteria of the heart (strength, purity, and directivity) are integrated with the tripartite Christian moral ideals of faith, love, and hope. Because of the brokenness of this world and human depravity, the heart is constantly tempted, tried, and inflicted by the vicissitudes of this world and our weakness. Keeping one's heart becomes the constant struggle for many believers. Facing these challenges, Asian American Christian ethics focuses on the internal restoration and reintegration of the heart so that they may continue to realize faith, love, and hope in their personal behaviors as well as in other social and communal relations. It is critical to note that the three moral criteria of the heart—strength, purity, and directivity—are not just given, in that they are eligible for their continuous reinforcement, refinement, and readjustment. Each Christian believer is therefore responsible for keeping his or her heart by holding on to the biblical, spiritual, and ecclesial teachings and guidance.

Conclusion

Above, I have argued that keeping one's heart is the moral foundation of Asian American Christian virtue ethics; I have also maintained that keeping one's heart means the continual restoration and renewal of the three qualities of the heart: strength, purity, and directivity. It is the Christian believer's responsibility to look continuously into the heart by critically examining its qualities. Given that the Spirit is received into the heart so that we can cry "Abba" as adopted children (Gal 4:6), keeping one's heart is further enabled by the advocating, counseling, and comforting guidance of the Spirit (Rom 8:2-6). For Asian American Christians, a virtuous Christian life leads also to a spiritual life. It makes sense, then, that the fruits of the Spirit are identified as the various virtues of the heart: love, joy, peace, patience, kindness, generosity, faithfulness, gentleness, and self-control (Gal 5:22-23). It should be noted also that due to the indwelling of the Spirit, the virtue of the heart is involved in the redemption of all creation beyond one's personal sphere (Rom 8:18-25). It remains to be seen how the further development of Asian American Christian virtue ethics will unfold with regard to various social issues of our world, including environmental preservation, global economics, and international politics.

DISCUSSION QUESTIONS

1. What are the three qualities of the heart that Ahn discusses and how are they characterized?

2. What are the similarities and differences between the Confucian and the biblical understandings of the heart? How does thinking comparatively in this manner illuminate your understanding of the Bible?

3. According to the author, why do we need the qualifier—"Asian American"—before Christian virtue ethics? How does the author answer this question?

4. What are the possible strengths and weaknesses of Asian American Christian virtue ethics in comparison with traditional Western Christian virtue ethics?

Peace and War

KEUN-JOO CHRISTINE PAE

Starting the car engine, I felt the smell of the New York metropolitan area. Since I moved to central Ohio some years ago, I have taken a road trip to New York City every summer where I could taste, touch, smell, hear, and see Korea, thanks to Koreatowns. One summer I decided to take Ohio state routes, instead of jumping onto interstate highways, to explore new areas of Ohio. As I drove through the woods in rural areas on Ohio State Route 36, I almost crashed into a signpost that read "Korean War Memorial Highway." Who could have imagined or predicted seeing Korea in rural Ohio? After all, Asians make up only 1.8 percent of the population here![1] That shock prompted me throughout my road trip to Manhattan to count how many times I had unexpectedly encountered Korea and Asia in Ohio: an old church-woman once told me that her late husband was a war prisoner during the Korean War, a middle-aged woman's sick father was a Korean War veteran, two of my students' families had been relocated to Columbus from Cambodia after the fall of Saigon, one church lady's grandson served the U.S. Air Force in Korea, and so on. Although I have rarely seen Asian faces in central Ohio, I have been surrounded by Americans' memories and experiences of Asia—or more specifically, America's wars in Asia.

My Asian American consciousness has been critically shaped in a small midwestern college town where I have participated in America's capitalist militarism through higher education. As I teach transnational intersectionality among race, gender, and class through the lens of U.S. militarism, I, a first-generation Korean immigrant, am no longer able to distance myself from the rest of Americans, Asian Americans in particular. My research and teaching often lead me to face the fact that the American public had racialized and gendered Asians long before Asian immigrants arrived on American soil. The racialized and gendered Asian American identity in the twentieth century has a lot to do with America's wars in Asia, especially during the early period of the Cold War. America's dominant memories and rhetoric of wars in Asia continue to affect Asian Americans' lives. These memories of wars are not simply about remembering the past. Just as Christians shape and reshape their religious identity by retelling the stories of Jesus, so the American public continues to shape and reshape the hegemonic imagination of Asian Americans by remembering and retelling the stories of (primarily white heterosexual male) Americans' experiences of wars in Asia.

It might not be an exaggeration to say that, in spite of diversity among Asian Americans, it has been various U.S. military engagements in the Asia-Pacific region and imperial aims through territorial expansion that brought all of us here from the Philippines, Pacific Islands, Taiwan, Japan, China, Korea, Vietnam, and so forth.[2] Therefore, the racialized and gendered history of Asian migration into the United States is, as Jodi Kim argues, inseparable from the U.S. military operations in the Asia-Pacific region, especially during the Cold War.[3] If this is the case, for Asian American ethicists like myself, theo-ethical contemplation on war requires an invocation of the most painful stories that have repetitively haunted our collective psyche. Peace, then, is only thinkable after we courageously mourn and look into the darkest pit of war stories that hold certain truths about who we are and toward where we are heading.

This chapter is my effort to dive into the bottom of America's war stories in Asia that may lead Asian Americans to contemplate how to re-remember, retell, and reshape our identities not in the memories of violent deaths but through those of the peace granted by a life-affirming God. In theo-ethically delineating this question, I first engage in the five major traditions of Christian reflection on peace and war. In particular, through reading Reinhold Niebuhr's Christian realism in light of the Asian American critiques of America's myths about Asia during the Cold War period, I will argue that our racialized and gendered Asian American identity is the product of America's imperialist wars in Asia. The purposes of reconsidering perceptions of Asian Americans during the Cold War are to deconstruct America's hegemonic imaginations of wars in Asia and to reimagine Christian ethical discourse on war. For these purposes, by rediscovering the unique place of the dead in early Christian Eucharist and theo-politically analyzing the Eucharist, I show why an Asian American Christian ethic of peace and war must begin with remembering history's victims, whose memories and tragic deaths still live with us. This remembrance of victims will help us reimagine Asian American identity at the Eucharistic table as a site for reconciliation, peace, and justice. Reimagining the Eucharist as ordinary Asian Americans' life-affirming ritual and political activism against war, violence, and destruction, this chapter makes an arduous effort to listen to Asian Americans' experiences of America's wars and accordingly map out possible directions to peace, not war.

Christian Ethical Responses to Peace and War: From Pacifism to Christian Realism

Since Christian theories of peace and war have been prolific, any summary of diverse Christian responses to war and strategies for peace will be found wanting. As these theories continue to exert influence over the American public's memories of and responses to America's wars in Asia, here I only highlight five selected Christian perspectives on peace and war: pacifism, holy war, just war theory, just peacemaking, and Christian realism.

Pacifism

Pacifism does not mean to "passively" accept the status quo, but to "actively" resist violence and injustice through the means of nonviolence. One might easily argue that pacifism is as old as Christianity. Christian pacifists argue that Jesus was a nonviolent peacemaker and that by revealing and resisting the ugly faces of violence on the cross, Jesus was a pacifist. Influenced by John Yoder's pacifism, Stanley Hauerwas accentuates that pacifism is not to be understood as a strategy for ending war but as a way of life for the followers of Jesus Christ.[4] His christological pacifism articulates the pacifist moral commitments to end war and to live alternatives to war, the foundation of which lies in the cross and resurrection of Jesus Christ.[5] Pacifism as active nonviolent resistance may jeopardize the resister's own life and security. Yet, borrowing Rev. Dr. Martin Luther King Jr.'s words, Hauerwas argues that unearned suffering can have redemptive power.[6] King's six principles capture the shared Christian values of nonviolence: (1) nonviolent resistance is not cowardly but is a form of resistance, (2) advocates of nonviolence do not want to humiliate those they oppose, (3) the battle is against forces of evil, not individuals, (4) nonviolence requires the willingness to suffer, (5) love is central to nonviolence, and finally (6) the universe is on the side of justice.[7]

The impact of Asian religious leaders such as Mahatma Gandhi and Thich Nhat Hanh on Christian pacifism in the West merits comment, and can be seen in the teaching of nonviolence as the religious and spiritual practice that continues to transform one's heart and mind as one actively participates in nonviolent peacemaking. Thich Nhat Hanh especially affirmed the possibility of nonviolent peacemaking only when the peacemaker empathizes with suffering beings and learns how to express compassion concretely.[8] His view is that since all living beings are interconnected, we cannot be indifferent to the suffering of others but must attempt to eradicate suffering. Furthermore, interconnectedness does not allow pacifists to demonize or feel morally superior to those who use violence; rather, it continues to challenge pacifists to critically reflect on their own deeds and thoughts.

Holy War

In spite of Christianity's historical engagements with war for the sake of God, most Christian ethicists today reject holy war. Holy war can be defined as "any war that is believed to be commanded by God or waged for religious reasons."[9] The most serious danger of holy war is that if war were waged in the name of God, there could be no limit for killing, for the world must be rid of evil. Thus, in order to wage holy war, one must absolutize one's moral goodness and divine favor over enemies, and in doing so demonize them.[10]

Although America has not actively rationalized its wars in the name of God, the holy war rhetoric as a form of U.S. exceptionalism has been found throughout American history. The founding fathers of the United States firmly believed that America was God's new Israel to create a new humanity; such a belief worked to rationalize the displacement and genocide of Native Americans.[11] As Jasbir Puar argues, U.S. exceptionalism infused with Christian triumphalism has often endorsed the country as "the arbiter of appropriate ethics, human rights, and democratic behavior while exempting itself without hesitation from such universalizing mandates," thus leading to the justification of America's overseas military operations.[12]

Just War Theory

St. Augustine's classic just war theory has been adaptive to ever-changing historical contexts of war. St. Augustine of Hippo took human sinfulness seriously into his theological consideration—this is why Augustine is often regarded as the father of both just war thinking and Christian realism.[13] In his work *The City of God*, St. Augustine argues for the necessity of the limited use of violence to keep the peace and order of the earthly kingdom against evils such as destruction and disorder.[14] Since the rulers of the earthly kingdom (e.g., the Roman Empire) who could use military violence in order to retaliate evils were also sinful human beings, Augustine insisted that there must be principled moral regulations on the use of violence and the declaration of war.[15] St. Augustine organized three core principles of just war theory, which are still relevant today: just cause (national self-defense or protection of the vulnerable), legitimate authority (only those responsible for the common good can rightfully declare war, not individuals), and right intention (the reason for going to war must be to advance the just cause, not to pursue an ulterior motive).[16] Just war thinking was further developed in the Christian tradition and in the modern West through sources including St. Thomas Aquinas, the medieval code of honor for knights, and other theorists of both natural law and international law (e.g., Hugo Grotius).

Contemporary just war theory today is normally divided into three parts: the conditions that must be obtained before a war can be "just" (*jus ad bellum*), the "just" ways that parties must conduct themselves in warfare (*jus in bello*), and the "just" way to cease or exit war (*jus post bellum*). There are six broadly recognized criteria of *jus ad bellum*: St. Augustine's aforementioned three principles and "last resort," a "reasonable probability of success," and "macro-proportionality."[17] *Jus in bello* refers to the rules of conduct in war. These rules include: (1) the need to discriminate between combatants and civilians and between legitimate and illegitimate targets, (2) the humane treatment of prisoners of war, and (3) the respect of the principle of micro-proportionality.[18] These classic principles of *jus ad bellum* and *jus in bello* are generally seen as requiring new interpretations in our time due to the complexities of contemporary warfare (e.g., the rise of terrorism, guerilla warfare, the proliferation of weapons of mass destruction, the reality of intrastate—not just interstate—conflict) and international politics (e.g., the role of the United Nations), as well as the ambiguity of those principles themselves.

Postwar Justice (Jus Post Bellum*) and Just Peacemaking*

Just as the primary ethical concern of just war is "justice," so peace in the postwar society requires justice. Though *jus post bellum* has been a part of classical just war thinking, it has remained comparatively underdeveloped until recently. Philosophical and Christian ethicists have recently produced sophisticated ideas of reconciliation, restorative justice, and political forgiveness to contribute to lasting peace in the postwar society and keep the state and social institutions (such as religion) accountable after the cessation of hostilities. One reason for this renewed focus is the growing acknowledgment that armed conflict is likely to reoccur in the postwar society if justice is not served. According to Daniel Philpott, the wounds of political injustice caused by armed conflict involve four parties: victims whose human rights are violated, perpetrators or wrongdoers who violate the human rights of the others, members of community at large who are neither victims nor perpetrators, and the governing institutions of the state.[19] Since war significantly undermines social structures and exasperates poverty, armed conflict can erupt again at any time without the healing of political wounds and the restoring of the humanity of victims. In short, peace does not automatically arrive after any given cease-fire; rather, peace depends on how successfully the postwar society establishes just relations among the members of society and completes the disarmament process, such as by eliminating land mines, uranium shells, and so forth.[20]

According to Susan Thistlethwaite, just peacemaking theory is "an emerging fourth paradigm or model beyond the historic ways of addressing peace and war."[21] Just peacemaking theory, which was first systematized by Christian ethicists Glen Stassen and Susan Thistlethwaite, focuses on "what causes conflict and therefore, sees peacemaking as the ever vigilant effort to establish justice."[22] These ethicists argue that just political economic structures, among other factors, are prerequisites for peace. So understood, just peacemaking intends to speak to adherents of "just war" and "pacifism" alike: just war theorists for filling out the parameters of "last resort," and pacifists for providing concrete ways that they can work for peace (beyond saying "no" to armed conflict). Today just peacemaking theory has become more sophisticated based on an Abrahamic understanding of "the love of God and neighbor" that consistently leads people of faith to seek out peaceful resolutions to conflict. Just peacemaking theorists suggest ten concrete actions to bring peace with justice, and these actions are applicable before and after war. These principles are believed to be universally applicable across the globe as well as capable of being grounded in multiple religious traditions.[23]

Christian Realism

Arguably, Christian realism has influenced America's perceptions of Asians the most. Asian Americans accordingly have compelling reasons to be concerned with this theory and its application to America's overseas military operations.

Reinhold Niebuhr, the modern representative of Christian realism, was an influential Christian thinker in the early Cold War period when the United States emerged as a global hegemonic power. In differentiating the moral principles that ought to govern states from those that ought to govern individuals, Niebuhr argued that we could not expect states who struggle for power and to augment their national interests in the international arena to conform to norms (such as love and self-sacrifice) that may be more appropriate for interpersonal relations. Thus states must learn to distinguish greater evils from lesser ones; they must also prudently use violence (i.e., not in such a way as to bring about the total destruction of humankind) to balance power among nations and to protect the weak.[24]

In the early Cold War period, Niebuhr may have been critical of American exceptionalism, but he did not give up on America's salvific role in Asia. In his theological understanding of the confrontation between free market democracy (i.e., the children of light) and communism (i.e., the children of darkness),[25] Niebuhr understood that humans lived in a new dimension of history, which had been created by the Cold War on the one hand and the absolute impossibility of resorting to nuclear war on the other. The greatest dilemma that the United States faced in the post–World War II world was that any military operation against the Soviet Empire, even for preventing future threats, might bring about the total destruction of humanity because of nuclear capabilities. It is this context of the dangerous world of vast nuclear powers wherein Niebuhr directed his concern toward Asia. In Niebuhr's eyes, the success of the U.S. strategy of containment depended on which side Asia would take; the problem was that the poor peoples of nonindustrial nations in Asia were vulnerable to Marxism, given its "preaching of the apocalypse of the proletariat victory over the bourgeoisie."[26]

Niebuhr's views on communism revealed his prejudice against Asia. He described Lenin as first accomplishing his communist revolution in "the semi-Asiatic" and almost wholly agrarian culture of Russia, his point being that Lenin's communist revolution would not have succeeded had Russia shared Western European, not Asian, cultural characteristics.[27] He regarded the ancient cultures of Asia as generally lacking in historical dynamism and thus interpreted the "hopeless people of the Orient" finding communism, a historically dynamic religion, as "the harbinger of a great hope."[28]

Many of Niebuhr's perspectives on American foreign policy were internally contradictory, especially when he was concerned about the destiny of Asia. On the one hand, he legitimized American hegemony in Asia. On the other hand, he also hoped that Asia would gain sufficient voice in the council of the free world to correct "the inevitable bias of the Western world" concerning its use of military and economic power.[29] Nonetheless, Niebuhr's views on Asians were consistent: they (1) were vulnerable to communism due to their slumbering culture, (2) were ignorant of the danger of communism, and (3) lacked scientific consciousness to determine their own destiny. In Niebuhr's imagination Asians shared similar traits with those of innocent children and vulnerable women living in mystical and exotic, yet lethargic, cultures. Unfortunately, his Orientalism was only possible through his denial of American capitalist imperialism in Asia, as well as the strategy of containment as a byproduct of American exceptionalism.

This is all to suggest that images of Asians as vulnerable and innocent populations could easily lead to justifications of America's military operations in Asia as "just" to protect the innocent. What is more, Niebuhr's Christian realism Asianized communism and accordingly constructed another image of Asia—the ideological enemy of the United States. Crucially for our purposes, the conceptualization of Asians as simultaneously innocent and vulnerable women and children needing to be protected *and* ideological enemies needing to be corrected or destroyed presented a challenge for garnering support for the war effort.

To be clear, it would be premature to simply discard Niebuhr's Christian realism for his Western elite bias against Asians, for his warnings against preventive war and critique of American exceptionalism are still valuable in our ethical assessments of war and warfare today. But in assessing Niebuhr's Christian realism through Asian American eyes, we see the dangers of permitting a powerful group of people (i.e., white male elites) to describe the realities of the entire world (including Asia).

So far, by focusing on the ways in which Christian traditions on peace and war have been applied to U.S. military actions, I have attempted to argue in this section that ethical reflection on whether to go to war, how to carry out war, and how to build peace should only be done with serious consideration on real people's lives. As I will describe further in the next section, Asian Americans have been shaped by U.S. military actions in the Asian theater, and they have accordingly re-remembered and retold America's wars in Asia in particular ways.

Asian American Investments and Reflections on Peace and War

Critically analyzing America's wars in the Asia-Pacific region, Asian American scholars have been particularly interested in how war narratives, produced either by the American public or by the real Asian bodies having experienced war, have affected the collective identity of Asian Americans. Here I present some themes and concerns that emerge either from the enduring legacies of those encounters or in contemporary military life today: the origin and labeling of Asians as "gooks," the creation of war orphans, the distinction between "good" and "bad" Asians, and the ongoing problem of racism in the U.S. military.

Reencountering the "Gook"

Among other valuable Asian American theorists' critical engagement with American imperialism in Asia, Jodi Kim's analytical reading of Korean American writer Chang Rae Lee's Native Speaker offers an interesting etymology of "gook," a derogatory term for Southeast Asians during the Vietnam War. Lee's novel theorizes that the term originated from American soldiers' earlier encounter with Koreans after World War II. When American soldiers entered villages in Korea, Koreans greeted them as their liberators, shouting "Mee-Gook" (the "United States" in Korean). Not knowing what these strange Koreans were saying, American soldiers interpreted Koreans as introducing themselves with "I am a gook" in their broken English. Thus, the "gook" originated from Americans' incorrect and arrogant assumption that all Koreans spoke English and were named "gook."[30]

Rather than simply be a mid-twentieth century neologism, the "gook" can be traced back further to America's colonization of the Philippines at the turn of the twentieth century, since Filipinos were also referred to as "gu-gu or goo-goo."[31] Whether applied to Southeast

Asians, Koreans, or Filipinos, then, the term "gook" racialized all Asians beyond their ethnic and individual diversity. It is also worth noting that the "gook" was etymologically gendered because it was applied multiracially to Asians, Arabs, and Haitians, and especially to female prostitutes who followed the men in the camps.[32] The racial epithet "gook" continues to associate Asians with the objects of American military intervention and thus to differentiate loyal citizens from "them" in this orientalizing way.

America's Wars and Asian Children

Asian war orphans have played important roles in bringing Asia into the hearts of middle-class white Americans. Transnational and interracial adoption was widely practiced as a consequence of the Korean War. The adoption of Korean War orphans in the 1950s and in the 1960s became widely known through periodicals such as *Reader's Digest* in popular stories about children fathered by U.S. military personnel as well as the altruistic activities of Bertha and Harry Holt. Harry Holt's "Dear Friends" letter in 1955 indicated the overwhelming number of "pure" Korean orphans as well as Korean children fathered by American soldiers. Emphasizing love as a Christian and American family value, this letter encouraged his supporters to rescue the little ones from Korea's cold winter, poverty, and tuberculosis.[33] Unfortunately, those biracial or pure Korean orphans were not always parentless children but "social orphans" created by war who were "legally" available for adoption.[34] Many of these children were either separated from their parents while fleeing from war or were left by their parents at an orphanage for what was supposed to only have been a temporary stay, as the parents had hoped to take them back at war's end. Most mixed-racial children were mothered by Korean prostitutes who had catered to UN soldiers. Ostracized in Korean society, these women had little choice but to give up their children for transnational adoption.

Operation Babylift toward the end of the Vietnam War was not too far different from the transnational and interracial adoption of Korean children. Due to widespread rumors that the Viet Cong would burn mixed-racial children alive, Vietnamese mothers were forced to give up their children fathered by American soldiers to Operation Babylift so as to have them subsequently adopted by (white) American families who were waiting for cute Asian babies.[35] But many children, including mixed-racial or "pure" Vietnamese children brought to the United

States through Operation Babylift, were not in fact biological orphans and would later be claimed by their Vietnamese parents.[36]

The transnational adoption of Korean and Vietnamese children reveals that adoption does not depend solely on any given families' benevolent actions or conscious decisions. Rather, transnational adoption of Asian children has in some cases been highly militarized to serve America's military and economic interests in Asia. Case in point: Operation Babylift successfully raised funds for the Vietnam War by manipulating sympathetic Americans who would do anything to rescue innocent children in Vietnam.[37] These (social) orphans from Korea and Vietnam generally experienced rapid assimilation with American society—a phenomenon reminiscent of the experiences of Native American children in the boarding school system in the nineteenth and early twentieth centuries. The Korean War and the Vietnam War thus added another portrait of Asian Americans: Asian Americans as once-hopeless children abandoned by their own parents but fortunately rescued by benevolent America.

"Good Asians" versus "Bad Asians"

As noted previously, despite the hatred and mockery associated with "gooks," America's mission to expand its military power and control of the economy in Asia was urgent enough to necessitate the creation of tolerable images of Asians in the minds of the American public. For without ordinary Americans' support for American military operations overseas, America's strategy of containment against communism would be impossible. The loss of China to communism in 1949 made the United States overdetermined to see Asia as a region "gathering increasing coherence and strategic importance for the United States in economic, military, and political terms."[38] For instance, as communist Chinese forces entered the Korean War, President Harry Truman declared a national emergency on December 16, 1950. According to Truman, if the goal of communist imperialism were achieved, Americans would no longer worship their God or enjoy God's blessings of freedom. He urged Americans to make every possible sacrifice for America's triumph over communism—specifically America's victory in the Korean Peninsula.[39] Truman's declaration confirms that the Korean War was America's war, and the destiny of Korea was inseparable from that of America. In addition, Truman equated Christian triumphalism with America's physical and ideological victory over communism.

While "Red Asia" still dominated the American public's imagination of Asia as Niebuhr's description shows, the United States also had
to remind Americans of the presence of "good Asians" whose safety was
dependent on American generosity. In fact neither the Korean War nor
the Vietnam War was conceptualized in terms as America fighting communist countries. Rather, both wars were largely seen as America's self-
sacrificial actions to save innocent South Koreans and South Vietnamese
from their communist counterparts. The U.S. strategy to differentiate
good Asians from bad ones did not work in combat zones, however, as
the massacres of civilians by American soldiers happened in both South
Korea and in South Vietnam. For example, the basic military training
for American soldiers often reminded them that all Vietnamese were
gooks, including Vietnamese women and children as potential gooks in
guerilla warfare, just as the massacre in the village of My Lai in South
Vietnam suggested.[40]

Furthermore, the American logic of the moral condemnation of
guerilla warfare and terrorism has a long history of racializing enemies.
Both in America's colonization of the Philippines and war in Vietnam,
Americans saw guerilla warfare as barbaric violence committed by a sav-
age race incapable of following civilized rules of warfare.[41] Therefore, the
racialized Asian enemies were condemned for their inherited immoral
character per se, rather than for their engagement with guerilla warfare.

Most importantly, U.S. economic and military imperialism and the
changing face of America's enemy in Asia had significant ramifications
for Asian Americans in the United States in terms of immigration patterns and the formation of Asian American identity. American citizens
of Filipino descent transitioned from being immigrants to colonized
nationals to foreigners, depending on the status of the Philippines with
respect to the United States.[42] To provide another well-known example,
the Japanese who were "good Asians" during World War I in their war
against Germany became "bad Asians" when they joined the Axis against
the Allied forces. Still, many American-born Japanese were recruited to
fight against imperial Japan during World War II.

During the early Cold War period, while presenting itself as the
model of democracy at home and abroad, the United States made itself
vulnerable to criticisms of its racism and hypocrisy. The Immigration
and Nationality Act of 1965 was one way to deal with these criticisms. By
removing the ban of and quota for Asian immigration, the United States
intended to integrate Asians ideologically with Americans at home and

abroad. The "good Asian" versus "bad Asian" trope, however, refuses to die and has been recast in different ways. Now Asian Americans as a whole might be seen as "model minorities" (good Asians); other times the same individuals or subgroups might be viewed instead as "perpetual foreigners" (bad Asians), thus revealing America's inability to accept the racialized other and (potential) enemy into American civil society.[43]

Differently from the pre-1965 Asian immigrants who were believed to migrate from "stable, continuous, 'traditional' cultures," most of the post-1965 immigrants have predominantly come from war-torn societies, including South Korea, the Philippines, South Vietnam, and Cambodia, "already disrupted by colonialism and distorted by the upheavals of neocolonial capitalism and war."[44] These post-1965 Asian immigrants return to the center of imperialism and yet retain the memories of imperialism that the United States seeks to forget.[45]

To be sure, the civil rights movement of the 1960s and the reality of post-1965 immigrants, especially from Asia and Latin America, have forced the American public to promote tolerance. Nonetheless, as Janet Jakobsen and Ann Pellegrini argue, tolerance could be a misleading social value that contributes to maintaining racially and sexually constructed social hierarchies.[46] Jakobsen and Pellegrini's argument leads us to question whether Asian Americans have freedom to be fully Asian or to be fully American; our racial difference is perceived as a threat to American security, and at the same time, our presence haunts America's guilt over imperialist wars in Asia.

Asian Americans in the U.S. Military System

Beyond the enduring legacy of America's wars in Asia on Asian Americans in the broader culture, the question remains how Asian Americans fare in the military today. The military is a unique microcosm of American society where racism, sexism, and homophobia can be aggrandized while attempting to unify soldiers under norms of white heterosexual warrior masculinity.[47] It is possible for many Asian American soldiers to experience forced assimilation by eliminating their racial differences, and at the same time the intrinsic impossibility of their belonging to the military system. As Anuradha Bhagwati, an American-born Indian woman and former marine official recounted:

> I met a lot of children of immigrants in the marines . . . we shared a common desire to prove ourselves to be just as American as the average white guy with a crew cut. The insecurity people of color have about

not quite belonging to the American way of life, however large or small it is, is really magnified in a white male institution like the marines. . . . The strange thing for me was witnessing the presence of young marines with roots in Southeast Asia, Vietnam, Korea, and also, after 2003, a handful from South Asia and the Middle East. There is an understandable sense among some immigrant children that they owe something to the country that they now call their own. . . . The United States laid waste, even genocide, upon Southeast Asia, but still, children of survivors of those wars feel they have something to prove about their American-ness. People will do surprising and sometimes awful things to feel worthy or respected in this country.[48]

Although Bhagwati's voice may not represent the entire body of Asian American soldiers, she raises two important questions that we ought to consider in our ethical reflection on war, militarism, and peace. First, the military continues to be used as a site to test Asian Americans' loyalty to the United States, and the military continues to function as a site to assimilate racially and culturally diverse people. Therefore, Asian American ethicists have reason to challenge the moral implications of the current military system that judges one's loyalty and legitimacy of American citizenship. Second, Bhagwati's words suggest that racial/ethnic/cultural assimilation, especially in the military system, is not simply nearly impossible, but undesirable. Forced assimilation of Asian Americans with the white heterosexual military system would not signal acceptance, but instead a cruel form of violence in separating one's body from one's mind by erasing personal (hi)stories, since what the military system might want is the well-disciplined body of a soldier and not his/her conscience, spirit, or particular story—namely, humanness. In fact modern military training known as "reflexive fire training" can transform a person into a killing machine who shoots before thinking.[49]

Racism in the military can be detrimental to Asian American soldiers. On February 21, 2012, the *Washington Post* reported the sad news about the suicide of Danny Chen, a Chinese American soldier.[50] The news report summarized the long history of racism against Asian American soldiers due to American soldiers' confusing them with their enemies. Still, some people questioned Chen's mental fortitude, figuring that had he been a soldier with strong body and mind, he would have been able to endure any racial slurs hurled at him. This excuse, of course, is problematic, for racial slurs should not be used to test one's mental status. Not only racism but also other forms of structural injustice such as sexism and homophobia oppress a group of soldiers who do not fit heterosexual masculine norms in the U.S. military.[51] If the military unit were truly cohesive (a desideratum), why does the U.S. military seek to hide racism, sexism, and homophobia perpetuated among soldiers? Don't the repeated incidents of racial, sexual, and gender discrimination in the military seriously undermine the formation of camaraderie among military personnel, or does the military consider Asian Americans to be incapable of forming comradeship with other soldiers?

Christian Theories of Peace and War through Asian American Eyes and the Making of an Asian American Ethic of Peace through Eucharist Alternatives to War

As we have seen, a critical analysis of America's wars in Asia and Asian American soldiers' experiences of the U.S. military system challenges the major Christian theories of peace and war that I surveyed previously in the "Christian Ethical Responses" section. More specifically, unless Christians committed to peace (be they pacifists or followers of the "just peacemaking" paradigm) critically analyze the multiple layers of oppression such as racism, classism, imperialism, and Christian triumphalism in the state war project, they cannot proactively work for peace. For peace is not a romantic or idealist word but must be grounded in critical analysis of complex social realities (e.g., the effects of America's wars in adoption, immigration, and contemporary military life). Christian realists might be better at including social realities in their contemplation of war. Yet they must humbly accept that their readings of social realities require more contextualization, given the complexities of the power systems in which we live. Similarly before, during, and after war, just war theorists must do a better job at considering the effects that any onset of war is going to have on real people, including civilians and soldiers whose lives will be dramatically changed. Finally, those who value postwar justice (*jus post bellum*) and just peacemaking may be encouraged to pursue the healing of the multiple wounds of Asian Americans as well as reconciliation among multiple racial groups in the United States.

No matter how we understand war, it inextricably involves killing, and thus any war story is haunted by its innocent victims. So-called official history, however, often intentionally erases the voices of these victims. What can we possibly do to be reconciled with these victims and listen to them? How can Asian Americans liberate ourselves from America's war history?

The first step is to rethink the meanings of Asian American identity. I previously argued that perceptions of Asian Americans have been deeply interwoven with America's wars in Asia. If we scrutinize how America's past and present wars in Asia have helped to construct internal and external perceptions of Asian American identity, "Asian" and "American" in this identity would not be mutually inclusive or exclusive but paradoxical. It is paradoxical because in order to be American, Asian Americans must learn how to remember America's wars in Asia in a similar way that the American public mourns fallen American soldiers overseas. When mourning fallen soldiers, Americans are often forced to be silent about the deaths of innocent Asian civilians or soldiers killed by napalm, nuclear bombs, and American tanks and guns. Without freedom to mourn history's victims in Asia, we may not fully enjoy the freedom to be "Asian Americans" but live in tension between being loyal Americans and being faithful Asians. How, then, would it be possible to make Asian American identity the site where history's victims of war are courageously embraced and alternatives to war are hopefully imagined? I submit that reconciliation between "Asian" and "American" in our identity is an ideal to enjoy full freedom to be Asian American. Namely, by being Asian, Asian Americans should not be perceived (by others) as racialized (potential) enemies to American society whose loyalty needs to be tested through the military service. By being American, Asian Americans do not need to mourn the victims of America's wars in Asia privately or to hide our Asianness in order to be faithful citizens of military empire. Freedom to be both Asian and American can on its own present some alternatives to war. In order to imagine these alternatives, I offer a reimagination of the Asian American church community as a political group, in resistance of U.S. military empire, that shares one common Christian practice: the Eucharist.

Reimagining the Eucharist and the Asian American Church Community

The Eucharist (also known as Communion or the Lord's Supper) originated from the Last Supper that Jesus had shared with his followers before he was arrested and crucified. Throughout his ministry on earth, Jesus shared many meals with social outcasts such as tax collectors, poor peasants, prostitutes, and so forth. The death of Jesus on the cross corresponds to his own teaching about the kingdom of God in contrast to the Roman apparatus of military occupation, cultural imperialism, economic exploitation, and massive taxation. Early Christian practices of the Eucharist were not only the important ritual to remember the life of Jesus but also the crucial way to build a community distinguished from Roman imperial power. According to Hal Taussig's analysis, "the social practice of early Christian meals was central to early Christian acts of resistance to Rome."[52] By giving thanks to God and remembering and retelling the death and resurrection of Jesus at the Eucharist meal, early Christians intentionally remembered the innocent deaths in the ruling of the Roman Empire.[53]

Hence, the Eucharist was early Christians' everyday political activism infused with spiritual practice. This kind of Eucharist is still celebrated today. During my field research of popular resistance to militarism in Jeju Island, Korea, I had the opportunity to observe and participate in the Eucharist celebrated on the street every day. A group of Catholic clergy and lay people gathered on the street across from the construction site of a naval base at Gangjeong Village. The Eucharist at Gangjeong was ordinary people's everyday resistance to the militarization of the island. Their resistance was also the memorial of the innocent deaths during Japanese colonialism, the U.S. military occupation in 1945, and the Korean War (1950–1953).[54] At the Eucharistic table at Gangjeong, the body of Christ in the consecrated bread was equated with all suffering beings—both human and nonhuman entities—whose suffering was caused by callous capitalism, militarism, war, violence, and so forth. While sharing the bread, the participants entered Christ's suffering and recommitted themselves to ending unnecessary suffering caused by unjust social structures. What impressed me the most was that the rite of Holy Communion ended with dancing—a symbolic action of celebrating and affirming life given from God.

My experience of the Eucharist at Gangjeong helps me reimagine a truthful practice of the Eucharist today, especially in the United States, one which requires remembering silenced victims of U.S. military imperialism spiritually supported by Christian triumphalism infused with American exceptionalism.[55] At the same time, the ritual must affirm and celebrate life over death, and peace over war.

In the Asian American context, Jonathan Tran's "Eucharistic memory" proposes how to truthfully remember the victims of history. He argues that America's Vietnam War domesticates the Vietnam War in "American mythos" while willfully forgetting Vietnamese people's memory of war (i.e., America's killing of the innocent).[56] In resistance

against this forgetfulness, according to Tran, we should practice "Eucharistic memory": a politics of "re-membering"—intentionally remembering the victims in the past whose identities merge into that of Jesus of
Nazareth by welcoming the unleashed ghosts of these victims of history
at the present table of the Eucharist.[57]

Furthermore, in order to be truthful memory, the Eucharist cannot
be privatized but must be practiced in community, because "memory
and forgetting go hand in hand, with every remembering a forgetting
and every forgetting a remembering."[58] Similar to Tran's proposal, Emilie Townes emphasizes the importance of resisting "forgotteness" as a
political action. By resisting willful "forgotteness," according to Townes,
people of color can open up "subversive spaces" within dominant discourses.[59] Both Tran and Townes may encourage the Asian American
church community to accordingly play a role of truthful community by
witnessing and remembering innocent deaths caused by America's wars
in Asia. Only then could we heal our own wounded identity interwoven
with horrific war stories and celebrate life sanctified by God.

One way to understand what the healing of "Eucharistic memory"
can do for Asian Americans is to consider the suffering of Asian Americans brought about by America's wars in terms of a transnational and
intergenerational haunting, as Korean American scholar Grace Cho has
persuasively argued.[60] It is not simply Asian Americans but also others
who may feel haunted by the "ghosts" of the victims of history whose
vengeance is unbearable. According to Cho, "studying ghosts allows us
to rethink a society's relationship to its dead, particularly to those who
were subject to some kind of injustice."[61] Therefore, the ghost and its
haunting effects act as "a mode of memory and an avenue for ethical
engagement with the present."[62] Perhaps in order to live every day during the time of America's successive wars, we do our best to pretend not
to see these "ghosts" living around us. However, ethical engagement
with the present in the midst of hauntings forces us to remember, welcome, and be reconciled with them because "haunting is a phenomenon
that reveals how the past is in the present" and forgetfulness is the fertile
ground to generate ghosts.[63]

How can we remember, welcome, and be reconciled with these
"ghosts," not only at the Eucharistic table but also in the political realm?
We might first recall that welcoming the dead at the Eucharistic table
was a common practice among early Christians, who did not see the
dead as being entirely separated from the living. Rather, the dead and

the living celebrated life together at the Eucharistic table—the dead even arrived at the table before the living.[64] The tragic wars in Asia and the willful forgetfulness about history's victims, however, prevent the living from celebrating life with the dead. We must thus exorcise these ghosts by welcoming them at our Eucharistic table and by remembering their stories just as we remember the death and resurrection of Jesus Christ. In other words, such an exorcism would not be to send away the ghosts with deep sorrow, but to let the ghosts be fully liberated from their suffering, traumas, and deep sorrow buried in our Asian American history so that they can celebrate life with us together. Exorcism further requires transforming perceptions of Asian American identity due to militarization into that of justice with peace, so that we will not repeat the same history of war that creates ghosts in the present and in the future.

Those who see the world through the positivistic lens might find my emphasis on reconciliation with ghosts or the dead at the Eucharistic table unsettling and uncomfortable. I do not simply reduce ghosts to the spirits of the dead. Although the most prominent images of ghosts in my mind are the silenced victims whose stories are barely detectable in written history, ghosts can have multiple faces. They can be our memories of or the secrecy of the tragic deaths of the innocent. Ghosts may include victims of our ongoing wars, such as ghost prisoners, ghost soldiers, and missing women, men, and children whose existences are intentionally erased to the public. The image of the ghost furthest from my mind is the cultic or supernatural figure found in horror films.

War and militarism are inevitably against the order of the Eucharist. While the logic of the Eucharist commands Christians to welcome strangers at the table of Jesus, militarism actively trains civilians to exclude others. As I argued earlier, modern military training transforms ordinary men and women into killers who should consistently differentiate themselves from enemies and suppress their human nature not to kill others. Rather than empathetically embracing "others" that the order of the Eucharist dictates, soldiers are forced to practice dehumanizing enemies, erasing their stories, and turning a blind eye to their interconnection to enemies in God's creation. What is more, while Susan Thistlethwaite has shown how military training (i.e., reflexive fire training) is only possible based upon the dualistic understanding or separation between body and spirit,[65] the Eucharist in the early Christian church trained "the whole person—body, mind, and soul and strength to know the world and the Spirit in it."[66] Hence, if the true Eucharist pursues unity between body and spirit by recognizing others in Christ's body (e.g., bread and wine) and by receiving Christ's body with gratitude, militarism actively seeks to destroy this unity by portraying others as threats and by claiming God exclusively for "us."[67]

I am particularly concerned about the consequences of reflexive fire training and the sacrifices that soldiers make of their will *not* to kill other human beings, which is to say combat encourages the severe separation between body and soul. In their book *Soul Repair*, Rita Nakashima Brock and Gabrielle Lettini unpack the concept of "moral injury," or what happens to soldiers when they act against their moral will not to kill.[68] Moral injury differs from post-traumatic stress disorder, although it can happen simultaneously with the latter. Moral injury is the result of "reflection on memories of war or other extreme traumatic conditions" when one has transgressed one's basic moral identity and violated moral beliefs such those derived from religion.[69] We do not know how many Asian American veterans suffer moral injury. But it may not be difficult to imagine that many Asian American soldiers might suffer especially from extreme feelings of guilt after firing at Viet Cong and Vietnamese civilians during the Vietnam War. A similar phenomenon might obtain a special kind of moral injury for American vets who have witnessed or participated in race- and gender-based violence in more recent conflicts in Afghanistan and Iraq, especially against Afghan or Iraqi civilians. Similarly, Danny Chen might have suffered moral injury, as many soldiers experience it out of deep sorrow and anger when their comrades violate their human rights.

I submit that the Asian American church community can play a role in creating public space where Asian American veterans candidly share their stories with other Asian Americans and look for pastoral care and counseling without a fear of judgment or receiving cheap absolution. In addition, the church can be a space for reconciliation between morally injured Vietnam and Korean War veterans and Vietnamese American and Korean American communities. According to Brock and Lettini, veterans living with moral injury seek out opportunities to be forgiven by their victims. Although reconciliation between veterans and victims is more complicated than we may think, the church can create a space where veterans build up genuine human relations with history's victims.[70] For this, as Brock and Lettini suggest, both clergy and laity must be trained and educated about moral injury and about how to interact with veterans.[71]

If the Eucharist ultimately calls for reconciliation between humans and God, between the dead and the living, and even between "us," the Asian American church community should consider how to bring reconciliation among Asian Americans. America's wars in Asia that followed imperial Japan have created divisions and distrust among Asian Americans. Chinese, Korean, and Japanese communities often find it difficult to work together for social justice and peace because various wars, historical conflicts, and territorial disputes among China, Korea, and Japan affect these ethnic communities' perceptions of one another. Korean (as well as the Pacific region physically occupied by imperial Japan) and Japanese American communities still experience conflict over the problems of Japanese military sexual slavery during World War II. Korean soldiers' atrocities against Vietnamese civilians during the Vietnam War have been rarely spoken of. Ongoing conflict between mainland China and Taiwan and Tibet is another obstacle for Asian Americans in need of reconciliation. Therefore, the Eucharistic table in the Asian American church community must continue to seek out opportunities to bring various Asian American groups together, to make difficult dialogue on war, and to continue to work for peace and reconciliation among us.

Furthermore, the reimagined Eucharist encourages us to attentively criticize the current military recruitment that targets people of color in impoverished areas. The military is often portrayed as the only option for poor youth to escape poverty, to earn college degrees, and to become loyal citizens of the United States. The Asian American church community should thus encourage the government to create better life opportunities for young men and women. At the same time, we must courageously criticize structural injustices such as racism, sexism, and homophobia in the military because our society cannot afford another Danny Chen. Just as both pacifists and just peacemaking theorists point out the importance of building up just social structures for long-lasting peace on a domestic and an international level, it is important to push for racial, class, sexual, and gender justice by resisting, struggling with, and attempting to dismantle oppressive power structures in the United States and abroad. So the Asian American church community must actively work for peace with justice, along with other racial ethnic minorities and others who seek to work for peace in these ways.

Conclusion: Vulnerability and Liberation

If the Eucharist is genuinely an alternative to war and a source to generate Christian ethical reflection on peace and war in ways that I have suggested, the question remains, What kind of theo-ethical reflection can Asian American Christians in particular produce? First of all, we can articulate that peace and war are antithetical to each other. War never brings peace. This is the lesson that Asian Americans have painfully learned. Asian American ethicists should continue to emphasize that we do not need war in order to know peace.

Second, we should more proactively imagine peace. Imagining peace requires remembering history's victims. As Kwok Pui-lan emphasizes, memory is a powerful tool in resisting institutionally sanctioned forgetfulness.[72] And based on a historical imagination of "the concrete and not the abstract," hope for peace is more practical and not so easily disillusioned.[73]

Finally, peacemaking may make us vulnerable to the unknown, as if we encountered the mystery of Christ at the Eucharistic table. However, this vulnerability is the only possible way for us to overcome the fear of unknown by thoroughly trusting our God who is present at the Eucharist. After interviewing women peace activists from eighty organizations over the world, British feminist Cynthia Cockburn wisely noted that peace activism is ultimately "liberation from fear."[74] Her sociological analysis offers a significantly theological meaning. During the Cold War period and even in earlier periods, fear of the communist military power allowed the United States excessively to militarize the Asia-Pacific region. Fear of terrorism and of losing their status as a global hegemonic power still drives the United States to ever-increasing militarization. The Eucharist forces us to face where our fear comes from. Just as Dorothee Soelle says, we have to remember that "the worst fear of creatures [i.e., human beings] is the fear of the authorities [i.e., the military system] wherein people are kept dependent. Imprisoned in it, people cannot fear God."[75]

Vulnerability that we experience at the Eucharistic table will eventually lead us to discern what to fear and what not to fear. Vulnerability humbles us by recognizing that the source of eternity and life is from God and not from military might. Vulnerability will also open doors for us to encounter others (both human and nonhuman entities) who are always transcendental to us and, therefore, we cannot help being in solidarity with them in their struggle for peace and justice. Being Asian in the United States is to be vulnerable, as I have argued previously. Yet this vulnerability is our power to heal America from war, violence, and lust for power.

DISCUSSION QUESTIONS

1. Of the traditional ways that Christian ethicists have thought about the morality of war (e.g., just war, pacifism, holy war, Christian realism, just peacemaking), which one most appeals to you and why? Given that standard training in the U.S. military today requires troops to dehumanize the enemy, can a Christian enlist or remain in good conscience in the military? Why or why not?

2. Pae argues that Asian Americans have reasons to be especially suspicious of American military activities in the Asia-Pacific region. If Pae is correct on this score, does that mean that the American society and government was and is right to question the loyalties of Asian Americans, as per the internment of Japanese Americans during World War II or the "perpetual foreigner" syndrome?

3. Pae notes that the military has historically been used as a site to test the loyalty of Asian Americans to the country but that the military is also a site of forced assimilation. Are there ways that the military can respect cultural differences of its members without sacrificing the order, discipline, and cohesion that is required for military effectiveness and success? How would the military system look if just human relations were emphasized in the system?

4. Pae commends the practices of the Eucharist for remembering, healing, reconciliation, and liberation. Can you paraphrase in your own words why? Do you agree with her assessment that remembrance is importance to manage the memories of the dead by the living? How would America's wars look if Americans actively remembered victims of war rather than war heroes?

✦ 6 ✦

Wealth and Prosperity

CHRISTINA A. ASTORGA

Wealth and prosperity cannot be separated from the transcendental concerns of people of faith. Touching every aspect of life, religious faith asks what the ultimate purpose of life is and how wealth and prosperity best serve or impede that. As Daniel Finn writes, "What can faith say to economics, about the nature of creation, about the value of work, about the purposes of prosperity, and the creation of wealth?"[1] Drawing from Scripture and tradition, this essay seeks to answer these questions as it develops an Asian American Christian faith ethics of wealth and prosperity. More specifically, in the first section, I discuss the range of Christian ethical responses to wealth and prosperity by drawing especially upon two sources. The first is the work of Sondra Ely Wheeler on the meaning of wealth from the perspective of the New Testament in her book *Wealth as Peril and Obligation*, given her expert reading of the New Testament's teaching on wealth and possessions and insightful discernment of the relevance of this teaching for contemporary times. The second is the Catholic social tradition, particularly its understanding of true prosperity as involving human goods other than income as well as its valuation of the principles of subsidiarity, solidarity, preferential option for the poor, and communal participation as constitutive of the common good.

My end goal is to bring to bear the faith ethics of wealth and prosperity on the life of Asian Americans in their own contexts. To do so I must first explain the ways in which Asian Americans are already invested in this topic; this I seek to do in the second section when I discuss the pursuit of the "American dream" for immigrant Asians, interrogate the myth of the model minority in terms of across-the-board financial success, and recount the ways in which wealth and prosperity for many

Asian Americans involve transnationalism. In the "Faith Ethics" section, I encourage Asian Americans to resist the lure of materialism in light of biblical and church teachings about the nature of true prosperity. I also raise a series of difficult questions about whether and to what extent those Asian American Christians who have experienced financial success may be complicitous in wrongdoing and otherwise led astray by the false teaching of the "prosperity gospel." I seek, in short, to move Christians toward a correct understanding of the responsibilities associated with wealth and a vision of true prosperity that is connected with the common good.

Christian Ethical Reflections on Wealth

As alluded to earlier, Scripture and tradition are two traditional sources of Christian ethical reflection. The Bible continues to be a source of moral wisdom for Asian American Christians and the wisdom of Catholic social teaching is especially meaningful for those of us who are Catholic. In what follows I will highlight a few themes from the Bible (particularly the New Testament) and from Catholic social thought as a way of capturing how Christian ethics as a field has wrestled with questions concerning wealth and prosperity.

Biblical Reflections on Wealth

Following the important work of Sondra Wheeler's discussion of wealth in the New Testament, we might organize our understanding of the portrait of wealth and prosperity that emerges in the New Testament under the following four themes: wealth as a stumbling block, wealth as a competing object of devotion, wealth in light of economic justice, and wealth as a resource for human needs.[2]

The first of these themes is that wealth can serve as an obstacle to discipleship, that is, living a way of life that is faithful to the vision of Christ's life. This theme is prominent in the story of the rich young man in Mark 10:17-22 (see parallels in Matt 19:16-22 and Luke 18:18-30) who, even in seeking what would make him gain eternal life, could not part from his possessions. As Jesus said when the young man went away sad, "Amen, I say to you, it is easier for a camel to pass through the eye of a needle than for one who is rich to enter the kingdom of God" (Mark 10:25). Wealth is also shown to be a hindrance or stumbling block to hearing and heeding the gospel in the parable of the sower: "the deceitfulness of wealth" (Matt 13:22), "the desire for other things"

(Mark 4:18-19), or "the riches and pleasures of the world" (Luke 8:14) choke the life out of the saving word, so that its seed, though planted into the soil, never had the chance to grow and bear fruit. In contrast, these stories suggest that dispossession enables the one being called to respond, since those who had "left everything behind and followed him" were the ones who responded to the call (Luke 5:11, 28; cf. Mark 1:16-17, Matt 4:18-22, and John 1:37-39).

The second theme that appears in the New Testament is of the danger of wealth becoming the primary object of one's attachment and devotion. When wealth has taken over one's heart this way, one falls into idolatry—not in the form of Baal worship but in the form of wealth taking the place of God as one's ultimate ground of security. The Gospels warn, "You cannot serve God and mammon" (Matt 6:24, Luke 16:13), and the disciples are counseled not to accumulate treasures on earth because where their treasure is, there also will their heart be (Matt 6:19-21). Even stronger language is used elsewhere: the wrath of God falls upon the sin of love for money (1 Tim 6:6-8, 2 Tim 3:2, Heb 13:5), which is described as the root of all evils. James warns against the lust for worldly things and, appropriating Isaiah's message, sees it as an adulterous act of making things as the object of devotion in the place of God (4:1-10).

To be clear, the lure of wealth is the sense of security that it offers, but the Bible describes it as deceptive because in the end this cannot save; this is why the individual who relies upon his wealth for security is called a fool (cf. 1 Tim 6:17-19). The point here is not to reject all treasures on earth but rather to work instead at storing up treasures in heaven "where rust cannot corrupt nor thief steal" (Matt 6:20). So understood, the New Testament can be read as affirming voluntary poverty as well as acts of openhearted generosity, such as giving alms to all who are in need (Matt 5:42), lending without any expectation of return (Luke 6:35, cf. Matt 5:42), offering our cloak to the one who takes our tunic (Matt 5:40),[3] and, as I will discuss further below, holding our possessions in common while placing them at the reach of any fellow believer who is in need or for the service of the church and its various ministries (Acts 2:44-45, 4:32-37).

The third theme that we can glean from the New Testament not only associates wealth with evil and oppression but also depicts the poor as the victims of the sins and abuses of wealth awaiting God's vindication. This theme is clearest in Luke, where the announcement of the gospel is portrayed as bringing blessing to the poor and woe to the rich

(Luke 1:51-53, 4:18-19, 6:21, 16:19-26, etc.). This similar portrayal of wealth is evident in the Apocalypse, where the whore of Babylon and those who feed on her vices are depicted in their opulent extravagance, while the faithful churches and martyrs under the throne are poor (Rev 2:8-10, 7:16-17). The Epistle of James presents covetous greed as the source of strife and murder (4:1-2), and his excoriation of the abuses of the rich, which echoes the scorn and rage of the prophets of the Old Testament, brings to sharp light the New Testament indictment of the rich (5:1-6): they deny the poor of the just wages for their labor and turn a blind eye to the crying needs of the poor while they wallow in their opulent wealth. The offense of the rich in James is comparable to the parable of the rich man and Lazarus (Luke 16:19-26) and the parable of the sheep and the goats (Matt 25:31-46) in that a failure to share one's wealth and possessions with the poor and needy is counted as defiance of God's demand for love and charity toward one's neighbor.

The final major theme of the New Testament regarding possessions is that material support of fellow believers is a necessary expression of Christian love. Any professed love for brothers and sisters in Christ must be embodied in the sharing of material resources. In the description of the Jerusalem community in Acts, such sharing is the testament of the fellowship of the saved (Acts 2:44-47) and of the unity of mind and heart forged in love (Acts 4:32-35). In the Johannine Epistles, the love of sisters and brothers in community is the sign of the love for God, which is manifested in the care of those in need, particularly in terms of material resources (1 John 3:16-17, cf. Jas 2:15-16). Elsewhere in the Pauline Epistles, the material service to fellow believers serves as proof or a test of the truthfulness of their confession of Christ who saves them: the sharing of wealth is portrayed as good for the whole community (Rom 12:6-8), infant churches are instructed to share all things with those who teach them the gospel (Gal 6:6), Gentile churches are told that they must come to the aid of the church in Jerusalem, and the sharing of resources between and among churches is described as something done for the sake of all (2 Cor 1–2).

To be sure, while these aforementioned texts have focused on the responsibilities to those within the Christian community, the Bible also speaks of the duty to care universally for the needy. We see this in the general admonition to "give to everyone who asks you" (Matt 5:42, Luke 6:30), the instruction to invite the poor to the feast (Luke 14:12-14), and the call to love the neighbor, including the stranger and the enemy (Matt 5:43-48, Luke 6:27, 32-35). This duty explicitly includes provision for material needs as exemplified in the parable of the good Samaritan (Luke 10:29-37) and in Paul's instruction, "If your enemy is hungry, feed him" (Rom 12:20).

How are we to synthesize or harmonize all four of these themes? Wheeler's position on the first two themes, which I believe to be correct, is that poverty neither defines discipleship nor ensures moral purity, for "possessions of themselves will no more bar admission to the kingdom than poverty of itself will secure it."[4] Instead, the problem with wealth is that it can lead to a paralysis of the heart in the face of the love of God that beckons. As it is possible "to give up everything one owns" and yet "have no charity" (1 Cor 13:3), it is thus possible ("with God") for even the rich to enter the kingdom. In the end what is morally decisive is the liberty or freedom of heart relative to wealth and possessions to love God and others, whether this be in voluntary poverty or in openhearted generosity. Still, the next two themes remind us that God will not only pass judgment on those "who actively rob and exploit the poor or use their wealth for corruption," but will also condemn "unjust distribution . . . along with unjust accrual and unjust use."[5] For Christians, then, attending to others' material needs is not an optional moral add-on or of secondary importance; it is what they are commanded to do if they are to faithfully follow Christ.

Ethics of Prosperity in Catholic Social Tradition

Catholic social tradition envisions true prosperity in terms not just of material goods but of all human goods necessary for flourishing. This is to say that true prosperity cannot be reduced either to material prosperity or any indexes of income (when measured as gross domestic product per capita). In developing an ethics of wealth and prosperity, this section first presents the limits of income as a measurement of prosperity and then proceeds to present the overarching principle of common good and its allied principles—the inherent dignity of the person, subsidiarity, solidarity, the preferential option of the poor, participation, socialization, and restoration—that lie at the foundation of the vision in Catholic social teaching of prosperity.

The Limits of Income as Index of Prosperity and Well-Being

Because income is easy to measure, it is commonly used as an index of prosperity.[6] Its singular value, however, cannot be equated with prosperity according to many Western philosophical and religious traditions, and even some economists, if prosperity is to mean the total well-being of persons, communities, and societies. Aristotle noted that income is of relative value: it is only good if it promotes happiness, but it in fact can lead to great unhappiness.[7] As discussed in the previous section, the Bible teaches that material wealth can delude one into believing that it holds the promise of ultimate happiness, displacing the worship of the one true God. Warnings against absolutizing the value of income for human well-being can also be found among economists, particularly those influenced by the capability approach of Amartya Sen, Martha Nussbaum, and others. In taking as its measurement of well-being what persons are able to be and to do, the capabilities approach reveals the limits of focusing on an index of income alone for three primary reasons: (1) there are other prerequisites or important capabilities for human flourishing (e.g., religious freedom), (2) people vary in their abilities to convert the resources they have into valuable functionings (e.g., a disabled person will require more societal resources than an able-bodied one in order to move around), and (3) a focus on GDP alone says nothing about equity in distribution.[8] All three of these concerns are present in Catholic social teaching, especially this last one, given the critique of income inequality resulting in the extreme material deprivation of the poor, who are then denied the basics of decent human life and are shut out of participation in the legal and democratic processes of society.

The skepticism of Catholic social teaching regarding income as a metric of human well-being is based on the belief that income and happiness are not perfectly correlated, because the market is not the place where one finds the human goods for a happy and purposeful life. The goods that are not attainable by one's purchasing power fall into three categories: character, social relationships, and public goods, which are in different ways components of the common good.[9]

The goods of character constitute the spiritual orientation of a rightly ordered life that is necessary for an authentic enjoyment of whatever material prosperity one has when acquired through virtuous means. A certain poverty of spirit is necessary for one not to be claimed by the allure of material goods. John Paul II points out how wealth can have such a hold on the human spirit that it can diminish it with the relentless drive for consumption. This superdevelopment, which consists in an *excessive* availability of every kind of material goods for the benefit of certain social groups, easily makes people slaves of "possession" and of immediate gratification, with no other horizon than the multiplication or continual replacement of the things already owned with others still better. This is the so-called civilization of "consumption" or consumerism, which involves so much "throwing away" and "waste."[10]

Consumerism consumes the person, rendering him or her at the mercy of forces that diminish or destroy his/her moral agency. In wanting for more, an individual is left incessantly dissatisfied with what is attained, and all the while, "deeper aspirations remain dissatisfied or even stifled."[11]

The goods of social relationships are the *telos* of material prosperity: self-gift and solidarity with those who have less. A crucial component of human fulfillment is the quality of relationships. If income is used in ways that destroy human relationships and communities, then it fails to achieve its *telos* (or end). Catholic social teaching emphasizes that society is not simply a "society of capital goods" but a "society of persons;"[12] thus its good cannot be measured simply in terms of output and income. John Paul II, in *Centesimus Annus*, notes that "it is possible for the financial accounts to be in order, yet for the people—who make up the firm's most valuable asset—to be humiliated and their dignity offended."[13] Thus material goods are universally destined: "riches fulfill their function of service to man [*sic*] when they are destined to produce benefits for others and for society."[14] The universal destination of goods is a clear requirement of charity and of justice, and the sharing of goods ought to take place within the broad scope of families, communities, nations, and the entire global community. Since in Catholic social teaching wealth is a means of enabling genuine human activity, including broader participation in the economic, civic, social, and political life of the community, the bishops teach that "efforts that enable the poor to participate in the ownership and control of economic resources are especially important."[15]

In addition to goods of character and social goods, a third sort of good—public goods—does not fall under the income metric of prosperity: "A public good is one that, because of its nature, is not efficiently provided by individually oriented markets. Examples include a well-functioning police and legal system, access to education and public health, and infrastructure."[16] The United Nations Development Program critique of income-based measures is largely focused on the importance of public goods, which includes in its index life expectancy as a measure of public health and literacy as a measure of access to education.[17]

Common Good and Its Allied Principles: True Prosperity in Catholic Social Tradition

Modern Catholic social teaching tends to avoid making concrete recommendations for the economy and to stay at the level of generality. As they address people in plural circumstances across the globe, these teachings offer prudential guidelines in the form of principles, the overall principle being the common good (with its allied principles) as constitutive of the tradition's vision of true prosperity.[18] John XXIII defines the common good as "the sum total of those conditions of social living, whereby persons are enabled more fully and readily to achieve their own perfection."[19] The "perfection" that human beings realize cannot be achieved in isolation; as David Hollenbach points out, "this shared life of communication and interaction . . . is good in itself. . . . It [the common good] cannot be broken down into individual goods but is a shared good that emerges from the participation of all for the good of all."[20] The allied principles, which are founded on the fundamental principle of the person as *imago Dei*, are those that promote the very conditions of social living that realize the common good, which is the flourishing of individuals and the prosperity of local, national, and global communities. As such, the person in his or her inherent dignity is someone and not something. All social life is rooted in human agency, and the end of social life is the good of human beings as subjects and not as passive objects.[21]

Catholic social tradition safeguards the free exercise of subjectivity through the principle of subsidiarity that states that "a community of a higher order should not interfere in the internal life of a community of a lower order, depriving the latter of its functions, but rather should support in case of need and help to coordinate its activities with the activities of the rest of society, always with a view to the common good."[22] Subsidiarity should compel individuals to take responsibility for their own integral human development to get involved in finding solutions to social ills without having to rely upon or wait for higher bodies (like the government) to act. Because the life and vigor of a prosperous community spring from the active participation of its members, the Catholic social tradition has always upheld personal initiative and the action of local communities. It does not, however, deny the necessity of government intervention and action, especially when it has to protect the rights of the poor and most vulnerable in society.

Solidarity is at the heart of the common good. It is an active and genuine concern for the welfare of others by the facts of our shared humanity and of our being sons and daughters of God. Moved by the spirit of compassion, solidarity involves making the problems of others one's own, helping to carry them, and to find solutions to them with all possible resources that are available. Solidarity is the very spirit of the preferential option for the poor (see below), by which, as the bishops at Medellín put it, "we make ours their problems and struggles."[23] According to Stephen Pope, "the virtue of solidarity has deep roots in Catholic social anthropology, as well as in the theological virtue of *caritas*, the love of friendship with God and the love of one another in God. It incorporates modern egalitarianism in a way that modifies the paternalistic dimension of pity and virtue of mercy (*misericordia*), at least as understood in figures like Augustine and Thomas."[24] Solidarity is the radical opposite of raw self-interest governing profit-driven market forces, which push to the margins those without purchasing power.

Catholic social teaching acknowledges that the deep roots of the principle of preferential option of the poor is in Scripture. Both the Hebrew and Christian Scriptures state again and again God's predilection of concern for the poor, downtrodden, marginalized, and oppressed. Yahweh, moved by their cries, lifts them out of their suffering and delivers them. In the Gospels, Jesus, who is himself poor, identifies with the poor: "whatever you do to the least of these you do to me" (Matt 25:40-41). This principle calls for the primacy of the needs of the poor at several levels. Affectively, it involves a profound love for the poor, and morally, it requires a deep reorientation that places the needs of the poor at the center.[25] Nothing could be clearer or more eloquent than the prophetic call for the preferential option for the poor found in the U.S. Catholic Bishops' letter on the economy: "Economic decisions must be judged in light of what they do *for* the poor, what they do *to* the poor, and what they enable the poor to do *for themselves*. The fundamental moral criterion for all economic decisions, policies, and institutions is this: They must be at the service of *all people, especially the poor*."[26] Despite the centrality of the principle of the preferential option for the poor in the Bible and in the church's social teaching, it is, as Donal Dorr writes, arguably "the most controversial term since the Reformers' cry, 'Salvation through faith alone.' "[27]

As alluded to earlier, the principle of the preferential option of the poor is intrinsically connected with the principle of solidarity; it is also connected to the principles of participation and socialization. The principle of participation calls for the inclusion of all in the life of the socioeconomic life of society. The social nature of persons, which is described as intrinsic to their nature and dignity, is at the base of the principle of participation: "to the extent that a society and its social structures (e.g., the economy) function in such a way as to push people to the edges of society, it keeps those persons who are marginalized from fully participating in community, and, hence, from fully experiencing their humanity."[28] The principle of socialization thus upholds the obligation of those who possess resources to intervene and provide assistance to those who, having fallen on hard times, are no longer able to function for their good or for that of the community. In our current economy, socialization is best seen in the many networks of solidarity—personal, local, national, and global—that embrace people who are in dire need.[29]

Lastly, according to the principle of restoration, the community is obliged to "attend to the adverse unintended consequences of market operations" such as when the "Hebrews sought to restore those who had fallen on hard times" through measures such as debt forgiveness, slave manumission, land return, redemption of a kin from bondage, and interest-free loans.[30] In contemporary times the principle of restoration calls for mechanisms and institutions to help ameliorate the consequences of market operations, particularly for those who could not protect themselves from the onslaught (e.g., trade-in adjustment assistance, job-training programs, bankruptcy protections, and credit assistance).[31]

As we have seen, the New Testament offers a multiplicity of ways to think of the value of wealth and poverty, and Catholic social tradition has interpreted the Bible in such a way as to have provided a conception of prosperity and human flourishing that far exceeds the question of income or material resources alone. Catholic social teaching not only lifts up the common good, with its attendant principles, but also insists upon the "preferential option for the poor" based on the prophetic concern in the Bible with the downtrodden. The vision that we can glean from the Bible and from Catholic social teaching is accordingly holistic as it is integral, given its basis on the foundational principle of the human person as *imago Dei* in her/his subjectivity and relationality.

Asian Americans and the American Dream

What is the marker of wealth and prosperity for Asian Americans? Realizing the "American dream" is what most, if not all, immigrants have left their home countries for in emigrating to the United States. It is also the same dream that those who were born in the United States not infrequently aim to attain. This is a dream of a life lived in material security and contentment where one's basic necessities are not only met but one is also able to live out a higher standard of living or "quality life." As I shall discuss in this section, recent studies and stereotypes of Asian Americans as the "model minority" suggest that this demographic may have realized the American dream, though the ascendancy of Asian Americans is just one side of the story, masking the real struggles of segments of the Asian American population who are among the poorest of the poor in America. Thus the narrative of Asian Americans is more complex than singular in its lights and shadows. Equally important in understanding Asian American realities and conceptions of wealth and prosperity are the transnational ties that many Asian Americans retain as they negotiate their ethnic identities in a highly globalized world.

The Rise of Asian Americans

"The American dream that we were all raised on is a simple but powerful one—if you work hard and play by the rules you should be given a chance to go as far as your God-given ability will take you."[32] With these words, then–President Bill Clinton brought into sharp light the deeply engrained mythos of the possibilities that life in the United States makes possible. The lure of the American dream has brought millions from all over the world to seek the promise of this dream across waters, mountains, and plains.[33] It has been observed, however, that "the American dream functions brilliantly as an ideology but provides a poor guide for practice."[34] Not all Americans share it, but the enduring power of this dream lies in those who believe it, if not as a reality than as an ideal. While the American dream of upward social mobility through hard work arguably predates the founding of the republic (e.g., consider the Declaration of Independence's "life, liberty, and the pursuit of happiness") and has changed throughout the course of history, the question remains whether the dream can hold up in the face of the profound transformation now underway in the racial and ethnic composition of the United States. More specifically, between 2000 and 2008, African Americans, Latinos, and Asian Americans comprised 83 percent of the U.S. population growth (U.S. Census, 2010). The question remains whether the American dream is even possible or desirable for those groups as well.

According to a recent survey conducted in Los Angeles, perceptions of achievement and optimism about reaching the American dream varied among racial, ethnic, and nativity groups, among other factors (e.g., age, economic factors of income and home ownership, education, citizenship status, and amount of retirement savings). Contrary to what their levels of income and education—comparatively higher than all other racial and ethnic groups—might lead one to conclude, Asian Americans were "less likely to believe that they have achieved the American dream."[35] Given that it was largely first- and second-generation Asian Americans who responded to the survey, researchers acknowledged that their nonregistering of higher levels of optimism provides fertile ground for future research.[36]

The findings of the Pew Research Center's recent report entitled *The Rise of Asian Americans* provides a sharp contrast with the ambivalence documented in the aforementioned study of Asian Americans regarding their attainment (or not) of the American dream by especially highlighting glowing statistics about their achievements. Asian Americans are the highest-income, best-educated, and fastest-growing racial group in the United States. The survey also finds Asian Americans to be more satisfied than the general public with their lives, finances, and the direction of the country; they also place a greater value on marriage parenthood, hard work, and career success.[37] They report great pressure to be successful. We might understand this reported pressure to do extremely well in school as connected to the same impulse to never be content with or stagnant about their current socioeconomic standing, thus resulting in feelings that that they have not (yet) achieved their full potential regardless of the reality of their (higher than average) material accomplishments.[38]

Asian Americans have reached astonishing milestones of economic success and social assimilation.[39] The number of U.S. businesses owned by persons of Asian descent increased 40.4 percent to 1.5 million between 2002 and 2007, which is an increase twice the national rate. Asian-owned businesses continued to be one of the strongest segments of the nation's economy, bringing in more than half a trillion dollars in sales in 2007 and employing more than 2.8 million people (Census Bureau Reports of 2011). To be sure, one of the major reasons for these impressive accomplishments is that many of the immigrants who came post-1965 were highly educated and highly skilled (n.b., nearly three quarters [74 percent] of Asian American adults who were surveyed were born in their native countries, and more than six in ten [61 percent] adults who have come from Asia in recent years have at least a bachelor's degree).[40] Recent Asian immigrants are three times more likely than other immigrants to get green cards (permanent resident status) on the basis of employer sponsorship rather than family sponsorship, even if family unification remains one of the most common ways that the majority of immigrants gain legal entrance to the United States.[41]

Behind the Statistics: The Other Side of the Story

While Asian Americans are commonly extolled as the "model minority" who have broken the racial ceiling to enjoy the American dream, Asian American scholars contend that this perception is more hype than reality, since it focuses only on the elite Asian Americans who have achieved financial success and/or graduated from prestigious universities and then made it to the top of their professional fields. Put simply, the model minority myth discussed elsewhere in this volume conveniently ignores the harsh realities of those Asian Americans who are slugging it out every day in factories and restaurants or toiling as store clerks, seamstresses, nail workers, and unskilled laborers with very little pay and often with neither job security nor health benefits. The model minority myth also fails to account for those contending with language difficulties and assimilation issues and who may be trapped in the vicious cycle of poverty and destitution in ethnic ghettoes.[42] A recent study entitled "Poverty Among Asian Americans in the 21st Century" confirms not only that Asian Americans are among the poor in America but also that both absolute and relative poverty are slightly higher among Asians than among whites overall (thus contradicting the misperception that Asian Americans as the model minority are uniformly outperforming whites).[43] More detailed analysis reveals that differences in the level of poverty are largely associated with factors relating to immigration (e.g., those who have greater or lesser fluency in English) and that certain subgroups, namely Cambodians, Thais, and Hmong, experience high levels of poverty.

As we have seen, then, the use of model minority with reference to Asian Americans is highly problematic and unsupportable by all the facts. It renders those who do not belong to the elite minority invisible, as it focuses only on this elite group by essentializing their success stories as representative of all Asian Americans.[44] Not only is this stereotyping founded on a false image and gross misconception, it can also be pernicious. Two Korean American sociologists, Won Moo Hurh and Kwang Chung Kim, have concluded that the model minority image of Asian Americans is racist, discriminatory, and ultimately anti-Asian.[45] Most importantly for our purposes, the model minority image can be insidiously used by the majority in support of institutional racism by granting affirmative preferences for other racial-ethnic minorities to the exclusion of all Asian Americans, including those who may have had tremendous social barriers to overcome (e.g., those who escaped war-torn countries as refugees). In other cases belief in the model minority might lead admissions committees or prospective employers to require higher standards for Asian Americans, thus depriving them of equal access to education and to social assistance. Finally, as many scholars have noted, the model minority myth is especially disastrous for undermining racial solidarity across racial-ethnic groups.[46] As Korean American theologian Andrew Sung Park astutely observed:

> This stereotypical picture of Asian Americans is dangerous when it is used for chiding other groups. The subliminal message says to other ethnic minority groups, especially to African-Americans, "This country is not racist. Look at *this* minority group. Why can't you make it in this great country of equal opportunity like this group? You are basically lazy and inferior to the model minority. You deserve your miserable lot."[47]

Still in many other cases, Asian Americans who attempt to ascend as high as their talent can take them (to refer back to President Clinton's words) will ultimately reach a glass ceiling, for they may be placed as a "middle minority" between the group at the top of the racial and socioeconomic hierarchy (whites) and other exploited racial-ethnic groups, such as Hispanics and African Americans. Thus Asians as middle minorities may find themselves as an "attractive target for the anger and frustration of the oppressed," but they themselves remain "also discriminated against, and unprotected by the dominant elite."[48] The 1992 L.A. Riots ("Sa-I-Gu," as it is known in Korean) is an unfortunate example of this, wherein several Korean American shop owners were targets of looting and arson by Africans Americans and Hispanics enraged by the Rodney King verdict (i.e., the acquittal of the police officers who had beaten him), and the police moved to protect (white) Beverly Hills instead of Koreatown. In such a case, the divide-and-conquer tactic pitted one oppressed minority against another instead of allowing them to see the underlying problem of white privilege and supremacy.[49]

Toward Transnationalism

In the twenty-first century, in a highly globalized world, Asian Americans are moving toward transnationalism as an alternative way of negotiating their identities, managing their business operations, and sharing their earnings and wealth to extended family members on both sides of the Pacific. Post-1965, patterns of immigration to the United States are no longer best understood as a linear move from one's original country to the newly-adopted one that would require a sharp rupture of communal ties with one's homeland. Asian immigration is better understood in terms of a circular movement, a going back and forth, as the bonds of relationship between and among family members, friends, and business associates continue to be nurtured through affordable international air travel, advanced telecommunications, and broadband technology (e.g., inexpensive international telephone calls, email, instant messaging, and social media).[50]

Might the hybridized identities and cross-Pacific ties that transnationalism facilitates only be available for those with education, wealth, and privilege? Against conventional wisdom, several recent studies suggest otherwise. Kenneth Guest's ethnographical study of Fuzhounese Chinese in New York's Chinatown reveals that many Fuzhounese also adopt the goods of transnationalism, even though they are "systematically marginalized in the United States, discriminated against because of their economic skills, legal status, language, and even ethnicity."[51] More specifically, undocumented Fuzhounese immigrants turn to transnational activities, such as forging networks between China and the United States, in order to "build identities that transcend their dead-end jobs, their transient lifestyles, and their local marginalization."[52] Beyond the Fuzhounese, Fenggang Yang's research on Chinese American evangelical churches with varying degrees of wealth reveals how multiple transnational ties are forged with churches and parachurch organizations (also with varying degrees of resources) in mainland China, Taiwan, and the wider Chinese diaspora.[53] Other studies report the ways in which Vietnamese Catholics and Buddhists in Houston have also forged similar transnational networks between Vietnamese temples and churches with their counterparts in Vietnam.[54] Transnationalism, in short, does not depend on having attained any model minority status of income or wealth.

The Faith Ethics of Wealth and Prosperity and the Asian Americans

In this last section of this chapter, I attempt to bring the faith ethics of wealth and prosperity to bear on Asian Americans' pursuit of economic success as propelled by visions of the American dream in the United States. The sociological findings in the previous section of glowing statistics about financial success (for some segments of the Asian American population) *and* ambivalence about their achievement of the American dream, about pressures to do well in school *and* to never be satisfied with their current socioeconomic standing, could point one to two possibilities. First, these findings might be taken as reminiscent of the warning about wealth in both the Bible and in Catholic social teaching. Second, they could substantiate the claim that wealth is not the index of true happiness and that there are other human goods that are necessary for one to live a truly prosperous life. Either way, an Asian American Christian ethical approach to questions of wealth and prosperity would seek to expose the falsity of the "prosperity gospel" and the temptation of materialism and consumerism to which many Asian Americans succumb.

As discussed in the "Christian Ethical Reflections" section, both Scripture and Catholic social teaching have warned against the lure of wealth: it is a lure that leaves the heart restless for more and more and can neither be truly satisfied nor give the heart rest because wealth is but a finite good. The warning about the quest for the American dream is that it can be mistaken as the ultimate goal in life, displacing what is the true *telos* of wealth and what is the true meaning of prosperity. The core question is how one can possess material things without being in the power of what is possessed. When one is claimed by one's possessions, one is bound by them; wealth takes over one's freedom. There is a need for a certain poverty of spirit for one to have a freedom of heart in relation to material wealth. And it is this poverty of spirit that enables one to discern the true meaning and purpose of one's life amidst the glitter of the material lifestyle one has attained.

To be clear, Asian Americans are not just susceptible to the lure of the American dream because of their immigrant ethos and continuing waves of immigration, but also because many Protestants in particular are involved in an immigrant church subculture that believes material success to be evidence of divine favor. As sociologist Sharon Kim has documented in first-generation Korean American immigrant churches in the Los Angeles area, the immigrant subculture "reinforces the idea that all truly spiritual individuals or 'good Christians' will work hard and succeed at what they do"—an assumption tied to the older (Calvinist) belief among those anxious about their predestined status that success in one's worldly vocation was to be taken as a "sign" of the elect.[55] While placing the origin less in terms of Calvinism and more generally in terms of popular white Western culture, Soong-Chan Rah concurs that many Asian American immigrant churches confuse the American dream for biblical standards and the will of God, for as "more and more wealth and possessions are accumulated by the Christian, there is an assumption that they are in the will of God and that more blessings are coming their way." Rah, among others, saw his own immigrant church as having chosen to "embrace the message of material success" as opposed to having provided a "spiritual and theological corrective" to this unbiblical teaching.[56] Whether adherents of the prosperity gospel are following the teachings of megachurch pastors like Joel Osteen, inheriting the "signs" of the elect teaching of their Calvinist forebearers, or drawing inspiration from the shamanistic-influenced prosperity gospel teaching in South Korea (as in the teachings of the "world's largest megachurch," Yoido Full Gospel Church),[57] an Asian American Christian ethical approach might be wise to follow Korean American theologian Sang Hyun Lee's condemnation of prosperity gospel teaching and the pursuit of the materialistic American dream in terms of the sin of worshipping idols and golden calves.[58] In short, an Asian American Christian ethical approach to wealth and prosperity would not shy away from clearing up these confusions: "prosperity gospel" is not the true gospel, and material or financial success is no indicator of divine favor.

To be sure, the ambivalence about the American dream could be taken as a sign that even Asian Americans caught up in the pursuit have an inkling that there is more to life than upward social mobility. Again, both Scripture and Catholic social tradition point to other human pursuits that are necessary for one to live a "purpose-driven" life. Scripture calls for one to live a way of justice and to use wealth as a resource for the needs of others. Catholic social tradition speaks of other human goods that are not attained by one's purchasing power, but which are the very conditions for true prosperity. It also speaks of the pursuit of the common good and its allied principles of solidarity and preferential option for the poor.

Asian Americans must look into whether their ways and practices meet the faith ethics of wealth and prosperity. How is their wealth obtained? Do they perpetuate unjust structures and institutions through engaging in practices that violate just wages or entering into contracts based on raw profits that are inimical to life, health, and environment? Do their work or business ventures contribute to the common social good, particularly in the protection of the poor and marginalized? How do they use the social power that comes with wealth? Do they use this power to make the lives of others better, or do they use it to take advantage of those who have no power, like other Asian Americans who are counted among those living in absolute or relative poverty? Furthermore, do they use their economic resources to manipulate the mechanisms of law and government to give unfair access or privileged treatment to those within one's inner circle of family and friends? Are idle assets being held that might be used to help those in dire need? Do they who benefit from society also bear their equitable share of its needs and burdens by paying their taxes honestly and justly? Do they strive to live simply so others can simply live? Or are their lives so governed by unbridled consumerism and their businesses conducted without social conscience and social responsibility?

To move from these general questions to more concrete references, an Asian American Christian ethicist would do well to ask: Are wealthy or middle-class Asian Americans hiring Hispanic nannies, housekeepers, or other aides and paying them low wages, in many cases "under the table"? If so, we might view them as willfully entering into their middle minority status and becoming for "brown" and "black" people new faces of exploitation. Or might Asian American Christians also be participating in structures of injustice against their own racial-ethnic peers? Korean American theologian Andrew Sung Park, among others, has drawn rightful attention to the ways in which Korean immigrants have exploited other Korean immigrants, many of whom are undocumented, for their cheap labor under unfavorable working conditions without adequate compensation, though the employers have not always recognized their actions as wrong because they paternalistically understand themselves as providing coethnics with jobs.[59] More specifically, Park and others have criticized the ways in which Korean business owners "survive on the cheap labor of newly arrived immigrants" and exploit the "catch-22 situation" of newly arrived immigrants that gives them very little bargaining power: "to get outside jobs [outside the ethnic ghetto], they need to speak good English; to speak good English requires work experience beyond the Korean immigrant communities."[60] That predicament, coupled with the cultural desire to "save the face" (che-myun) of the reference person who introduced them to their employers and their own aspirations to own their own businesses someday keeps workers unable or unwilling to press for better working conditions, and thus wages are low in these ethnic ghettoes. These are all concrete instances that the faith ethics of wealth and prosperity confronts and calls to conversion and transformation.

The rise of U.S. businesses owned by Asian Americans is phenomenal. In bringing in half a trillion dollars in sales and employing more than 2.8 million people, these businesses have become powerful engines of the American economy. However, Asian American Christian ethicists would want to know whether they were operating on the principles of human dignity and distributive justice. Of course corporate institutions must operate with goals of profit, since profit is the engine of growth, but the profit earned should also be with a social conscience and social responsibility. But institutions can commit gross corporate injustices, such as when ethical principles are rendered as totally irrelevant or when the corporations are run in technical compliance with extant labor laws but in ways that allow them to amass wealth on the backs of more impoverished others. For instance, the wildly successful clothing retailer Forever 21 has been hailed by the media and by members of Korean immigrant communities as a "Christian" company—its Korean Christian immigrant owners go to church at 5:00 a.m. every morning to pray, include "John 3:16" at the bottom of every Forever 21 bag, and consider their success a blessing from God.[61] But their trendy, mass-produced, and cheap clothes are hardly "Christian" in that they are manufactured by workers who toil under desperate conditions that are no better than the near (secular) industry standard of sweatshop labor (as the Emmy-winning documentary *Made in L.A.* about a lawsuit and boycott by Latinas against Forever 21 recounts).

Scripture teaches that wealth must be used as a resource for human needs in the light of love as material care for our neighbor. What is asserted here is the responsibility that ownership of wealth and possessions entails. There is a special focus on meeting the needs of those one calls brothers and sisters in the faith, but the love for one's neighbor through material care must be cast with a much wider net to include strangers and even enemies. There is also the call of sharing of resources for the end goal of equality in the meeting of needs. This calls for an uncalculating generosity in sharing one's material resources so that the basic needs (decent food, housing, and clothing) and access to goods (education and health) of all may be met so that some do not have too much while others too little or nothing at all. With reference to this call of Scripture, an Asian American Christian ethical approach to faith and prosperity would seek to inquire how Asian Americans rank in tithing and offering in their churches. Such an approach would want to know how Asian Americans are involved in the hospitality and sharing of their resources. Is the outreach to others as fullhearted and generous? Is self-gift and solidarity at the heart of their life of faith in terms of the sharing of their material resources to others? To be clear, while my "negative" examples above emerge from Korean American contexts, it is less that this subgroup merits special attention and blame and more that Korean American theologians (who are well represented among Asian American theologians) have not shied away from prophetically calling their communities to repentance.

The model minority accolade given to Asian Americans is a myth; it is not borne out by facts. It is more a bane rather than a blessing. Only the elite Asian Americans live in material abundance while many are living in poverty, trapped in the vicious cycle of social marginalization. What is more, nearly all Asian Americans, rich or poor, must contend with enduring racial discrimination and prejudice as they are considered by many of their non-Asian counterparts as the perpetual foreigner or "other." What then is the promise of prosperity for Asian Americans under this human condition as envisioned by Catholic social tradition? We recall that prosperity cannot solely be measured by the index of material prosperity, for it is the total well-being of persons, communities, and nations. It is founded on the common good, which requires the interconnectedness and interdependence of people in the pursuit of the good of all. It is built on the principles of subsidiarity, solidarity, preferential option for the poor, socialization, participation, and restoration. This vision of prosperity cannot be realized when people are isolated from each other. They have to come together in community, in what John Paul II called networks of solidarity, in the sphere of civil society.

The phenomenon of transnationalism brings together people in their fragmented and broken lives as they renew their bonds of affection and friendship across time and distance in a world that has become so globalized. No longer are they separated from their homes even as they remain in their places of work. Transnationalism goes beyond the paradigm of uprooting and assimilation as people are able to negotiate their identities through multiple and hybrid ways of interacting and interconnecting. To live a life of prosperity is first to know and to be known as someone and not as something, to love and to be loved as a person of worth, to be connected with people who are home and family, and to be able to participate in the building of a global community. For Asian Americans this may mean not only staying connected to their families and friends in their "ancestral" lands but also forming real relationships with those around them in their American context—their neighbors, employees, and employers, many of whom may not be coethnics.

In conclusion, economics is not beyond the reach of faith ethics. The questions regarding wealth and prosperity are questions about faith as much as they are about ethics. Wealth is not an end in itself. Its *telos* gives it meaning and purpose. Prosperity is not only measured by income or wealth. Its index is the full human flourishing of persons and communities. When the faith ethics of wealth and prosperity is brought to bear on the life of Asian Americans, it brings to light the complexity of such a life within the promise and peril of living as Asians in America in the pursuit of the American dream, and the prophetic call for meaning and purpose in the midst of it all.

DISCUSSION QUESTIONS

1. Astorga discusses both New Testament teaching and the Catholic social tradition on wealth. Is there a limit to how much money one can have in order to remain faithful to the Gospel, or is the matter less about total amount or salary and more about one's attitudes toward wealth and possession?

2. Astorga discusses how many Asian Americans are intent on pursuing the American dream, but that true happiness may not be found in the accumulation of wealth. In what ways are Asian Americans themselves ambivalent about their supposed financial success? In what ways should they be?

3. Do wealthier and more successful Asian Americans have special obligations to care for Asian American groups who are less financially well-off? Why or why not?

4. If stores like Forever 21, founded by Korean American entrepreneurs, really do pay low wages to their workers under unfavorable—even oppressive—working conditions, do Christians have obligations not to shop there? What else might Christians do to stand in solidarity with such workers?

Racial Identity and Solidarity

KI JOO (KC) CHOI

Is Asian American Christian ethics up to the task of advancing race relations? More specifically, is it up to the task of facilitating and supporting racial solidarity and cooperation, by which I mean the disposition to identify with persons of different racial backgrounds as one's neighbors and participate in the sustained advancement of their good?[1] In this essay I do not presume that Asian American Christian ethics by virtue of its disciplinary nature is indeed capable of furthering the kind of disposition outlined. Rather, my premise is that the capacity of Asian American Christian ethics to advance racial solidarity and cooperation depends on whether its conception of Asian American identity and, therefore, its work as an ethical enterprise, sufficiently acknowledges the enduring reality of ethno-racial prejudices, asymmetries, and ideologies of power.[2]

This essay moves in three parts. In the first part, as a point of reference for Christian responses to racial solidarity, I turn to a select number of black liberationist approaches to race. I focus on how these accounts utilize race, particularly the concept of blackness, as a means of social analysis and resistance. Understanding the general contours of this employment of race against racism provides a helpful way of assessing the extent to which accounts of Asian American identity can empower racial solidarity and cooperation, particularly between Asian Americans and other persons of color. This assessment is the subject matter of the second part of the essay, where, based on a reading of certain sociological trends and indicators, I cast doubts on the ultimate moral value of conceiving of Asian American identity in hybrid terms especially when it comes to matters of racial justice. Despite its virtues, an emphasis on the hybrid identity of Asian American experience can too easily serve as blinders to the threat of Asian American reinscriptions of whiteness, with its racism and privilege (or what I shall refer to as Asian American whiteness). In the third part, I propose the importance of turning to a more sobering account of hybridity for Asian American Christian ethics. Such an account presses the importance of naming on two fronts: naming the ways in which racism against Asian Americans persists and naming the ways in which Asian Americans participate in racism itself. This twofold task of naming is critical if Asian American Christian ethics is to be committed to advancing just racial relations.

Christian Responses to Racial Solidarity: Taking Cues from Black Liberation Theology

Whether Asian American identity can be conceived in a manner that advances solidarity and cooperation between Asian Americans and non–Asian Americans of color may not be immediately obvious, especially in light of numerous negative appraisals of ethno-racial identity. Representative of such appraisals are the efforts of Catholic moralist Bryan Massingale and Protestant ethicist Jennifer Harvey at delineating the sin of racism, specifically the role white racism and privilege play in shaping attitudes, judgments, and policies against nonwhite persons and groups in religious institutions.[3]

More particular accounts of the negative social, political, and economic impact of white racism and privilege range from the historical to the contemporary. For instance, Katie Cannon's ethnographic accounts of the lived reality of African women during Euro-American colonialism and institutionalization of slavery; M. Shawn Copeland's account of how the objectification of blackness (specifically black bodies) persists in contemporary popular culture, especially with respect to cultural attitudes about beauty and male-female relationships; and Emile M. Towne's exploration of how the structural legacies of slavery and segregation affect health care delivery and access for African Americans.[4] More recently, Michele Alexander's account of the African American experience with the U.S. justice system and incarceration provides a scathing and provocative reminder of the extent to which white racism and privilege endures at the personal and structural levels of society despite the contemporary rhetoric of postracialism.[5]

While many authors who critique white racism and privilege do so in order to cast a negative light on race and delegitimize it as a category of identity, a number of other critical approaches to white racism and privilege reappropriate race in such a way that race itself serves to call society's attention to the sin of white racism and privilege. These accounts are certainly not dismissive of the insidious legacy of Euro-American slavery and discrimination. However, they are equally concerned with what might be lost to human personhood and the goal of liberative praxis without acknowledging ethno-racial difference.

A provocative and deeply influential expression of such a position is found in the works of James Cone and Cornel West, among others. Cone's argument rests on the claim that the thematic trajectory of the Bible, particularly in the Hebrew Scriptures, is one of God's preferential treatment of Israel, which forms a hermeneutic lens of judgment against the sin of modern racism. While Cone claims that as a formal theological point God is colorblind, the God of Scripture is at the same time a God who is of and for the Israelites and, thus, of and for those who "labor and are laden"—the oppressed.[6] In the modern era that means God is siding with blackness as an "ontological symbol" of what oppression and suffering means in its most insidious and pervasive form (i.e., white racism and the explicit and implicit imposition of whiteness as the standard of being [white privilege]). Thus, whether we are talking about the "extermination of Amerindians, the persecution of Jews, the oppression of Mexican-Americans, and every other inconceivable inhumanity done in the name of God and country . . . [b]lackness . . . stands for all victims of oppression who realize that the survival of their humanity is bound up with liberation from whiteness."[7] As an ontological symbol of such oppression, blackness is to be regarded as a reappropriation of "the oppressor's definition of blackness . . . so that the past may emerge as an instrument of black liberation" and, by association, the liberation of others who suffer similarly.[8]

West sounds a similar tune in referring to blackness, especially as it is grappled with in black intellectual culture. Rather than a symbol, he thinks of blackness as a kind of metaphor for "the problem of evil in its concrete forms in America." In West's judgment, "American society prefers to deny the existence of its own evil. Black folk historically have reminded people of [this] prevailing state of denial."[9] As metaphor for racial evil, then, blackness facilitates awareness of white racism intellectually and, more importantly, affectively to all persons in society, black and white alike. And like Cone, West is insistent that only when we are aware of the kind of racial evil blackness affords, justice and solidarity are possible.[10]

For Cone and West, race—reconceived as symbol or metaphor—functions as a kind of hermeneutical lens for moral judgment and action. As such, race is reconceived prophetically; its sociopolitical visibility and recognition is meant to witness against racism, thereby amplifying society's acknowledgment and ultimately resistance to white racist ideologies. Such resistance is not simply for the benefit of black persons or bodies but affects all who suffer similarly insofar as they are subject to the normative push of whiteness (whether that push is felt in terms of standards of beauty and self-worth, economic and political opportunity, and so on). Race is also reconceived dialectically in the sense that the prophetic employment of race must not be taken to mean that race is an essential feature of human identity (biological or otherwise). Race is contingent all the way down (a function of white racism and privilege); the contingency of race, therefore, tightly constrains the legitimacy of race to the sphere of social analysis and action.[11] In that way race is not unlike a social novel: while fictitious, a social novel's analytic and moral force resides in the kind of narrative power the genre of fiction often yields.[12]

Assessing the Prospects for Racial Solidarity and Cooperation: Asian American Hybridity as Racial Metaphor?

Cone's and West's approaches to the concept of race provide a useful comparative point of reference for Asian American Christian ethics. If we were to approach Asian American experience prophetically and dialectically, that is, as a kind of racial symbol or metaphor, what kind of social reality would Asian American identity punctuate? Would it illumine a social narrative that converges or diverges with the narratives of blackness, as Cone and West describe? Wrestling with such questions requires a better sense of the contours of Asian American identity and how Asian American experience ought to be characterized. In the following, as a case study, I turn to one proposal for a hybrid conception of Asian American identity. While there is much to commend in such a proposal, the question I raise is whether the embrace and construction of a hybrid Asian American identity sufficiently illumines and, perhaps more importantly, avoids the hazards of what I shall refer to as Asian American whiteness. That question in turn calls into question whether the "turn" to hybridity in Asian American self-understanding can advance just racial relations, particularly between Asian Americans and non–Asian Americans of color.

From Liminality to Hybridity

Is there a shape to Asian American experience? Is there a defining feature to Asian American identity? How should Asian Americans understand themselves as Asian American? To these questions, consider the Korean American systematic theologian Sang Hyun Lee's efforts at constructing an Asian American theology.[13] Following the observation made by Vietnamese Catholic theologian Peter C. Phan and others that Asian Americans are "betwixt and between,"[14] Lee describes Asian American identity as substantially formed by the experience of liminality (a term he borrows from the anthropologist Victor Turner). The experience of liminality, while it can stand on its own, can also arise as a consequence of social marginalization. It is the latter notion of liminality that applies particularly to Asian Americans. For Lee, Asian Americans can identify with liminality to the extent that Asian American social marginalization takes place on two fronts: "not fully accepted by, or fully belonging to, either the [white] American world or the Asian [world, their ancestral homeland and heritage]."[15] Inasmuch as Asian American liminality— "the situation of being in between two or more worlds"—is a function of this twofold marginalization, Asian American liminality "includes the meaning of being located at the periphery or edge of a society."[16]

Liminality captures the fullness of the social reality of Asian Americans, but only the acknowledgment and acceptance of their liminality opens Asian Americans to the creative potentials of their liminal situation. For Lee the creative potentials of liminality are grounded theologically in the way liminality is characteristic of God's intratrinitarian life. Drawing on his groundbreaking and influential work on Jonathan Edwards' philosophical theology, Lee argues that in God's delighting and loving Jesus as truly other, this "otherness and distance between the Father and the Son are the liminal space between them. The Father out of love for the Son enters into a liminal space in meeting the Son. Out of the liminal space between them emerges (proceeds) the communion of the Father and the Son—namely, the Holy Spirit."[17] The Spirit, as proceeding from the liminality that God occupies, is taken as underscoring the threefold creative potential of liminality for marginalized persons in society: (1) openness to the new, (2) openness to *communitas* (or genuine community), and (3) prophetic knowledge.

Lee suggests that one way in which the threefold creative potential of Asian American liminality can be realized is through the embrace of hybridity in Asian American self-understanding. (In this way, liminality and hybridity are mutually reinforcing ideas.[18]) Following the lead of the postcolonial thinker Homi Bhabha, Lee argues that constructing Asian American identity in hybrid terms expresses resistance to the "hegemony of any one of the diverse elements out of which Asian American identity is constructed."[19] Conceiving Asian American identity as hybrid, therefore, means keeping Asian American identity multivalent and elastic, that is, "permanently open."[20] Striking in this regard is Lee's claim that Asian American hybridity must encompass racial inclusivity and capaciousness:

> To construct an Asian American identity is to embrace all these different kinds of Americans in our own conception of ourselves [Native Americans, African Americans, Hispanic Americans, English Americans, Italian Americans, and many others]. The cultures and histories of the peoples of all the different ancestral backgrounds cannot be, in a mechanical way, the content of what constitutes the Asian American identity. But none of those peoples can be excluded from the meaning of an Asian American identity.[21]

To construct hybrid identities is to participate in the relational process of negotiating multiple racial and cultural encounters rather than simply existing in a racially and culturally static state.[22] As such, Lee's account of Asian American hybridity presents itself as an Asian American analogue to thinking about blackness symbolically or metaphorically, at least on one level, that is, in nonessentialist terms. Hybridity expands the perimeters of Asian American identity, destabilizing reductive, insular, and parochial perceptions of Asian American life. In so doing, the goal of hybridity is racial and cultural exchange and synthesis. To be hybrid goes beyond simply exposing oneself to and adopting a multiplicity of racial and cultural beliefs and practices. Rather, it is to embrace those beliefs and practices in such a way that new, inventive forms of being and self-understanding as Asian American emerge.

Yet while Asian American hybridity functions similarly to the metaphor of blackness in its shared resistance to ethno-racial essentialism, it remains to be seen whether Asian American hybridity can also, like the concept of symbolic or metaphoric blackness, function to motivate Asian American social action in the direction of interracial solidarity and cooperation. This is not to discount Lee's insistence, as noted above, that constructing hybrid identities (as a creative expression of liminality) promises transformative ways of being in society. More specifically, as Lee asserts, Asian Americans embracing hybridity, and, thus, the goal of racial and cultural exchange and synthesis, would be "an act of rejecting and resisting" Euro-American notions of who counts as "real Americans."[23] Hybridity, therefore, becomes one way to promote common ground with the kind of discrimination non–Asian Americans continue to face and illuminates how Asian Americans fit into the larger narrative of American racism. Accordingly, the embrace of hybridity as a form of resistance to white racialized hierarchies should be regarded as a form of racial solidarity: a way of identifying and cooperating with others who have suffered the force of whiteness through cultural, political, and economic marginalization.[24] Is this not in the spirit of Cone's claim, as we saw earlier, that to be for blackness in modern society is to be for those who have been subject to the oppression of white racism and privilege? For Lee, being for hybridity functions similarly to being for blackness, as Cone understands it. But the trickier question is whether Asian Americans being for hybridity would *indeed deliver* in the way Lee proposes. In other words, what are the prospects for achieving the kind of moral promise Lee ascribes to Asian American hybridity? What are the prospects for the kind of ethno-racial, cultural inventiveness that expresses and embodies Asian American resistance to white racialized hierarchies? Attending to how intercultural and interracial encounters have and continue to play out in Asian American life offers a challenging response to those questions and raises the additional question of whether pursuing Asian American hybridity is sufficient in regards to advancing Asian American solidarity and cooperation with non–Asian Americans of color.

The Statistical Reality of Asian American Hybridity

To better appreciate the kind of challenges that stand in the way of the moral promise of hybridity (as Lee conceives of this promise), we do well to first turn our attention to the extent to which hybridity is already a reality in Asian American life. Consider the rise of the mixed raced population in the United States. According to the 2010 U.S. Census, the mixed race population has grown approximately 35 percent since 2000.[25] Moreover, 9 percent of all marriages in the United States were interracial, or double the percentage in 1980.[26] With respect to Asian Americans, the U.S. Census reports that in 2010, 2.6 million Asian Americans counted themselves Asian in combination with one or more additional races, which is almost 1 million more since the 2000 Census.[27] That 2.6 million persons count themselves Asian-multiracial in the 2010 census is not insignificant considering that only 17.3 million persons counted themselves as U.S. residents of Asian descent.[28]

The rise in multiracial identification among Asian Americans is increasingly felt in Asia as well. Consider the case of South Korea's recent increase of "international" marriages. Spurred by a low female birth rate during the 1980s (due in part to an increase in abortions of girls in favor of boys) and the desire of more educated Korean women to delay if not reject marriage altogether, an increasing number of Korean men have turned to marrying "foreign" Asian women. In 2004, for instance, "the number of Koreans marrying foreigners rose 38 percent to 35,447, or 11 percent of the newlyweds that year. Most of these marriages involved women from Vietnam, China, the Philippines, Mongolia, Nepal, and Uzbekistan." Many of these marriages have failed: the non-Korean Asian wives were abused by and socially isolated within their husband's extended family and larger Korean society, due in part to the inability to negotiate differing expectations of the meaning of marriage, family, masculinity, and spousal responsibilities, all of which were made more difficult by the inability to communicate.[29] Yet these failures at bridging cultural differences have at the same time brought into public discussion questions of what it means to be Korean, specifically whether a Korean would forfeit some genuine sense of Koreanness if he/she does not follow "traditional" familial patterns and customs.[30]

Hybridity: From Promise to Peril

The growth of multiracial Asian Americans (as well as Asians) certainly underscores the difficulty of talking about race in descriptively and conceptually coherent ways. That difficulty does not necessarily undermine race talk to the extent one cannot talk about Asian American identity per se. Rather, it simply undermines stereotypical and prejudicial ways of talking about Asian American identity (or accounts of identity that reinforce and promote stereotyping and discrimination). Consigned to the flames, then, are battle hymns of so-called tiger mothers,[31] the myth of model minorities, and perceptions of seemingly inherited intellectual aptitude,[32] among other pop-culture perceptions of Asianness.

Furthermore, the trend toward Asian American hybridization complicates the question of Asian American authenticity, particularly at the cultural level of particular ethnicities. What makes a Filipino genuinely Filipino, or what is the Korean way of doing this or that—these are questions that cannot be answered in some direct, straightforward manner in light of the increasing hybridization of Asian American identity. Korean Americans who marry "outside the race," who practice yoga and enjoy the music of southern rock—are they "less" Korean than those who speak fluent Korean, socialize primarily with fellow like-minded Koreans, excel academically, and make it a point to venerate their ancestors in a formal, customary way? Hybridity resists a singular measure of Koreanness (or other Asian ethnic identities for that matter), perhaps insisting more on the priority of hospitality—to be Korean American is to be hospitable to racial and cultural variation, fluidity, and innovation. Such hospitality takes on particular significance for multiracial Asian Americans. As a father of children who are of Korean, English, German, and Norwegian descent, there is something particularly liberating about hybridity. It invites my children to understand themselves, if they so choose, as Korean American in ways that forgoes the litmus test of cultural purity and loyalty.[33] Hybridity invites the both/and, that is, the cohabitation of multiple cultural forms wherein cohabitating beliefs and practices (modes of being) mutually challenge, expand, and revise each other's meanings and significance.

Yet despite the virtues or positive possibilities of Asian American multiracialism and multiculturalism, the actual picture of hybridity in Asian American communities is more complex and less encouraging. Consider three sites in which Asian American (and Asian) hybrid cultural encounters and multiple belongings have been *in actuality* less than creative and mutually engaging.

Site 1. For starters, turning to the view of hybridity in Asian and Asian American religiosity from the Asian feminist theologian Kwok Pui-lan is instructive. Taking the Chinese experience of Christianity as a point of departure, Kwok draws attention to the ways in which Asian Christianity "has always been a hybrid."[34] By hybrid she means the experience of belonging to multiple religious traditions in dialogue with one another, and thus not simply an assimilation of one tradition into another. Case in point: the Jesuit missionaries to China in the sixteenth century, including Matteo Ricci, who caught the ire of Pope Clement XI in 1715 for his support of "the Chinese practice of veneration for ancestors."[35] Or consider the nineteenth century Protestant missionaries who adopted the Chinese Buddhist use of "religious tracts to propagate their beliefs."[36] In more contemporary times, the practice of "inter-spirituality and multiple belongings" is on stark display in "ethnic minority Christian churches" in the United States. "Here different cultures, festivals, and customs come together, and new immigrants find a place for negotiating their identity."[37] But despite her often enthusiastic and optimistic portrayal of hybridity in Asian and Asian American religious experience, Kwok does acknowledge numerous historical instances, particularly in China, where cultural, religious encounters led to exclusion and marginalization, as in the ninth-century shunning of Buddhism by the Confucian emperor of China.[38] Furthermore, even though Kwok cites Soong-Chan Rah's study of Asian American evangelicalism as exemplifying multicultural religiosity, Rah also documents the extent to which the contrary is true. Russell Jeung suggests that multicultural religiosity is perhaps more so the case in mainline Protestant Asian American congregations rather than many evangelical ones.[39]

Site 2. In addition to the descriptively complex reality of Asian and Asian American religiosity, we do well to remember that intra-Asian rivalry, prejudice, and racism are not uncommon features of Asian history and contemporary Asian American relations. Longstanding historical animosities continue to express themselves today, subtly and overtly. Take for instance the continuing controversy between the Korean American community in Palisades Park, New Jersey (just outside of Manhattan) and the Japanese government over the placement of a memorial dedicated to Korean women taken as sex slaves by Japan during World War II; the Japanese consulate in New York City has been seeking its removal.[40] While Japanese government officials are driving this dispute, it reflects enduring historical tensions among ordinary Koreans and Japanese in the United States and abroad. Telling in this regard is the recent mass popularity of comic books in Japan depicting Koreans (as well as Chinese) in demeaning ways. According to one account of these comics, a Japanese character who appears in a comic book titled "Hating the Korean Wave" claims, "It's not an exaggeration that Japan built the South Korea of today!" Elsewhere the comic declares, "There is nothing in Korean culture to be proud of."[41] In the United States, the Virginia legislature, in response to pressure from many Korean Americans in Virginia (approximately 80,000 reside in Virginia), passed a bill requiring Virginian history textbooks to note that the Sea of Japan is also called by others (e.g., South Koreans) the East Sea.[42] A similar effort is afoot in Albany, the state capital of New York, by state legislators from districts primarily in New York City with large Korean American constituents.[43]

To be fair, intra-Asian hostility, particularly in the United States, is not widespread, at least according to a recent Pew Research Center report; *only* 11 percent of Asian Americans polled in 2012 indicate that their particular Asian American group gets along with other U.S. Asian groups "not too well or not well at all."[44] Yet if the above examples of Korean-Japanese sentiments are any indication, the strains that do exist between Asians as well as Asian Americans should not be regarded simply as cosmetic. Hybridity (or interracial and intercultural encounter or cohabitation) may indeed be a feature of Asian and Asian American experience, but so too are interracial and intercultural tension, division, and misunderstandings.

Site 3. Intra–Asian/Asian American rivalries are not the only examples suggestive of Asian and Asian American hybrid encounters that have gone and continue to go awry. The continued encounters Asians and Asian Americans have with Westernized cultures of affluence is one area that deserves special scrutiny in light of alarming suicide rates, particularly among Koreans and Japanese.[45] While some analysts have pointed to internal cultural values that make suicide an honorable way of resolving particular situations (Korea and Japan are often cited on this point),[46] a growing number of investigators into the phenomenon of suicides among Asians are pointing to the kind of social and economic pressures and expectations contributing to suicide; more specifically, the supplanting of certain long-held Confucian values with that of more perhaps alluring values of Westernized material prosperity introduced with industrialization. Revealing, even if anecdotally, is one highly reported account of the suicide of a Korean American couple on September 11, 2009, in Queens, New York City. The couple left the following short letter to the daughter they were leaving behind: "I love you, my daughter. I'm sorry to leave you alone. It would've been much better if you had a wealthier father." "Along with the note, they left $40 in cash for her."[47]

From Hybridity to Asian American Whiteness

Suicide may be an extreme consequence of less than constructive encounters and exchanges with Westernized cultures of affluence. The more pervasive consequence may be the unassuming embrace of attitudes, values, and practices mirroring white racism and privilege by Asian Americans. Consider the kind of socioeconomic advances so many Asian Americans have achieved and the hazard of adopting prejudicial racial paradigms in light of that achievement. More specifically, 12–18 percent of the student body at Ivy League schools is Asian American while Asian Americans are only 5.5 percent of the population.[48] As the

U.S. Census Bureau reveals, in 2011, 50 percent of the Asian American population over 25 years of age held bachelor degrees versus 28.5 percent of the U.S. population over age 25. Beyond college, 20.7 percent of the Asian American population 25 years and over had graduate or professional degrees versus 10.6 percent for all Americans 25 years and older.[49] Additionally, the findings from a Pew Research Study show that between 2008 and 2010, Asian-White and Asian-Asian marriages in the United States had the highest median combined annual earnings than any other marriage pairings ($70,952 and $62,000, respectively).[50]

While statistics neither serve as absolute predictors of behavior nor reveal the fullness of reality, such statistics ought to encourage Asian Americans to reflect on how their achievement has been and should be expressed. That it can be expressed in a manner that reinscribes the prejudicial, marginalizing dispositions and attitudes of white racism and privilege is not impossible. Consider a recent incident at the University of Michigan as reported by the *New York Times*:

> [On February 23, 2014] at the undergraduate library . . . hundreds of students and faculty gathered for a 12-hour "speak out" to address racial tensions brought to the fore by a party that had been planned for November [2013] and then canceled amid protests. The fraternity hosting the party, whose members are mostly Asian and white, had invited "rappers, twerkers, gangsters" and others "back to da hood again."[51]

Consider further a series of events reported once again by the *New York Times*, this time, protests by Chinese immigrants, standing alongside white Americans, in the summer of 2014 over the housing of approximately 180 homeless families, mostly African American and Hispanic, in a former hotel in the Elmhurst community of Queens, New York City. According to one account of the events in the *Times*,

> The [Chinese] residents [said they] felt nervous around the new arrivals [the homeless families]. . . . There were reports of shoplifting from the Good Fortune Supermarket, public urination and panhandling—all things, they said, that had been unheard-of in their neighborhood until now. . . . "When you see them, it looks like they're going to mug you," Linda Chang, 50, said in Mandarin. "It makes me feel uncomfortable." . . . Mark Gao, 32, a wok chef at a Sichuan restaurant in Manhattan, said that his wife was nervous to walk home alone at night from her restaurant job, and that he had told his nieces not to play outside without an adult. "Why does the government want to support this group?" Mr. Gao said in Mandarin. "Why do they want to give them free money?"[52]

Surely, these two incidents hardly establish definitively a larger pattern of Asian American marginalization of others. (Regarding the protests in Elmhurst, Queens, the *Times* does report other Chinese Americans who disagreed with the protests.) But they do offer a cautionary tale of how Asian Americans are not wholly immune to embodying white racist perceptions and modes of behavior, whether wittingly or not.[53] Asian Americans, as much as anybody else, can (and in fact do) embody racism; racist attitudes and actions are not peculiar to any one particular person or group of persons. Asian Americans inhabiting new instantiations of white racism and privilege (an Asian American version of whiteness) is part and parcel of Asian American experience.

A recent assessment of Asian American attitudes toward non–Asian Americans is additionally suggestive. Asian Americans "are most positive about relations with whites . . . [and] less positive about relations with Hispanics and most negative about relations with blacks," according to a 2012 Pew Research Center study.[54] More specifically, according to this Pew study, 61 percent of Asian Americans say they get along "pretty well" with whites (26 percent say "very well"). In comparison, 56 percent of Asian Americans see themselves as getting along with Hispanics "pretty well" (16 percent say "very well"). With respect to African Americans, 48 percent of Asian Americans say their group gets along with African Americans "pretty well" (15 percent say "very well"). Strikingly, "Korean Americans have an especially negative view of group relations with blacks." Only 39 percent of Korean Americans surveyed say they get along "pretty well" with African Americans (and just 4 percent say "very well"). This may be in part the legacy of racial clashes in L.A.'s Koreatown in the wake of the Rodney King verdict (April 29, 1992). But whatever the reasons, Korean Americans' particularly negative attitudes are still reflective of the generally negative views Asian Americans of various origins (Vietnamese, Filipino, Chinese, Indian, and Japanese specifically) have of relations with African Americans. According to a number of sociological studies, such negative views between Asian Americans and African Americans, and to a slightly lesser extent Latinos/as, are attributable in part to the distances that exist between Asian Americans and other minorities in "residential areas, workplaces, networks of friends, and public places." So, Claire Jean Kim and Taeku Lee conclude, "Asian Americans and Blacks, in particular, appear to lack extensive contact and shared experiences that facilitate coalition building."[55]

Hybridity and the Opacity of Asian American Whiteness
and Discrimination

The overall negative attitude Asian Americans have toward relations with African Americans and Hispanics raises interesting if not difficult questions. At the very least, it provokes examination of how Asian American hybridity may be playing out in contemporary U.S. society (in troublesome ways). To that extent I do not contest that Asian American experience is largely hybrid if that is taken to mean an experience of interracial and intercultural encounter and dialogue. First-generation Asian Americans immigrating to the United States is a hybrid experience of sorts.[56] The experience for succeeding generations is perhaps "hyper" hybrid insofar as second- and third-generation Asian Americans not only are affected by the hybrid legacies of their parents but also must make sense of those legacies in their own encounters and dialogues with other Asian Americans and non–Asian Americans at school, work, houses of worship, and the larger public sphere of American life. However, the consequences of Asian American interracial and intercultural encounters and dialogue are myriad and eschew a straightforward regard for Asian American hybridity. While we should welcome and encourage the positive possibilities of hybridity, the promise of hybridity should not lead to an underestimation of actual hybrid experiences that have resulted in messier outcomes. Hybrid encounters can and do go awry.

The growing Asian American exposure and access to Western cultures of affluence, both economic and educational, offers a particularly interesting lesson on the perilous possibilities of hybrid encounters. That Asian Americans are not impervious to the threat of what I refer to as Asian American whiteness underscores the extent to which hybrid encounters can veer easily away from creative exchange and synthesis. To be sure, Lee is far from oblivious to the ways in which Asian Americans have inhabited and continue to inhabit forms of white racism and privilege. As such, Lee suggests that the moral promise of hybridity (as offering one important way of calling out and resisting Asian American reinscriptions of whiteness) is not automatic but requires intentionality, vigilance, and courage.[57] Lee is quite right, for simply affirming as morally positive the multicultural and multiracial features of Asian American experience is not enough and can lead to a form of hybrid essentialism or a complacency in the notion that Asian American self-identification with hybridity means Asian Americans are outside rather than a part of the realities of American racism. In that respect an uncritical embrace of hybridity can too easily draw attention away from less than attractive realities of Asian American life as if they do not exist.

Realities of Asian American life that are especially difficult to accept are Asian Americans' embodiments of conscious and unconscious attitudes and patterns of behavior that mimic white racialized hierarchies as a consequence of their growing socioeconomic achievements. Inattention to such realities is problematic inasmuch as Asian Americans may find themselves sleepwalking into the very forms of life that perpetuate exclusion and marginalization, *including* their own marginalization, by engendering a false sense of social empowerment and equality with their white peers because of their educational and economic gains. To be sure, this is not an uncontroversial claim, for not all Asian Americans would agree on the extent to which discrimination is felt, especially at the personal level. But collectively, Asian American discrimination is not absent, and its reality is not trivial. For instance, consider the hot-button issue of Asian American access to higher education. While, as we saw above, Asian American college enrollment, particularly at elite U.S. institutions, is remarkable relative to non–Asian Americans, high-achieving Asian Americans are not necessarily treated fairly in the college admissions process. Citing a "2009 study of more than 9,000 students who applied to selective universities, the sociologists Thomas J. Espenshade and Alexandria Walton Radford found that white students were three times more likely to be admitted than Asian Americans with the same academic record."[58]

Such an outcome is not necessarily problematic for many middle class and affluent white adults, according to recent research conducted by Frank Samson, a sociologist at the University of Miami. As reported by Scott Jaschik of *Inside Higher Ed*, Samson's research shows that white adults surveyed in California think that college admissions should be based on quantifiable measures of merit (e.g., grade point average and standardized test scores). But such an opinion shifts when "these white people are focused on the success of Asian-American students." As Jaschik explains Samson's study:

> The white adults in the survey were also divided into two groups. Half were simply asked to assign the importance they thought various criteria should have in the admissions system of the University of California. The other half received a different prompt, one that noted that Asian Americans make up more than twice as many undergraduates proportionally in the UC system as they do in the population of the state.

When the other half of white adults are informed of how many Asian Americans make up the student population in the UC system, "the white adults favor a reduced role for grade and test scores in admissions—apparently based on high achievement levels by Asian-American applicants."[59]

In calling attention to the example of Asian Americans and college admissions, my intent is not to endorse one form of college admissions standards over another. Rather, I am simply calling into question the perception that some Asian Americans may have of themselves as fully integrated into mainstream white America and thus fully equal to their white American peers. On the contrary, as Mia Tuan has argued in her ethnographic studies of Asian Americans (specifically second– and third-generation Japanese and Chinese Americans), Asian American acceptance into the white American mainstream has not been identical to the experience of white ethnic Americans (Italians, Irish, Germans, Czechs, etc.). One important reason why Asian American material success has not necessarily translated into full social acceptance into mainstream white America is that Asian Americans do not "look" (or cannot so easily pass for) white, unlike many other ethnic Americans.[60] This may explain in part the popularity of Asian American cosmetic "whitening."[61]

A false sense of Asian American empowerment, or an inaccurate assessment of Asian American parity with mainstream white America, poses a particular obstacle to Asian American solidarity and cooperation with non–Asian Americans of color. So long as Asian Americans are neglectful of their collective marginalization, it remains to be seen whether Asian Americans possess the kinds of evaluative resources to resist and transform a society in which one's lot is so deeply determined by the arbitrariness of skin color and how one "looks" yellow, brown, black, or white. This is not to say that discrimination against Asian Americans is identical to the kind of discrimination felt by African Americans and Latinos/as. But it is to recognize that all persons of color are disciplined by the racialized hierarchies of white racism and privilege in one way or another. The history of black chattel slavery in North America, the history of Jim Crow and de facto segregation—these are not direct links to Asian American history per se. But the Chinese Exclusion Act of 1882, the Immigration Act of 1924 (which continued the immigration restrictions on Chinese and other Asians and established new restrictions, particularly on Japanese immigration), the U.S. internment of Japanese Americans during World War II, the Alien Land Law of 1913 (which barred Asians from owning property in California), the Cable Act of

1922 (which revoked the citizenship of white U.S. women upon marrying Asian or other foreign men), and so on—these are important aspects of Asian American history. And this history, like that of the history of African Americans, was motivated by a similar kind of white suppression of otherness, the legacy of which is felt in various ways and in varying degrees to this day. If Asian Americans are unwilling to examine or consider the ways in which white racialized hierarchies continue to impact Asian Americans, despite their socioeconomic achievements, then to what extent does that unwillingness desensitize Asian Americans to the kinds of marginalization experienced by others? Alternatively, *to what extent does it desensitize us from the ways in which we may be marginalizing others by mimicking whiteness* in believing that we are in fact just like our white American peers and, correlatively, expressing, explicitly or implicitly, greater affinities with them? Difficult questions indeed. Highly noteworthy are numerous empirical studies that suggest racial solidarity and cooperation between Asian Americans and other persons of color is strained particularly by Asian Americans' general lack of belief in their own discrimination.[62]

The Task of Asian American Christian Ethics in Light of "Tragic" Hybridity

What does the foregoing discussion imply for Asian American Christian ethics and racial solidarity? To the extent that Asian American Christian ethics is a mode of moral reflection informed by Asian American experience, clarity on the shape of that experience is tantamount. Whether moral reflection that is informed by Asian American experience can promote racial solidarity, however, will depend significantly on the kind of description and conceptualization of Asian American identity that Asian American Christian ethics assumes or adopts and the extent to which that identity illumines the reality of American racism. That is the basic proposal for Asian American Christian ethics drawn from our earlier survey of black liberation theology and ethics, in its conceptualization of blackness as metaphor or symbol. Such a proposal is not to imply that the racial situation of Asian Americans is identical to that of African American life. Instead, it is to suggest that the impact of white racialized hierarchies is pervasive and systemic in ways that make Asian American and African American (as well as Latino/a) experiences of race a shared experience of white ideologies of race, power, and privilege, though from distinct directions and positions.

With that proposal in mind, the foregoing section questions whether Asian American Christian ethics, if it approaches Asian American experience primarily in terms of hybrid identity, is up to the task of acknowledging and delineating the specific ways white racist ideologies and assumptions frame Asian American life. While we focused on Lee's conception of Asian American hybridity as a point of departure and also encountered briefly Kwok's account of Asian and Asian American hybrid religiosity, they represent a larger number of Asian American theologians and ethicists who are increasingly turning to hybridity as not only the interpretative frame of Asian American life but also the normative ideal for Asian American self-understanding.[63] To that extent, sustained assessment of whether the concept of Asian American hybridity can inform the work of Asian American ethics in the service of racial justice and cooperation takes on new and increasing importance.

Does the concept of Asian American hybridity sufficiently facilitate the work of unpacking the contours of racism as it is actually felt by Asian Americans, or does it make the relevance of that work more opaque? My contention has been that affirming hybridity makes that work more challenging if affirmed uncritically. As indicated earlier, the cultural and ethno-racial diversity of Asian American experience indeed encourages a conception of hybridity as central to Asian American self-understanding. But hybridity in itself does not necessarily result in creative synthesis and self-determination, or as Lee might put it, a way of being that resists the dominance of any one system of values. Consequently, simply acknowledging and affirming the hybrid character of Asian American identity cannot amount to an adequate protest against the normative push of racist ideologies of power and privilege. And considering the many ways in which Asian American intercultural and interracial encounters have played out negatively *in practice* (especially, for instance, toward Asian American instantiations of whiteness), whether the promise of hybridity is a *realistic* prospect remains an open question.

Accordingly, Asian Americans Christian ethics may do better to work with an account of Asian American experience that is interpreted through a tragic conception of hybrid identity. Tragic in the sense that the promise of hybridity is often less than promising: Asian American hybridity holds the promise of creative self-determination as resistance to white racialized hierarchies, but in reality Asian American hybridity often devolves into less than liberating life scripts. In this respect, a tragic account of Asian American hybridity echoes Brian Bantum's reflections on the mulatto in American history. The mulatto challenges the irrationality of modernity's insistence on white racial hierarchical boundaries while also calling attention to the difficulty, perhaps impossibility, of being mulatto (embodying self-creative becoming) due to the entrenchment of whiteness as the standard of being in modern society.[64] Others suggest that the inescapability of whiteness (or the kind of limitations that such inescapability represents) is an inherent liability in identity construction.[65]

To embrace the tragedy of Asian American hybridity is to embrace a metaphoric understanding of Asian American identity that calls specific attention to the discriminatory traps Asian Americans fall victim to despite the creative potentialities of their hybridity. These traps are threefold: (1) Asian Americans are not insulated from being racist or, minimally, assuming racist attitudes; (2) Asian Americans are perhaps inattentive to that reality, intentionally or not, to their detriment; and (3) such inattentiveness is detrimental because it enables and bolsters further inattention to the ways inequality persists between Asian Americans and their white peers. Theologically speaking, the persistence of these traps for Asian Americans underscores the reality of temporal existence. But perhaps more than the limitations of our finitude, the reality of sin (the inexhaustible tug toward the self and private affections) punctuates further the fragility of our endeavors toward creative synthesis and innovation, the goal of hybrid existence. That does not preclude, however, the hope that Asian American hybridity can express itself creatively or offer witness to a way of being that transcends whiteness. The point, rather, is the need for honesty and perceptual clarity about the present racial realities of Asian American life as the grounds for the pursuit of that hope.

What, then, does the tragic character of Asian American hybridity recommend (perhaps demand) with respect to the task of Asian American Christian ethics? First and foremost, tragic hybridity informs Asian American Christian ethics in such a way as to dispel any notion that its work is inherently liberatory (*against* convention or the status quo and, instead, *for* new possibilities) because it is Asian American Christian ethics and by definition contrastive to mainstream Christian ethics as such. Rather, Asian American Christian ethics can be liberatory and support, specifically, racial solidarity and cooperation only if it is committed to interpreting Asian American experience through the sustained self-criticism that the concept of tragic hybridity calls for.

What might such self-criticism entail? Methodologically speaking, Asian American Christian ethicists must prioritize the task of excavating Asian American experience past their own preconceptions and beliefs of themselves and bring to bear the findings of that excavation on their normative work in ethics. To prioritize such a task is to acknowledge that simply being Asian American does not mean that one necessarily has access to the actual, complete contours of Asian American life, even his or her own. Moreover, it means that Asian Americans, whether ethicists or not, cannot be ambivalent about race. Excavating Asian American experience, therefore, entails, more specifically, confronting and wrestling with the ways Asian Americans continue to be marginalized and, perhaps more unpleasantly, struggling with how recognition of Asian American marginalization is made difficult by the ways Asian Americans themselves perpetuate marginalization of other persons of color, particularly by reinscribing patterns of white racism and privilege as expressions of Asian Americans' rise in economic and educational affluence.

I will be the first to admit that excavating Asian American racial realities, at least at the personal level, is genuinely difficult, especially as one who has benefited from the kinds of opportunities "elite" education affords and lives comfortably in a relatively affluent suburb of New York City: that I am subject to white racialized discrimination would hardly sound defensible to many, even to myself, perhaps no more than crying wolf, succumbing to a pernicious culture of victimization. But confronting and wrestling with Asian American discrimination (that is, making it visible when oftentimes it goes unnoticed or ignored) requires coming to grips with and making sense of a variety of personal experiences: for instance, the not-so-uncommon experience of people wondering (out loud!) where my children have been adopted from (my biracial children apparently look very Asian when they are with my wife, who is Caucasian); or when I am told that their preferred minorities are Asians (on the premise that since I am Asian American it is safe to say as much and I would find it flattering).[66] At the same time, making visible Asian American discrimination requires discerning the ways in which I too endorse the discriminatory disposition of white racialized hierarchies: perhaps, for instance, when I reflexively assume that a "racially diverse" school district is necessarily poor performing and less desirable and not thinking twice about the fact that many of the highly rated schools (at least in my neck of the woods) are anything but racially diverse.

However challenging and uncomfortable the task of unmasking and struggling with both racism against Asian Americans and Asian American complicity in racism, the urgency of such work is obvious if Asian American Christian ethics is to offer resources to advance the work of racial solidarity and cooperation. This should not be taken to mean that Asian American Christian ethics must be limited to simply identifying, making sense of, and constructing theological-ethical responses to the racial realities of Asian American life. Yet, at the same time, Asian American Christian ethics must not avoid and discount the task of naming how Asian Americans participate in the reality of white racism and privilege.

The task of Asian American Christian ethics cannot simply amount to making visible the fact that there are ethicists who self-identify as Asian Americans, just as there are black and Latino/a ethicists. Instead, the task ought to be making visible how Asian Americans are indeed disciplined by and also perpetrators of whiteness as a means of disrupting truncated and complacent perceptions Asian Americans may have of themselves. Disruption in this sense presses reflection on the racial assumptions and attitudes that may be informing the work of Asian American Christian ethicists or their deliberations about what the ends of Asian American Christian ethics ought to be. Failing that kind of self-critical reflection may make it more difficult for Asian American Christian ethics to identify with, complement, and deepen the emancipatory work of non–Asian American Christian ethicists, creating intellectual and affective distance between Asian-American and non–Asian American disciplines of ethics in ways that reflect and reinforce white racist hierarchies in society at large.

DISCUSSION QUESTIONS

1. Choi discusses how the concept of Asian American hybridity can obscure the racial realities of Asian Americans. How so? Do you agree with this proposal?

2. Choi contends that Asian Americans who discriminate against others, particularly African Americans and Latinos/as, are perpetuating patterns of white racism and privilege. Do you agree that this is the case?

3. Choi argues that the Asian American perpetuation of white racism and privilege can mask the kind of discrimination and marginalization Asian Americans continue to experience. How so?

4. How does Choi describe Asian American discrimination and marginalization? Do you agree with this description? Whether from firsthand experience or those of others, can you think of other ways that Asian Americans continue to be discriminated against that are not named in this essay?

5. Choi ultimately commends a "tragic" conception of hybridity for Asian American Christian ethics. Can you paraphrase in your own words what he means by this concept and what that means for Asian American Christian ethics? Do you concur with his prescription?

✦ 8 ✦

Health Care

SUEJEANNE KOH

On February 12, 2013, the *New York Times* reported that SungEun Grace Lee from Queens, New York, had died after suffering from terminal brain cancer. She was twenty-eight years old. The focal point of interest, however, was not her relatively young age at the time of death, but how she had been entangled in a court dispute five months earlier over the question of her removal from life support. While the hospital where Grace was receiving treatment argued that they wanted to follow Grace's wishes, her family insisted that she had been unduly influenced and heavily medicated by her hospital caretakers. Furthermore, for Grace's deeply devout Christian parents, the concept of a patient's "right to die" was anathema—from their perspective, this was tantamount to committing suicide and would therefore consign her to hell. After the courts upheld Grace's mental competence to make her own decisions, Grace's lawyer reported that Grace had changed her mind and decided to remain on life support in order "to make peace with her parents and to make peace with God."[1] She spent the last five months of her life at her parents' home in her childhood bedroom; her brother, Paul, stated that he believed that interval of time had given Grace and her family the opportunity to say good-bye.

This particular situation, secondhand though it was, resonated with me because of the ways in which it powerfully revealed the knotted convergence of distinct ethical concerns with which many Asian American Christians grapple. Grace's story raises questions not only about physical well-being but also about what constitutes a life well lived; her dilemma surfaces questions not only about her identity as an autonomous patient but also about the obligations she had as a daughter who had been loved and nurtured from birth by an Asian immigrant Christian family. What made these questions particularly difficult to answer is that no one was the villain here. On the one hand, hospital administrators were acknowledging Grace's legal rights to determine end-of-life care as an adult fully in charge of her decision-making capacities;[2] her family as well as community church members, on the other hand, asserted that such a declaration on Grace's part was out of character: "She is the most hopeful, positive and persistent person there is and encourages others to do the same."[3] In the context of Grace's entire life and religious convictions, a declaration to die simply did not make sense to her family and friends. In contrast, the hospital testified that Grace had expressed "in no uncertain terms that she [could not] bear to go on living as she [was]" and upheld her mental competency to make such a decision. In such a view, the hospital tacitly affirmed a distinction between a life well lived (i.e., defining quality of life) and merely living (what Giorgio Agamben might call "bare life").[4]

While I will revisit Grace's story at the end of this chapter, for now I employ this narrative to frame a more general description of Christian health care ethics. Theological concerns can become entangled with advances in medicine and, indeed, be shaped by them. While Christians might often think of salvation merely in terms of the afterlife, what Grace's story and the etymological origin of "salvation" suggest is a more holistic understanding of the term. "Salvation" derives from the Latin root *salus*, which means "health, safety, and well-being."[5] The perception that medicine and religion inhabit distinct spheres of influence is a modern viewpoint that arose in the wake of the Enlightenment; but in reality, over most of the course of the history of medicine the issue of physical health was often intertwined with religion, as will be detailed in the next section. The framing of health care as a *theo-ethical* concern, although an unfamiliar contextualization in our present-day environment, is completely justifiable given health care's history; it is the modern "secularized" distinction that is the aberration.[6]

Nevertheless, this aberration arguably discloses the relationship between theology and medicine *implicitly*,[7] even while modern science may explicitly assert that the two are distinct. Modern science's strategy of mapping out health care's close relationship to the configuration of living spaces (thus acknowledging the role of hygiene) as well as the transformation of illness into disease (thus helping to distinguish between physical sickness and moral causality) overall increased quality of life as well as extended life-spans for large swaths of the human population.[8] At the same time, the strategy of containment—the isolation and taming of contagion through bounded physical spaces and the modern empirical calculus of disease—also has had social implications for the body politic along with the individual human body. To the extent that Christianity has been involved in the development of modern medicine, it has been complicit in defining what are and are not normative bodies. Health care policies and initiatives have revealed how health care is not merely about the "objective" administration of scientific knowledge. Instead, health care often is entangled with ideas about race, ethnicity, class, sexuality, and gender. The Tuskegee Syphilis Experiment (1932–1972) and North Carolina's State Eugenics Program (1929–1972) stand as the most notorious examples in the United States of a larger eugenics movement, of how ideas of racial and sexual normativity along with class issues explicitly motivated clinical studies and experiments done in the name of scientific and medical progress. And while we may think that such examples are far from our everyday lives, Christianity has often been the driving force behind certain moralizing ideas about healthy families and societies.[9]

Any constructive Christian health care ethic consequently must consider a confluence of social, racial, economic, cultural, and theological factors. In other words, the shaping of a body politic affects the health of individual bodies. Like others, Asian Americans have been shaped by the construction and administration of health care in the United States. But while an extensive and growing body of sociological and epidemiological literature on Asian American health care issues exists (as referred to throughout this essay), the research conducted for this essay revealed only a few resources on the intersection of Asian American health and Christianity, mostly focused on mental health and mostly from a sociological perspective. This essay addresses this lacuna by offering a constructive Asian American Christian health care ethic.

This ethic is an "Asian American Christian" one in two ways. One, it is attentive to the particular conundrums and challenges that Asian Americans face in health care—this is the descriptive part.[10] Two, it contextualizes the relationship between the body and the body politic as an ambivalent one—that is the constructive part. By ambivalence, I draw upon not only the common sense of the word as meaning "mixed" or "two-sided," but also how it has been employed as an analytical framework. Ambivalence, to be sure, is a familiar Asian American interpretive strategy that emerges from postcolonial theory regarding the formative encounter between the colonizer and colonized; but precisely the uneven character of this relationship renders it dynamic and open to productive possibilities.[11] However, I also argue that ambivalence is particularly suited as a strategy for an overarching health care Christian ethic in two ways. One, ambivalence helps one to critically engage with how Christianity has participated in the development of health care, both in its failures and successes. Two, as will become apparent in the last section, an ambivalent approach opens up our vision of the Christian body and body politic, providing a corrective to the ways in which Christianity has colluded with social forces to define the "normal body." An Asian American health care ethic addresses and advocates for the particular concerns of Asian Americans, but it also engages in critical self-reflection on how Asian Americans have engaged in constructing boundaries, hedging off those who seem to belong from those who do not.

The rest of the chapter will unfold in the following way: In the first section, a selective overview of Christianity and the development of health care will be given, paying particular attention to the ways in which Christians were either adaptive or countercultural in their approaches. The "Yellow Peril" section will provide a survey of salient health care issues for Asian Americans. The final section will offer a constructive Asian American Christian health care ethic, employing an ambivalent hermeneutic of the body and body politic.

Christianity and the Development of Health Care

Christianity has indisputably made distinct and positive contributions to the development of health care as we know it today along with its adaptation of medicinal models from its surrounding milieu. While my overall discussion will be framed through an ambivalent lens, this section first provides a brief and selective discussion of some of these positive contributions. While debate continues regarding the perceived importance of medicine over against religious healing during Christianity's origins, at minimum one can conclude that the two approaches were not seen as contradictory.[12] Like others within that context, early Christians accepted that physical illness, while not always divine in origin, was intrinsically linked to the spiritual world. The distinction between Christians of that time and others primarily lay in attribution of healing to the one God, and God alone.

However, first we should acknowledge what Christianity adopted from Greek medicinal therapeutics. Greek physicians generally approached illness and disease from a naturalistic perspective, meaning that they derived remedies and treatments from a physiological understanding of the body. More specifically, they attributed an individual's illness or disease to an imbalance in the body's humors (black bile, yellow bile, phlegm, blood) that needed to be adjusted through a prescribed regimen of behaviors, drugs, or even surgery. At the same time, Greek physicians also employed magic and folk remedies for diseases that were not thought to be divine in origin. The Greek cult of Asclepius (and later the Roman cult of Aesculapius) reflects a development in thought about the source of illness and disease. During the earlier stages of the Asclepius cult, the Greeks thought sickness to be divinely caused and thus treated through appeal to the gods; later, although Asclepius was still consulted for cures, the idea of natural origins for sickness gained traction.

Given its origins in Judaism (which possessed no native system of therapeutics), Christianity readily adapted much of Greek medical practices. Greek medicine was ultimately perceived as offering a "value-neutral" approach rather than one fundamentally derived from religion or magic. However, in contrast with Greek and Roman societies at large, early Christians understood themselves as having a particular mandate to care for the vulnerable, particularly the sick and poor. Although the Greeks possessed an understanding of *philanthropia*, a concept which came to be understood in terms of the generosity of rulers toward their subjects as well as in friendly relations between citizen-subjects, *philanthropia* did not extend to gift-giving to the poor or sick. There was no concept of private charity: the concept of pity was not directed toward the poor or sick but instead reserved for the powerful who had calamitously fallen from power.[13] In short, the resultant feelings of pity from the giving of help or gifts was contained within a quid pro quo basis within one's class. Consequently, while physicians were encouraged to exhibit *philanthropia*, this virtue was isolated to a general attitude of friendliness or compassion as part of the art of practicing medicine. *Philanthropia* was more of a philosophical ideal of minor virtue regarding the physician but not central to the art of medicine—competence, above all, was to be pursued.[14] The Greeks accepted inequality as an inevitable part of life, and the presence of physical incapacitation translated for them into a life not worth living, for "health and physical wholeness were essential to human dignity."[15]

As a result, the critical distinction between Christian and Greco-Roman approaches to medicine arose from Christianity's *theological* motivations for treating sickness for several reasons. First, in contrast to Greco-Roman thought regarding the basis of human worth, Jewish and Christian thought understood each human being to have been created in the *imago Dei* and thus inherently valuable and worthy of protection. Second, although Christians appropriated the Greek concept of agape, they infused this "previously little-used and colorless word" with new meaning to reflect God's nature.[16] God's love was above all reflected in Christ's self-sacrificial act on the cross, and from this perspective *imitatio Christi* translated into compassion and care for others. Finally and critically, Christians identified these "others" with the vulnerable who were directly identified with Christ: "I was hungry and you gave me food, I was thirsty and you gave me something to drink, I was a stranger and you welcomed me, I was naked and you gave me clothing, I was sick and you took care of me, I was in prison and you visited me. . . . Truly I tell you, just as you did it to one of the least of these who are members of my family, you did it to me" (Matt 25:35-36, 40). This new paradigm for health care ethics grew as Christianity spread; in fact as Gary Ferngren, Guenter Risse, and Rodney Stark argue, Christianity's rise can be strongly linked to the creation of social support structures, including those that treated sick persons and populations (n.b., recall that Acts 6:1-6 recounts the creation of deacon positions to focus on serving vulnerable populations, and Justin Martyr also describes how a collection was taken up for the sick and indigent).[17]

Christianity's rapid growth in urban empire settings facilitated the development of large-scale health care initiatives. Given the overcrowded, often unsanitary conditions of city living, disease spread rapidly through urban areas as epitomized by plague. Cities were not equipped to provide support for urban populations without family or social networks; churches therefore attracted such populations through their provision of a variety of care. Ferngren specifically notes the Cyprian plague (A.D. 250–270) as requiring a larger response on the church's part to administer to the sick and dying since civil authorities rarely implemented emergency measures. Despite the Decian persecution, as well as accusations that Christians were responsible for the plague, presbyters actively organized efforts to aid plague victims, who were often thrown out onto the streets or refused burial (for fear of contagion) by mainstream populations.[18] Christians and their persecutors alike were

treated, rich and poor were called upon for service, and churches under-
took burial for the dead. During this period the church began to see such
services expanding to include both non-Christian and Christian vulnerable populations, resulting in large numbers of conversions and the
creation of new social bonds in light of the decline of traditional ones.[19]
Consequently, especially after Christianity became the official religion
of the Roman Empire, the state became increasingly reliant on churches
to provide medical care for the sick and dying.

Christianity continued its role in shaping medicine into its modern-
day form through the creation of what we now know as hospitals.[20] The
first institutions that could be recognized as such were the Basileias,
completed in 372 and created under the direction of Basil the Great (ca.
A.D. 330–379) in response to a famine. In turn the creation of these hospitals could arguably be connected to the already established presence of
monastery infirmaries: establishments that greatly detached stigma from
illness and provided medical care without charge. Still, these establishments differed from modern-day hospitals in at least two ways: one,
most staff administering care were laypeople rather than physicians; and
two, health care addressed spiritual concerns as well as bodily ailments.
The soul and body were considered as inseparably intertwined in determining a person's health.[21]

The explicit consequences of institutionalized medicine corresponded with transformations and developments in medical procedures—
most significantly the increase in surgical procedures with the successful
introduction of anesthesia after 1850, and more recently technological
advances in treatment such as the pacemaker and robotic prosthetics.
Undoubtedly such technological advances have been a boon to a larger
swath of the population and improved overall quality of life. Christianity's part in transforming medical care as the provision of ad hoc care in
response to famine and epidemics to one of a large-scale, institutionalized response focused on maintaining the health of a population is arguably an enormous one.

Such large-scale, institutional responses can also be found in the
United States. Catholic social thought was a major driving force in the
development of health care as the country increased in size and population. Some significant examples of pioneering work in United States
health care by Catholics include sisters staffing the first university-
affiliated infirmary at the University of Maryland in 1823, the development of prepaid health plans by several Catholic institutions in the late

nineteenth century, and Catholic schools comprising 40 percent of all nursing schools in 1933. In 1915 the Catholic Health Association (now known as the Catholic Hospital Association) was founded, and out of this organization, the *Ethical and Religious Directives for Catholic Health Care*.[22] While the early versions of this document were essentially lists of dos and don'ts, later versions gave theological expression to Catholic emphases on the dignity of the human person and the ministry of healing as an expression of the gospel.[23]

While Risse, Hauerwas, and others point to the Enlightenment as the era during which medicine began to diverge from its Christian roots, others have argued that the increasingly precise scientific classifications that came to characterize medical practice as a whole itself emerged from the disciplinary discourses of Christianity. Such technologies and mechanisms by which the containment of disease was accomplished are what Michel Foucault identifies as biopolitics. As he asserts, "Western man was gradually learning what it meant to be a living species in a living world, to have a body, conditions of existence, probabilities of life, an individual and collective welfare, forces that could be modified, and a space in which they could be distributed in an optimal manner."[24] Health was a matter not only of the individual but also of populations within geographical territories, and to be part of that population was to successfully present oneself as contagion free. Others who failed to exhibit this were understood as deviant, aberrant, abnormal. Health was no longer just a matter of survival but of "the imperative to live"[25]; an "avoidable flaw" rather than "an inevitable condition of living."[26]

Consequently, the presence of disease translated to *moral* as well as physical disorder. As John Wesley could affirm, "Cleanliness is indeed next to godliness."[27] So while Christianity must indeed be credited in terms of improving overall health and extending life-spans to the point that even the phrase "life expectancy" could be understood as a normed reality, the legitimacy of this achievement necessitated the identification of what was *not* normative, of what needed to be bounded off for the safety of the overall population. The history of medical missions, in particular, sheds light on physical health as a barometer of moral health. While Christian doctors and nurses often worked against colonial bureaucracy, acculturated to new environments, and provided much-needed medical services and supplies, religious historians have also done critical work in dismantling the romantic vision of the medical missionary who brought both physical healing and spiritual salvation to the heathen. Medical missions was a harbinger of order for both the body and soul; as Megan Vaughan writes, "Healing . . . was part of a programme of social and moral engineering through which 'Africa' would be saved."[28] As a result, hospitals were emblematic of scientific progress and Christian virtue; conversely, the empirical presence of disease meant the absence of moral or religious integrity. As a result, we should be cautious in solely attributing positive outcomes to Christianity's role in the creation of institutionalized health care. The more accurate reality is that Christianity was deployed in the name of health care in ambivalent ways, and the relationship between the two must be continuously negotiated.

A number of overarching themes as well as ongoing questions in presenting a Christian ethics of health care can be given at this point. The first is of Christ as the great physician (*Christus medicus*). Identification of Christ as physician started at the beginning stages of Christianity (ca. 117 being the earliest source). However, while some of the motivation of this arose from an apologetic desire to attribute Christ as the divine source of healing, this metaphor more often identified Jesus as healer of the soul-sick, referring to Scripture: "Those who are well have no need of a physician, but those who are sick; I have come to call not the righteous but sinners" (Mark 2:17; cf. Matt 9:12, Luke 5:31). The mission of Christian hospitals was therefore to provide health care ultimately in the service of spiritual care.

At the same time, the adoption and adaptation of the Hippocratic oath by early Christians recognized the practice of medicine as a practice with goods intrinsic in itself[29] rather than as a collection of skills to be merely administered according to the directives of the state or marketplace. Allen Verhey clearly identifies the reformist character of the oath, and he argues that it provides an opportunity for Christian health care professionals to provide a similar reformist perspective in our current environment so that doctors understand themselves not only as simply beholden to principles that accent the autonomous but also as accountable to a larger ecclesial context.[30] Stanley Hauerwas provides a complementary (or some might argue, a contrasting) perspective in that he accents the church as a community of witnesses that can demonstrate the practice of presence to those in pain, often further isolated in their pain as a result of the structures of institutionalized medicine: "Medicine needs the church not to supply a foundation for its moral commitments, but rather as a resource of the habits and practices necessary to sustain the care of those in pain over the long haul."³¹ Both, however, turn to the formative promise of practice as providing the necessary basis for administering theologically coherent health care.

From early times, Christian admittance and treatment of patients has often included prayers, confession, and washing, in acknowledgment of one's sin as well as trust in God's providential will. However, this does not translate into a Stoically derived passivity in the face of pain, nor does it mean that personal sin is necessarily etiologically related to illness. Rather, such practices put the ill in intimate contact with the healthy. Such contact disrupts notions that the body—individual or social—is a hermetically sealed off entity, turned in on itself. In identifying the sick with Christ, the sick become more than merely an "object" or "patient."

The early Christian response to plague, famine, and individuals cast out onto the streets was to assist non-Christian and Christian alike. Early Christians answered the question of who deserved health care in a way that countered the ethos of the time; in their own way, they upended the social hierarchy of the time. In our contemporary context, where health care is administered by the state, nonprofit, and private organizations, we can find U.S. Christians on both sides of the debate of whether universal health care is a Christian responsibility toward which to work, with both opponents and proponents referring to Christian mandates to bolster their reasoning (e.g., whether certain contraceptives should be mandatorily covered by Christian institutions or businesses and whether caring for the sick poor is a matter of Christian justice for all). Given as it is that access to health care is often offered through employment, this particular arrangement also raises the question of whether health care is a good or right in itself or the reward and consequence for a certain level of workplace productivity.

Christian ethical reflection on health care, then, is not simply about the actual act of medical assistance or the health care professional-patient dyad but includes broader reflection on how the body and body politic are shaped through institutional, government, and marketplace policies. In other words, health care ethics concerns itself with decisions about social inclusion and exclusion along with accompanying analyses on how we understand health and normativity. It involves the distribution of power and knowledge in social networks, and this distribution has both direct and indirect consequences for one's health.

I have suggested throughout this section that there is no one, definitive Christian health care ethic. It is true that all Christians hold life to be sacred; but there are contrasting Christian perspectives about if and when contraceptive usage and abortion are permissible, whether physician-assisted suicide is ever acceptable, and whether reproductive technologies invariably contravene the natural law. Some Christians affirm the direct link between sin and disease while others reject it. There are disagreements between Christians about the conditions for access to health care. Ultimately, however, any Christian health care hermeneutic would affirm that physical and spiritual well-being are linked together, and toward that end, the administration of health care is a vital expression of Christ's love in this world. Health care ethics is both a matter of love and justice—or, as Margaret Farley describes, "compassionate respect."[32]

From Yellow Peril to Model Minority: Asian American Health Care

The enterprise of public and personal hygiene has often accompanied the project of modernity. The creation of clean and "uncontaminated" spaces were in line with the vision of a civilized nation whose people knew how to practice the necessary social restraint or ability to "self-govern" (habits, practices, and so forth) in order to exemplify progress, prosperity, and promise. Inversely, peoples and spaces that failed to meet these codes of health were pathologized. Nayan Shah's study of health epidemics in San Francisco's Chinatown at the end of the nineteenth century describes how the public health campaign to make San Francisco the "healthiest city in the known world" was paired with "the image of Chinatown as a noxious and degraded space."[33]

Shah's work helps us to limn the relationship between theology, race, and health care. In the United States, the Naturalization Act of 1790 was explicit in terms of who it deemed worthy of citizenship: "a free white person" who was proven to be of "good character" residing in the United States for two years.[34] As Matthew Frye Jacobson notes, however, this seemingly precise definition actually opened the door to American nativism.[35] The large-scale immigration of Irish, Polish, Italians, and others from Eastern Europe raised questions of whether the identification of "free white person" was overinclusive. While the nativism debates of the 1840s and 1850s were primarily about Catholicism and economics, by 1870 the discussion had explicitly turned to race; with the acceptance of African Americans to the naturalization process, the concept of "white" became the point of exclusion for Asian

Americans, deemed as "unfit" for "self-government" within a republic.[36] In reaction to the inaccurate perception of Chinese workers as a threat to white productivity and prosperity, the Chinese Exclusion Act was passed in 1882 and not fully repealed until 1943.

Self-government was a statement not only on one's complexion but also on one's features, habits, and beliefs. As the question of self-government became a racial one, American exclusionists turned to the sciences in order to justify racial categories, creating a hierarchy of races as well as a list of racially derived "social inadequacies": for example, feeblemindedness, epilepsy, tuberculosis, deafness, and "dependency."[37] In short, whiteness became both the standard and the goal toward which one strived.

This racial conceptualization did not emerge ex nihilo but was intertwined with a theo-logic that worked toward the formation of a nation-state, an extensive telling of which J. Kameron Carter has given in *Race: A Theological Account*. Specifically, the racialized theology that emerged when Christianity was severed from its Jewish roots became a racist theology when Kant sought to legitimate Christian theology in light of the Enlightenment's challenge to religion. By identifying Christianity with scientific rationality (which was in turn a sign of modernity), those nations and peoples who did not exhibit signs of that rationality were deemed as racially inferior, as peoples who were insufficiently modern or capable of achieving whiteness as associated with rational religion. Religious rationality and whiteness, in other words, were two sides of the same coin. Becoming a modern citizen-subject was as much a theological project as it was a racial one. An 1870 Congress session debate clearly displayed concern about the rising (especially Asian) immigrant population by voicing this racial-theological perspective plainly: "Does the Declaration mean that the Chinese coolies, that the Bushmen of South Africa, that the Hottentots, the Digger Indians, heathen, pagan, and cannibal shall have equal political rights under this Government with citizens of the United States?" As Jacobson notes, the inference about whiteness was that whiteness equaled freedom, civilization, and Christianity.[38]

As a result, the adaptation of mainstream health care norms by Chinese immigrants during the first half of the twentieth century played a large role in the transformation of Asian Americans from "yellow peril" to a "model minority." As previously mentioned, Chinese immigration into the United States during the eighteenth century, which was initially welcomed as a cheap source of manual labor, was later met by hostile resistance as the immigrants were perceived as a threat to white American workers. Unease about the growing Chinese immigrant population directly translated into strategies for "containing" it—Shah effectively demonstrates how spatialization became an indicator of racialization through mapping, enumeration, and classification. Such strategies allowed for the empirically based and "objective" justification to portrayals of the Chinese as living in ratlike squalor and as sources of virulent disease.[39]

Moreover, Chinese males overwhelmingly populated late nineteenth-century Chinatowns due to immigration restrictions on Chinese women. The living arrangements of groups of men, women, and children who were not married couples with families translated into "queer domesticity and deviant heterosexuality."[40] Together with the Chinese's apparent inability to conform to American hygiene and public health standards, the widely held conclusion was that the Chinese were unfit for citizenship.

Given this backlash, during the interwar period between World Wars I and II, "Chinese American social workers took up the discourses of hygiene, domesticity, and gender and reworked them in their advocacy for access to municipal social services and for improved housing."[41] Moreover, as the few Chinese immigrant women began to marry and have children, they took up models of American motherhood as a way to have more "conventional" families. With the United States' entrance into World War II and the subsequent internment and vilification of Japanese Americans, public sentiment began to portray the Chinese as the "good Asians" in contrast. Chinese Americans advocated vaccination campaigns, and Chinese social workers attempted to dispel fears among certain Chinatown subgroups that public health officials were dangerous, a natural fear in reaction to public health officials' characterization of Chinatown overall as a "menace."[42] The opening of the Ping Yuen housing community in 1951, in a reformed San Francisco Chinatown, marked a decisive point in the eventual development of the idea of Asians as the model minority. The Chinese families selected for this community project were "picture perfect" Chinese American families, usually composed of husbands who had served in the military in World War II and wives who were models of American taste and domesticity. As Shah writes, this event helped to mark the "ambivalent process by which ghettos created through racial segregation became valorized as ethnic cultural enclaves. During the middle of the twentieth century, descriptions of Chinatown as a site of danger, deviance, and epidemic disease were eclipsed by visions of sanitized exoticism."[43]

Such narratives of Chinese Americans helped to reinforce the popular belief that Asians were paradigmatic, assimilable citizen-subjects. The model minority myth was reinforced by governmental health reports that asserted the healthy status of Asian Americans, but were in fact reliant upon limited data that focused on only a handful of Asian American populations. J. S. Lin-Fu argued in a 1988 article that inadequate and misleading data masked the ethnic and socioeconomic diversity of Asian American populations and therefore the varying health statuses within the Asian American community. Her article marked the beginning of sustained advocacy efforts to better serve the Asian American community's health care concerns through more extensive research on local levels as well as through the leadership of community-based organizations where large populations of Asian American communities existed.[44]

Another significant development in Asian American health care came about with the publication of Anne Fadiman's *The Spirit Catches You and You Fall Down*, an account and analysis of her meetings with a Hmong refugee family who lived in Merced, California. The family's youngest daughter, Lia Lee, had suffered from violent epileptic seizures from a young age. Her Western-trained physicians wanted to treat her condition with medications; her parents, while concerned, also believed according to Hmong tradition that epilepsy was a sign of spiritual power. Fadiman's account highlighted the communicative gap—both linguistic and cultural—between Lia's doctors and parents, with both parties desiring what they perceived as the best for Lia's health.[45] A direct result of Lia's story was the creation of a community-based organization (CBO) that initiated a cross-cultural training program to facilitate communication between Hmong shamans and Western-trained health providers. Moreover, Fadiman's account helped to bring about a watershed moment in medical training regarding cultural competency, with her book now assigned as required reading in many medical schools across the country. Arguably, though, Fadiman's story should not overshadow the reality that advocacy organizations were already promoting Asian American health care issues, as generated by Fu's earlier article.[46]

Significant Statistics and Themes for Asian American Health Care

I turn now to provide a selective overview of significant statistics and themes for Asian American health care. In my selection of these themes and statistics, I have tried to strike a balance between those themes that are widely known and those themes that cut against popularly assumed notions about Asian American health. The following are highlighted: health insurance, employment in the health care industries, complementary alternative and traditional medicine (CATM), health conditions, hepatitis B, tuberculosis, HIV/AIDS, occupational and lifestyle hazards, and mental illness.

Insurance Rates and Access to Health Care. One of the most significant barriers to quality health care in the United States is the inability to access or afford health insurance, and Asian Americans are also affected by this reality. In 2010, 18 percent of Asian Americans were uninsured, compared to 11.7 percent of the nonwhite Hispanic population. However, percentages of the uninsured vary widely within the total Asian American population. For example, while South Asian Americans enjoy a high percentage of employer-covered insurance (75 percent), Korean Americans have one of the lowest rates of employer-covered insurance (49 percent) due to the fact that nearly half of all Korean Americans are employed in workplaces with 25 employees or fewer.

Two other factors also influence insurance coverage rates and access to health care—questions about eligibility according to immigration status and language and cultural barriers. English language fluency varies among Asian American subpopulations: 52 percent of Vietnamese, 46 percent of Chinese, 22 percent of Filipinos, and 21 percent of Asian Indians are not fluent in English.[47] In 2010, 76.9 percent of Asian Americans indicated that they spoke a language other than English at home. However, despite these challenges, early figures indicate that Asian American health care advocacy groups have been efficient and successful in signing up Asian Americans under the Affordable Care Act.[48]

Employment in the Health Care Industries. A number of studies have demonstrated that racial-ethnic physician-patient concordance, or the option to seek out health care professionals of a similar ethnicity or race, improves the quality of health care.[49] Overall, Asian Americans are well represented in the health care professions, with Chinese, Asian Indians, and Korean Americans being the three largest subgroups from 1978 to 2008 (however, it must also be noted that across this same time range, those categorized as "other Asians" [excluding Vietnamese, Filipinos, Koreans, Chinese, and Asian Indians] comprised 42.1 percent of the entire Asian American physician population). Although gender parity is gaining, the three subgroups with the lesser percentages of women physicians are Vietnamese, Korean, and other Asian.

A recent study reviewed data collected over a six-year period in California to determine how the relative under- or overrepresentation of minority physicians in any given geographical area impacted movement in or out of those areas. While black physicians on average remained in areas as underrepresentation increased, Asian American physicians tended to move to areas that had similar levels of representation as the previous area. Tentatively, this seems to indicate that Asian American physicians[50] are more sensitive to market trends. While the study itself does not examine the reasons for these differences, these findings suggest that the Asian American response to the model minority myth is complex and varied. Although recent Asian American scholarship has argued against the assignation of the model minority status and demonstrated its social and psychological debilitation, it is also well documented that medicine remains a highly prized profession within the Asian American community.[51] Consequently, further questions must be asked about how the model minority myth is generated by Asian Americans as much as it is externally imposed.

The representation of Filipinos in the nursing profession is another facet of the complicated relationship between ideas of progress, gender, race, and class. Filipinos (especially women) comprise an unusually high percentage of those in the health care practitioners and technical services category; for example, statistics from the Bureau of Registered Nurses in California show that while Filipinos represent approximately 5 percent of the California population, they make up close to 20 percent of the overall nursing population.[52] Additionally, these nurses are overwhelmingly women, reflecting the long migrational histories of Filipina nurses to the United States.

This migration, as Yen Le Espiritu has demonstrated, was entangled in colonial ideas about gender and race. Nursing, convincingly established in the United States as a feminine profession, was initially exported to the Philippines to "civilize" the Filipinos into certain norms about femininity and Western progress. Over time, in order to strengthen the relationship between the two countries as well as to have access to a "cheaper" labor force, the United States encouraged the education of and emigration of Filipina nurses to the United States. This overrepresentation of Filipina nurses, however, has not necessarily translated into more egalitarian marital and family relationships; the impact of this particular workforce arrangement remains to be seen.[53]

Complementary Alternative and Traditional Medicine. Analysis indicates that more than any other racial group, Asian Americans turn to complementary alternative and traditional medicine (CATM) in addition to consulting Western-trained health care professionals.[54] Although studies on the reasons motivating such turns to CATM are few, they suggest that cultural ideas about health and well-being are behind them, as well as skepticism about institutionalized medicine as practiced in the United States. Greater research on and professional knowledge of CATM is necessary by health care professionals, especially as such medicines may contraindicate with pharmaceutical drugs or present safety hazards due to lack of regulation.

Health Conditions and Occupational Hazards. Asian Americans are most at risk for the following diseases and conditions: cancer (especially cervical for Laotian, Vietnamese, and Cambodian women),[55] heart disease, stroke, unintentional injuries, and diabetes.[56] Illnesses that disproportionately affect Asian Americans are: hepatitis B, HIV/AIDS, illness as a consequence of smoking, tuberculosis, chronic obstructive pulmonary disease (COPD), and liver disease. The following is a brief and selective overview of the various factors that contribute to some of these illnesses.

Hepatitis B. Although Asian Americans make up approximately 5 percent of the U.S. population, they comprise more than 50 percent of hepatitis B cases overall. This is attributable to a number of factors: (1) nearly 70 percent of Asian Americans either were born to or had parents who were born in countries where hepatitis B is common (n.b., hepatitis B is easily transmissible through blood); (2) since hepatitis B symptoms do not often manifest themselves until the later stages of the disease, people often go untested and unvaccinated; and (3) people often avoid testing and vaccination because of the stigma attached to a positive hepatitis B diagnosis, as well as language and cultural barriers regarding health care access. However, hepatitis B can contribute to manifestation of liver cancers and cirrhosis if not treated.

Tuberculosis. The Office of Minority Health states that in 2012, tuberculosis was "24 times more common among Asians, with a case rate of 18.9 as compared to 0.8 for the non-Hispanic White population."[57] While U.S.-born Asians constitute only 3 percent of TB cases, foreign-born Asians comprise 43 percent. Four of the five top countries for foreign-born TB cases are Asian: Philippines, Vietnam, India, and

China.[58] This disease proves challenging to combat for several related reasons: latent TB infection is not symptomatic, and infected individuals without access to regular health care can go without screenings for years. Moreover, poor rates of regular medical care may impact the proper completion of TB treatment, which extends over several months.[59]

HIV/AIDS. Although Asian Americans as a group have a lower prevalence of reported HIV/AIDS cases in comparison to other racial groups, the incidence of such cases is increasing more than any other group—in fact Asian and Pacific Islander women in the United States have the highest rate of increase for new HIV infections.[60] The rising Asian American population, an increase in sexual risk behaviors, as well as greater reporting and surveillance certainly may be factors.[61] At the same time, cultural stigma around same-sex orientation and sociocultural mores regarding sexual behavior may result in testing avoidance and contribute to an underreporting of cases. In 2011, 86 percent of Asian American men reported with HIV/AIDS were gay, bisexual, or engaging in sex with other men; 92 percent of women received it through heterosexual contact. Most strikingly, Asian American women are 20 percent more likely to be diagnosed with HIV/AIDS than their white counterparts.[62] A part of this percentage is also composed of the underground economy of Asian American sex workers, who often face threat of physical violence or unemployment if they do not accede to clients' requests to engage in high-risk sexual behaviors.[63]

Occupational and Lifestyle Hazards. Here, I briefly note particular workplace issues that may affect the health of Asian Americans, particularly those who work in the service sectors or are self-employed. While it is true that Asian Americans on the whole are well represented in management, professional, and related occupations, this conceals the reality that many Asian Americans also participate in the service industries. For example, Vietnamese comprise one-fifth of the personal service sector, reflecting the fact that many work in nail salons. Chinese American restaurant workers may face frequent exposures to bleach, secondhand smoke from cigarettes, and cooking fumes. Self-employed Korean Americans make up about a quarter of the self-employed sector, many of them small-business owners of laundry services, convenience stores, or restaurants. Exposure to chemicals in these various environments may lead to skin and a variety of respiratory problems, including lung cancer, COPD, and nerve-related damage.

Mental Illness. Mental health issues among Asian Americans have increasingly received more attention in the past decade or so, not only among Asian Americans but also in the larger media as well.[64] Psychologists and psychiatrists remain underrepresented among Asian Americans, and Asian Americans seek out professional help the least when compared with all racial and ethnic groups. In general, reports of mental health issues increase from the first to second generation.[65] Two subpopulations among Asian Americans have been identified as particularly vulnerable to mental illness: young Asian American women born in the United States and Asian American women between 65 and 84 years of age. The former group exceeds national rates regarding suicidal ideation and attempts, while the latter possesses the highest of suicide rates among women of all racial groups, even though overall Asian American women enjoy the longest life expectancy in comparison to all other groups.

For young Asian American women, imbricating factors include racial discrimination and stereotyping, the pressure to uphold a family's honor through academic and professional achievement, and the persistence of the "model minority" myth (which may feed into the first two factors). Elderly Asian American women face a different kind of double-edged sword, where making financial and physical sacrifices for their children may leave them impoverished and reliant on their children, who in turn are often reluctant to seek out external support structures from a sense of filial piety.[66] As well, both the idea of maintaining "face" (upholding honor) for one's family and the association of mental illness with sin may prevent Asian Americans from seeking out help outside of the home. Although stigma around mental illness is experienced among all American subpopulations, the lack of information regarding mental illness and cultural values tend to exacerbate it among Asian Americans.[67]

The challenge that persists across a number of health care categories for Asian Americans is data disaggregation, although this has improved since 1985.[68] As evidenced above, certain subpopulations are more vulnerable to particular conditions and diseases than others. More granular data allows for communities to mobilize health care workers and community-based organizations, increases awareness among communities about preventable diseases and conditions, and provides evidence for the need of greater funding for research and program implementation from foundations and government agencies.

At the same time, while data helps to mobilize advocacy efforts, further sociological studies need to be conducted to explore the impacts of race, gender, and class for Asian American health care. Even within the Asian American community, questions of inclusion, exclusion, and normativity arise from differences in socioeconomic status, competition for resources, cultural and historical histories, and varying amounts of time spent living in the United States. In other words, despite a prevailing perception that the Asian American population is monolithic, no one strategic approach is sufficient to address the whole of Asian American health care issues.

As Grace Lee and Lia Lee's stories demonstrate, an Asian American health care approach thus highlights the necessity to negotiate a number of world views instead of merely focusing on the acculturation of populations to the strictures of Western medicine and institutions. On the other hand, such acculturation—e.g., in increasing the percentage of Pap-smear tests for Asian American women, or increasing the percentage of hepatitis B screenings—is critical for improving health outcomes. Even while identifying the pressing challenges that Asian Americans face, arguably what racial and ethnic health care advocates have highlighted so effectively is that health care is a holistic concern where the physician-patient dyad, often focused on efficiency and outcomes, is only one piece of the puzzle. Community-based organizations and community-based participatory research (CBPR) have led the way in advocating for a holistic (or "ecological") approach where multiple partners—community health workers, schools, physicians, nurses, churches, and clinics—collaborate to approach health in a more organic, grassroots way, lending texture to the material contours of salvation.

Toward an Asian American Christian (AAC) Health Care Ethic

As I noted in the beginning, a Christian health care ethic helps to develop an understanding of salvation where physical and spiritual health are mutually constitutive of each other. Although the early Christians were not unique in perceiving health in this way, I understand their distinctive response to physical suffering in their environments as arising from their experience of the risen Christ. The reality of Christ resurrected—an enfleshed man who nevertheless carried tangible and visible reminders of his wounds—suggests not a hermetically sealed off entity but rather a body suggestive of openness and porosity, where distinctions between others and the self become blurred and the health of the individual's body depends on the body politic and vice versa. This blurring of distinctions implies at least two things. One, while disease and suffering are not to be glorified, as Paul writes, "The body does not consist of one member but of many. . . . If one member suffers, all suffer together with it; if one member is honored, all rejoice together with it" (1 Cor 12:14, 26). Christ's suffering acknowledges and embraces the reality of our suffering. The suffering of others is not their own but also ours.

Consequently, while Ferngren asserts that the early Christians appropriated agape to reflect God's love, I add that Christ's love is also about eros (God with us, meaning God's desire to be with us and for us). Such love overflows, dissolving polarizing distinctions that arise from powers that contend those distinctions are necessary for our protection, well-being, even salvation. This blurring of distinctions between self and others therefore means an uncoupling of a necessary relationship between morality and health as well as the ways this relationship is deployed not only spatially but also psychologically. A Christian health care ethic will be concerned with the protection or preservation of the health not only of oneself but also of the community; in fact it will stretch our ideas of exclusion and inclusion within that community.[69]

As I have demonstrated throughout this chapter, acknowledging the mind-body connection in itself does not necessarily translate to a life-giving ethic. Considerations about one's health status have often shaped corresponding thoughts about one's soteriological status, and vice versa. In other words, the presence of disease has often meant judgment about one's moral as well as bodily fitness, and one's successful acclimation to bodily normativity has often had soteriological implications. I argue, then, that a Christian health care ethic should embrace a both/and approach that recognizes the spirit-body connection but will eschew an either/or approach that encourages moral judgment about who we should help (e.g., only those who "deserve" our help), or why (e.g., because they need saving). In other words, an either/or approach has resulted in Christianity's ambivalent track record regarding the salvation of souled bodies.

However, it is precisely the acknowledgment of this ambivalent track record that allows for the presence of productive possibilities. By questioning and unsettling the ways in which sociopolitical power and Christian authority have colluded to define the normative body, an ambivalent approach consequently opens up the possibilities for new visions of salvation. An Asian American Christian (AAC) health care

ethic embraces a both/and approach in a spirit of renewal and reconstruction.[70] In retrieving the spirit of the early church and recognizing that history as part of its own, an AAC health care ethic will both
involve itself in the medical care of vulnerable populations as well as
advocate for equitable access to health care. Toward this end, an AAC
health care approach will work for further disaggregation of data on
behalf of vulnerable Asian American populations but not *reduce* understanding of health care to an empirical level. To reduce health care to
the empirical level would open up the risk of reinforcing a quantitative
envisioning of being, the very thing that an ambivalent health care ethic
resists, particularly given the ways in which such quantitative approaches
have been linked to sanitized and sanitizing visions of humanity.

In a similar vein, Asian American Christians will also critically
reflect on how ideas about status and socioeconomic stability affect the
envisioning and discernment of vocational and avocational identities,
and how such envisioning affects the health of not only the Asian American community but also the community at large. Explicitly, this would
involve how resistance to the model minority myth includes acknowledgment of the ways in which the myth affords certain Asian Americans
with socioeconomic privileges through its "positive" stereotyping. Part
of the danger of the myth is that it perpetuates the temptation to enclave
oneself off from those who may threaten the security of those privileges in some shape or form. An AAC health care ethic would therefore
incorporate an openness to risk by challenging Asian American health
care practitioners to consider serving rural or other vulnerable populations, as well as work on increasing physician–patient concordance for
underrepresented populations.

Overall, given the ways the Asian American community itself has
been subject to an either/or approach to health care, Asian American
Christians will resist from imposing this approach on others. It will critically assess the ways in which the church itself has also supported such
projects in domestication and work against definitions of normativity
that translate to homogeneity. More concretely, an AAC ethic will help
to uncouple disease from shame and stigma, particularly in (but not limited to) two cases. One, although research and media have increasingly
brought attention to Asian American mental issues in the past decade or
so, broadly speaking, Asian Americans still commonly rely on family
and community in order to address mental health issues, when at all. A
recent study indicated that while Asian American pastors do sometimes

refer their congregants to external mental health services, such referrals often corresponded to greater knowledge of mental health issues on the pastor's part.[71] More collaboration between pastors, physicians, psychologists, and social workers is necessary for dialogue, education, support, and action around mental health issues.[72]

AAC communities can also participate in shaping a healthy sexual ethic. While current conversations frequently focus on same-sex relations or sex trafficking, honest, theological discussion on responsible sexuality is equally important. Such discussions would not only focus on the prescriptive but also help to place sexuality in a larger intersectional framework. As Foucault would argue, it is not that sexuality is a suppressed issue within AAC communities; rather, it is regulated and disciplined by a network of official and unofficial authorities so that certain models of sexuality become normative while others are not, reinforcing a cycle of shame and stigma. Theologically responsible sexuality, however, is not entirely equivalent to normative sexuality. These discussions must be conducted in a spirit of protection (especially for children and youth) but not devolve into a spirit of fear; ultimately, the goal of such conversations would be to help contribute to a flourishing ethic of life.

At the heart of both Grace Lee and Lia Lee's stories is the reality that health care is not merely about the application of precise principles or empirical metrics. Agape, eros, respect, and care—no matter how carefully we attempt to parse out these words, we cannot fully describe the everyday realities in which both Grace and Lia's families participated to sustain and nourish these women (e.g., bathing, massaging, transporting, feeding, and praying for them). Nevertheless, shifting all decision-making authority to a person's family or community may create its own set of ethical quandaries. The conflation of religious with familial authority, as in Grace's case, can be in danger of creating a closed system that not only denies the will and desires of the individual but also prevents the possibilities for thoughtful discourse and counsel, thus degenerating into paternalism. In other words, as Farley notes, an ethics of care—in this case, as represented by family and community— must be held together with respect for the embodied individual; in fact care and respect illuminate the other.[73] An AAC health care ethic, characterized by a productive ambivalence, will not only work to transform the Asian American communities of which it is a part but also open up those communities to the possibilities of being transformed when critique is necessary.

Ultimately, an AAC ethic will work toward the goal of shalom—peace, prosperity, well-being—while continuing to critically reflect on the shape of salvation. It does so by remembering the reality and promise of the resurrected Christ; his flesh, as John Updike writes, is ours: "The same hinged thumbs and toes / The same valved heart / That-pierced-died, withered, paused, and then regathered."[74] A Christian health care ethic, then, is not about a disembodied, eschatological future but includes the work of healing the corporeal present for a life abundant.

DISCUSSION QUESTIONS

1. Who or what have primarily shaped your visions of (1) salvation and (2) "the good life"? How do these two visions overlap, and where do they diverge? Has this chapter broadened your ideas of what a health care ethic involves?

2. This chapter distinguishes between an "either/or" and "both/and" approach to health care and the ways in which Christianity has shaped both approaches. Can you reflect on how various faith communities (specifically Asian American) have espoused either approach?

3. What issues have seemed particularly important to Asian American Christian communities, and what issues do you feel should be more important? Do ideas about the connection between sin and disease discourage discussion about certain illnesses versus others?

4. In what ways have you been taught to reflect theologically about the body (i.e., the human body, the body of Christ), and how does this differ from or overlap with cultural or historical constructions of the body? How does the author's argument challenge your current thinking about the body?

Immigration

HAK JOON LEE

Rallies for immigration reform and demonstrations against prolonged detention or deportation of undocumented immigrants continue in many cities of the nation as some eleven million undocumented immigrants desperately await the freedom to travel, gather at family reunions, gain better job opportunities, and obtain the right for their children's public education, all while Congress drags its feet on immigration legislation. As the national debates on immigration mostly focus on the issues of border patrol, the barrier fence along the U.S.-Mexican border, deportation, and undocumented immigrants, the public conception of immigrants is largely that they are Hispanic. This public perception, however, is not entirely accurate. Asians actually make up the largest group of new immigrants in the United States, surpassing Latinos.[1] In many ways persons of Asian heritage are silently reshaping not only the demography and racial composition of the nation but also its social and cultural fabric. Asian immigrants are bringing new capital, skills, motivation, entrepreneurship, and cultural products to the United States. Vibrant Asian ethnic communities are rejuvenating urban areas by reversing displacement and ghettoization, population decline, and job losses in manufacturing in many U.S. cities; other effects of Asian immigration include the suppression of crime rates and the mitigation of certain social pathologies. Beyond that, Asian immigrants continue to build economic and cultural bridges between the United States and their countries of origin, which in turn invites new capital investments, trade, and cultural and educational exchanges.[2]

This essay studies the distinctive characteristics of Asian immigration to the United States along with its ethical meanings and implications from an Asian American Christian perspective. Immigration is a complex, multifaceted social phenomenon, precluding any simple causal explanation. Multiple factors—political, economic, cultural, religious—contribute to the immigration of people. Although immigration ultimately belongs to the decision of individuals and their families, other factors such as political ideology, immigration and labor policy, popular media, global economy, and trade agreements affect the flow of people.[3] Therefore, the study of immigration requires the examination of not only the particular history and dynamics of the relationship between the sending and hosting countries, but also the changing nature of immigration in a global context.

In studying Asian immigrants this essay focuses, among many factors, on the dynamics of globalization (economy), transnationalism (interconnectivity), racialization, and Asian communal tradition (e.g., Confucian emphasis on education), examining how these variables together give rise to culturally distinctive practices of "goose families," "parachute kids," and "maternity tourism," while shaping the unique patterns in the settlement, adaptation, and social mobility of Asian immigrants. In particular, it pays close attention to the unique role and function of Asian ethnic communities as the hub of enclave economies and social networks—the source of Asian American cultural identity and social capital. Finally, I explore how an Asian American Christian approach that adopts a covenantal ethics model can address the challenges and moral concerns facing Asian immigrants. As a method of reconciling strangers or alienated parties and of building unity out of diversity, covenantal ethics helps Asian immigrants and U.S. citizens to build mutual trust and to work together for the common good.

Christian Responses to Immigration

It is no surprise that Scripture offers rich resources for immigration ethics as its major human characters, such as Abraham, Jacob, Joseph, Moses, the people of Israel, and early Christians were migrants, nomads, or experienced exile and life in a diaspora. In a sense migration is central to the biblical drama, which is plotted by the stories of leaving home, seeking a new settlement, and later returning home. Even God in Jesus Christ is understood to have come to a far country and dwelt with humans to establish the eternal home of shalom. The prominent biblical metaphors of the pilgrim people, exile, the promised land, and the ethical values of hospitality, justice, and basic human dignity were developed out of the experiences of migration.

One such example is the hospitality toward strangers and charity toward the disadvantaged (Jer 7:4-8, Zech 7:8-10). In the book of Exodus, the people of Israel were commanded not to mistreat the sojourner out of profound concern for the sanctity of life bestowed by God at creation as well as out of their own experience as migrants and slaves in Egypt (Exod 22:21, 23:9). Moses told his people that God said: "You shall treat the stranger who sojourns with you as the native among you, and you shall love him as yourself, for you were strangers in the land of Egypt: I am the LORD your God" (Lev 19:34). The Torah stipulated in great detail the protection of aliens, strangers, and sojourners from abuse and discrimination, fair treatment for them in legal cases, the guarantee of timely and fair payment, rest on the Sabbath, and special care to receive a portion of special tithes that were collected every three years for the poor (Deut 14:28-29, 26:12-13; Lev 19:10, 23:22; Deut 24:19-21; Ruth 2:5-9).[4] The law was based on the awareness that aliens and sojourners were vulnerable to the whims and abuses of the hosting society because of their lack of full membership and their unfamiliarity with customs, laws, language, and topography. Though not fully developed as the contemporary idea of human rights, a deep concern for the dignity of strangers and aliens in the Old Testament points to a seminal form of human rights.

This biblical teaching on the special care for the disadvantaged even further intensifies in the New Testament.[5] There are many passages that emphasize the hospitable treatment of strangers. Among them, Jesus' parable of the final judgment in Matthew 25 shows the depth of commitment by the early Christian commitment to this value (Matt 25:35). God's commandment to care for strangers and migrants still binds all Christians today because they are called to welcome and care for strangers, and by doing so they are judged eschatologically as having welcomed and cared for Christ himself.

Among various Christian approaches to immigration, such as hospitality and care for strangers, this chapter proposes covenantal ethics as a plausible Christian approach to Asian immigration. I turn next, however, to a discussion of immigration from the perspective of Asian Americans so as to provide the contextual backdrop for this constructive approach.

U.S. Immigration and Asian American Experiences

In studying Asian immigrants, one cannot ignore the broader historical narrative of emigration to the United States. Immigration has been integral to its identity; the United States was born out of and shaped by immigration. With the exception of Native Americans, all other ethnic groups are the descendants of voluntary or involuntary (African Americans, in particular) immigrants. The United States has redefined and renewed itself again and again through immigration. Furthermore, because of immigration, American society is not based on a single religious, racial, or ethnic tradition, but has been multicultural in nature. The United States is comprised of people with diverse languages, cultures, and religions who form a single polity through their allegiance to the Constitution.[6]

The vast land of the United States, its rich natural resources, and its successful free market economic system have also greatly affected the dynamics of immigration. The idea of the "American dream" and the trope of America as the "promised land" have drawn immigrants from all over the world who have helped to keep the United States highly competitive and innovative.[7] Immigrants have constantly rejuvenated the nation with their creativity, hard work, and entrepreneurship, making the American dream a credible story to many people. Leonel Castillo, a former director of the U.S. Immigration and Naturalization Service (INS), confirms the attraction of the American dream by saying:

> We've always managed, despite our worst, unbelievably nativist actions to rejuvenate ourselves, to bring new people. Every new group comes in believing more firmly in the American Dream than the one that came a few years before. . . . They go to night school, they learn about America. We'd be lost without them. . . . The old dream is still dreamt.[8]

Just as a new marriage changes the dynamics of the two newly related families, immigrants have remolded the nature and character of the nation. Even today, the growing population of Latino and Asian immigrants is changing the political and cultural landscape of the nation.

Racism

Unfortunately, however, immigration in the United States cannot be discussed apart from racism; the two have been intertwined from the beginning and continue today in different forms and dynamics.[9] Starting with white European settlers' conquest and subjugation of the native peoples, through the forced transportation of African slaves and the exploitation of Asian and other immigrants, the history of immigration in the United States has been deeply entangled with racism, and the history of Asian immigrants is far from being an exception.[10] Since the first Asian immigrants landed in the United States around 1763, Asian immigrants have endured generations of strict legal sanctions and harsh discrimination. Beginning in the mid-nineteenth century, when scores of new immigrants from several Asian countries arrived to do difficult and often dangerous work on sugarcane plantations and other farms, in mining, and in railroad construction, they were legally discriminated against and exploited for their cheap labor. When their projects were complete, they were then abandoned without any social or legal protection. For legislation had been passed that specifically prohibited Asians from becoming naturalized: the Chinese Exclusion Act of 1882, the Immigration Act of 1917, and the National Origins Act of 1924. These laws not only effectively barred virtually any major immigration from Asia until 1965, thus consigning the (mostly) male workers to so-called "bachelor societies," but they also prevented Asian immigrants from "getting ahead" from the fruit of their labor: the California Alien Land Law of 1913 prohibited "aliens ineligible for citizenship" from owning agricultural land, thus disproportionately affecting Chinese, Indian, Japanese, and Filipino farmers.[11]

One sees in the history of Asian immigrants in the United States the tension between the universal constitutional ideals (of life, liberty, and the pursuit of happiness) and entrenched racism, which has engendered tortuous, complex, and paradoxical dynamics of race, identity, and culture. Put differently, the tension is between openness and exclusion, acceptance and discrimination. Even today, Asian immigrants become the frequent targets of abuse and exploitation for cheap labor and their financial and entrepreneurial contributions. A particular type of stereotype against Asian Americans as "perpetual foreigners" is still prevalent among the citizenry. Popular media images of Asian Americans are still commonly limited to dippy shop owners, martial arts experts, math/science/computer whizzes, and international students who are socially awkward, submissive, or those FOB (fresh off the boat) who speak broken English.

The stereotype also reveals some notable patterns of bias toward Asian Americans—as a submissive, hardworking, but ultimately a foreign group. No matter how long Asian Americans have lived in the United States or how fluent their English is, the stereotype of the perpetual foreigner constructs Asians as not "real" Americans and thus untrustworthy. Unlike other, particularly white, immigrants (e.g., Irish, Italians, Jews, etc.) who shed their "foreign" status within a single generation, the racialization of Asian Americans as perpetual foreigners has not only stuck to Asian Americans across decades but has been continually reinforced by the large influx of Asian immigrants in recent decades.

This stereotype of Asian Americans as perpetual foreigners has continued to render Asian Americans vulnerable to abuses and mistreatment,[12] as the public tends to dismiss injustices committed against Asian Americans on the belief that "foreigners" are not entitled to full or equal legal protections. The vulnerability of Asian Americans is evident in the fact that racism against Asian Americans (by whites and other race groups) is still quite pervasive and seldom discussed in the media, although the same cannot be said about racism directed against other groups. More specifically, while the genocide of Native Americans and the slavery of Africans are now well-known to the public, racism and abuse against Asian Americans still do not commonly receive adequate attention in school textbooks and the media, thus contributing to the misperception that Asian Americans have not experienced, or do not experience, racism at all.

Globalization and an Economic Dimension of Immigration

If the immigrant history and racism of the United States work together to show a domestic side of Asian immigration, then globalization is the transnational, structural force that shapes and dramatically transforms the nature of immigration. Migration may be as old as human history itself. It probably started when a nomadic tribe of early human beings moved from one place to another searching for food and security. However, what makes contemporary migration distinctive is its massiveness and speed due to globalization and the technologies of communication and transportation. Immigration today is part of the global exchange, interdependence, and international division of labor as the world is turning into a single market system of production, investment, distribution, and consumption.

People constantly chase jobs, better economic and educational opportunities, and a safer society with good health care and welfare systems. Today, thanks to global media and the Internet, those looking for better opportunities are exposed to the situations of other countries far more extensively than before and are able to make a move because of the common availability of transportation and many open borders.

Globalization is profoundly affecting the shape and dynamics of Asian immigration. The advance of transportation and communication technologies and the end of the Cold War are transforming many Asian countries into industrialized, consumer-oriented societies, increasingly integrated into the global economic system. As a result of global economic integration, the wider availability of global media, and the available resources and means around them, more and more Asians are exposed to Western, or specifically U.S., culture and lifestyles, which raises their expectations and aspirations and leads them to decide to emigrate to seek better economic and educational opportunities or security.

Transnationalism

Globalization not only offers more opportunities for immigration but also is radically transforming its very nature and dynamics. Traditionally, immigration was viewed as leaving one place to settle into another place permanently. A conventional metaphor of immigration was transplanting—uprooted from old soil and replanted into new soil. This is no longer the case. In the global era, the idea of permanent settlement is losing its currency. Today immigrants are turning into transmigrants. Many immigrants are embedded in more than one society simultaneously. In other words, even after their departure, immigrants still keep their ties with their countries of origin.

Furthermore, in many cases immigrants are no longer viewed as defectors by their home countries but rather as important assets abroad. The sending countries are taking a more active attitude toward the diaspora communities by granting new statuses and benefits (e.g., dual citizenship, business opportunities, and political participation) in order to keep immigrants' connections and interest in their home countries. This facilitates and expands the flow of remittance, business investments, and informal lobbying power for the sending countries' national interests in the United States. As a consequence, such immigrants no longer feel restricted, evicted, or displaced; they mobilize and capitalize their connections and resources to create or find the most optimal scenario for their survival and success. They continuously compare their achievements and positions in one place to those in another place because no one place is truly secure due to the constantly changing nature of economy in the global era.

A transnational character of immigration is also prominent among Asian immigrants in the United States. The economic growth in their countries of origin stimulates their entrepreneurship and economic opportunities. Many Asian self-employed immigrant businesses arise in the very interstices of two nations and locales, such as import-export firms, shipping and air cargo companies, retail trade, and labor contractors. Personal networks, economic social ties, and social capital are no longer confined to a single ethnic immigrant community but are instead stretching beyond national borders. Immigrants reconfigure, stretch, and activate their family and community networks across national boundaries for the maximization of their business and economic opportunities, utilizing their labor and resources in multiple settings.

Distinctive Characteristics of Asian Immigration

So far we have examined the U.S. history of immigration and racism and the impact of globalization. The question remains how Asian immigrants respond to these pressures and forces and how their responses shape the pattern of settlement and the cultural identity of Asian immigrants.

Asian immigrants are far from being a homogeneous group, as they include peoples from various countries on the Indian subcontinent, East Asia, and Southeast Asia. Asian immigrants are culturally and religiously diverse with different nationalities or ethnic backgrounds and a variety of languages, from Filipino nurses in Iowa to Indian engineers in Silicon Valley, from Korean shop owners to Chinese workers in garment factories to Vietnamese political refugees. Despite massive demographic, historical, and cultural heterogeneity, however, Asian immigrants in general manifest some common cultural and moral characteristics, in particular a communal tradition that emphasizes the centrality of the family and the primacy of community goals over individual desires, respect for social propriety and formality, sexual modesty, and conservatism.[13]

Motivation for Immigration

Asian immigrants come to the United States for a variety of reasons—the different combinations of push and pull factors in their countries of origin and settlement. However, their cultural communal tradition is partly reflected in the motivation of their immigration.[14] With the exception of the Vietnamese, who have come to the United States in large numbers as political refugees, many Asians have come primarily for economic, educational, and family reasons. In particular for those from East Asia (the region with a strong Confucian culture) in the post-1965 era, education is a major factor for immigration to the United

States. With several of the world's most competitive colleges and universities, the United States is very appealing to many East Asians who aspire to higher education, especially since today education is considered a crucial tool for social mobility in the competitive global economy. If they can afford to do so, many Asians want to send their children to the United States and other Western countries. One example is known as "a goose family" among Korean immigrants. A goose family in Korean idiom does not refer to a tribe of migrating birds frequently observed in Northeast Asia. It metaphorically describes a married couple virtually living in separation, sometimes for a decade, and often only visiting once a year, between Korea and the United States or Canada simply to offer better educational opportunities to their children. A goose father is usually working in South Korea to support the family financially, while a goose mother takes care of the children who attend schools in the United States or Canada. As the *New York Times* reported and President Obama also mentioned, this zeal for education is shockingly weird to the eyes of Americans.[15]

The other practice that reflects East Asian passion for education is known as "parachute kids." East Asian parents send their young children alone, some as young as twelve years old, to stay with a relative (e.g., an aunt or uncle) or in a boarding school in the United States for their education; both parents stay behind in the home country and just send money and checks from time to time to that relative or boarding school. While families who do this believe they are doing what's best for their children, the absence of parental influence in the formative years of their identity formation could lead to lifelong adverse effects. While separated from their parents and siblings and without proper supervision, these kids often suffer from loneliness and the stress of adjusting into a radically different social environment. Some even struggle with addiction and juvenile delinquency.[16]

Another example is "maternity tourism," the practice of some rich Chinese families who come to the United States in order to obtain citizenship for their newborn babies in the belief that a U.S. citizenship brings legal protections and economic benefits (e.g., free public education in the future) to their children. After giving birth, mothers and new baby American citizens return to China, but now the mothers expect that their children can return to the United States anytime they want. For example, one sees Mexican mothers crossing the border to give birth to obtain U.S. citizenship for their newborn children. Their difference is a class factor. These Chinese mothers are not poor; they pay tens of thousands of dollars to make a trip to the United States for a few months and receive medical care.

Non–Asian Americans would be surprised to find that behind these unusual family practices is the unique Asian cultural tradition where the parents sacrifice to provide the best education for their children; better education is believed to lead to their children's better professional and economic future. Education is not considered an individual activity but a family project. Parents and older siblings often sacrifice time and money for children and younger siblings to receive the best education they can get. Asian Americans' strong belief in the rewards of hard work, including in education, are reflected in recent statistics: 93 percent of Asian Americans identify themselves as very hardworking, and nearly 70 percent believe that hard work will propel them toward success and financial security (n.b., compare that latter figure to 58 percent of the American public that feel the same way).[17]

Although not unique to them, one sees a strong functional affinity between Asian immigrants and the American capitalist spirit: they are ambitious, self-motivated, hardworking, and entrepreneurial or risk taking. They buy into the ideology of the American dream and the free market economy, and bring and inject creativity, new energy, capital, and skills, thus contributing innovation and productivity to the U.S. economic system.

Legal Status of Immigration

Because of the emphasis on education and hard work, the education level of Asian immigrants is high, even higher than whites, making them the most highly educated group of immigrants in U.S. history. About 61 percent of adults aged 25 to 64 among Asian immigrants have a bachelor's degree or higher, which is double the percentage of other recent immigrants from other parts of the world.

Because of their achievements in higher education and their professional skills, and because current U.S. immigration policy privileges workers with specialized skills (e.g., in the granting of H-1B visas), Asian immigrants resort more to formal legal channels, rather than illegal routes, when immigrating. For example, while Latinos account for a large part of the undocumented population living in the United States, Asian and Pacific Islanders account for about 10 percent of the undocumented population.[18] Recent Asian immigrants are three times more likely than other immigrants to obtain permanent residency status on the basis of employer sponsorship. For example, Asian immigrants in the United States hold about 75 percent of H-1B visas, as many U.S. corporations need highly skilled workers.[19]

Settlement: Ethnic Community

Like other immigrant groups, Asian immigrants have maintained strong ethnic communities in major cities of the United States. The formation and growth of Asian ethnic communities was not only the result of a logical consequence (natural embodiment) of their communal disposition, but also an inevitable response to institutional discrimination and systemic racism. Asian ethnic communities play several important functions for Asian immigrants in settling in a new land:

Function 1. Asian ethnic communities serve as the place of social network and collective agency that are not otherwise available in the United States for Asian immigrants. Immigration and settlement take place through various webs and channels of family, and their social and ethnic networks serve as reliable sources of information and ways to adjust to a new land. These networks connect people across the Pacific; many Asian immigrants come directly to their ethnic communities and stay there until they find better places to settle.

Function 2. Ethnic communities are the place where immigrants' Asian cultural identity is maintained and cultural heritage is celebrated. In response to the challenges of the immigrant life, Asian immigrants mobilize their communal tradition by actively discovering or newly building various solidaric subgroups (which sometimes do not exist in their country) around common roots, networks, and affiliations such as their native hometown in the country of origin, school alumni/ae connection, and church membership. In the postmodern era of dwindling social capital (n.b., Robert Putnam's thesis of "bowling alone") and the demise of community, ethnic community and networks offer a precious source of social capital for Asian immigrants.

Function 3. Asian ethnic communities also become for Asian immigrants the basis for a vibrant enclave economy with its own distinctive distributors, traders, and consumers. Enclave economy constitutes a kind of a subeconomy that is built upon family and various communal and social networks that generate jobs, incomes, and business opportunities, not only domestically but also increasingly transnationally. For example, Korean immigrants work as self-employed business owners of small, family-run, labor-intensive retail stores. They invite coethnic immigrants for joint business ventures or hire their coethnics and provide services within their own and other surrounding ethnic communities to build and sustain vibrant enclave economy. Many Asian Americans, especially newcomers, find their jobs and economic opportunities in enclave economies. Asian professionals (medical doctors, financial advisors, bankers, insurance agents, lawyers) initially perform their practices in their own ethnic community while businessmen open small businesses to serve coethnic customers.

In short, for Asian immigrants, ethnic communities have been the backbone of their social and economic survival and success as it serves as the locus of emotional comfort, a shield from blatant racism, a positive ethnic affiliation, a social and information network, a vibrant enclave economy, and a nurturing social capital and political agency, giving them a greater sense of identity and social control over their immigrant life.[20] By building a distinctive ethnic community, Asian immigrants carve out their own social space where they experience freedom (relative autonomy), cultural learning and self-expression, training and exercise of leadership, and economic subsistence free from white controls.

An Asian American Christian Perspective on Immigration: The Search for a New Social Covenant

So far we have briefly examined the distinctive history, dynamics, and characteristics of Asian immigration in the United States in the context of globalization and transnationalism. What, then, is an appropriate Asian American Christian ethical response to the challenges and issues surrounding Asian immigrants? Despite their hard work, entrepreneurship, optimism and significant contributions, in many cases Asian Americans are still perceived by others as strangers—as outsiders or guests at best who are permitted to stay (as resident aliens) but only under the generosity of the host people. Furthermore, Asian Americans find themselves caught between the intricate, complex, conflicting forces of whites and other minority racial groups, as the stereotype of "model minority" indicates.[21] How can Asian Americans overcome this stereotype? Here, I would offer covenant ethics as an appropriate Asian American Christian ethical response to these problems.

According to Daniel Elazar, "Covenant is a morally informed agreement or pact based on voluntary consent, established by mutual oaths or promises, involving or witnessed by some transcendent higher authority, between peoples or parties."[22] Covenant is a biblically grounded ethical mechanism that brings formerly alienated or unknown parties to a peaceful or reconciled relationship—in our case, a peaceful relationship between immigrants and others in the United States—by overcoming misunderstanding and alienation. Specifying mutual obligations and responsibilities on the basis of agreement, a successful covenant cultivates the goodwill, trust, and communal bonds among different groups.

The Christian idea of the covenant (grounded in the new covenant of Jesus Christ) is based on some core moral premises, in particular the sacredness of human life, unity of humanity in God, reciprocity, and the promotion of the common good:

Premise 1. Covenant is predicated on the conviction that all humans are created in God's image and thus have worth irreducible to any instrumental value. Every person deserves respect and is entitled to basic human rights regardless of nationality, religion, or gender. As we will see shortly, the biblical ethics of hospitality to strangers and the love of neighbors as oneself reflect the deep biblical commitment the sacredness of life.

Premise 2. Covenant is based on the interconnectedness of humanity in God as the creator. Solidarity is woven into the fabric of God's creation. God is the foundation of solidarity—the source of all life and the parent of all humanity, for indeed, all humans are brothers and sisters with each other. As creator and parent, God watches over how we treat each other. The idea of God as the creator is associated with God's sovereignty and ownership of the planet. In Scripture the land belongs to no one group. It is a gift from God. This religious understanding of the land has enormous socioeconomic implications. The land should not be controlled by one group but shared by and with everyone.[23] For Christians the covenant has a new meaning in Jesus Christ. All Christian ethics flow out of the new covenant with God in Jesus Christ—His unconditional love and sacrifice on the cross for us. God's unconditional love compels us to show the same kind of care, love, and compassion to everyone, in particular the poor, the oppressed, and the strangers. Hospitality to the strangers is our naturally grateful response to God's grace.

Premise 3. However, solidarity in creation is not mechanically undifferentiated; it is a highly differentiated and complex, organic solidarity. The metaphor of covenant is particularly effective in addressing immigration in a pluralistic society because the covenant is a nonviolent method of reconciling cultural-social differences, misunderstandings, and competing interests. Covenant respects the freedom and particularity of each participant while seeking the common ground under the assumption that respect for diversity is indispensable for the promotion of the common good.

Premise 4. Dialogue is a primary means that covenant ethics relies on. Identifying common interest and goodwill in each party, dialogue leads each party to have deeper understanding of the other party beyond superficial knowledge or social stereotypes. Dialogue is a method that harmonizes the common good and particularity: covenant forges a new unity out of diversity when the participants reconcile their differences through dialogue. To achieve the agreement (the unity out of diversity), people must respect universal norms (e.g., human rights, equality, solidarity of humanity, justice). Predicated on these universal norms, covenant ethics seeks to build an intentional, new, inclusive moral community beyond the narrow confines of race, ethnicity, class, and sex.

Premise 5. Successful dialogue leads to the agreement of the participants on the specific terms of mutual behaviors and actions, indicating rights and responsibilities. Collective will is formed and strengthened when these covenantal terms are respected and abided by. This means that covenant is not only a mechanism of mutual understanding, but it also could be instrumental to community organizing, networking, and coalition building; it could serve as a building block of local grassroots politics for justice while strengthening the moral infrastructure of civil society.

The covenant offers a holistic biblical category that encompasses and illuminates major ethical values of Scripture in their mutual connections, including those associated with immigration: the sanctity of human life, solidarity, reciprocity, gratitude, care for strangers, and hospitality. In a covenantal framework, hospitality is a concrete practice of one's covenantal relationship with God expressed through generosity toward aliens and strangers. The biblical idea of hospitality is based on gratitude of God's prior deliverance; it is responsive (not proactive by human initiative) to the divine grace. Therefore, no group can claim absolute privilege and exclusive right to the blessings, such as a land, that they received from God.

More importantly, covenant ethics overcomes the difficulty that the ethics of hospitality faces in addressing a moral issue that Asian immigrants face. As discussed previously in the "U.S. Immigration" section, marginalization characterizes the *Sitz im Leben* of Asian Americans; Asian Americans are treated as perpetual strangers—regarded as not eligible to full membership, equal voice, or decision-making power. An ethics of hospitality does not properly address the problem of marginalization that Asian immigrants experience but rather may end up reinforcing it by turning them into the object of pity and even paternalism. By emphasizing the reciprocity between immigrants and the people in the host country, however, covenant ethics challenges the danger of this unequal, hegemonic moral assumption implied in the ethics of hospitality. Unlike the idea of hospitality that highlights only the agency of people in the hosting society, covenant ethics attends to the agency of immigrants as well. From a covenantal perspective, true hospitality should begin with the acceptance of Asian immigrants as actual and full members of a society, rather than treating them merely as the beneficiaries of charity or compassion.

Covenant ethics can help to undo the stereotype of perpetual foreigners and to untangle the triangulation by clarifying moral issues and identifying the responsibility of each group in seeking reconciliation and the common interest. The core moral norms embedded in the covenant—respect for human dignity, solidarity of humanity in God, reciprocity, and dialogue—offer directives for Asian Americans in engaging within their communities and with other racial groups.

Covenant ethics regards all human beings, either immigrants or residents, as free, equal members of God's beloved family. Ephesians 2:14 says, "For he is our peace; in his flesh he has made both groups into one and has broken down the dividing wall, that is, the hostility between us." In other words, in the new covenant in Jesus Christ, there is no Jew or Gentile. Everyone is an equal member of God's family. The idea of covenant offers a theological basis of basic rights but within a far more organic moral imagination and framework. In this covenant Asian immigrants cannot be treated as perpetual foreigners simply due to their physiological and cultural differences, because they are equal members of God's household.

Notions of covenant can facilitate reconciliation by overcoming alienation and enmity through dialogue, mutual understanding, and the exchange of pledges. The covenant directly addresses the question of alienness, alienation, or distrust that is central to the syndrome of perpetual foreigner and the model minority. Covenantal thinking is antithetical to alienness or alienation, for the latter indicates the estrangement or nonexistence of relationship at all, whereas the former means the establishment or reconciliation of relationship on the promise of commitment. Put simply, the covenant is a trust-building mechanism. It brings alienated parties together to mutual trust. As a mechanism of reconciliation, covenant ethics challenges Asian immigrants and all racial groups to actively engage with each other to find common ground rather than avoiding, blaming, or competing with each other. The first step toward a covenantal relationship is to build basic trust through dialogue or an exchange of truthful information by learning about other cultures and discovering common interests.

The following section explores what covenant-making concretely would entail in Asian immigrants' relationships with other racial groups in the United States, first with other minority groups, and then with whites.

Asian American Relationships with Other Minority Groups: Competition versus Coalition

It is important for Asian immigrants and other minorities to get to know one another through dialogue and mutual learning because interracial tensions between Asian immigrants and other minority groups are, to a significant degree, the result of mutual suspicion and misunderstanding resulting from racial stereotyping due to white hegemony.[24] Therefore, clear understanding of the nature and dynamics of triangulation and white hegemony is critical in overcoming alienation and misunderstanding, enabling the groups to move toward reconciliation and covenantal relationships.

Obligations of Asian Immigrants

Asian Americans need to recognize the loaded social meanings and perilous racial-political implications of the myth of model minority. They need to place the myth—its intention and social function—in the context of racial relationship and hegemony in the United States. More specifically, some Asian immigrants perceive other minority groups as uneducated, lazy, and even dangerous due to their very limited observation of some poor inner city residents' behaviors or through their buying into white stereotyping of them through mass media. A major source of this misunderstanding is the limitations of Asian immigrants' historical knowledge. Recent Asian immigrants come to the United States with very little understanding of its racial history and dynamics. Their image of the United States is mostly from Hollywood movies or television shows. A classic example of the deficiency in their knowledge of

U.S. history is that many of them mistakenly think that "real" America is white and therefore they mostly identify the American dream with the white middle-class dream. Their pursuit of the American dream is unknowingly a desire to be like whites—in terms of wealth, power, fame, and lifestyle. In the process, they may not show sufficient interest in lower or underclass people in their community or businesses, which conveys the perception that Asian businesspeople do not have much concern for other residents in their business areas.

This means that Asian immigrants need to learn to empathize with the frustration, pain, and suffering of other minority groups, respecting them as the fellow children of God, and perhaps intentionally to choose to form solidarity and coalitions with other minority groups for the expansion of democracy, human rights, and the freedom and equality of all. In the case of small-business owners in urban areas, they may begin this task of mutual understanding and reconciliation by sharing life and building bonds with the residents in the area. Asian immigrants should strive to learn the history of the community and the specific environment of their businesses and make emotional and moral investments in the community in order to establish a strong and enduring relationship with residents as well as local churches and civic organizations.[25]

Obligations of Other Minority Groups

Misunderstanding of Asian Americans is equally to be found among African Americans and Latinos/as.[26] For example, many African Americans believe that Asian immigrants are either taking their jobs or expending the financial resources that they badly need and that Asian immigrants receive special treatments from the government or banks.[27] They may also mistakenly believe Asian Americans do not experience racism. Because of this misinformation, some Black Nationalists harbor strong enmity or jealousy toward Asian immigrants, viewing them as exploiters or foreigners who do not deserve their respect.

This information is not true. As we have seen, many Asian immigrants draw upon their own ethnic, class, and human resources (education, skills, and financial capital that they bring with themselves) for their business activities rather than receiving secret special treatments from the government or banks. Some work from sixty to seventy hours per week to save enough money for the down payment of their own small businesses. They do not extensively compete for jobs with other racial minorities because many Asian immigrants open businesses in their ethnic communities and/or blighted areas where no one wants to go or work in a professional or knowledge-based industry.[28] Asian immigrant businesses bring benefits to the communities by revalorizing the urban spaces, creating jobs for workers, and stimulating the local economy.[29]

In addition, not all Asian immigrants live affluently; many struggle with poverty. Many of their small businesses are facing stiff challenges due to dwindling resources and growing competition within and without their communities as the Great Recession continues. Racism is not the pain and injustice of African Americans or Latinos/as alone. Asian Americans are also the victims of racial discrimination and stereotyping.

Other minorities should not treat Asian immigrants as foreigners. The history of their immigration goes back several centuries, and they are here to stay. Other minorities should show hospitality and inclusiveness toward Asian immigrants to build solidarity with them. Asian immigrants should not be the target of the frustration, anger, or racial insensitivity of other minority groups.

One very recent example of such insensitivity is the incident around Jeremy Lin, an Asian American NBA player. Two sports commentators, ESPN writer Anthony Federico and the anchor Max Bretos, used racial slurs in referring to Lin as "Chink in Armor," though both apologized later under criticism. This incident belies that racism is not just the white-black issue, and that racism against Asian Americans is serious.

From a covenantal perspective, racism against Asian immigrants contradicts the core covenantal values of dignity, solidarity, and reciprocity; it not only denigrates the dignity of Asians but also undermines the unity of humanity, harming all of us.

Our brief observation shows that while victimized by white racism, ironically both Asian immigrants and other minority groups internalize and perpetuate white stereotypes toward each other. They see others through the lens of white stereotype rather than making the effort to discover them with their own, fresh eyes. Asian Americans and other minority groups should cooperate to overcome these stereotypes and misunderstandings and to confront white hegemony. They should remember that major progress in a political realm and the fight against hegemony is not possible without the support of other minority groups—their experience, networks, and organizations.

As aforementioned, the process of covenanting usually includes the development of the specific terms of interaction, namely the guidelines of mutual behavior and actions. Following are some possible terms that Christian churches of Asian immigrants and other minority groups may consider in their covenantal relationship in order to overcome stereotypes and to build mutual trust:

1. Respect the dignity of the other groups and their members. Remember that every person is created in the image of God and thus deserves proper respect and protection of his or her rights.
2. Learn and understand the history, culture, struggles, and aspirations of the other racial groups in order to reduce mutual misunderstandings and overcome the stereotypes.
3. Practice zero tolerance toward any form of racism and discrimination: when a church becomes aware that one of its members discriminates or uses racial slurs, it condemns the behavior as inconsistent with the gospel.
4. Collectively work for justice, recognizing the common stakes that all minority groups share with each other.
5. Include the other minority groups in various public discussions and conversations taking place in every level of society.[30]

Asian American Relationship with Whites: Inculturation versus Interculturation

Obligation of Whites

In U.S. history immigrants have always been suspected of being a threat to the unity and homogeneity of the hosting community. There is some legitimate concern behind the suspicion because the lifestyle and the culture of immigrants are obviously different from those of the host country, and their differences challenge and contest the cultural boundaries and social customs of the hosting community.[31] This fear and suspicion is usually expressed in the form of nativism, especially in the time of economic difficulty, demanding the complete assimilation of immigrants to the culture of a hosting country by giving up their ethnic cultures and identities.

Although whites' psychological fear of or anxiety toward otherness is partly understandable, nativism is closer to the desire to maintain hegemony than it is to an expression of a genuine concern about national unity. This is evident by the fact that white nativists demand complete assimilation yet have never accepted non-European immigrants as full, equal members of the society. This hypocrisy has been a consistent pattern—demanding the loyalty of racial minority groups while simultaneously segregating or discriminating against them.

This hegemony of whites creates a deep social tension within Asian Americans—a tension between their communal tradition and assimilation under white hegemony. The question is how to reconcile the conflict between assimilation and ethnic identity/tradition, especially when white suspicion of Asian American loyalty is still acute. A moral dilemma is that because Asian immigrants rely on their communal traditions (family, ethnic community, enclave economy) for survival and meaning, they are suspected of ethnocentrism; when they try to assimilate, however, they are still not fully accepted; furthermore, they lose the cultural source of their survival and resistance against racism.

In the era of transnationalism and globalization, the idea of uncritical assimilation is not plausible. It is not practical for immigrants to cut their ties with their countries of origin and eschew their cultural identity, customs, and mother tongue. In U.S. history assimilation has seldom taken place in such a way. Instead, a certain preservation of distinct cultural identities has been the case. We need to alter our conceptual framework from acculturation to interculturation, for which the covenantal idea of *E Pluribus Unum* (out of many, one) offers rich moral resources. The idea of covenant is very fruitful because growing interdependence and multicultural reality keep the pressure on every group to celebrate their particularity while also forging social unity on the basis of God's norms of justice, equality, and peace.

Unlike inculturation, interculturation is reciprocal rather than unidirectional; it is also based on equality rather than superior-inferior relationship. Interculturality is based on the principle of *convivir* (a Spanish word that means "to live with" or life-together). According to Orlando Espín, "*Convivir*, 'to live with,' implies, among other things, that those who *conviven* are actually present with and to one another for a sufficiently prolonged period of time and, further, that their presence with and to one another engages them with and in one another's daily lives in ways that each considers sufficiently meaningful and sufficiently mutually respectful."[32] As the United States anticipates a major demographic change around 2040 where whites will no longer be the majority, intercultural learning is critical for justice and peace among diverse racial groups in the country. Rather than privileging their cultural patterns and social customs as the norm for all others, whites also need to learn how to live together with others by learning cultures and histories of other racial-ethnic groups. They should accept that Asian Americans would not be Asian Americans without this particular flavor and spice of life coming from their culture and tradition.[33]

Obligations of Asian Immigrants

Asian Immigrants have moral obligations to the nation and other groups. Scripture teaches that strangers and sojourners have to carry out all social responsibilities that come from their residence.

Obligation 1. Asian Americans should reject white hegemony. Rejecting hegemony may not sound like a covenantal obligation, but actually it is; it is the expression of tough love toward whites. Rejection of hegemony also demands that Asian Americans dismantle their internalization of white standards of beauty, goodness, and stereotypes toward other minority groups. Racial hegemony works in disguise to the extent that white symbols, standards, and justifications are naturally accepted by the minority groups.[34]

Asian Americans should confront racism and assert their equality before the law through collective actions. While African Americans, through the civil rights movement, have established certain standards of racial sensibility and respect by the media, Asian Americans are still struggling to achieve such a level. Resignation, passivity, or exercise of the virtue of deference are not the best way. History shows that the powerful do not voluntarily share their power. Equal respect and treatment must be demanded: unfortunately the idiom is still true that the squeaky wheel gets the oil. As far as white racism is concerned, proving their adequacy to whites through self-improvement or being a model minority goes nowhere; Asian Americans have already proved themselves through hard work, educational and professional achievements, and myriad contributions to U.S. society, yet they are still treated as foreigners and discriminated against. Given their lack of political power, Asian Americans need to focus their efforts on political participation and representation. Instead of occupying themselves with economic success alone, they need to translate their education and economic power into political power by empowering the existing Asian American advocacy groups and building coalitions with other racial minority groups.

Asian Americans need to own up to a new sense of responsibility as their numerical power and economic influence grow. Their communal and family orientations and personal economic success should not deter them from participating actively in political and civic activities to protect their own rights as well as to enhance the common good.

Jeremiah's teaching (29:4-7) for the exiles is very instructive for Asian immigrants in this respect. The Israelites in their exile faced the danger of being self-enclosed and tribalistic—detaching themselves from the issues of Babylon and remaining nostalgic for their homeland, collectively introverted. Jeremiah instructed them not to do so but rather to actively participate in the life of Babylon while contributing to its common welfare. This teaching is relevant for Asian immigrants in their life in the United States. Although they face alienation and discrimination, and they may be occasionally nostalgic for their countries of origin or remain with their ethnic communities, Asian immigrants also need to overcome these challenges and actively participate in and contribute to the democratic, multicultural America.

Asian Americans should use their rising political and economic power to influence the future course of the nation and to promote justice for those who are historically oppressed. This suggestion is plausible given the fact that Asian Americans today will exercise significant political power in coming years. Although Asian Americans made up 5.1 percent of the population in 2012, they will grow up to 8 percent of the total U.S. population by 2041. Furthermore, record numbers of Asian Americans are eligible to vote today. Their voting-eligible population grew by 16 percent over four years, from 6.9 million voters in 2008 to 8 million voters in 2012. Even so, more than half of eligible Asian American voters did not exercise their right on election day.[35] This means that more active political and civic participation of Asian Americans is needed.

Obligation 2. At the same time, Asian Americans need to continue to affirm, nurture, and celebrate their cultural identity and heritage through the empowerment of ethnic community and building of a pan–Asian American coalition. Their distinctive history and culture should be not only "the first point of reference from which to know and say what is [theirs]," but also the base from which to reach out to others.[36] To do so is to walk a fine line. While ethnic culture should be respected, the culture and its particularity should not be absolutized, nor demand exclusive loyalty from members.[37] Frank Wu notes,

[T]he integration of Asian Americans should further integration, not Asian Americans personally. Our empowerment cannot be for our sake alone, to acquire power and install Asian faces in political office. We must have a principled agenda if we are to be a moral group. The substance of Asian American political identity cannot be raw self-interest if we are to be legitimate at all.[38]

Asian immigrants, in particular, need to be careful lest their communal tradition, a major source of their survival and success, further complicate their relationships with other racial groups (racial triangulation). They should keep a delicate balance between celebration of their cultural tradition and the acknowledgment of the contingency of their own culture. That is, in enhancing their collective identity and political agency (which is necessary to counter white hegemony), their communal tradition should not deter dialogue and cooperation with other racial groups for the common good and deepening of life together.

Obligation 3. Covenant ethics provides some good insights on how Christians should address the practices of goose families, maternity tourism, and parachute kids that we discussed above. Before jumping to condemnation, we should understand the social contexts of these practices. They are, after all, the responses to a growing global pressure for survival and success (amplified by the traditional Confucian emphasis on education that is revered especially in East Asian cultures) in the midst of intensifying competition. All three practices, distinctive in the era of transnational migration, are driven by a long-term strategy for economic success in a global society where market logic and materialism triumph. Citizenship and competitive education in the United States are considered valuable assets for not only children but also their parents; the U.S.-born babies and parachute kids offer the parents future opportunities to enter into the United States because their children provide legal connections or social networks that could make their entrance and settlement in the United States easier.[39] In particular, the phenomena of goose families and parachute kids reveal the desperation of people living in small, resource-scarce countries such as Korea and Taiwan where human capital (i.e., education) is virtually the only resource for global competition.

However sympathetic we may be for the reasons behind these practices, ultimately they are not commendable from a covenantal ethics perspective. No matter how justifiable the motivations behind parachute kids, such practices are undesirable because they make the family or well-being of children secondary to economic success in a capitalist society. These practices instrumentalize and commodify education for personal, familial, and even national success, for which even the sanctity of family is compromised, with a profound devaluation and alienation of social relationships in general. From a covenantal perspective, educational pursuits should neither override the harmony and health of the family nor the psychological and physical well-being of children, for the family remains foundational for the emotional and moral well-being and development of its members.

What now of maternity tourism? Although the practice is not technically illegal, it is not consistent with the spirit of U.S. immigration law. It abuses a legal loophole in that the law was not originally written in any awareness of a highly mobile society where a rich pregnant woman could visit the United States only to obtain citizenship for her baby. This practice violates the covenantal rules of reciprocity and solidarity. From a covenantal perspective, citizenship—a key marker of membership—and responsibility cannot be separated. Membership always entails certain corresponding duties. Driven by crass self-interest, maternity tourism obtains rights (free public education, legal protections) without having to discharge any duties (paying taxes). Hence, it undermines the solidarity of a society where all the members are supposed to work together for the advance of the common good. The practice also violates fairness because it is the option available to rich people alone, thus alienating those who cannot afford it.

Toward the Beloved Community of E Pluribus Unum

The federalist vision of *E Pluribus Unum* (out of many, one) is the organic metaphor that overcomes the two extremes of assimilation (a melting pot) and pluralization (balkanization). This vision rejects any sectarianism, tribalism, white hegemony, or racial violence that would deny the unity of humanity and any hegemonic ideology and tyrannical power that denies diversity of human cultures. This organic vision taps into and draws out the best potential of each racial group and the creative energies and goodwill of people for the unity and the common good of the nation. In this moral framework, *Pluribus* does not mean disorder, just as *Unum* should not be tyranny. The vision seeks the unity out of diversity, not by imposing, but through inviting voluntary participation of many different groups. The metaphor of *E Pluribus Unum* is covenantal in nature; it envisions a society that builds unity among diverse groups through mutual agreement.

This metaphor is more appropriate than "a melting pot" or "a salad bowl" in dealing with the tension between assimilation and identity. It is more organic than the metaphor of a salad bowl while more deferential to the freedom/particularity of each group than the metaphor of a melting pot. Stressing the particularity of culture, custom, and identity of a racial group, the metaphor of a salad bowl does not emphasize enough the significance of the common good and unity, including reciprocity among different groups, while the metaphor of a melting pot denies the significance of the distinctiveness of each racial and ethnic group.

The vision of *E Pluribus Unum* indicates that people of all different races are called to build a free, inclusive, solidaric community in the United States. When globalization raises a fundamental question about the boundary of human community and its membership, this motto offers a plausible common vision by saying that racial justice, prosperity, peace, and justice cannot be achieved by one racial group but requires the collective efforts of all groups. I believe that this vision is relevant because all groups have the same stake in the well-being of the nation as the latter is increasingly multicultural and no one group will be the majority soon. Common sense attests that no single culture should be idealized as "the definitive locus of truth or as the best vehicle for the expression of truth."[40]

Because globalization, high mobility, and the evolution of communication technologies are loosening the tie between rights and responsibility, isolating individuals from their families and communities, Asian immigrant churches need to preach this covenantal vision as God's vision for humanity because it reflects the Christian ecclesiological metaphor of the body of Christ (1 Cor 12). As the spiritual and moral center of immigrant life, Asian immigrant churches have a profound calling and responsibility for reconciliation and just peacemaking among different racial groups. Through their prophetic and priestly ministry, they can make a difference in the life of Asian immigrants. In particular, they may preach a subversive hope for God's kingdom and the sacredness of human life against white hegemony while serving as the ambassadors of reconciliation in the interracial, interethnic relationships;[41] they could work for the making and renewal of the national covenant between Asian immigrants and other racial groups by utilizing their denominational connections and religious networks.

Covenant ethics equips Asian immigrants for the task of active civic engagements and a new theological appropriation of their communal traditions. When equipped with covenantal vision and ethics, Asian Americans will avoid the pitfalls of both individualism and collectivism and continue to contribute to the betterment of both their new home and the world with the rich resources and energy they brought with them across the Pacific.

DISCUSSION QUESTIONS

1. In comparison to other immigrant groups, such as Latinas/os, what are the distinctive cultural characteristics of Asian immigrants in the United States?

2. How have racism and such distinctive stereotypes of Asian Americans as model minority or perpetual foreigner been complicating the cultural-political relationships of Asian immigrants with other racial minority groups?

3. What particular Asian cultural features do you think are operating under the practices of goose families, maternity tourism, and parachute kids, and what are your critical ethical responses to these practices as Christians?

4. How is the idea of the covenant, or a similar notion such as *E Pluribus Unum*, specifically helpful for Asian immigrants' constructive relationship with other racial groups?

The Environment

HANNAH KA

My mother was the matriarch not only of her human family but also of all other organic and inorganic members of our household. She ingrained in me how to be friendly to our surroundings by investing her time and physical energy for and with them. She gathered the last cycle of the laundry water to clean the bathroom. She carefully unwrapped the gifts she had received from others to reuse the wrapping paper. She taught me to finish my food so as not to create too much waste, and put the food scraps in her compost to make nutritious fertilizer for her vegetable garden. She befriended not only our birds and dogs but also the rocks, plants, and soil. Although confined in her last days to a high-rise condominium complex due to the socioeconomic environment of South Korea, my mother lived then as she always had with the deepest concern for her surroundings to which her life was deeply indebted. While her life was and continues to be one of the most invaluable texts in my search for an Asian American Christian environmental ethic, her individual story can be broadened through shared experiences among other Asians and Asian Americans. For example, the eulogy given by Taiwanese American ethicist Grace Yia-Hei Kao on the occasion of her Taiwanese grandmother's funeral vividly recollects her memories of her grandmother meticulously salvaging grains of rice from a dust pan after sweeping the kitchen floor, cleaning them, and storing them for later use.[1]

Now I have come to believe that my mother and Kao's grandmother were living in accordance with sound eco-theological principles in their embrace of the ethical values espoused by nature, their cultures, Christianity, and their own spirituality. No matter how fearful the signs of global ecological destruction, they continued to salvage grains of rice and scrub the bathtub with laundry water. Although Kao and I live an ocean away from our foremothers, our relationships as well as our Asian American Christian environmental ethics, to a certain recognizable degree, continue to bear a resemblance to their eco-theological life principles. Yet, following Kwok Pui-lan's suggested methodology for doing postcolonial feminist theology, I will begin by reviewing how the Christian tradition has traditionally responded to the environment before elaborating on its significance for shaping Asian and Asian American Christian environmental ethics.[2] Then I will find an intersection where Christian theology can converge with Asian and Asian American understandings and experiences of the environment.

Canvassing the Range of Christian Responses to the Environment

What have we heard so far from ecological theologians and Christian environmental ethicists within the contexts of Europe, North America, and their colonies? After centuries of globalized industrialization, human residents of this planet increasingly became concerned with environmental deterioration during the latter half of the twentieth century. In particular, two indictments alarmed Westernized Christianity, prompting serious responses from churches and theologians. In 1967, in "The Historical Roots of Our Ecologic Crisis," Professor of History Lynn White Jr. argued that Christianity was responsible for "our ecologic crisis," highlighting the fact that since the late Middle Ages, many Christians had become negligent in their concern for this world as a result of Western Christianity's "implicit faith in perpetual progress," disenchantment of nature, anthropocentrism, and unbalanced emphasis upon the afterlife.[3] In 1974 Australian philosopher John Passmore made a similar claim that Christian belief that the next world is more important than this one renders Christians less obligated to this world, even to the extent that otherworldly piety fosters in them "a hostility toward nature."[4]

While we can bracket for the purposes of this essay the legitimacy of White's and Passmore's arguments,[5] it is important to underscore the ways in which the Christian tradition within European and North American contexts have responded defensively to these criticisms. In admitting that historical Christianity and Westernized Christianity are complicitous in the deterioration of the environment, Christian scholars have begun to reinterpret biblical passages to formulate a theory of Christian stewardship to illuminate humans' place on earth in relationship to God and to see how our responsibilities extend not only to humanity as a whole but also to all of creation. They have also anticipated with hope the future development of ecological theologies and Christian environmental ethics based upon the ways in which Christian theo-ethical reflection has historically been responsive to contemporary issues and concerns.[6] According to Roman Catholic process theologian John F. Haught, ecological theology in the Christian tradition can be categorized into one of three types: the tradition-centered (or "apologetic") approach, the sacramental approach, and the cosmic promise (or the "cosmological-eschatological") approach.[7]

The first of these approaches, the tradition-centered approach, recognizes that Christianity has neglected "the wealth of ecologically relevant material in the Bible and Christian tradition," and thus directs its theological focus on retrieving "this lost wisdom" within the Christian tradition to address current environmental issues.[8] The most common biblical bases for responsible Christian stewardship include, but are not limited to, the creation story recounted in Genesis and the lived presence of Jesus himself depicted in the gospel as demonstrating a compassionate relationship to all of creation. Christian churches and theologians within the scope of the tradition-centered approach most likely begin their advocacy for Christian stewardship with Genesis 1–2 where God creates not only humans but also the whole world and then puts humans in charge of the garden of Eden. Despite its creative interpretations of the Scriptures and Christian theologies, the tradition-centered approach can be faulted for falling short of making a profound impact on the current human manipulation of the earth for a few reasons.

First, more often than not, it is those authors with more conservative leanings who employ this approach in calling for responsible Christian stewardship. Their discussions generally take place within European and North American countries and are framed implicitly by viewing the rest of the world from the perspective of their own colonial interests and histories.[9] The upshot is that this approach does not adequately address the culture of hyperconsumption in the economic north that demands heavier resource extraction and causes heavier pollution in the economic south. Put simply, their discussions remain more focused on the interpersonal level of environmental ethics per se, without undertaking other related social issues. Second, it is also difficult, or impossible, for these scholars to engage in dialogue with others whose perspectives and life situations differ from those of European and North American

Christians. Third, when addressing current environmental crises, the authors who employ the tradition-centered approach often utilize an anthropocentric binary framework that consists of the dominating and the dominated, the oppressor and the oppressed, humanity and nature. While its call for responsible Christian stewardship highlights agential responsibility of humans, it fails to revere the agential power that the rest of creation has upon us.

Despite the contribution this tradition-centered approach makes to an interpretation of Scripture and theology, Haught claims that this approach alone is not enough and must be supplemented by two other approaches, namely the sacramental and the cosmic promise approaches.[10] The second of Haught's three approaches, the sacramental approach, views nature as a place where the divine is revealed and where all forms of life are interrelated with one another and with the divine. When nature is seen as such, the natural world can no longer be manipulated solely for human purposes. Within this approach the traditional Christian understanding of sin and redemption is broadened to include humanity's relationship to nature, without which we lose "an impression of the divine" or "a symbolic disclosure of God" revealed in nature.[11] Although this sacramental theology reunites humans with the rest of long-estranged nature, and, therefore, allows us to attend to the ecological crisis, Haught asserts that this approach alone, which is deficient in its biblical foundation for eschatological fulfillment, cannot serve as "a distinctively Christian ecological theology."[12]

John Hart's *Sacramental Commons* fits into Haught's sacramental approach. In *Sacramental Commons*, Hart criticizes the anthropocentric stewardship model and underlines the sacredness of all places and of nature. From an arguably more solid Christian standpoint, Hart ascribes sacramental meanings to all of God's creation by developing a "creatiocentric consciousness" that emphasizes the interrelatedness and interdependence of all creation.[13] In order to present an ecocentric ethic of relation, he investigates how the nature of interrelatedness among all creation is voiced in other times and traditions by reflecting on St. Francis of Assisi; two Native American leaders, Black Elk and Phillip Deere; and secular naturalist John Muir. Hart's articulation of the sacramental approach is invaluable in affirming the interrelatedness and sacredness (sacramentality) of all of creation, especially for those whose traditions are grounded in the sacraments. Yet I suggest that his ecological theology, as expressed in Haught's analysis of the sacramental approach in general, is not well-grounded in Christian eschatological promise and fulfillment.

Complementary to both the tradition-centered and the sacramental approaches is the cosmic promise approach, the last of Haught's three-part typology. This approach broadens the scope of eschatological promise once made to Israel and to the church, now toward "the entire universe," by arguing that "the divine promise . . . pertains not only to the 'people of God' but also . . . to the 'whole of creation.' "[14] Thus, subduing and taking dominion over the earth is not only "a violation of nature's sacramentality" but also a denial of God's eschatological promise for all of the creation.[15] As such, Haught himself places a heavier emphasis upon the cosmological-eschatological approach whose complementary synthesis of the first two will surely strengthen future Christian ecological theologies.

Christian theologians Willis Jenkins, Jürgen Moltmann, and Sallie McFague provide concrete examples of the tradition-centered and the sacramental approaches, finding their complement in an environmental ethics of cosmic promise. In *Ecologies of Grace*, Jenkins embraces the cosmological-eschatological approach by integrating narratives of salvation for Christian environmental ethics by means of three ecologies of grace: eco-justice theologies (sanctification), stewardship theologies (redemption), and ecological spiritualities (deification).[16] In *The Source of Life*, Moltmann modifies a sacramental approach embedded in the cosmological-eschatological approach. While affirming the sacredness of all creation as an indwelling place of God that is sustained by God's spirit, Moltmann also finds hope for "the rebirth of the whole cosmos" through the resurrection of Christ to eternal life.[17] Similar to Moltmann's work, yet more nuanced with a feminist perspective, Sallie McFague synthesizes Haught's three approaches in *The Body of God*. With an emphasis on the significance of embodiment, she rectifies the issues imposed on historical Christianity by White by arguing that the universe, as the body of God, is the locus of redemption within the common creation story, thus providing a rich rationale for Christian environmental ethics. While her ecological theology still rests in Haught's third category, her cosmological-eschatological approach alludes to a new possibility for a dialogue with other cultural traditions, and thus is open to a fourth categorization of ecological theology. Therefore, McFague's *The Body of God* holds particular importance for Asian American Christian ethicists in regard to the manner of Christian faith and environmental ethical practice within Asian American Christian communities.

McFague highlights the significance of body by retrieving early Christianity's emphasis on embodiment concealed in the Westernized interpretation of the Bible. By recognizing the world as "our meeting place with God," where God's transcendence is physically expressed and immanently embodied, McFague restores its sacred meaning by reclaiming all the physical aspects of life in the universe, which she calls "the body of God."[18] McFague's ecological theology is among the most interesting ecofeminist approaches to environmental problems today. Her use of an organic model of cosmology can inspire Asian American theologians and ethicists to look into other organic models of cosmology abundant in the lived experiences of many Asians and Asian Americans. Her eco-theology, therefore, can function as a point of engagement with Asian and Asian American feminists and theologians, while her application of this reclaimed importance of the physical aspects of life remains pertinent to deconstructing the traditional theology and to underlining postcolonial Asian American Christian theologies. McFague's organic model of cosmology, revised anthropology, Christology, and eschatology can be particularly useful for Asian Americans for the reasons I will further explore in the next section. My analytical retrieval of her work will be worked out in the third section with greater complexity as a point of departure for my own construction of Asian American Christian environmental ethics.

How Are Asian Americans Specifically Invested in This Topic? And Why?

Many Asian American Christian communities have been disproportionately focused on the transcendental God who alone is in complete charge of his creation (independently of humans), on salvation that is available only for humans (exclusive of the rest of creation), and on the divine immanence (too spiritualized) that does not fully encompass the socioeconomic, political, cultural, and physical aspects of all life. In order to rectify this unbalanced emphasis on this anthropocentric, otherworldly salvation prevalent in the majority of Asian American Christian communities, many Asian and Asian American Christian theologians have emerged among progressive Christian voices over the past few decades. Theologians and biblical scholars including C. S. Song, Peter C. Phan, Sang Hyun Lee, Andrew S. Park, Kwok Pui-lan, Gale

Yee, Rita Nakashima Brock, and Kah-Jin Jeffrey Kuan, among others, have made tremendous contributions to Asian American Christian theology and biblical interpretation with respect to Asian American identity, spirituality, racism, sexism, sexuality, classism, poverty, immigration, democratization, war and peace, economic globalization, and postcolonial critique of imperialism. They are also now nurturing the next generation of Asian American Christian scholars.

While making explicit impact on the socioeconomic, political, and cultural aspects of the lives of Asian Americans, the challenges that Asian American theological and biblical scholarship has proposed to Asian American environmental ethics remain implicitly focused on human issues with few exceptions.[19] To these Asian American Christian communities whose theo-ethical interests are more devoted to human issues, McFague's ecological theology can speak more deliberately to our Asian American Christian understanding of God, Christ, and salvation in our relationship to the environment as well as invite Asian American Christians to be more invested in the environment. Through a critical engagement with McFague's ecological theology, progressive Asian American Christian theologians and ethicists will surely give birth to a unique Asian American Christian environmental ethic that may speak to the heart of many Asian American Christians.

The relevance of McFague's ecological theology in constructing an Asian American Christian environmental ethic includes her organic model of cosmology, anthropology, Christology, and eschatology. Initially intended to correct the traditional model, McFague's organic model of cosmology nevertheless disrupts many Asian American Christians' unexamined adaptation of the traditional, anthropocentric, and hierarchical binary human/nature relation, and, subsequently, our justification for unilateral dominion over the rest of creation. After criticizing the traditional model of spiritualized, Christian, anthropocentric, homogeneous, and hierarchical cosmology for its failure to recognize differences and diversities of life, McFague offers an organic model of cosmology, in which diverse forms of life are radically interdependent and interconnected.[20] Once diversities and differences are fully recognized, a theology of nature gives rise to a new meaning of salvation closely linked to creation, available to all aspects of its diverse forms, directing us toward acknowledging the unity of its "infinite differences and diversity."[21] With its compatibility with other organic models of cosmology, her ecological theology also inspires Asian Americans to look into other cultural models of organic cosmology.

McFague's revised anthropology is informative to Asian American Christians in the sense that it offers an insight into how Christian faith can be reconciled with postmodern science to embody the common creation story within the context of a long evolutionary process. Whereas postmodern science assigns the evolutionary process on this planet Earth to billions of years, the common creation story recounts it over only thousands of years. When she introduces five features of the common creation story to suggest humans' place in the scheme of things, humans' place is radically diminished, especially because the human species is placed not only as one among many other organic and inorganic inhabitants and existents but also in relation to the fifteen-billion-year evolutionary history of the universe.[22] Hence, it is clear that humans cannot be portrayed as masters of the world.

With respect to Christology and eschatology, which are relevant to Asian American Christians' move toward an ecological theology, the universe for McFague as the body of God is also "the place of salvation." That is, God's transcendence can only be revealed to us immanently in the cosmic Christ whose liberating, salvific, compassionate, empowering, and all-inclusive love is expressed immanently in creation as the physical body of God and is extended to all creatures. McFague's Christology directs us toward welcoming this extended meaning of salvation that is available not only to the human species but also to all other forms of life. Salvation is no longer exclusively available to humans. Nor does it point us to otherworldly salvation alone, apart from our own and others' physical bodies. Rather, salvation can be realized on earth in "the healthy functioning of all inhabitants and systems of the planet" through "our solidarity with other life-forms."[23] Closely related to this revised Christology, McFague further suggests a new eschatology, one that does not look forward to the otherworld, but envisions a hope for a new creation here and now.[24] Accordingly, this eschatology obliges humans to live as the body of God by transforming our current ways of life and taking responsibility for this eschatological vision in the continuing creation narrative.[25]

Delineated as such, McFague's Christology and eschatology can collaborate with the emerging progressive Asian American Christian theologians to undercut the conservative theological beliefs of Asian American Christians commonly found in many immigrant churches, and help these Asian American Christians find God's redemptive power through the cosmic Christ whose radical expressions of love are immanently embodied in all forms of life in the universe. This new meaning of salvation, made available to all forms of life, now invites Asian American Christians to join other ecological theologians and Christian environmental ethicists to participate in the continuing creation, the cosmic Christ's redemptive love for all other life, and an ongoing journey toward salvation here and now.

Once Asian American Christians are fully aware of our interdependence and interrelatedness in the physical body of God, there is no way for Asian Americans not to be invested in the environmental ethics both locally and globally. Let me offer a tangible example. Asian and/or Asian American ways of eating, especially feasting, requires a critical theological and ethical reflection on our food culture and on our patterns of consumption, which directly result in the degradation of environment both around the corner and around the globe. Feasting, sometimes extravagant feasting, is integral to the cultural lives of many Asians, Asian Americans, and other people of the Asian diaspora, from routine gatherings of family and friends on cultural holidays and anniversaries of the death of loved ones, to celebrations of major milestones in life, such as the first birthday, the wedding, the sixtieth or the seventieth birthdays, the funeral, and the like. These feastings fuel the ever-increasing material and food consumption among many Asians and Asian Americans.[26] Added to these are the weekly church meals provided at many immigrant religious communities, especially in Korean American churches.

These Asian and Asian American cultural practices generate a further destruction of the ecosystem; specifically, the excessive use of disposable dinnerware (e.g., Styrofoam cups, plates, containers, and disposable chopsticks) further aggravates the natural environment. Although feasting is a part of nearly all cultures, this excessive use of disposable tableware during communal meals becomes a special environmental concern for many Asian Americans.[27] Asian American consumption patterns parallel, perhaps exceed, the patterns of food consumption in the economic north, which has negatively influenced the agriculture in the economic south by destroying "the cultural diversity of food and the biological diversity of crops," thus impairing the local environment.[28] The excessive consumption of seafood and fish of many in the Asian American feasting culture, along with the demands made by other racial/ethnic groups in the economic north, may have a direct impact on fishery farming in Southwest Asia, causing reduced food security for local Asians and ecological destruction in Asia.[29] These environmental issues resulting from current food consumption patterns in the economic north cannot be confined to exploited Asian countries; in reality it is a critical condition that we are experiencing together around the globe and thus must face together.

As one of many Asian American ethicists who have inherited eco-theological life principles from our forebearers, our living today in an overconsuming culture without deep ethical reflection makes me increasingly uneasy. As mentioned earlier, Asian American environmental concerns are not as explicitly and fully theologized as other social ethical issues have been. Yet environmental awareness has not been completely absent from the lives of Asian Americans and their Christian communities. On a practical level, for example, for the sake of animal welfare and the health of marine ecology, many Chinese and Taiwanese Americans, including Taiwanese American film director Ang Lee, join their counterparts in various parts of Asia in standing against shark finning and boycotting the consumption of shark fin soup (a delicacy commonly served in high-end weddings, state banquets, or other formal events).[30] Some Asian American Christian congregations also make a fervent effort to reduce the material consumption and food waste in their weekly church meals.

On a theological level, Chinese American theologian Kwok Pui-lan addresses the impact of environmental degradation on "the lives of marginalized women."[31] Even though environmental ethics per se is not her primary research area, she is nonetheless deeply invested in how colonialism and the concept of empire have made an impact on the socioeconomic, political, and environmental lives of the colonized. Kwok also offers an invaluable tool for those who wish to develop Asian American Christian environmental ethics; her methodology of postcolonial imagination allows Asian and Asian American ethicists to weave Christian themes through particular experiences of one's community to reconstruct postcolonial Christian theologies and environmental ethics.[32] Despite her efforts, the problem continues unabated because of Asian American Christians' lack of attention to her postcolonial theological articulation.

Korean ecofeminist theologian Chung Hyun Kyung exemplifies such a postcolonial imagination of Buddhist-Christian eco-theology, as she concludes *The Letter from the Future: Goddess-spell According to Hyun Kyung* with a salimist manifesto. In this volume she subversively uses the Korean noun *salim*, meaning "making things alive," which has been often imposed on women in the household, and identifies herself as a "salimist" or a Korean ecofeminist. According to Chung, a salimist whose gift is "making things alive" also takes good care of the earth; salimists strive to make things alive by "creating peace, health, and abundant living for the family (the very large extended family of all forms of life) and a beautiful living environment."[33] Salimists touch everything and recycle whenever possible, they are peace activists, and they love women, nature, earth, and goddess.[34] Chung's interfaith, transnational, and postcolonial imagination candidly captures the lives of my mother, Kao's grandmother, and many other Asian women whose lifelong dedication to a respectful relationship with the environment is truly genuine. This will certainly shed light on those who are losing their cultural wisdom of being salimists in this globalized hyperconsumption culture. Stated as such, Asian and Asian American concerns for the environment are not only local but also global. Their concerns are expressed in their daily practices as well as in their theological articulation.

The export-oriented food production in Southwest Asia has a direct environmental impact on the consumers in the economic north as well as on the residents of the Asian region. The Chinese food culture expressed in shark fin soup and the Korean celebration of life expressed in milestone birthdays raise environmental concerns not only for Asian Americans but also for all global citizens whose lives are both directly and indirectly involved in the well-being of the ecosystems of our shared planet. Consequently, an Asian and Asian American approach to the environment voiced in this chapter cannot help but be a transnational approach. At the same time, as diverse as are the environmental concerns around Asian and Asian American food cultures, this transnational Asian and Asian American approach to the environment must embrace diverse perspectives. While constructing a transnational Asian Christian approach to the environment in this chapter, I will not attempt to provide "the" Asian and/or Asian American Christian approach to the environment, as if there could be only one valid approach. Instead, the Asian American Christian environmental ethic that I offer will be firmly grounded in my social, cultural, and religious location—a first-generation Korean immigrant Protestant Christian living in the United States—in the hope that other Asian American Christians will offer their distinctive wisdom on our shared mission of constructing Asian American Christian environmental ethics.

Developing an Asian American Christian Ethics Approach to the Environment from a Korean American Christian Perspective

In constructing an Asian American Christian approach to the environment, let me begin by stating the following: *humans cannot survive even a day without the animals, the plants, and all other inorganic and organic existents on earth, while others can all flourish without humans.* This statement may sound parallel to, if not identical with, McFague's statement: "[t]he full truth is that we cannot live without the plants and animals and the ecosystem that supports us all" and "the plants do very nicely without us, . . . but we would quickly perish without them."[35] Yet there is a significant difference in our further elaborations of this dependent relationship. In this section I will briefly explore the shortcomings of McFague's ecological theology—her unconscious inclusion of anthropocentric, hierarchical, action-oriented and binary elements—and suggest my own construction of an Asian American Christian environmental ethic. This construction will be grounded in the lived experiences and the cultural traditions of Asian and Asian Americans while addressing issues about Christian ecological theologies and environmental ethics that developed within European or North American cultures and their colonial contexts.

We Are Utterly Indebted within Multifariously and Unequally Inter/dependent Relations in a Flux of Time

While acutely aware that the higher and more complex levels of existence have a more serious dependency on and vulnerability in regard to the lower levels of entities or events, McFague nonetheless defines the relationship among them as merely interrelated and interdependent. To deepen her understanding of interdependent relationships among all forms of life, I argue that if one is more dependent on and more vulnerable to others for sustenance or for survival, one's relationship to others is not merely interdependent but unequally dependent and, thus, radically indebted. That means humans are more radically dependent on the rest of the universe.

While her sentiment of radical dependency is well encapsulated in McFague's statement quoted above, her ecological theology does not fully reflect the unequally indebted relations when she places humans

at the top of the hierarchical order in the multileveled universe, reinforcing an anthropocentric binary on an epistemological ground.[36] By
positioning the epistemological agency of humans above the ontological
agency of others, she unintentionally tempers the import of other kinds
of agential capacities that the other, larger parts of the sacred body of
God have upon humans.[37] She thus falls into the trap of the stewardship
model when appealing to the use of human capacity for self-conscious
reflexivity to eradicate the bodily oppression imposed on the rest of creation by urging capable humans to be planetary guardians and caretakers
and more active partners in the continuing creation.[38] Although in fact
we humans are physically more vulnerable and dependent upon all other
forms of life for our bodily survival, we have rationalized ourselves into
believing we have been placed in a higher position within this anthropocentric hierarchical scheme; humans are charged with the higher call,
or the deeper sense of responsibility, on the basis that we have been created in the image of God. With this agential capacity, humans, who take
the upper hand in this epistemological human–other relation, choose to
conserve, preserve, and consume other living and nonliving materials
more responsibly.

Does this anthropocentric, action-oriented, Christian environmental ethic ring true to Asian and Asian American Christians who do not
consider themselves to be charged with the higher call, but still live with
sound eco-theological life principles? Answers to this question can be
traced in the lived experiences of many Asians and Asian Americans
I have mentioned earlier in this chapter: my mother, Grace's grandmother, Taiwanese and Chinese Americans who stand against shark finning, Chung's Korean Buddhist-Christian ecofeminist theology, and
some Asian American Christian communities. Although many of them
may identify themselves as Christians, their inherited religious and cultural traditions are much more complex than their European and North
American Christian counterpart. As I look into their ethical values
espoused by nature, cultures, Christianity, and their own spirituality,
the common thread that binds them together is not exclusively Christian
faith but partly a Confucian model of organic cosmology; embedded in
their eco-theological life principles is the Confucian idea of "the unity
of Heaven and Humanity" that many of us also believe encompasses the
earth as well.[39]

Similarly to McFague's organic model of cosmology, Confucian cosmology in its variety of breeds is an organic one that emphasizes the unity

of heaven and earth—the interrelatedness and interdependence among all parts of the universe as well as the unity with heaven. Let me take a Confucian metaphor of the holy rite (禮: li: ritual) as an image for the universe.[40] Imbedded in this metaphor is an interrelated and interdependent nature among all participants whose participation with equal dignity in the ritual constitutes the holy rite. Yet this Confucian cosmology goes deeper than McFague's by prioritizing the existential value over the functional significance of each participant.[41] Let us recall McFague's emphasis upon the self-conscious reflexive function of humans as a basis for her anthropocentric action-oriented ecological theology. In contrast Confucius highlights the existential significance of each part over the functional value. By being a part of the holy rite, one is contributing to the life of others and vice versa. When this existential value of all parts is well recognized, their relations cannot be ordered by a hierarchical scheme of things based on the differing capacities of each participant but must be mutually indebted to each other's presence for constituting the whole. Thus, a sense of mutual indebtedness can arise among all parts of the universe for sustaining the whole.[42] From this cosmology arises a sense of indebtedness among the intricately intertwined parts of the whole.

Thus, I claim that a sense of "indebtedness" must be highlighted in all relationships, especially from the human side to the planetary relationships that sustain and support human life.[43] With the notion of indebtedness, I would press McFague's interrelated and interdependent nature of all life-forms a little further, while adopting her understanding of the universe as the body of God and of the cosmic Christ. All parts of this universe—living and nonliving, organic and inorganic—are not only interconnected and interrelated but also indebted to the whole within a vast range of shared communities, whether their relationships are intentional or unintentional, direct or indirect, and observable or unobservable. If we humans cannot survive "without the plants and animals and the ecosystem that supports us all," we are more radically indebted to their presence in this world.

There are two inseparable yet distinctive aspects of indebtedness: the existential—or ontological in Jane Bennett's term—and functional levels. The indebted relation understood existentially concerns one's indebtedness to the presence of others for one's existence, while the indebted relation understood functionally captures the instrumental contributions that others make for one's well-being.[44] The former precedes one's indebtedness to others' functional contributions. One may say that we can be functionally indebted to others without realizing it, and that the functional relationship holds even if one is unaware of the existential connection. Yes, that is true. But the functionally indebted relation to others without realizing it also requires the existence of others. Although this indebtedness is germane to all existents, let me first conceptualize it from a human perspective. For example, I am existentially indebted to the photosynthetic nature of trees, air, water, sunlight, and microorganism for the air I breathe, although I may not be fully aware of my functional indebtedness to the trees around me. Yet unless trees exist, I cannot be functionally indebted to them. Humans must recognize that we are, first and foremost, existentially indebted to others whose mere presence among others organically constitutes our planetary community, prior to discussing how plants, animals, and the ecosystem functionally support human life. Without their vital presence, the human species would not exist, and, therefore, we would not be in a position to conceive of interdependent functional relationships. Without them our existence would be impossible because our survival utterly depends on, and is inherently and profoundly indebted to, their presence.

This realization of existential indebtedness, then, is followed by our functional indebtedness to others whose "performative differences" in an ongoing and constantly changing environment sustain and enrich not only human life but also the lives of each existing other as well as the existence of the whole.[45] Functional indebtedness exists within the symbiotic system of nature that is mutually interdependent and mutually beneficial. However, the functionally indebted relationships among persons and plants, animals and other aspects of the ecosystem are unspecified, multilateral, and utterly unequal. Situated in a flux of time, the nature of our functionally indebted relationships is not mutually equal or reciprocal but always unequal, multilateral, multidimensional, multidirectional, and multicentric, adding more fluid complexities to the intricate web of life.[46] These complexities of indebted relations intertwined with diversities and differences of all life-forms disrupt an anthropocentric binary relation and dismantle any hierarchical ordering of beings by a singular standard such as "subjectivity or the ability to experience and feel."[47]

To illustrate this complexity of indebted relations in a concrete way, let me give a lengthy example. My mother raised many Asian orchids in her condominium, some wild and others cultivated that were potted individually and given to her as gifts. For twenty years or more, my mother collected and took great care of them until she died of cancer.

During my mother's last few months, my daughter and I flew out to Korea to stay with her, taking care of her physical, emotional, and spiritual needs, and any other needs she might have, and also receiving care from others along the way. We soon began to argue: I complained that caring for her and her household was too much work, while my mother scolded me for not taking care of everything in the house precisely as she would, including nurturing dozens of orchids. Even though they were cultured, they were nonetheless delicate natural existents. Already too busy to take care of a dying mother and a toddler and with my own work to contend with, I was exhausted and simply could not remember to spray water on the pebbles in the orchid pots once a week or to bathe them once a month. In addition to meeting her personal needs, all I could remember to do was to feed our family and to keep the thermostat at twenty-six degrees Celsius at nighttime, which was higher than usual, but I had noticed my mother covering herself at home in December in Korea because she would usually turn the thermostat off during the day. During the weeks my mother was in and out of the hospital, I remained at her bedside twenty-four hours a day during the week until my brother came to share the shift with me on weekends. Simply too busy and preoccupied with other things, I did not think to turn the heater off during the day, nor to pay attention to those delicate orchid pots. When she came out of the hospital to celebrate Korean New Year's Day at home one last time, we were surprised and delighted to see that one of the orchids had blossomed into a flower in late January after weeks without water. When we opened the sliding glass doors to the windowed veranda to smell the flowers, we discovered that the veranda was quite damp and the pebbles in the pots were moist, apparently from a combination of natural forces: the humidity of the snow in the air outside the building seeped in through the ventilation of the outer window and combined with the heat rising from the heated floor in the living room that was adjacent to the veranda with only a sliding door in between. That, along with sunlight during the day and colder temperatures at night, had coaxed her orchid into flower at just the right time. My mother told me that the orchid usually blossoms only once a year in late May. She was very happy to see this unusual, special treat from this Asian orchid. During this holiday, as the rest of our family was busy preparing to host our relatives, she was left alone on a couch, dozing off most of the day, but talking to this blossomed orchid when she was awake, quietly smiling and tearing up.

Although I cannot speak for the blossomed orchid or the pebbles, the existents in the story possess, to different degrees, passive, inactive, receptive, and objective aspects as well as generative, active, and subjective aspects in their individual modes of existence that are beyond the scope of this touching story. But surely all aspects of these days, whether included, omitted, forgotten, or excluded in the above story, better capture the complexities of mutually and multifariously indebted relations than I am able to identify. The complex relationships that exist within and among all existents, whether human, cultivated plants, or materials living or nonliving would not have been possible without their mutual existential support. This story reminds us of functional indebtedness among diverse indebted existents whose presence constitutes the whole. This is true not only at the level of the body of God but also in the household of my mother, signifying the reality of functional indebtedness that involves the whole of creation. This mutual indebtedness is universal and ongoing, whether it be unarticulated or articulated, indefinite or determined, infinitely existential or functional. It occurs between my mother, the orchid, and the collective pebbles. It is also to be found among all others, however variously gifted or limited, fulfilled or deprived of opportunity, but in all cases indebted existents, deeply involved in their own stories.

In retrospect my mother was wrong—there was not just one way to keep the orchids alive; it was actually an act of "negligence" on my part, or "nonaction" (wu-wei) in Taoist thought, that brought about the chain of events that led to the miraculous bloom.[48] So the lesson here is that we humans may try to control nature to get it to do what we want, but sometimes it is our very activity and inactivity that leads nature to do things we would not have expected. This lesson leads us to move beyond McFague's emphasis upon the moral responsibility of humans by entrusting ourselves to the agential influence that collective planetary life has upon us.

My goal is to inspire us to be respectful of all our surroundings, and, subsequently, to act accordingly, broadening ways of acknowledging and responding to that indebtedness beyond a binary, anthropocentric, and action-oriented scope of interrelatedness and interdependence. Greater awareness of human indebtedness to the environment in both natural and cultural senses must, if we are wise, move us beyond the limited utilitarian calculation that has thus far shaped our relationship to our planet. We must reduce the risk of anthropocentric self-centeredness concealed in binary interdependent relations.

Respectful Grace and Graceful Respect: An Asian American Christian Environmental Ethic

My Asian American Christian environmental ethic goes deeper into the heart than does McFague's ecological theology of liberating, healing, and caring by drawing from the respectful adaptation of nonhuman existents to their surroundings and also from the graceful sharing of their indebted life.[49] When plants encounter changes in the environment, whether it be a sudden change of weather for a day, an external invasion inflicted upon them, or a long-term climate change, they respond to such changes respectfully by dying or modifying their life to accommodate the changes primarily in order to ensure their existential continuation, and, then, secondly to maintain their functional indebted relationships to all other existents within the surrounding environment. As I attempted to articulate their adaptive ways of being, I could not find any better way to translate their response into human language than to refer to them as "respectful" responses. In these planetary existents, the best way to describe their ways of encountering and adapting to changes/challenges is to say in the way they live, they are deeply respectful.

When the interrelated and interdependent life among all planetary existents is viewed as indebted, their interactions cannot be evaluated simply on the basis of whether their actions are just or caring; at a deeper level they must be perceived as the "graceful" sharing of their indebted selves with those to whom they are unequally indebted. Humans, more gifted in the self-conscious reflexive, active, and subjective way of being, but deficient in other aspects, must be able to see the support we receive from the nonhuman existents as graceful "liquidation of debt," rather than approaching this complex indebtedness merely as a justice issue, as if we were dealing with economic transactions and fair trade.[50] Humans can also experiment to expand an ethics of radical hospitality to other forms of life in the universe by reducing our subjective roles that give us an upper hand in a hierarchical ordering of agential capacities.

Our moral responsibilities should not be unilaterally aimed at taking care of the earth, but must become respectful and graceful responses to our radically and multifariously indebted relations. Then we may be able to find grace there, in the complexities of our indebted relations. When humans learn to embody the passive, receptive, or objective aspects, or *wu-wei* in Taoist terms, that reflect the true status of our radically indebted relations to other forms of life, we may learn to appreciate and embody their ways of being graceful and respectful.

Therefore, I would like to expand the sentence I wrote at the beginning of this section: *Humans cannot survive even a day without the animals, the plants, and all other inorganic and organic existents on earth, while they can all flourish without humans. Accordingly, the life of the human species is not merely interdependent with, but utterly indebted to, all the other existents on earth, rendering humans more vulnerable than any others.* Humans are more indebted to the plants, the animals, and all other parts of nature on earth in a highly complex manner in both existential and functional senses than the rest of nature is, in fact, indebted to humans. Once we recognize our existential indebtedness that leads to a secondary, functional indebtedness, we may be able to discover how indebted we humans are to their presence in this intricate web of life. All other parts of nature— simply by being present among us—exercise more profound agency than we have acknowledged in the manner in which we have impacted our environment.

McFague's and others' action-oriented approach to the environment is limited to the active, rational, and subjective aspects of the universe. Thus, to Asian Americans, her language of Christian environmental ethics remains, to an important degree, only partially true to Asian Americans, as well as to other planetary forms of existence. I have noted earlier that many Asian and Asian American theologians and biblical scholars have not been very explicit in articulating Christian environmental ethics. Similarly, organized environmental activism holds only marginal interest among Asian and Asian American Christian communities compared to our sound ecological ethic ingrained in us implicitly (nonverbally, nonsubjectively and nonactively).

There are a few reasons for this implicit disposition of Asian American Christian environmental ethics. First and foremost, as a Korean American Christian ethicist, I find my mother's and our forebearers' lives as the most relevant texts in my search for an Asian American Christian environmental ethic. Their ways of living with the deepest concern for their surroundings have taught us well. It was not their theoretical articulation or intentional actions but their ways of being indebted to their surroundings that have sustained this planet; my mother or Grace's grandmother would hardly rationalize themselves as acting justly or caringly, yet they still lived with utmost respect for

their natural environment. So my environmental ethic of being respectfully graceful and gracefully respectful as a derivative of the concept of
indebtedness developed partly from reflecting on the lived experiences
of our forebearers.

Closely related to the first, my Asian forebearers' implicit ecological ethic is grounded in Asian cultural roots that ultimately influenced
me to retrieve and reappropriate some Confucian and Taoist sources.
These cultural sources run deep within me and my fellow Asian American Christians—often deeper than the words we confess on Sundays—
immersing us in a deeper appreciation of implicit ways of being related
to other existents on this planet. If we conceive of our world as a ritual, or the holy rite as imagined by Confucius, we cannot help but live
wholeheartedly to be in harmony with other parts of the universe. If
Asian and Asian Americans embrace any environmental ethics or eco-
theological life principles, paraphrasing Neo-Confucian philosopher
Wang Yang-ming's words, "it is not because we deliberately want to do
so, but because it is natural for us to live that way."[51] Laozi nurtures us
in his wisdom that if we could center ourselves in the Tao, "the whole
world would be transformed by itself, in its natural rhythms."[52] All these
cultural teachings did not equip many Asian and Asian Americans to
articulate and rationalize our relationship to the other existents, yet nurtured us to seek the depths rather than the surface in our relationship to
other existents on this planet.[53]

Last but not least, the deepest sense of indebtedness and being
respectfully graceful and gracefully respectful comes from the respectful adaptation of nonhuman existents to their surroundings and also
from the graceful sharing of their indebted life, as I sketched out at the
beginning of this section. The stream water does not intend to nurture
lives around it, yet it continuously sustains life. Trees do not plan to
provide the air we breathe, yet they are the reason that humans and animals can breathe. By ourselves, humans, because we are more vulnerable
and more radically indebted, lack the capacity to take care of the earth.
From that unalterable fact, we must become more gracefully respectful
and respectfully graceful to each and all members of the constituency
of the environment to which we are deeply and irretrievably indebted.
Asian American Christian environmental ethics should not be limited
to actions that are outwardly just and caring but must foster an inner
transformation especially of humans whose radical indebtedness to others challenges us, first and foremost, to be more respectfully graceful and

gracefully respectful for any genuine Christian liberation, healing, and caring of the earth.

Epilogue

I hope this essay is helpful to readers who are interested in constructing their own particular environmental ethics or in transforming their environmental awareness. I invite them to find the intersection of their Christian faith within their own distinctive cultures and to journey with me to find ways of relating to the environment in graceful and respectful ways. This approach to indebted planetary existence, although in its infant stage, may also suggest a new direction for others who are interested in broadening and deepening their ways of doing environmental ethics or ecological theology. With all due respect, I can only hope that each of us can learn to imagine our own ways to address the environmental issues near and far, mindful of being grounded in the natural and cultural environment that surrounds us.

DISCUSSION QUESTIONS

1. What are some of the distinctive characteristics of this particular Asian American Christian environmental ethics that speak most poignantly or persuasively to you?

2. Can you articulate why you embrace—or reject—the sense of indebtedness introduced in this chapter?

3. Are there changes you might recommend in Christian communities as a result of this construction of Asian American Christian environmental ethics? Speaking from your own cultural and religious position, can you construct your own Christian and/or religious environmental ethics?

4. What does your tradition say about your relationship to the environment?

Education and Labor

IRENE OH

This essay examines the topics of education and labor as they may apply to the development of an Asian American Christian ethic. The overarching aim of this research is to provide a more nuanced understanding of both labor and education for Christian communities with Asian American members. Divided into three sections and followed by a short list of questions and resources for further reading, I provide a brief introduction to education and labor in the general realm of Christian theology and ethics and then discuss their relevance to Asian American populations. The concluding section describes how an Asian American Christian ethic with regard to education and labor might evolve and pays particular attention to specific issues to consider in the development of such a theological ethic. Where possible, I include specific information and analyses about Asian American subgroups because of the significant disparities that exist between and among different Asian American ethnicities.

What Is the Range of Christian Responses to the Topics of Education and Labor?

Christian views toward work and education reflect both shared textual sources and unique social contexts. As such, Christian perspectives on these topics include a range of responses to questions regarding the place of learning and labor. Christian Asian American communities may find themselves at a crossroads with regard to Christian ideals regarding work and the purpose of education. At a minimum, Christian Scripture values manual labor and a day of rest; Christian theological views on education tend to emphasize the affirmation of faith. While education and labor may serve specific theological purposes, both also have much broader functions in contemporary U.S. society. Education and work are fundamental to economic survival in the United States. With few outliers, people who have higher levels of education are far more likely to be employed, and to be employed with higher salaries, compared to those with fewer years of education. Beyond economic necessity, schooling functions not only to impart academic skills but also to create a democratic citizenry with shared civic virtues. Work in the United States, as elsewhere, also serves multiple purposes beyond the benefit of wages (and other benefits such as health insurance and retirement funds). Workplaces are important points of social connection, and one's occupation is often shorthand for one's social standing in the United States. For all of the above reasons and more, education and labor are important topics for reflection.

Christian Views on Education

Christian views on education tend to converge on the idea that one of the primary purposes of learning is to allow humans to grow closer to God. However, there is tremendous variation across the history of Christianity as to the purpose of formal education given the changing nature of human society. The multiple goals of Christian communities in promoting literacy and establishing schools include creating and preserving biblical texts, furthering knowledge of God and creation, facilitating the conversion of non-Christians, and "democratizing" Christianity through biblical literacy. In this section I will focus primarily upon contemporary views of schools in the United States as opposed to topics such as the history of Christian educational institutions, theological treatises on the proper use of the rational faculties, religious curricula, or seminary education. Examining the purpose of schools from Christian perspectives provides insight into the aims of education, and, moreover, relates to the lives of many, if not most, Asian Americans today given that formal education is so closely linked to future labor and employment. We are all invested in schools in the United States whether we are students ourselves, parents, educators, coworkers, employers, taxpayers, or some combination of the above.

My personal experiences as a student, as a professor, and as a parent of school-aged children undoubtedly affect the ways in which I view education and how education relates to one's work. Having attended private, independent schools my entire life (with the exception of the University of Virginia, where I obtained my doctorate), and having taught at two private, research universities, my firsthand experience with educational institutions are undoubtedly limited. I have, however, spent many more years in school than most, and I also have been either a student or a teacher at schools in a very wide variety of cultural settings. The schools that I have attended include an Episcopal prep school in Honolulu, a Quaker liberal arts college in suburban Pennsylvania, and nondenominational research universities in Berlin and Chicago. With the exception of the school in Honolulu, Asians and Asian Americans were minorities in all of the others. Being born and raised in Honolulu as a fourth-generation Korean American, I was aware from a very young age of differences among the ethnicities, socioeconomic classes, religions, and generational stages of Asians and Asian Americans. Honolulu in the 1970s was one of the very few cities in the United States where such diversity among Asian Americans existed and the only city in which persons of Asian ancestry made up the racial majority. My own family was in many ways "typical" of Asian Americans in Honolulu with family members exhibiting this kind of diversity. The members of my extended family include my great-grandmother, who immigrated to Hawaii over a century ago as a picture bride to a sugarcane laborer; an uncle who is a third-generation Japanese American (married to my third-generation Korean aunt); and my mother who immigrated in the 1970s from South Korea. My extended family includes white-collar professionals and blue-collar union workers, Shinto Buddhists and Korean Presbyterians. Despite this extraordinary diversity, in many ways I was raised in a very stereotypical Korean American household that emphasized excellence in education with the expectation that my siblings and I would become highly-paid (or at least well respected) white-collar professionals. Our family—like many others among my Asian American peers—emphasized learning for the sake of achievement rather than for its own sake. While I attended an independent, Episcopal school that required weekly chapel attendance and that placed a heavy emphasis on public service, the primary reason my parents selected the school for me was its academic reputation, not its religiosity. It is with this background that I contemplate the nexus of Christian theology, education, and labor.

Christian theologians generally view education and literacy in particular as serving multiple purposes. These include deepening one's knowledge of God, strengthening the rational faculties endowed to humanity by God, expanding the reach of the Bible, and building Christian communities. John Calvin, following Martin Luther, saw education as a means "to the glorification of God and the edification of the church through the exposition of God's truth in such a way that the people of God might learn to worship and serve him as they ought."[1] From the perspective of the Reformers, teaching congregants how to read enabled them to learn how to read the Bible and other religious texts. The Catholic Church in Vatican II states in *Gravissimum Educationis* ("The Importance of Education") that the principal purpose of a Christian education is that "the baptized, while they are gradually introduced [to] the knowledge of the mystery of salvation, become ever more aware of the gift of Faith they have received."[2] As institutions, churches have always needed well-educated clergy not only to expound theological content but also to keep accounts and handle other mundane transactions required for any institution.

Some of the most controversial aspects of Christian education historically have surrounded the missionary activities of both Catholic and Protestant sects. While adherents of many of the major world religions have, to some extent, spread their religious beliefs to other parts and peoples, Christianity has an especially notorious history of evangelism because of its association with European colonialism. Beginning around the sixteenth century and concurrent with the exploration of lands abroad, European and British Christians were complicit in the colonizing of the native inhabitants of Africa, Asia, and South America. They often viewed their pedagogical work abroad not simply as teaching non-Europeans in Africa, Asia, and South America how to read and write, but as a "civilizing" mission with the intention of replacing "barbaric" native cultures with the "enlightened" customs and values of European Christianity. While such blatant condescension toward non-Europeans is certainly no longer acceptable, the legacy of European Christian missions and the destruction of native cultures lingers.

The purposes of education today are far more varied, even for Christian communities. While for some the purpose of education may be explicitly theological, for others the purpose of education serves much broader purposes that are only remotely theological in nature. Because formal education, referring to schooling in institutions from the primary years to postgraduate, is often partnered with the state, education serves multiple purposes that may not be explicitly Christian. The vast majority of children in the United States attend public schools, that is, schools that are paid through government taxes. According to the Department of Education, approximately 90 percent of U.S. children attend public schools, with close to 9 percent attending private religiously affiliated schools (approximately 2 million children attend Catholic/parochial schools), and the remainder enrolled in private independent schools.[3] Regardless of the type of school one's children attend, the education they receive will very likely have multiple aims to enable them to function in our democratic society. Given the constitutional separation of church and state, public school curriculums do not teach theology, although they can teach *about* different religious traditions in appropriate academic contexts. For example, public schools may teach about Puritans seeking religious freedom and the establishment of colonies in North America, but may not require students to read the Bible as daily school routine.[4]

Philosopher Amy Gutmann argues that public education "at its best would teach children to understand their rights and responsibilities as citizens, to think for themselves, to develop skills and virtues that enable them to live a good life of their own choosing and reciprocally contribute to society."[5] Inspired by John Stuart Mill, other educators view the aim of education as creating "a state of individuals where citizens are educated to choose their own conception of the good life consistently with the equal freedom of other individuals to so choose."[6] Still others recognize that children are not simply autonomous citizens but extensions of families as well as larger communities—including religious ones—within the state. As such, families, and not the state, ought to be the primary arbiters of values that are taught in educational settings. Each of these settings—family, community, and school—communicate the tools of "deliberative citizenship" by imparting in multiple ways the skills required of responsible, critically thinking members. Learning to be a responsible member of the family unit or a religious community, for example, entails instilling norms like reciprocity that are likely valued in the larger society. Likewise, secular, public schools can aim to instill certain habits or virtues, such as patience, that are also valued in Christian thought. In other words, the skills and values that are found in both secular and religious schools often overlap, even though explicitly theological language and content would only be found in the latter.

Because education serves both private and public purposes, families that choose a Christian school for their children will find a broad curriculum that attends to nonreligious topics necessary for academic achievement. The Catholic Church affirms in *Gravissimum Educationis* that

[a]ll men of every race, condition and age, since they enjoy the dignity of a human being, have an inalienable right to an education that is in keeping with their ultimate goal, their ability, their sex, and the culture and tradition of their country, and also in harmony with their fraternal association with other peoples in the fostering of true unity and peace on earth. For a true education aims at the formation of the human person in the pursuit of his ultimate end and of the good of the societies of which, as man, he is a member, and in whose obligations, as an adult, he will share.[7]

In Christian schools within a pluralistic society such as the United States, teaching children the religious values of their particular tradition may not necessarily adversely affect democratic values required of our citizenry. Specifically, Christian schools must be able to balance endorsement of Christianity with impartment of the important civic value of toleration of other religious traditions. In parochial schools, for example, "the perspectives and concerns of other cultures" are an essential part of the curriculum, even while maintaining a commitment to Catholic teachings.[8]

Christian Views on Labor

The topic of labor covers myriad subjects, and writings from both Catholic and Protestant traditions address many of these, ranging from biblical injunctions on work and rest to support for labor unions and fair wages for migrant workers. In this section I will touch upon several of these topics with the aim of demonstrating the breadth of Christian thinking on labor. This breadth is particularly helpful when considering Asian American populations, given their diversity in the labor market.

Perhaps the most persuasive theological writings on the topic of labor in the contemporary era concern the protection of workers in a capitalist market. These writings are meant to alleviate the work conditions of those who work in difficult, if not outright dangerous, environments, are paid poorly, are not unionized, and have no legal recourse should they suffer harm on the job. Scripture and other religious sources can also inform Christians who sit at the opposite end of the spectrum— highly educated, well-compensated workers who may view their careers as a means to prestige and financial gain, without consideration of the ethical compromises at stake.

In sources ranging from the Bible to "prosperity gospel" sermons of some megachurches, we find a variety of views on labor and wealth. While there seems to be little disagreement that workers ought not to be exploited, there is a very wide range of views on the accumulation of wealth as a result of work. In his papal encyclical, *Rerum Novarum*, Pope Leo XIII urges that "remedy must be found quickly for the misery and wretchedness pressing so unjustly on the majority of the working class."[9] Although written over a century ago, much of the suffering Leo describes still applies today to many: insufficient wages, grinding work, and poor working conditions. Leo XIII suggests that the state allow for labor unions and collective bargaining so as to enable workers to obtain fair living wages and decent work conditions.

Rerum Novarum notes that wages and working conditions should be enough to allow for a workman (assuming that "he be a sensible man") to support himself, his wife, and his children, as well as save a part of his income. Moreover, work should not be so strenuous that it does not afford a day of rest. Protection of the Sabbath enables the worker for one day a week "to turn his thoughts to things heavenly, and to the worship which he so strictly owes to the eternal Godhead."[10] Christian sources, including Scripture and monastic (specifically, Benedictine) practices, indicate that manual and creative labor are to be celebrated and that a day of rest is sanctioned. Many of these cite Genesis, in which God creates the world in six days and rests on the seventh, in claiming that the Bible is the basis of the Sabbath and that both work and rest are fundamentally part of human existence.

Of course, theological views on work and wealth vary tremendously, and Weber's observations of the Protestant work ethic and its frugal mindset remind us that hard work and wealth are firmly established values in the panoply of Christian practices.[11] However, even such strongly capitalist views do not emerge at the expense of mandated rest and manual labor. Rather, they expand Christian notions of the good life so as to accommodate a wider variety of types of work within a changing society. Observation of the Sabbath serves as a reminder that human connection and reflection outside of work are vitally important to religious life. This broader acceptance of ritualized rest and types of work as "successful" provide a needed change of perspective for success-driven upwardly mobile Christians. In the early church, the apostles are described by their profession, which suggests while that a person's trade is vital to identity, persons of even the most humble of professions are worthy before God.

Importantly, differences in wealth and social status are generally recognized as a natural part of creation. Leo XIII heavily criticized socialists who argued that all wealth ought to be distributed equally, essentially negating the notion of ownership of private property. Given that all those who are able to work can do so under fair conditions, it is theologically acceptable for employers and the owners of capital to be wealthier than laborers. The wealthy nonetheless have an obligation to use their assets responsibly. Echoing major principles of *Rerum Novarum*, the 1908 Social Creed issued by the Federal Council of Churches endorses a living wage, protections from the harshness of industry, and the abolition of poverty.[12] Updated a century later by the National Council of Churches, "A Social Creed for the 21st Century" recognizes more fully the roles of the environment, peace and war, and universal human rights in an era of industrial globalization. Neither of these documents seeks to abolish differences in economic standing, but rather emphasize the need for "grace over greed in economic life."[13]

While the above views, or slight variations, are commonly found in theological literature, there has long existed a strand within Christianity that views the accumulation of even extraordinary amounts of wealth as divine blessing. From the second century theologian Clement of Alexandria ("the inheritance of the kingdom of heaven is not quite cut off from [the rich] if they obey the commandments") to Joel Osteen, one of today's most well-known megachurch televangelists ("God wants us to prosper financially, to have plenty of money, to fulfill the destiny He has laid out for us"[14]), a number of theologians have taken the view that so long as a Christian does not idolize money or material possessions, then the riches one earns or receives ought to be viewed as God's grace. The general consensus, despite the frankly ostentatious displays of wealth by popular pastors of megachurches (T. D. Jakes, e.g., drives a Rolls-Royce, owns an airplane, and lives in a lakefront mansion), is that so long as one's wealth did not come from the illegal harm of others, then one's enjoyment of one's wealth is morally acceptable.

How Are Asian Americans Invested in the Topic of Education and Labor?

Statistically, Asian Americans seem to be surpassing other racial groups in terms of educational achievement, income, and employment. The percentage of Asian Americans who hold college degrees is higher than any other racial group, and the median household income of Asian Americans is also higher than any other racial group in the United States. Delving more deeply into these numbers, however, reveals a far more complex portrait of Asian American educational attainment and labor. While Asian Americans, as a whole, indeed are well educated and compensated, the statistical studies of Asian American subgroups uncovers a "dumbbell" graph, with a few subgroups (notably Indian Americans) attaining extraordinarily high rates of higher education and earnings, while other subgroups experience below-average rates of high-school graduation and high rates of unemployment and poverty. This section describes an intricate portrait of Asian Americans in terms of educational attainment, employment, and occupation. I provide below a general snapshot of Asian Americans in each of these categories, followed by a more detailed analysis that breaks down the aggregate numbers by various subgroups (or ethnicity, gender, and/or generation).

The image of Asian Americans as a "model minority" emerges as a result of fairly broad statistics on education and labor. Forty-nine percent of Asian Americans aged 25 and older hold a bachelor's degree, compared to 31 percent of whites and 28 percent of the United States population overall.[15] The median household income of Asian Americans in 2010 was $66,000, which is $12,000 more than white Americans and $16,000 more than the United States population. According to the Pew Research Center, Asian Americans today comprise the "highest-income, best-educated and fastest-growing racial group in the United States."[16] These statistics are further validated by surveys of Asian American attitudes toward work and education.

Recent surveys of Asian Americans suggest that behind the education and income statistics lies an ardent belief in hard work. The attitude that hard work—which includes children working hard at school—is important to getting ahead is pervasive among Asian Americans. Sixty-nine percent of Asian Americans believe that most people "who want to get ahead can make it if they're willing to work hard," as opposed to 58 percent of the general public; and an incredible 93 percent of Asian Americans believe that "Americans from my country of origin group are very hardworking."[17] The belief that hard work is vital to success is not lost on Asian American children. In fact nearly 4 out of 10 Asian American parents believe that parents from their country of origin subgroup place "too much pressure" on their children to perform well in school, while 6 out of 10 Asian American parents perceive other American parents as placing *too little* pressure on their children in school.[18] Amy Chua's provocative memoir, *Battle Hymn of the Tiger Mother*, points to these widely divergent cultural attitudes.[19] Chua, a Yale Law School professor and a Chinese American daughter of immigrants, details in this auto-biographical book the intense pressure and extraordinary expectations she has placed upon her high-achieving children: no playdates, no TV, nothing short of As on their report cards. The upshot of such parenting, she claims, is her children's sense of confidence through real achieve-ment, including a Carnegie Hall music performance by one daughter and admission into Ivy League colleges for both. The popularity of the book (she was interviewed on *Oprah*) and the lively debates that ensued indicate that for all its controversy, Chua hit on a topic that touched a nerve for Asian American and non–Asian American parents alike.

While the statistics for Asian Americans as a whole indicate that, as an aggregate group, we are currently succeeding at realizing the American dream, the educational history of Asian Americans in the United States and current differences among Asian American subgroups tell a complex story that belies the image of the monolithic rise of Asian Americans in the United States. For much of our time in the United States, Asian American schoolchildren, like their African American counterparts, were segregated from white students and often districted to inferior pub-lic schools. The Supreme Court held in *Lum v. Rice*, 275 U.S. 78 (1927) that school segregation applied to Asian Americans as well as it did to Blacks:

> We cannot think that the question is any different, or that any different result can be reached . . . where the issue is as between white pupils and pupils of the yellow race. The decision is within the discretion of the state in regulating its public schools, and does not conflict with the Fourteenth Amendment [of the U.S. Constitution].[20]

Only with *Brown v. Board of Education* (1954) were Asian American children, along with other American children of color, integrated into public schools. About a decade later, with the influx of immigrants from Asia after the liberalization of immigration and naturalization laws in 1965 and a significant wave of immigrants seeking refuge from war in Southeast Asia in the early 1970s, a large number of Asian American chil-dren with vastly different socioeconomic backgrounds and educational needs began to attend school in the United States. Predictably, those Asian families from professional backgrounds and/or who spoke English (as was the case with Indian immigrants) arrived in many ways far bet-ter equipped to navigate the educational systems and professional labor market of the United States. The children who grew up in these homes often became the students who performed well in American schools and were portrayed in media as math geniuses, violin virtuosos, and computer whizzes. These children became the face of the mythical model minority. On the other hand, families that arrived as refugees from desperate wartime circumstances—families who were poor, undereducated, and traumatized—not surprisingly had children who performed below average in American schools. These trends remain apparent even today. University of California researchers recently found that in the state of California, with the largest and most diverse numbers of Asians and Asian Americans in the United States, 45 percent of Hmong and 40 percent of Cambodians and Laotians have not completed high school. (Twenty-five percent of Cambodians and Hmong live in poverty—twice the rate of any other ethnic group in California.[21]) Along those same lines, Laotians, Cambodians, and Khmer have college graduation rates of 5 percent and Vietnamese Americans have 16 percent, which is a stark contrast to the 42 percent college graduation rate for Asian Americans overall. These numbers tell us that there is a tremendous gap in the education achievements of Asian Americans. The lumping together of Asian ethnicities as a model minority in education is not only misleading but also completely inaccurate.

Indian Americans, as suggested above, are far more likely than Americans with Korean, Chinese, Filipino, or Japanese ancestry to have a college degree. Although the median income level of Asian Americans is far higher than that of the average American, Asian Americans of Korean, Vietnamese, or Chinese origin are also more likely than the average American to live in poverty.[22] The wealth gap within the Asian American community is sizable. The percentage of Asian Americans living in poverty is actually higher than the United States average (12.6 percent versus 12.4 percent). The poverty rates among the Hmong, Cambodian, Laotian, and Vietnamese are among the highest in the country, ranging from over 16 percent to nearly 38 percent.[23]

Approximately 7 million Asian Americans work in the United States in a broad range of industries. As with education and income, labor statistics confirm that Asian Americans are more likely than the average American to be employed than either whites or blacks.[24] Weekly earnings of Asian Americans are higher than either whites or blacks, and unemployment rates are lower. Not surprisingly, these trends are likely attributed to the fact that Asian Americans as a whole are more likely to have college degrees; and college graduates were more likely to weather through the most recent economic recession than those without undergraduate degrees. As the Department of Labor points out, however, the "aggregate data for Asian-Americans is more likely to hide the challenges of some in the community. While a large portion is highly-skilled, those with fewer skills face significant challenges that are too easily overlooked when focusing on the larger group."[25] Indian Americans, for example, who have the highest rates of college education, are the most likely to be employed (64.7 percent), while other Asian American subgroups had lower employment rates.

In parsing out the data with regard to Asian American women, unexpected statistics emerge. In stark contrast to the data with regard to Asian Americans overall (men and women), employment rates for Asian American women have declined at twice the rate of white women between 2009 and 2010; Asian American women were thus less likely in 2010 to be employed than white women. Moreover, Asian American women earn only 73 percent of their male counterparts' wages (compared to 81 percent for white women), even as Asian American women are more likely than white women to hold college degrees (49.4 percent versus 45.8 percent).[26] It is unclear why in the last few years Asian American women's rate of unemployment has risen. One reason may be because a disproportionately high number of Asian American women work in service industries, which were especially hard hit during the recession. Data indicating that the number of Asian American women who earned at or below minimum wage doubled between 2007 and 2012 reinforces the probability that the high rates of low-wage service industry workers among Asian American women lends to their high rates of unemployment.[27] Also, differences in gender norms among Asian American subgroups may account for relatively high rates of unemployment among women (Bangladeshi women, for example, are employed at only half the rate of Bangladeshi men).[28]

In terms of type of employment for Asian Americans generally, data from the Department of Labor shows that Asian Americans are more likely to work for the private sector than white or black Americans.[29] About 80 percent of Asian Americans work for the private sector, while approximately 6 percent are self-employed and 11.5 percent work for the government (local, state, or federal). In looking at subgroup data, variations emerge. For example, approximately a quarter of Korean Americans are self-employed, more than twice the number of any other Asian American subgroup.[30] In terms of occupation, Asian Americans are overrepresented in scientific and engineering fields, with approximately 14 percent employed in those areas compared to 5 percent for the United States population overall. Among Asian American subgroups, we find a wide disparity with 28 percent of Indian Americans in the sciences and in engineering.

While it remains true that Asian Americans disproportionately pursue careers in the STEM (science, technology, engineering, and math) fields, distinctions in occupational choice emerge when looking across generations of Asian Americans. Larry Shinagawa, Director of the Asian American Studies Program at the University of Maryland, has found that second-, third-, and fourth-generation Asian Americans today are bucking the trend of entering into STEM fields. Unlike Asian Americans of previous generations, they are more likely to major in the humanities in college and to enter into other fields. Also, because "many Asian Americans do not feel they can compete with immigrant Asians in STEM fields . . . they opt for law and business."[31] While later generation Asian Americans enter into law and business because they believe that they offer similar pay and prestige, according to Shinagawa, there is actually no evidence that law and business pay more than the sciences.

Just under half of employed Asian Americans work in white-collar occupations, that is, in management or in a profession typically requiring higher education, including STEM-related fields. Of employed Asian Americans, 21.3 percent work in sales and in office support and just 17 percent work in service industries. Among the service occupations, the majority (6.3 percent) work in food services, and the second largest group works in the "personal care" field. As with other labor statistics, the data about occupation when tracked by subgroup reveals highly divergent portraits of Asian Americans. In the personal care field, for example, we find only 1.3 percent of Indian Americans listing this as their occupational area compared to 21.8 percent of Vietnamese Americans.[32]

The challenges facing Asian Americans are varied. A "bamboo ceiling" may prevent further advancement for high-achieving Asian Americans, despite their having equally strong or even better qualifications than those from other racial groups. Ranging from admissions to elite colleges and universities to breaking into corporate management ranks at Fortune 500 companies, the presence of the bamboo ceiling prevents Asian Americans from populating the highest ranks of our society. Of course, for the many Asian Americans who are not represented by the model minority myth, the challenges are formidable. Both the lack of education and poverty among immigrant groups that are scarred by a legacy of war in their home countries (e.g., among the Vietnamese and the Hmong) create a cycle of despair that is perpetuated from generation to generation. Given the wide variations among Asian American subgroups, there is no singular Asian American theological ethic that addresses adequately the issues of labor and education. Instead, multiple ethical frameworks are necessary to accommodate the multiplicity of challenges facing the extremely diverse Asian American community.

Asian American Christian Ethics: Bringing Justice to Education and Labor

Although the term "Asian American" serves as a convenient demographic umbrella, the use of the term should be used cautiously when attempting to develop an ethic for what is in fact an extremely diverse community. Crafting an Asian American Christian ethics concerning education and labor requires sensitivity to a wide range of life situations. Socioeconomic status, ethnicity, gender, age, and other variables affect both values and visions of "the good life." Drawing from the writings of Asian and Asian American theologians, I suggest various approaches to education and labor that reflect the different struggles of very diverse Asian American subgroups. The development of Asian American theological ethics, in other words, requires that we honor the particularities and differences among ethnic subgroups and individuals. At the same time, because Asian Americans are joined together in the same racial category in law, historical narratives, and culture, Asian Americans can justifiably stand in solidarity with one another as well as with others who are similarly marginalized. On a practical level, so long as Asian Americans continue to be viewed as a singular entity in the United States and subject to laws and programs that treat us as monolithic group, Asian Americans will need to unite across ethnic subgroups to bring about ethically motivated political action.[33] Asian American Christian ethics need to balance, therefore, awareness of diversity within the Asian American population and the practical need to present a united front as agents of change within the American political system.

The plight of the most disenfranchised of Asian American subgroups, those who are the least educated and with the lowest paying, most dangerous jobs (or who are chronically under/unemployed), requires an ethic that affords them access to educational resources, a living wage, and safe working conditions. Indeed the situation of these

Asian American communities is so dire that one might prioritize this aspect of Asian American Christian ethics among others. This ethic entails not only campaigning for policy changes that would address these issues but also correcting ways in which Asian Americans may be complicit in the subjugation of others, whether they be Asian American or not. While there are many school systems that fail to meet the needs of Asian American students, and many businesses that exploit Asian Americans, an Asian American Christian ethic must emphasize the complicity of Asian Americans in the subjugation of other Asian Americans. One notable example involves the labor violations committed by the clothing company Forever 21, which is owned by a Korean American evangelical Christian family. The Department of Labor found "dozens of manufacturers producing goods for Forever 21 under sweatshop-like conditions."[34] It is ethically unconscionable and theologically inconsistent for self-proclaimed Christians to violate repeatedly laws that protect the safety and well-being of employees.

A theological ethic that gives voice and, in particular, political influence to enable positive changes would be especially important to marginalized Asian American subgroups. Such an Asian American theological ethic resonates with other liberation theologies in addressing concrete societal problems of economic and political inequality through the lens of a Christ who acts on behalf of the marginalized members of society, particularly those who lack political and economic power. When addressing these members of our community, a theology that emphasizes justice would seem most appropriate. Notably, a number of Asian American feminist theologians have emphasized the necessity of a Christian ethic that takes up the causes of the oppressed in both North America and abroad. As the editors of *Off the Menu: Asian and Asian North American Women's Religion and Theology* state, a number of Asian American feminist theologians are deeply committed to "justice and work for social change. . . . [O]ur work takes on many dimensions, attuned to specific locations and issues as well as to the global implications of such work."[35] The vision of Christian ethics articulated in these theological accounts is concerned primarily with just relationships between and among humans. As such, an Asian American theological ethic concerned particularly with education and labor would focus upon access to quality education for underserved children, acquisition of skills required to enter and succeed in the workforce, and social services necessary to support individuals and families who are undergoing hardships.

An Asian American Christian ethic applied to the topic of education and labor might also turn to narratives and virtues that would resonate with Asian American experiences and cultures. Peter Phan, a Vietnamese American Catholic theologian, suggests that Asian Americans imagine Jesus as the "immigrant par excellence"—one who crosses borders and exists in a liminal state, both belonging and yet not belonging.[36] First-generation immigrants may "readily relate to this figure of Christ the immigrant from their experiences, sometimes painful, of living as marginalized immigrants in the United States."[37] This narrative of Christ as one who is able to move between, reconcile, and join two worlds, Phan argues, emboldens Vietnamese American Christians in particular, but Asian Americans and immigrants more broadly, to create a new identity that honors both America and home countries.

In forging this new identity, Phan suggests that Vietnamese American Christians reconsider the moral virtues that are found in both Vietnamese and American cultures. While cautious to note that "Asian" virtues such as "love of silence and contemplation, closeness to nature, simplicity, detachment, frugality, harmony, nonviolence, love for learning, respect for others, filial piety, compassion, and attachment to the family" may be exaggerated or caricatured, Phan urges that Vietnamese Americans nonetheless lay claim to these virtues, while at the same time avoid "the risk of yielding to leisurely quietism, political and social withdrawal, avoidance of public responsibilities, and spiritual escapism."[38] He advises that Vietnamese Americans use so-called "Asian" values to balance and correct materialism and the "the excesses of the American way of life."[39] Using the image of the strong yet flexible bamboo tree, Phan calls on his fellow Vietnamese American Christians "to develop a way of uniting the best of the two cultural and moral traditions while avoiding the excesses of both."[40]

Phan's understanding of Christian values can apply to Asian American populations in different ways. The conceptualization of Jesus as an immigrant can be especially comforting for first-generation Asian Americans, who are most directly impacted by the movement between two different lands, cultures, and peoples. Seeing that Jesus struggled with "dual" identities, ultimately transcending and yet embracing both may inspire immigrants who, too, struggle with double identities and the attempt to forge a new one in a new country. The other values could readily apply to Asian Americans of any generation, Vietnamese or not. The image of the bamboo tree as strong yet flexible exemplifies the virtues of resiliency, which is valuable universally. The danger of materialism, of which Phan warns, might be especially applicable to Asian Americans who are finding themselves sacrificing important values in the quest for more material comforts. As it applies to education and labor, this can be borne out in pressure placed upon students to obtain high grades and attend prestigious colleges as a means to lucrative careers, even if the students are miserable. It can also be applied to adults who consistently prioritize work over other important commitments, such as family, friends, and community involvement.

Considering an Asian American Christian ethic theologically, we must remain vigilant of the tensions between the particular and the universal. While it is very important, especially when considering ethical action, to be aware of unique circumstances, it is also critical not to lose sight of the universality of Christianity. On the one hand, incorporation of specific details for Asian American subgroups allows for the creation of an ethic that is potent in its specificity. Developing a targeted and effective strategy to overcome a particular problem requires that we have specific details about the situation. Thus, when dealing with, for example, very low high-school graduation rates among Hmong youth, it is vital to understand specific reasons for this problem in order to provide effective solutions. The solution to such a problem differs if the cause is due to long working hours of teens as opposed to truancy, teen pregnancy, language acquisition, or other factors. An ethic that arises in tandem with consideration of this problem would differ based upon the diagnosed problems.

On the other hand, the development of an overarching Asian American Christian ethic may result not only in losing sight of the differences among Asian Americans subgroups, but also in ignoring the universal message of Christianity. Any Christian theology ought always to reflect at its core universal principles. In other words, a theology that is too closely aligned with a specific ethnic or racial group may appear to be stereotyping based upon ethnicity or race. In order to avoid this danger, a Christian ethic that responds to the specific needs of a particular community needs to balance targeted messages with values, images, and principles that apply to all of humanity. As Korean American theologian Anselm Kyongsuk Min explains:

> The theological bottom line is that God is the universal creator of all reality, that Christ died and was raised for all. All Christian theology must live the tension between embodiment and transcendence,

particularity and universality, and strive for concrete universality, a universality that is effectively concretized in the particular, a concreteness that seeks to transcend its particularity. Without this tension, theology falls into either oppressive tribalism or impotent universalism.[41]

In any case, it is apparent that certain Christian themes—compassion, justice, and hope—apply across specific communities. A Christian ethic ought never to claim that "God, Christ, salvation, grace, and the Church, objects of theological reflection, exist only for the needs of a particular group or can be grasped in their truth only from the perspective of a particular group."[42] Rather, a theological ethic must advance these universal claims while at the same time "reflect[ing] the perspective and needs of a particular group, especially those of a group whose voice has been suppressed and absent."[43]

An Asian American Christian ethic with regard to education and labor must take on multiple forms in order to acknowledge the vast diversity among the Asian American community. The ethical needs of the least-educated and the poorest of Asian Americans differ vastly from those of the most well-educated and well-off. At the same time, there remains a need for solidarity across Asian American subgroups for practical reasons and for theological integrity. The practical reasons for solidarity include legislative and political change, as Asian Americans are often subject to laws as a monolithic group; also, Asian Americans ought to work together to confront and address the extremely wide socioeconomic disparities among ethnic subgroups. Theological integrity requires that we not lose sight of the Christian narrative as a universal message that offers a transcendent, salvific grace to all humanity.

DISCUSSION QUESTIONS

1. What are the priorities of a good education? What are the benefits and drawbacks of Christian schools? Ought the primary purpose of education be to prepare students for the labor market?

2. What positive lessons can be learned from the contemporary focus among many Asian American groups on education and, in particular, getting admitted to selective colleges? Or should we instead consider high-achieving Asian Americans a "cautionary tale" from a Christian point of view?

3. What are some guidelines for ethical treatment of workers? If workers voluntarily consent to receiving low wages or working long hours, should such a scenario prove problematic from a Christian point of view?

4. Why ought—or ought not—Asian American Christians feel a greater moral obligation to assist other Asian Americans with regard to education and employment than people of other races or ethnicities?

Cosmetic Surgery

JONATHAN TRAN

I am, in this essay, concerned with thinking through the phenomenon of elective plastic surgery among Asian American women. I first describe the phenomenon and then analyze it from the perspective of Asian American Christian ethics. In describing the phenomenon, I relate plastic surgery epiphenomenally as occurrences among Koreans (in Korea) and Asian Americans, showing how the two cohere as separate expressions of a continuous phenomenon. In analyzing the phenomenon, I initially offer what I take to be a possible Christian approach aided by the work of Gerald McKenny and then examine how Asian Americans might respond both to the phenomenon and to McKenny's approach to the issue. In conclusion, I advance a conception of performativity as a uniquely Asian American *and* Christian perspective on elective plastic surgery.[1]

* * *

An online ad for the elective cosmetic procedure Valentine Mouth Rejuvenation (valentine anguloplasty) begins, "With advancing years . . . the upper lip lengthens, lip vermilion thins and lines appear, lip 'pucker' disappears, corners of the mouth turn down, bony support shrinks, the nasal tip drops, and the columella-labial angle narrows." To which you might respond, "Who cares?" Clever as it is, the ad lets you know why the "smile surgery" might be for you: "Since the mouth and peri-oral region play a dominant role in conveying disposition, this age-related negative line can be misinterpreted, turning messages of openness into rejection, receptiveness into hostility, pleasure into pain, joy into sadness, understanding into misunderstanding, comprehension into confusion, delight into despair." Accompanying images remind the viewer that an upturned smile is "happy" and its opposite, "sad." Going further, the ad critiques competing cosmetic options, as if to cannibalize its own profession: "For years, plastic surgery has been obsessed with facelifting, casting it as the ultimate solution to facial aesthetics. Actually 'facelifting' does little or nothing to correct many problem areas, especially the area around the mouth." After describing how the procedure works—"Its name comes from the small heart-shaped excision made at the corner of the mouth"—the ad ends with a smile. All's well that ends well, so long as one's end is achieved through elective plastic surgery.[2]

In what context is such a practice coherent, much less enticing? According to an August 27, 2013, *Wall Street Journal* piece, "Cosmetic surgeons in Seoul say they are seeing a sudden rise in demand for the so-called smile surgery this year among men and women in their 20s and 30s, most of whom are concerned about facing criticism at work because of their expressionless miens."[3] Already the nation with the highest per-capita plastic surgery rates—one in five women elect cosmetic procedures—South Korea has proven ripe for ads like the one just described. While nailing down actual plastic surgery numbers is notoriously difficult, consumer interest in the smile surgery has been widespread enough for physicians and journalists to take notice and controversial enough for its practitioners to come to its defense.[4] Veteran plastic surgeon Dr. Kwon Taek-keun said, "Even when you are looking like your normal self, people keep asking you: 'Why are you frowning?' That's a lot of stress." If you weren't already worried, Dr. Kwon's ominous suggestion—"Why are you frowning?"—could do the trick. This strategy of prescribing a therapy, the prescription of which *creates* its pathology, is par for the course in a global medical culture that consistently blurs the lines between curative procedures and procedures that go by other names: circumventive, preventative, elective, enhancement, and so on.[5] Not surprisingly, valentine anguloplasty is envisaged as restoring—"It's going against gravity. [. . .] We're restoring the original lip line"—rather than distorting that which is natural.[6]

Also in the fall of 2013, a story about South Korean beauty contestants gained much attention on the Internet. Displaying photos of twenty *different* women, the story exhibited in full and discomfiting view how plastic surgery was making South Koreans literally look alike (see Figure 1).[7]

FIGURE 1

Even granting the racialized purview which opines all non-Caucasians "look the same," these women actually *do* look alike. Or perhaps they have been *made* to look alike. When it was revealed that the previous winner of the Miss South Korean pageant had gone under the knife—with the rationale, "I wasn't born beautiful"—the impression arose that all these women had been *made* to meet a common standard, making them look alike, and only as such did they qualify for pageant contention.[8]

What is the relationship between plastic surgery in Korea and in America, specifically among Asian Americans? Given the broad influence of Western and specifically American culture, both historically and within the present context of globalization, one might interpret the phenomenon as a product of cultural imposition. Along with valentine anguloplasty making one look happier, these surgeries might be interpreted as procuring a Caucasian look for non-Caucasian women. American plastic surgeon Dr. Anthony Youn, native to South Korea, articulates this interpretation:

> The majority of facial cosmetic operations performed on Asians are considered "Westernizing" procedures. Two of the most popular, nose jobs (rhinoplasty) and double eyelid surgery (blepharoplasty), are specially

designed to make these features look more Caucasian. Asians generally have wider and flatter noses. Asian rhinoplasty narrows the nose and makes it project more, similar to a European look. Asian blepharoplasty creates an extra fold in the upper eyelid, therein creating a crease. While present in nearly all Caucasians, this extra fold occurs naturally in only 15 percent of East Asians. While Asian plastic surgeons claim that these procedures are meant to retain their patients' ethnicities and make them generally more attractive, I don't buy it. To put it bluntly: Facial plastic surgery on Asians is about making a person look as Caucasian as possible.[9]

Even though he speaks generally of Asians, it's safe to assume that Dr. Youn's observations stem from his *American* context and so include Asian Americans. After all, desiring distinctly Caucasian physical features has been for some time now the driving hypothesis explaining elective cosmetic surgery among Asian American women. Anthropologist Eugenia Kaw penned the authoritative study for this hypothesis, conducting significant research among Asian Americans in the San Francisco area, concluding the following:

> The desire to create more "open" eyes or "sharpen" noses is a product of racial ideologies that associate Asian features with negative behavioral or intellectual characteristics like dullness, passivity, or lack of emotion. With the authority of scientific rationality and technological efficiency, medicine is effective in perpetuating these racist notions. The medical system bolsters and benefits from the larger consumer-oriented society not only by maintaining the idea that beauty should be every woman's goal but also by promoting a beauty standard that requires that certain racial features of Asian American women be modified. Through the subtle and often unconscious manipulation of racial and gender ideologies, medicine, as a producer of norms, and the larger consumer society of which it is a part encourages Asian American women to mutilate their bodies to conform to an ethnocentric norm.[10]

Kaw does not find it surprising that among Americans those of Asian heritage are proportionately the most likely to take up plastic surgery.[11] Kaw's research comes from the early 1990s, at which point two million Americans opted for plastic surgery, 20 percent of whom were Latino American, African American, or Asian American, with Asian Americans the most disproportionately represented. Not only was plastic surgery more likely for Asian American women, but they tended toward specific kinds of procedures. While Caucasian women gravitated toward liposuction, breast augmentation, or wrinkle removal, Asian American women pursued eye and nose procedures that gave them more characteristically Caucasian features.[12] As difficult as it is to establish causal relationships between ethnicity and actual practices, the associations, as Kaw said at the time, are hard to avoid: "While the features that white women primarily seek to alter through cosmetic surgery (i.e., the breasts, fatty areas of the body, and facial wrinkles) do not correspond to conventional markers of racial identity, those features that Asian American women primarily seek to alter (i.e., 'small, narrow' eyes and a 'flat' nose) do correspond to such markers."[13]

As compelling as it is, the evidence of Kaw's ethnographic research bears out only some of her hypothesis. Kaw admitted that at the time of her data gathering, statistics for ethnic trends in plastic surgery were not considered relevant and so remained largely uncollected, such that her research by necessity tended toward the anecdotal. There has, since Kaw's study, been a large growth in the numbers of Asian Americans electing cosmetic surgery, especially so in the last ten years which saw a 57 percent change from 2004 to 2005 and a 21 percent growth from 2011 to 2012.[14] Simultaneously, there is notably more data regarding ethnic trends, but in a way that makes Kaw's causal hypothesis less straightforward. According to the American Society of Plastic Surgeons, the aggregate number of Americans electing cosmetic plastic surgery was approximately 14 million in 2012, with Asian Americans still disproportionately represented at roughly 8 percent (of those surgeries) against their 3 percent of the U.S. population. Procedures that produce features characterized as Caucasian remain popular among Asian American cosmetic patients.[15] However, it is also the case that the overwhelming majority of people who elected eye and nose procedures, 80 percent and 73.3 percent respectively, were Caucasian; though some of this can be accounted for by the proportional majority of Caucasians in America, there remains no easy causal relationship between ethnicity and plastic surgery. For instance, Asian Americans were about as likely to elect breast augmentation, liposuction, and tummy tucks as nose and eye procedures.[16] As well, since Yaw's article, surgical technologies have had to keep up with demand for procedures that produce features that are explicitly non-Caucasian (e.g., eye surgeries that correct for fattiness while retaining the distinctly oval shape of Asian eyes), suggesting that previous numbers reflected practical as much as cultural considerations. None of this debunks Kaw's hypothesis as much as returns it to the complicated racialized and gendered context from which it was drawn and on which it was meant to comment. On the question of whether Asians and Asian Americans want to "look white," perhaps Asian American writer Andrew Lam gets closest when he characterizes Asian American self-image regarding whiteness as "traditionally schizophrenic and contradictory."[17]

Whereas in the past, when one could map American aesthetic influences from Hollywood and Madison Avenue to places like East Asia, today the influences follow these schizophrenic and contradictory lines. Consider what is now called "Asian medical tourism" whereby Asian American women go to Asia, often for the first time, for plastic surgery in places like South Korea, which is more technologically advanced and where such surgeries are more culturally acceptable, and, at one– to two-thirds less expensive, significantly more accessible.[18] Going abroad for cosmetic surgery has the added benefit of anonymity, a relative asset considering the misgivings still associated with plastic surgery in America. Asian countries have been quick to profit from these considerations. Case in point: the Philippines-based Belo Medical Group, a well-established cosmetic practice, recently partnered with the Philippine Department of Tourism in order to attract more Americans to the country for cosmetic surgery.[19]

In the last three years, medical tourism to South Korea has tripled, a fact attributed by many to the enthusiastic reception of Korean popular culture.[20] The sensation known as "K-Pop" is epitomized by the enormous musical smash "Gangnam Style," which in 2012 set an Internet milestone by becoming the first Youtube video viewed by a billion people.[21] "Gangnam Style" is about a Seoul district that has come to be known as the Beverly Hills of South Korea, in part because it boasts over five hundred cosmetic surgery centers.[22] One sees, in the case of K-Pop, a complex but important shift in the patterns of global influence, as Asians increasingly determine aesthetic sensibilities and Americans under the influence of Asian culture go to Asia. In a report for *The Atlantic*, Zara Stone observes, "K-Pop has created a completely new beauty aesthetic that nods to Caucasian features but doesn't replicate them."[23] While an easy causality remains as elusive in this case as it did twenty years ago for Kaw, the numbers attest to a significant development. In 2012, 30,582 Americans, the vast majority of whom were Asian American, traveled to South Korea for plastic surgery, and by 2015, an expected 400,000 medical tourists from all over the world will be visiting South Korea each year, over half of whom will seek cosmetic services.[24] Hugely profitable, Korean medical tourism grossed $453 million in 2012, with projected numbers reaching a staggering $4.2 billion by 2020.[25] Today, rates of cosmetic surgery among Asian Americans pale in comparison to rates among Koreans, one in twenty versus one in five respectively, according to the International Society of Aesthetic Plastic Surgery. Still, with influences like K-Pop, one can anticipate these numbers drawing closer as cultural realities produce a dynamic of continuity whereby American beauty, which is to say Caucasian beauty, sets standards and Asian women receive and reimagine those standards; all the while, Asian American women find themselves as "medical tourists" negotiating agency amidst this unmappable dynamic.[26]

Christian Responses to Medical Technology: Rethinking our Capabilities to Eliminate Suffering

Coming up with ethical critiques of plastic surgery is easy enough, but accounting for those critiques is a bit more challenging. For example, many Americans have been quick to carp on South Korea's seeming obsession with plastic surgery, and some of those criticisms have been mindful of how Caucasian these women are made to look.[27] Yet those consternations often stop short by failing to acknowledge the complicit role Western conceptions of beauty play in Asian and Asian American women's lives. Caucasian critics have failed to see themselves, literally and otherwise, in these women's new faces. As Asian American writer Haruka Sakaguchi said in commenting on the harsh response to the Asian American broadcast journalist and talk show host Julie Chen's admitting to plastic surgery, "The same critics who comment on the morality of Julie Chen's actions, or rudely accuse her of a cultural inferiority complex, would be better off examining the social configurations of our society that led her to make that decision in the first place."[28]

As intimated, one way to respond to the phenomenon of Asian American plastic surgery is to attribute imposed notions of beauty as driving Asian American women toward these kinds of procedures. In this view only the source of imposition changes, from Madison Avenue and Hollywood to the Gangnam district of Seoul, South Korea. This is basically the argument that Kaw makes, and to great effect. Yet, as stated, Kaw's data suggests associations that entail causal arguments that are difficult to manage. Hidden in these suggestions of imposition are certain premises about female agency, premises which seem to me to be somewhat wrong and somewhat right. Further analyzing this phenomenon, or at least going forward from where Kaw leaves us, then, requires that we wade through the more interesting if also more complex questions around agency and how these women use plastic surgery as a form of agency, not only as instances of being determined but also as uniquely late capitalist modes of self-determination, a kind of agency that both responds to and acts on culture. Kaw's hypothesis presumes that these women are being acted upon, that the surgery stands in for Western impositions of beauty, the submitting to which plastic surgery seems to indicate. This, as I said, seems somewhat right, but precisely where it is right, on this point about imposition, requires further analysis because imposition is not a straightforward affair—as I have tried to indicate by passing references to causality—unless our theorizing refuses even a conceptual nod to agency.

Kaw's hypothesis doesn't quite get to the ways electing plastic surgery enacts a kind of agency. Such agency is meager to be sure, but perhaps meager agency is what remains available to us within globalizing cultures, of which medical tourism is surely an instance. We might shift our question, then, from "What is being done to these women and why?" to "What are these women doing and why?" Accordingly, we should acknowledge that viewing South Korean plastic surgery as *only* subservience is a kind of arrogance, as if Americans are the origin of all things, even the damnable things.[29] For instance, though it is true that Asians prefer fairer complexions and have pursued technologies for gaining unnaturally what hasn't been given to them naturally, still this preference can be traced back long before Madison Avenue and Hollywood started broadcasting fair-skinned Caucasian images.[30] To be sure, native preferences found further footholds in these cultural prompts, but there's enough complicity to go around. Social theorist Hejiin Lee writes, "There's a real problem when you make generalizations about a whole country full of women, that they're all culturally duped." Lee continues, "Often times when Asian American women opt to get surgery, people automatically assume it's because they want to look white, but often you find the pressure to engage in these surgeries coming from their own families, from their connections abroad."[31] Tracing out accounts of agency amidst this glut of complicity becomes the task of figuring out what it means to be a person amidst the pressures operating on our bodies. Kaw herself saw this, writing, "On the one hand, the women are rebelling against the notion that one must be content with the physical features one is born with, that one cannot be creative in molding one's own idea of what is beautiful. On the other hand, they are conforming to Caucasian standards of beauty."[32]

* * *

Hence, considering Christian responses to Asian American cosmetic surgery necessitates first examining the context in which elective plastic surgery bespeaks agency—coming into the world by self-showing, as Heidegger spoke of. What is the quality of that agency, what does it achieve for those for whom the self shows itself by such measures? I approach these questions by reviewing a possible approach to these questions in Gerald McKenny's work, and then by assessing that approach by offering an Asian American perspective on it.

In *To Relieve the Human Condition*, Gerald McKenny describes modern medicine in terms of "the Baconian moral project" in which medical technology is imagined as enabling the elimination of suffering and the expansion of human choice.[33] Professor McKenny's assessment is critical if we are to come to grips with what has befallen us in modern medical cultures. There is a double development here: first, the eclipse of a prior moral universe, the stock of criteria by which normative judgments were hitherto rendered, and then its replacement with a newly regnant moral universe. To accept this, one does not need to be committed to *ressourcement* declension narratives that have as of late emplotted rival moral regimes.[34] One need only be willing to grant that modern medicine is powerful insofar as it operates with a high degree of moral autonomy even though we can be sure that challenges to its authority remain extant. One may wonder how medicine gained this sovereignty, but for my purposes here it need be only permitted that it, or something like it, obtains. Modern medicine advances beyond moral reproach such that the vast majority of its practices and commitments are not so much debated as counted as obvious. McKenny's approach gives theological footing to Kaw's observation that "the Western medical system is a most effective promoter of the racial stereotypes that influence Asian American women, since medical knowledge is legitimized by scientific rationality and technical efficiency." Kaw reports how many prospective cosmetic surgery patients are given medical reasons, rather than elective and cosmetic ones, for their procedures, as if the medicalization of the procedure legitimated it: "For example, many patients were told that they had 'excess fat' on their eyelids and that it was 'normal' for them to feel dissatisfied with the way they looked."[35] When questions are put to medicine's authority (e.g., stem cell research, reproductive technologies, rationales for euthanasia, and so on), the manner in which these questions are handled depict them as exceptions to a rule, ethical tinkering that will be permitted so long as the entire complex of medicine remains intact.[36] And all this because modern medical technology has not so much outpaced ethics as much as produced its own ethics, ethics the warrant of which we currently presume—the idea that it is morally right, and undeniably so, to eliminate suffering and expand human choice. The reason medicine no longer requires moral intervention is because it has proven itself up to the task; if anything, control of suffering and human choice were in jeopardy until modern medicine arrived on the scene, showing prior ethical commitments wanting, or so the story goes.[37]

The self in such a world is then a self insofar as it remains free from suffering. So much so that when suffering cannot be staved off, when medical therapies have reached their limit and "nothing more can be done," questions arise as to whether one should go on; the self has become less than itself and so may not be worth preserving.[38] Once you stake personhood on the absence of suffering and you enact personhood as the pursuit of therapies that will ensure that absence, then it is quite natural to assume that any life that entails suffering is not worth living. One of the implications of Professor McKenny's assessment is that insofar as human life is a life from which suffering cannot be eliminated, hence the double entendre of "to relieve the human condition," the Baconian moral project is either Manichean, for it will teach us to regret our lives as bodies that cannot go on completely devoid of suffering, or doomed to failure. But to the ears of Baconians, the latter suggestion can't help but be heard as a dare, the former just pedantic. If it is the moral enterprise we all take it in faith to be, then it will, like any enterprise worth its salt, pursue relentlessly its goal; no amount of suffering will deter its vocation; suffering will only further inspire its work. We should acknowledge the profound moral responsibility physicians assume; to them, and to us patients as their beneficiaries, there can be no higher calling. The embarrassingly high regard with which we hold physicians tells us we too believe in this calling. Nothing less than the self is at stake, and it is the genius of modern medicine that it has actually kept pace with the ambitions to which it has given itself. Here, we should notice how hope operates situated almost entirely in terms of the medical establishment's ability to come through for the sufferer; what is asked of the patient is not to give up hope, that is, to believe some therapy will come available. The modern self, then, is the one able to perform these rituals of promise and hope hinged to questions of suffering and the expectation that human life is worth living insofar as it avoids suffering.[39]

The self, to be a self, also determines itself, which explains McKenny's portrayal of the self as chooser. Medicine's role is to ensure that choosing continues. Notice that on this score the self in pain is cast as a problem to the self as chooser; most immediately, the self cannot choose out of pain, making the question of pain internal to the question of indeterminacy. It becomes a conundrum for this line of thought to account for the self as anything other than chooser, a person able to assert the self amidst the determinations against which agency is established. And medicine expands and therefore enables this choice, so that the description of what it means to be a chooser—a person—itself expands (the significance of this expansion will be taken up later). What was once seen as luck or fate or providence can no longer be left to chance, or *should* no longer be, hence the moral ascription of the Baconian project. That is why we late moderns, when we look back, tend to lament our predecessor cultures' lack of choice and even begin to wonder whether life was worth much then, or at least we are glad we no longer need to live that way. It is no problem that conceptions of selfhood keep changing, and the point here is that change is now almost entirely accounted for in terms of technology, against which any culture's conceptions of selfhood now need to answer and against which no culture's pace of life can long compete. We don't regret simply the past but any culture unable to offer what modern technological culture now can, which may answer that prior wonderment about medicine's autonomy.[40]

Before turning back to plastic surgery, we should consider the ethical reach of the Baconian moral project. Consider for a moment children. It used to be the case that some things could not be controlled and so weren't viewed as within the provenance of human agency. For example, cystic fibrosis or Down syndrome were fates we suffered when children were born with these systemic chromosomal disorders. We took advantage of modern medicine's abilities to treat their challenging living consequences, but there was little we could do to preclude the occurrences of cystic fibrosis and Down syndrome as such. Now we, or more specifically those of us with access to medical technology, can. We can eliminate them altogether. We do so, among other ways, by the triple screen, a medical diagnostic tool deployed usually in the second trimester of pregnancy to detect these kinds of abnormalities. Not only that, but if a true positive is found, those involved can, if they choose, intervene and abort. Wanting to avoid those unpleasantries, we can also trace out and then leave out those chromosomal realities altogether; we have been involved in these kinds of activities as long as we have been screening viability through in vitro processes. While the latter saves us from having to abort pregnancies, both approaches will have the effect of eliminating the presence of cystic fibrosis and Down syndrome children from the world, because there is no Down syndrome without Down syndrome children. We can offer all the sentimentalities we wish about the gifts these children are, but the fact is that at the pace with which we are pursuing these interventions, these children will be gifts we have not much longer. As regrettable as that sounds, it's simply the continuation of modern medicine's moral enterprise. No one would deny that great suffering attends the life of the cystic fibrosis child and family. In the past nothing could be done, and so these sorts of questions about interventions were not yet questions. But now that we can know, even if we elect to do nothing with that knowledge, the question then becomes *shouldn't* prospective parents be able to know and thereby possesses those choices such knowledge avails? One can imagine a situation where technology made knowledge possible for individuals while the options they had in response still remained limited. But at this point it's the case that, among the various options available to a family that receives a true positive, abortion remains. And it's also the case that in America upward of 85 percent of families will choose to abort these pregnancies.[41] *And* we can understand why, if we're honest with ourselves. Because of technology, the issue is not simply choosing *not* to abort; the issue rapidly has become choosing to *have* these children, the choice to have but the inverse of the choice not to abort. That is how responsibility is weighed in the Baconian imagination—the presence of the technology issues with moral compulsions; in these cases the burden of proof more often than not lies with the family that chooses *not* to abort.[42]

Finally, consider the following comments from the noted Oxford bioethicist Julian Savulescu:

> Fancy a child who's likely to be altruistic? Then look for a version of the COMT gene. Want them to be faithful and enjoy stable relationships? Avoid a variant of AVPR1A. Steer clear of a certain type of the MA0A gene, too—it's linked to higher levels of violence in children who often

suffer abuse or deprivation. Screening embryos like this is illegal at present, but isn't rational design something we should welcome? If we have the power to intervene in the nature of our offspring—rather than consigning them to the natural lottery—then we should. Surely trying to ensure that your children have the best, or a good enough, opportunity for a great life is responsible parenting? Some people believe that babies are a gift, of God or nature, and that we shouldn't mess with their genetic make-up. But most of us already implicitly reject this view. We're routinely screening embryos and foetuses for conditions such as cystic fibrosis and Down's syndrome, and there's little public outcry. What's more, few people protested at the decisions in the mid-2000s to allow couples to test embryos for inherited bowel and breast cancer genes, and this pushes us a lot closer to creating designer humans. Children with these genes are healthy. They don't develop cancer until later in life and it's often preventable.[43]

Professor Savulescu believes that insofar as these technologies are available, it is morally irresponsible *not* to utilize them. His is a viewpoint further along than many of ours on these matters in that the use of these technologies to control cystic fibrosis and Down syndrome serves, for most of us I imagine, as examples for extensions of the proposition that it is morally responsible to eliminate suffering and expand human choice. While we may still find ourselves wrestling with these matters, Professor Savulescu is perfectly comfortable eliminating any further Down syndrome children.

Instructively, the one worry Savulescu does register is the standard one where these kinds of medical interventions smack of the eugenics associated with Nazi and other racist pogroms. There is, however, a critical difference, Professor Savulescu reminds us: whereas those machinations imposed eugenics for their own purposes and thus forced them upon the unwitting and powerless, we *chose* these technologies; no one is forcing us. Specifically, he writes, "what was especially objectionable about [Nazi eugenics] was the coercive imposition of a state vision for a healthy population. Modern eugenics, from testing for diseases to deciding whether you want a girl or boy, is voluntary. So where genetic selection aims to bring out a trait that clearly benefits an individual and society, we should allow parents the choice. To do otherwise is to consign those who come after us to the ball and chain of our squeamishness and irrationality."[44] Notice how the argument works. First, the primary difference between what the Nazis did and what Professor Savulescu is proposing is that his proposal involves our choosing; agency-as-choosing becomes the primary arbiter. Secondly, insofar as this is true, insofar as we can choose, we would be foolish *not* to choose, to, as he puts it, "consign" ourselves "to the ball and chain of our squeamishness and irrationality." Choice then does double-duty, first absolving the technology of moral concern and then imposing upon us the requirement of its deployment. Again, what some might take to be monstrous, or at least questionably monstrous, Professor Savulescu takes as a matter of course, the difference predicated on agency even if the technology and procedures do practically the same thing.

Using the ethical paradigm offered by McKenny, one can imagine elective plastic surgery as a form of moral agency insofar as it fulfills the conditions of what he calls the Baconian moral project. Remember that veteran plastic surgeon Dr. Kwon Taek-keun said to the *Journal*, "Even when you are looking like your normal self, people keep asking you: 'Why are you frowning?' That's a lot of stress." If the smile surgery can alleviate this stress and its consequences, then isn't it alleviating human suffering? Sure, the cynic can argue that such an appraisal is highly subjective, making it that anything will count as suffering. But this is where the Baconian moral project's second goal of expanding human choice cashes out, by expanding moral description: only *I* can say whether I am in pain; no one else can tell me the moral status of my suffering.[45]

As for how plastic surgery made all those female beauty pageant contestants look the same, remember that pageants are but especially public exhibitions of societal standards; we are *all* constantly being judged by those standards; pageants just display the criteria in an intensely visible venue. So the same criteria that would make all those contestants elect plastic surgery would be operative on all who live in the society where those criteria govern.[46] We might think of these contestants as those most able to appease those standards, rendering the ugliness of the criteria less than ugly; or at least some think of them that way, else they would not have made it to television. And while it would be banal to claim inability to achieve societal standards of beauty as a kind of suffering that needs assuaging, it would be more difficult to deny that subjection to those standards of beauty have ill effects. All teenagers know this. If we examine the manner in which those standards of beauty issue, often in socially pernicious ways, then a serious consideration comes into view. Toni Morrison illustrates these dynamics hauntingly in *The Bluest Eye*, a crushing story about how brutal self-hate emanates in communities dominated by white conceptions of beauty.[47] One cannot read *The Bluest Eye* and deny the suffering created by these societal standards.

Of course, there is suffering and there is suffering. But that's just like saying there's beauty and there's beauty. One can no more choose what one takes as suffering than one can choose what one finds beautiful, or whether one feels pain altogether; the pain is immediate; we are not given to interject; there is no room for consideration. Hence, it goes without saying that elective plastic surgery is a kind of choosing. I will return to this later, but for now it is enough to note that most people who elect these procedures would readily say, "I'm not forced to do this; I'm choosing to," and would feel as absolved, and maybe as responsible, as Professor Savulescu does because of the ostensible presence of choice.

Returning to our question, where is the self in these practices? One answer, the one I have been considering, is in the very enactment of suffering's elimination and choice's expansion. In the vacuum where medical culture now dictates moral terms, agency is now procured by adherence to this moral project: inasmuch as I do not suffer and choose for myself, I am a person. Indeed, one could even posit that elective plastic surgery is the act par excellence of the modern moral self, where one is freed from aesthetic suffering as the ultimate act of choosing, where one can become—at least on the surface, though a surface with depth—whoever one wants to become. In this light plastic surgery becomes the definitive instantiation of the Baconian moral project.

I have been reviewing the manner in which the Baconian moral project constructs selves through elective medical procedures like cosmetic surgery. Namely, since selfhood is established as freedom from suffering and of choice, so that to lack either of those qualities jeopardizes one's hold on selfhood, then modern biotechnology can be seen as productive of selfhood in a way underappreciated in Kaw's hypothesis, inasmuch as it is able to provide these qualities.

Elective Plastic Surgery among Asian Americans: Trends, Performance, and Performativity

Having considered McKenny's ethical reflection of our phenomenon, it is now time to assess that account from an Asian American perspective. In doing so I first assess that account through the conceptual lens of what critical theorists have called "performativity" and then, concluding, advance that concept toward an understanding of Asian American cosmetic surgery that makes use of McKenny's ethical responses and its Asian American appropriation.

In *The Melancholy of Race*, Anne Anlin Cheng utilizes a distinction that critical theorist Judith Butler previously delineated between "performativity" and "performance."[48] "Performativity" would be descriptive of acts where individuals subscribe and conform to scripted requirements for roles bequeathed by society. In line with "performativity" then, Asian American women who elect plastic surgery subscribe to conceptions of beauty imposed upon them by others—Kaw's thesis where society does violence to them by compelling them to do violence to themselves. Performativity as a conception, then, would have us believe that selfhood is gained, but in an extremely circumscribed way.[49]

However, Professor Cheng, following Butler at this point, offers the possibility that one performs an imposed script, but in ways that stretch the bounds of that script: "some kind of agency has irresistibly emerged in the unpredictable dynamics between an individual's performance and the performativity that scripts her."[50] In this way, "performance" in contradistinction to "performativity" inscribes the self within imposed conditions of performativity *and* also reinscribes the self beyond those initial possibilities. The suggestion here is rich and the argument goes like this: selfhood comes about through performance of socially managed scripts; there is not an account of selfhood that is free of scripting; to be a person is to be acknowledged as a person, which occurs when one has satisfied criteria of selfhood that scripts put on offer. At this point the argument is working under performativity, and it is dogmatically familiar enough. However, Cheng's point presses further. She is not saying that selfhood is claimed at the moment when the individual sheds oneself of allegiance to selfhood totally, as if one could escape social criteria altogether. To be free in this vein is to be undetermined by anything other than agency as assertion. Avoiding those Cartesian presumptions, Cheng instead turns to the question of whether performance of social scripts needs to be as narrowly conceived as performativity suggests. Instead, she asks the question whether one can perform a script in ways that surpass the respective script's possibilities, not to the effect of freeing the individual from all scripts, but rather to write alternative scripts within the terms offered by the dominative script. Isn't the whole point, for Cheng, of turning to performativity as a conceptual metaphor to highlight the multitudinous ways a role can be performed (well or poorly, creatively or flatly, etc.)? Judgment of performance is not a simply either an up or down proposition but one of expanding boundaries, the possibilities of which expand the various criteria for judgment. Analyzing elective cosmetic surgery through the contrastive concepts of performativity and performance grants the possibility that, sure, these women may be subjected to societal norms, and in these violent ways, or they may be acting as subjects within conditions that imagine subjectivity in novel ways. If the latter is the case, then presupposing all elective cosmetic surgery as only performativity enacts its own kind of violence, where women's lives are forced into the service of unbending conceptual categories.

What Might an Asian American Christian Ethics Approach Look Like?

I want to figure Christian ethical life as situated between performativity and performance as Cheng would have it. Consider here the philosopher Stanley Cavell's *The Claim of Reason*, a text I find endlessly useful for Christian moral reflection. After having shown why the regular formulations of societal obligation turn up empty, Cavell writes,

> What I consent to, in consenting to the contract, is not mere obedience, but membership in a polis, which implies two things: First, that I recognize the principle of consent itself, which means that I recognize others to have consented with me, and hence that I consent to political *equality*. Second, that I recognize the society and its government, so constituted, as mine; which means that I am answerable not merely to it, but for it. So far, then, as I recognize myself to be exercising my responsibilities for it, my obedience to it is obedience to my own laws; citizenship in that case is the same as my autonomy; the polis is the field within which I work out my personal identity and it is the creation of (political) *freedom*.[51]

What I want to conclude with is the point that elective plastic surgery bespeaks *not* belonging to a field of equality and freedom by which agency can be reimagined, reidentified, and reenacted over against the aesthetic norms that govern society. In this way Christian consternation of such practices, what I previously characterized as a type of cultural carping, needs to account for its own complicity in these realities. In the same way that the belittling of plastic surgery misses its own role in aesthetic imposition, so Christian concern about these matters needs to account for the complicity of its failure to supply alternative frameworks for construing agency; the mistake of ethical carping is a mistake of commission, while Christianity's is a mistake of omission. Self-making is the fate of persons who no longer feel like they effectively belong with others, and subscription to the Baconian moral project is the fate of individuals absolved of moral commitment beyond agency as assertion, which medical technology will quickly absorb in the absence of competitor regimes and then renarrate in terms of suffering and choice as McKenny so astutely observes.

Cavell's vision, in contrast, is that agency is something to be worked out and membership in a common life is such a working out; membership is not construed here in terms of the obligation of individuated duty (consider Kant's categorical imperative), but rather belonging (consider Cavell's revision of Kant, what he inverts as a "categorical declarative").[52] When that is in place—no small achievement, to be sure—then equality proves the footing necessary to imagine freedom as not opposed to equality, the animating question of much political liberalism, but mutually informative: on this register equality allows freedom to be envisaged within a framework of mutuality where freedom is configured beyond self-assertion and equality allows freedom to be envisaged as regard for whom I am mutually committed to, where my equality *with* others does not depend on my freedom *from* others.

The relentlessly inequitable treatment of women (and precisely here Christianity's aforementioned sins of omission disastrously follow its sins of commission) makes for conditions that divorce freedom from equality. Within these conditions freedom becomes plastic surgery's self-assertion against the imposition of Western standards of beauty, just as equality becomes isolation from those very others who might otherwise *with me* reimagine criteria for beauty and, hence, the moral mission of medicine. Given all this, we cannot be surprised, much less carp about, feminine agency procured by elective plastic surgery.[53]

Cavell helps us see this. Cheng helps us see the productive possibilities within this divorce and in doing so raises further possibilities for what I signaled as certain ecclesial negotiations between performance and performativity that Cavell's mutuality of freedom and equality lays bare.

While one can imagine a variety of communities constituted in these ways, the Christian church is the field of equality and freedom I have in mind when I speak of places where agency is worked out in a common life. This may sound vague, and for those who have actually been to church, misleading. But what I'm imagining is an account of agency whereby persons belong to one another, and where whatever selfhood is given to mean, that meaning gains traction in terms of, and never devoid of, others to whom one belongs.

Claiming one belongs to another will strike some as outrageous, especially if one considers the history of violence against women where "belonging" justified all manner of imposition. Yet in considering our history, it would also be problematic to assert selfhood as a counterweight to communal belonging, a sense which political liberalism has been pushing for some time now and which will increasingly employ medical technology as the extension of human choice vis-à-vis the Baconian moral project. Yet for those not raised in liberal democratic cultures, belonging may simply speak to something like family, which begins with communal obligation and only from there ventures into selfhood. This may again sound vague, and, if one catches my drift that Asian Americans, among others, are these ones not raised in liberal democratic cultures and so comport to communal belonging where selfhood gets worked out, again misleading. After all, isn't it the notion that children "belong" to their parents that allows Asian American parents to impose aesthetic norms on their children? (It is not uncommon to hear Asian and Asian American parents pressuring their children to get their eyes "fixed.") Yet notice that I said that church is "something like family" though its family-like status is a necessary but not sufficient condition of the church. Church is like family inasmuch as it holds that communal belonging is individuality's condition of possibility. In a family, a child belongs to a family long before it asserts anything about itself. Likewise, in church, a person emerges as a Christian at the point of baptism where he or she is born into the community as new creation. In family and church, individuality grows from the family's or the church's respective development of that individual, whereby the individual develops traits that both form—Cheng's notion of performativity—and transform—Cheng's notion of performance—communally governed standards for personhood. But church goes further than family in that it requires belonging that in turn entails mutuality of authority. In many families the daughter "belongs" to the father, and so his authority, not hers, is presumed; in church the daughter belongs to the father only inasmuch as the father also belongs to the daughter as a mutual entailment of their baptisms. This mutuality where freedom and equality are worked out in relation to each other is the description of the new creation the Apostle Paul thinks is the New Testament church.[54]

Mutuality of authority will have the effect of simultaneously affirming the kinds of communal belonging familiar in Asian American family life and breaking open what that belonging entails. Just as family life, where children are reared into societal scripts, often operates as ground zero for performativity (and so the common scenario of the

Asian American mother arranging cosmetic surgery for her daughter), so Asian American family life as extensions of the baptismal liturgy just might rewrite those scripts and rearrange lines of authorization (and so the less common scenario of the Asian American child invoking her fraternal authority to praise the beauty of her mother's wider and flatter nose, "Eomma, you *were* born beautiful").

I have been moving toward an account of church that both develops from the characteristic belonging of Asian American family life and obtains to the mutuality resident to the church's sacramental life. Let me conclude by saying how this might inform how we think of the phenomenon of Asian American plastic surgery described earlier in my essay. McKenny's account of the Baconian moral project enabled us to see how plastic surgery secures, *pace* Eugenia Kaw's authoritative hypothesis, a kind of agency for women, though in a decidedly a-theological way. Cheng's distinction between performance and performativity was meant to assess the moral status of that agency, whereby some agents primarily rehearse and repeat societal expectations while others reform and even transform those expectations. With McKenny's account and Cheng's assessment both on board, I can now say that Christian performance of Asian American life goes beyond simple performativity and so goes beyond rehearsing and repeating social expectation. These performances take place on the stage where aesthetic demands, racial and otherwise, conscript some to plastic surgery. Resetting this stage will require an account of selfhood that is answerable to those to whom one belongs; otherwise one will be left alone to answer to the dictates of aesthetic performativity. These dictates are no small thing, and I have tried to describe them as a continuous, if causally unmappable, phenomenon stretching between Asia and America. In this vein the church can be seen as an expanding repertoire of practices that reconceives—over and against these conscriptions—ethnicity, gender, beauty, agency, happiness, responsibility, and so on.

This can take any number of forms. Imagine the parents of a child born with a cleft palate. These parents might be tempted by social demands to baptize their child in front of the church congregation only *after* first societally baptizing their child through so-called "reconstructive" plastic surgery.[55] However, as Christians, these parents envision their lives as primarily belonging to their congregation and so might first submit the demands of performativity to the congregation's performance of faith, within which the congregation might respond by claiming

Psalm 139, that the child has been fearfully and wonderfully made, cleft pallet, poopy diapers, piercing wail, bald head and all. Receiving those words, the parents might imagine baptizing the child in front of the congregation as performing Psalm 139 and resisting the performativity of plastic surgery as societal baptism, the former exploding the demands of the latter. At the point of baptism, the congregation receives the child as one of their own, and as one of their own, theirs to treat by way of plastic surgery, theirs to raise without the societal benefits of plastic surgery, or whatever direction life in the Spirit might take them.

So it goes for the Asian American Christian woman who feels compelled to kowtow to societal pressures regarding Caucasian notions of beauty or the sacral power of Gangnam style. For her, Psalm 139 offers a different script. In this staging she has been searched and is known, even as she is seen publicly and sees herself privately, as one whose deeds will never take her from the presence of the Lord, and whose very body witnesses to the wonder of the Lord, the liturgy (as "the work of the people") rendering her a self that when surgically altered for cosmetic reasons surrenders something of that witness and wonder. Psalm 139 tells her that the circumscribed performativity that demands something other than that which is given might be a type of enmity toward God, warring with the one who made her fearfully and wonderfully.[56] In these ways, Asian American women who refuse the demands and promises of elective cosmetic surgery might just be liturgically performing the psalms' script and enacting a performativity-exploding agency.

By gathering Asian Americans together, Christian churches honor Asian American bodies, their goodness and beauty—a basic notion, but one that cannot be underestimated given the biopolitical pressures of performativity. Gathered with others by the female pastor whose faithfulness is esteemed as beautiful *and* Asian American (beautiful *as* Asian American), this community localizes aesthetic judgment over against universalizing standards unforgiving of the particular. No doubt local forms of socialization are powerful in their own right, but these modalities offer alternative ways of being, which in this case means alternative ways of looking. Ruled by the rites of baptism, the criteria for membership in these churches follow their liturgical birthing of selves who as selves belong to the one corporate body of Christ, whose Jewish body catechistically engrafts into itself all kinds of faces.

DISCUSSION QUESTIONS

1. How convincing is Eugenia Kaw's hypothesis that Asian Americans seek cosmetic surgery in order to look Caucasian? How does the explosive growth of Asian medical tourism, inspired by the likes of "Gangnam Style," confirm or challenge Kaw's hypothesis?

2. In issues of bioethics, how much should the presence of "choice" make us feel better about an otherwise morally questionable practice? For example, if one can claim with fair certainty that one *chose* to undergo rhinoplasty (a nose job), that one was not being pressured to do so by societal standards, does that make an act that would otherwise smack of cultural acquiescence morally acceptable?

3. Are Asian Americans, with their high commitments to community, more or less likely to bow to the pressures of societal aesthetic norms? How can the Christian church ethically challenge those norms? Is the Asian American church more or less prone to those norms, more or less able to challenge them?

4. Is there something more questionable or troubling about the use of plastic surgery to enhance physical appearance than, say, the use of makeup, alterations in hairstyle, dieting, or exercise? If so, what is it (e.g., medical risks, costs, use of medical resources, permanent alteration of one's God-given features)? Is there a moral difference between surgically altering one's eyes or nose versus surgically augmenting one's breasts and butt? Where does the line between acceptable grooming and inappropriate vanity fall?

Conclusion

The Future of Asian American Christian Ethics

GRACE Y. KAO AND ILSUP AHN

Readers who have tarried with us through *Asian American Christian Ethics* have now been armed to look at moral problems with an Asian American lens. They have seen how the problems of gender relations and sexuality are compounded for both Asian American men and women by racism and imperialism; how abstract Christian considerations of the ethics of peace and war cannot capture the special concerns that war, particularly America's wars, continues to have on this particular demographic; and how any adequate discussion of the ethics of marriage, family, and parenting for Asian Americans must factor in common patterns and issues among the Asian American population (e.g., transnationalism, multigenerational households, biculturality among immigrants and refugees, "tiger mom" parenting pressures to excel).

Attention to the distinctive histories and concerns of Asian Americans has accordingly equipped readers to go beyond the black/white binary. This polarizing and dichotomous understanding of race and race relations in the United States has never been descriptively adequate; it is increasingly less so as more and more racial-ethnic minorities who are neither (or neither fully) black nor white populate America's shores. Still, as society continually compels Asian Americans to choose sides—e.g., with (mostly) black protests against (mostly) white police brutality? With blacks and other racial-ethnic minoritized communities for continued affirmative action, or with whites alleging reverse discrimination?—Asian Americans have long known that their interests and experiences cannot be fully captured in these ways. Asian Americans have particular histories and concerns not reducible to those of others, in part because their race grants them privileges in some cases and occasions to be discriminated against in others. Now non-Asians who have read our book will know such things, too.

We hope you have enjoyed reengaging the Christian tradition of ethical reflection with us. We are especially eager to see in successive years whether Asian Americans, Christian or not, will continue to find the reflections and perspectives presented here true to their own. As this emerging subfield of study is taken up by a wider diversity of Asian American Christian scholars—later generations, Asian adoptees, "hapas," LGBTIQ, and so forth—we expect that the topics and concerns that Asian American Christian ethics will be tasked to cover will deepen and expand. Moreover, as scholars become more comfortable working on problems of special concern to Asian American communities, we hope to see sustained reflection on issues not typically covered in anthologies of Christian ethics, including some of the ones surfaced here in these pages (e.g., plastic surgery; the phenomena of "parachute kids," "goose families," and "maternity tourism;" the use of complementary alternative and traditional medicine (CATM) in health care ethics; an ethical and environmental scrutiny of feasting).

Now the work of inaugurating the subfield of Asian American Christian ethics is complete. To paraphrase a well-known philosopher, however, the point has never been only to understand the world, but to seek to change it. Going forward, then, and to paraphrase Irene Oh's remarks in this volume, the task for Asian American Christian ethicists will be to balance an awareness of the tremendous diversity that exists among us with the strategic need to present a "united front" as agents of change for the good and justice for all.

Notes

Preface

1 A more detailed account of this origin story can be found in Grace Yia-Hei Kao, "Prospects for Developing Asian American Christian Ethics," *Society of Asian North American Christian Studies* 3 (2011): 91–92. Our thoughtful, and at times painful, process of collective self-reflection involved us exploring these and other possible explanations: Was the small fraction of us doing this kind of explicitly contextualist work at the time we first met in 2008 tied to the lack of Asian American faculty mentors in ethics? Our training in graduate school that had neither encouraged us to study this kind of scholarship nor do it ourselves? Our rejection of any essentialist assumption that "authentic" work for us scholars of Asian descent would have us pursuing "Asian" concerns instead of whatever most sustained our intellectual curiosity? Ironically cultural reasons for not wanting to make a "big deal" about our social location as racial-ethnic minorities? An uncritical assumption on our part that mastery of and ongoing work within the white, Euro-American canon of scholarship was the key to our success in academe?

2 The SCE has committed to support the Asian and Asian American Working Group (alongside the earlier established African and African American Working Group and Latino/a Working Group) as part of its Twenty-First Century Initiatives—commitments that the SCE has undertaken since the dawn of the new millennium to address the evolving needs of the Society.

3 We especially thank SueJeanne Koh for helpful feedback on an earlier draft of this preface.

Chapter 1: Introduction

1 More specifically, our book is the first of its kind *from scholars whose primary training and discipline is ethics.* We undoubtedly stand in the debt of Asian American scholars in theology, Bible, and related fields, who, since the 1960s, have been doing the work of ethics all along in providing moral responses to social and theological questions and in pursuing justice and liberation for all. The

269

relationship that Asian American Christian ethics has to broader scholarship by Asian American Christians is thus comparable to Miguel De La Torre's understanding that the emerging discipline of Latina/o Christian ethics is "rooted in forty years of Hispanic religious scholarship." See De La Torre, *Latina/o Social Ethics: Moving beyond Eurocentric Moral Thinking* (Waco, Tex.: Baylor University Press, 2010), 69.

2 Paul Lauritzen, "Emotions and Religious Ethics," *Journal of Religious Ethics* 16, no. 2 (1988): 314.

3 The idea of subdividing human experience along the lines of sex, gender, race, nationality, culture, and so forth as a source of ethical reflection might still be seen as especially problematic for Christians, given the theological proposition that cultural variation and social distinction among Christians are ultimately irrelevant before God as per Gal 3:28 ("There is no longer Jew or Greek, there is no longer slave or free, there is no longer male and female; for all of you are one in Christ Jesus"). Some skeptics might accordingly invoke the principle of Christian unity to call into question any ethical approaches that foreground racial-ethnic particularity or other markers of social differentiation, including the enterprise of Asian American Christian ethics articulated here. In response to these and other concerns about unnecessarily dividing the body of Christ, we would note first that all claims in Christian ethics, like all studies in ethics, are anchored in specific social contexts (whether or not these are acknowledged) and thus an understanding of those contextual factors is necessary for doing Christian ethics well.

4 *Asian Americans: A Mosaic of Faiths* (Washington, D.C.: The Pew Forum on Religion and Public Life, 2012), 11, 17–18, http://www.pewforum.org/Asian-Americans -A-Mosaic-of-Faiths.aspx, reports that Asian American Christians exceed their U.S. counterparts in frequency of worship attendance and in concurring with the belief that living a very religious life is an important goal.

5 See Elizabeth M. Hoeffel et al., *The Asian Population: 2010* (U.S. Census Bureau, 2012), 1–23, http://www.census.gov/prod/cen2010/briefs/c2010br-11.pdf. According to the 2010 Census, 14.7 million people or 4.8 percent of the total U.S. population, reported being "Asian alone" and 2.6 million people (0.9 percent) additionally reported being "Asian in combination with one or more other races." In sum, 5.6 percent of the total U.S. population report having some Asian heritage.

6 See Paul Taylor, ed., *The Rise of Asian Americans: Updated Edition* (Washington, D.C.: Pew Research Center, 2013), 1, http://www.pewsocialtrends .org/2012/06/19/the-rise-of-asian-americans/, for these and other statistics. The 2010 Census confirms that the Asian alone population increased more than four times faster than the total U.S. population, growing by 43 percent from 10.2 million to 14.7 million. Asians who reported multiple races also grew at a faster rate than the Asia alone population, growing by 60 percent in size since 2000.

7 To be sure, Christian ethicists vary from one another not only in the way they relate the four traditional sources of the "Wesleyan quadrilateral" to one another, but also to the extent to which they draw upon the disciplines of secular

learning (including natural and social sciences and philosophy) and the wisdom and practices of other religious traditions.

8 Thus in characterizing our work as Asian American Christian ethics, we push back—as Stacey Floyd-Thomas observes that womanists have done in womanist theology and ethics—against the "assumption of Christian ethics that one must transcend one's social location in order to speak to the universal condition of [our] humanity." See Floyd-Thomas, *Mining the Motherlode: Methods in Womanist Ethics* (Cleveland, Ohio: Pilgrim Press, 2006), 3.

9 Taylor, *Rise of Asian Americans*, 31–32. There is nonetheless considerable variance among Asian Americans: Filipinos (33 percent) and households headed by someone who is Vietnamese (34 percent) are most likely to be arranged multigenerationally, whereas households with Korean (20 percent) or Japanese (18 percent) heads are least likely (33).

10 See Mark Chiang, *The Cultural Capital of Asian American Studies: Autonomy and Representation in the University* (New York: New York University Press, 2009), 6; and Henry Yu, "The 'Oriental Problem' in America, 1920–1960: Linking the Identities of Chinese American and Japanese American Intellectuals," in *Claiming America: Constructing Chinese American Identities during the Exclusion Era*, ed. K. Scott Wong and Sucheng Chan, 192–93 (Philadelphia: Temple University Press, 1998).

11 Chiang, *Cultural Capital*, 7.

12 Chiang, *Cultural Capital*, 7.

13 Mary F. Foskett and Jeffrey Kah-Jin Kuan, eds., *Ways of Being, Ways of Reading: Asian American Biblical Interpretation* (Atlanta: Chalice, 2006), xiii.

14 Grace Yia-Hei Kao, "Prospects for Developing Asian American Christian Ethics," *Society of Asian North American Christian Studies* 3 (2011): 98. The quoted passage is taken from Rita Nakashima Brock et al., "Introduction," in *Off the Menu: Asian and Asian North American Women's Religion and Theology*, ed. Rita Nakashima Brock et al. (Louisville, Ky.: Westminster John Knox, 2007), xiv.

15 Foskett and Kuan, *Ways of Being*, xiii.

16 Hoeffel et al., *Asian Population*, 2. While the six largest Asian ethnic groups today in the United States are the Chinese, except Taiwanese (at 4 million), Filipinos (3.4 million), Asian Indians (3.2 million), Vietnamese (1.9 million), Koreans (1.7 million), and Japanese (1.3 million), the Census also tracks data from numerous other Asian groups (e.g., Bhutanese, Okinawan, Sri Lankan). See U.S. Census Bureau, "2011 American Community Survey," table B02018, http://factfinder2.census.gov/bkmk/table/1.0/en/ACS/11_1YR/B02018.

17 Examples of this phenomenon include the expansive definition of "Asian American" provided by our aforementioned colleagues in biblical studies and the acronyms APA (Asian Pacific American) and API (Asian Pacific Islander) that have been used elsewhere to signal the inclusion of Pacific Islander concerns under the Asian American canopy, such as in the U.S. Conference of Catholic Bishops' 2001 pastoral statement "Asian and Pacific Presence: Harmony in Faith" and the official Congressional designation of the month of May as "Asian-Pacific American Heritage Month."

18 Chiang, *Cultural Capital*, 7, 231n4.

19 Eric Yo Ping Lai and Dennis Arguelles, eds., *The New Face of Asian Pacific America: Numbers, Diversity, and Change in the 21st Century* (Berkeley, Calif.: Asian-Week, 2003), 29.

20 An annotated bibliography commissioned by the SCE Asian and Asian American Working Group and produced by James W. McCarty III entitled "Tilling the Field: An Annotated Bibliography of Asian American Christian Ethics Five Years In," August 14, 2012, http://scethics.org/groups/92/tilling-field-annotated-bibliography-asian-american-christian-ethics-five-years, draws this very distinction. A small section of our publications fell under the first category, "Asian American Christian Ethics," while a much larger body of our work was categorized under "Work by Asian American Christian Ethicists." McCarty shares our understanding that scholarship produced *by* Asian American Christian ethicists is not necessarily to be counted as scholarship *on* Asian American Christian ethics.

21 K. Scott Wong, *Americans First: Chinese Americans and the Second World War* (Philadelphia: Temple University Press, 2008), 79–83.

22 Sociologist Russell Jeung has shown how Asian American evangelicals on college campuses and other ministry settings are more likely to pursue friendships and ministry opportunities with one another (than with non–Asian Americans) because they assume that Asian Americans share similar values, goals, familial systems, pressures, lifestyles, immigrant experiences, and so forth. See Jeung, *Faithful Generations: Race and New Asian American Churches* (Piscataway, N.J.: Rutgers University Press, 2004).

23 Nami Kim, "The 'Indigestible' Asian: The Unifying Term 'Asian' in Theological Discourse," in Brock et al., *Off the Menu*, 23, 37.

24 Kwok Pui-lan, *Postcolonial Imagination and Feminist Theology* (Louisville, Ky.: Westminster John Knox, 2005), 40.

25 Kwok, *Postcolonial Imagination*, 40, cf. 58.

26 There is a large and ever-increasing body of Asian American (not just Asian) theology. A sampling of work includes Peter C. Phan, *Christianity with an Asian Face: Asian-American Theology in the Making* (Maryknoll, N.Y.: Orbis, 2003); Sang Hyun Lee, *From a Liminal Place: An Asian American Theology* (Minneapolis: Fortress, 2010); and Mihee Kim-Kort, *Making Paper Cranes: Toward an Asian American Feminist Theology* (St. Louis, Mo.: Chalice, 2012).

27 E.g., nearly all Asian Americans today encounter "model minority" stereotypes or expectations, with their attendant misconceptions and distortions (though the myth does not apply to all Asians in Asia or elsewhere). To provide another example, Asian Americans must also frequently contend with the "perpetual foreigner" syndrome, wherein our status as real or loyal Americans is held in suspense, regardless of length of residence, fluency in English, acculturation to mainstream cultural values, contributions to society, or American citizenship (n.b., in contrast, the right of belonging of, say, ethnic Japanese in Japan does not arise in analogous ways, though Japan and other countries have their own struggles with ethnic minorities and indigenous peoples). Finally, Asians in America are gendered in very specific ways (i.e., emasculated as men, portrayed as submissive or as fetishized objects as women) in ways they generally are not

in Asia because of the historically particular ways they have been racialized in the North American context and in the West more broadly.

28 Chiang, *Cultural Capital*, 13; Jeung, *Faithful Generations*, 63; David Lopez and Yen Espiritu, "Panethnicity in the United States: A Theoretical Framework," *Ethnic and Racial Studies* 13, no. 2 (1990): 198–224.

29 This is important to acknowledge in light of the tendency among some second- and later generation Asian Americans to distance themselves from either their Asian roots or their first-generation counterparts by shedding ethnic markers of food, language, physical appearance, mannerisms, and so forth. See Jonathan Tran, "Why Asian American Christianity Has No Future: The Over Against, Leaving Behind, and Separation From of Asian American Christian Identity," *Society of Asian North American Christian Studies* 2 (2010): 18.

30 It is also worth noting that the U.S. Census Bureau aggregates data about the Asian population in the United States according to residence alone, not citizen- ship status.

31 This sentence is formulated based on Tat-siong Benny Liew's initial definition of Asian American biblical hermeneutics, which he deconstructs in chapter 1 of his seminal book *What Is Asian American Biblical Hermeneutics? Reading the New Testament* (Honolulu: University of Hawaii Press, 2008), 3.

32 As Liew explains, "If there is a consistent body of work that refers to the schol- arship of a Frank Yamada or a Mary Foskett, if the interpretive work of a Devadasan Premnath or a Seung Ai Yang is cited time and time again, if there is a recognizable trail of publications where we find a Bundang, an Iwamura, a Kim, a Kuan, a Sano, a Seow, a Yee, or a Yieh going back and forth in dialogue and exchange with each other, there will before long surface a tradition, even a canon, of Asian American biblical hermeneutics that is not so easily dismissible" (*Biblical Hermeneutics*, 7–8).

33 Liew, *Biblical Hermeneutics*, 2.

34 Liew, *Biblical Hermeneutics*, 2.

35 One reason for the limited applicability of Liew's methodology for Asian American Christian ethics has to do with the different stages of development of our two disciplinary subfields. Asian American Christian ethics is only in its infancy: while approximately two decades of scholarship in Asian American biblical hermeneutics had been published before Liew proposed his "reference without referentiality" methodology in 2008 (n.b., the Asian and Asian Ameri- can biblical hermeneutics group was formed in the mid-1990s in the Society of Biblical Literature), we Christian ethicists of Asian descent in the United States have only begun self-consciously developing Asian American Christian ethics since the formation of the Asian and Asian American Working Group of the Society of Christian Ethics that same year (2008) and thus cannot yet draw upon an extensive body of literature for our purposes.

36 See Kao, "Prospects," 96; and Gale Yee, "Yin/Yang Is Not Me: An Exploration into an Asian American Biblical Hermeneutics," in *Ways of Being, Ways of Read- ing: Asian American Biblical Interpretation*, ed. Mary F. Foskett and Jeffrey Kah-jin Kuan, 152–63 (St. Louis, Mo.: Chalice, 2006). We have already referenced Yee's "by us" criterion in our previous "Question of Identity" section when

noting the ways the "us" is something not so much biologically determined but deliberately chosen by those who willfully adopt a pro-Asian American stance "as discernable in thematic content or point of view" (Kao in idem, 98–99; Yee in idem, 158).

37 Kao, "Prospects," 97.

38 Jonathan Tran, among others, has noted the ways in which the social upheavals of migration, the struggles for survival, and enduring anxieties about belonging render many Asian American Christians especially susceptible to conflating Christianity with security, the gospel with the "false promises of the American Dream," and discipleship with upward mobility. See Tran, "Response: The Possibility of an Asian-American Christian Ethics," *Society of Asian North American Christian Studies* 3 (2011): 103–10.

39 Kao, "Prospects," 99.

40 A comparison to Asian American theology may help illuminate this point: Andrew Sung Park's career-long work on the concept of *han* to supplement the traditional Christian focus on sin has transformed more than just Korean attitudes on what forgiveness and reconciliation require, and Rita Nakashima Brock's feminist and Asian American-inspired alternative to atonement theology has made lasting contributions to systematic theology in ways that benefit more than women or Asian Americans.

41 The point made here, that interrogating the model minority myth is good not only for Asian Americans but also for others, can be extended to other common Asian American stereotypes: as "perpetual foreigners" (as all but Native Americans are "foreign" and immigrants), "honorary whites" (as equally problematic for "whitewashing" Asians and pitting them against other racial-ethnic groups in the granting of special privileges), and "middleman minorities" (in keeping Asian Americans in conflict with other racial-ethnic minorities instead of allowing them to see the deeper root of white supremacist hegemony as their common problem).

For a discussion of the perpetual foreigner stereotype, see Frank H. Wu, *Yellow: Race in America Beyond Black and White* (New York: Basic Books, 2002). For a discussion of Asian Americans as "honorary whites," see Mia Tuan, *Forever Foreigners or Honorary Whites? The Asian Ethic Experience Today* (New Brunswick, N.J.: Rutgers University Press, 1998); and Min Zhou, "Are Asian Americans Becoming White?" *Contexts* 3, no. 1 (2004): 29–37. For a discussion of Asian Americans as "middleman minorities," see Pyong Gap Min, "A Comparison of Pre- and Post-1965 Asian Immigrant Businesses," in *Mass Migration to the United States: Classical and Contemporary Periods*, ed. Pyong Gap Min, 285–308 (Walnut Creek, Calif.: AltaMira, 2002).

42 Kao, "Prospects," 100.

43 Kao, "Prospects," 100–101.

44 Michael Walzer, *In the Company of Critics: Social Criticism and Political Commitment in the Twentieth Century* (New York: Basic Books, 1988), 20. As Walzer insightfully continues, "the passion for the truth will not be a sufficient reason unless it is matched by a passion to tell the truth to these men and women" (20).

45 For a sampling of helpful ways to understand this concept of traditioning, see Jonathan Y. Tan, "From Classical Tradition Maintenance to Remix *Traditioning*: Revisioning Asian American Theologies for the 21st Century," *Journal of Race, Ethnicity, and Religion* 3, no. 2 (2012): 1–22; and Orlando Espín, *Idol and Grace: On Traditioning and Subversive Hope* (Maryknoll, N.Y.: Orbis, 2014).

46 Among others, Grace Ji-Sun Kim invokes the "wisdom of [her] forebears" as she selectively retrieves *prajna* and *Kuan-yin* to offer a "Christology that is relevant to Korean North American women," Young Lee Hertig retrieves the Taoist notion of *yin-yang* to prescribe a version of feminism that can speak to Asian American women who lack "affirmation from both the Asian American and the mainstream communities," and Amos Yong insists that Asian American evangelical theology must "responsibly engage that which is distinctively Asian," which is why he "return[s] to the wellsprings of Asia" to selectively retrieve several Confucian, Taoist, and Buddhist ideas to "allow the gospel to be more deeply rooted in the Asian heart and mind." See Grace Kim, *The Grace of Sophia: A Korean North American Women's Christology* (Eugene, Ore.: Wipf & Stock, 2010), 83, 104; Young Lee Hertig, "The Asian American Alternative to Feminism: A Yinist Paradigm," in *Mirrored Reflections: Reframing Biblical Characters*, ed. Young Lee Hertig and Chloe Sun (Eugene, Ore.: Wipf & Stock, 2010), 14; and Amos Yong, "Whither Asian American Evangelical Theology? What Asian, Which American, Whose Evangelion?" *Evangelical Review of Theology* 32, no. 1 (2008): 34–36.

47 Here, we would add that our contributors did not necessarily follow Ahn's *ordering* of the steps, as they may have logically begun with the experiences and traditions of Asian Americans first, but they nonetheless sought to bring the history of Christian ethical thinking and Asian American traditions in critical dialogue as per his method.

Chapter 2: Gender and Sexuality

1 Christine E. Gudorf, "The Erosion of Sexual Dimorphism: Challenges to Religion and Religious Ethics," *Journal of the American Academy of Religion* 69, no. 4 (2001): 863, 866–67.

2 Virginia Ramey Mollenkott, *Omnigender: A Trans-religious Approach* (Cleveland, Ohio: Pilgrim, 2001), 1.

3 Plato, *Republic*; *Laws* 896a 1–2.

4 Aristotle, *On the Generation of Animals*, 2.4.738b20–23 and 2.716a5–7.

5 Stoic philosophers Musonius Rufus, Epictetus, Seneca, and Marcus Aurelius are examples of such extensions of dualism. Margaret A. Farley, *Just Love: A Framework for Christian Sexual Ethics* (New York: Continuum, 2006), 33.

6 Mark D. Jordan, *The Ethics of Sex* (Malden, Mass.: Blackwell, 2002), 4.

7 St. Augustine, *Confessions* 2:2; see Elizabeth A. Clark, *St. Augustine on Marriage and Sexuality* (Washington, D.C.: Catholic University of America Press, 1996), 4–5, 13–15; "Your voice" is referring to Holy Scripture.

8 St. Augustine, *The Good of Marriage*, chap. 3; see "The Good of Marriage," in Roy J. Deferrari, ed., *Saint Augustine: Treatises on Marriage and Other Subjects*, The Fathers of the Church 15 (New York: Fathers of the Church, 1955), 13.

9 St. Augustine, *The Good of Marriage*, chap. 5, 24:32; *On Continence*, chaps. 9, 12.

10 Farley, *Just Love*, 138–39; note that St. Thomas Aquinas did not share in this understanding. While he kept the dualism about gender intact, he eliminated the idea that even sex in marriage is sinful. Thomas Aquinas, *Summa Theologiae* II-II. 153, art. 2; see note 12 below.

11 Rosemary Radford Ruether, *Sexism and God-Talk: Toward a Feminist Theology* (Boston: Beacon, 1983), 158.

12 Farley, *Just Love*, 44; cf. Thomas Aquinas, *Summa Theologiae* I-II.34.1 ad. 1; II-II.154.11; II-II.26.11; *Summa Contra Gentiles* III.122.4–5; III.123.

13 Farley, *Just Love*, 46.

14 Quoted in Jordan, *Ethics of Sex*, 118.

15 Quoted in Jordan, *Ethics of Sex*, 60.

16 Quoted in Jordan, *Ethics of Sex*, 60.

17 See the review of Luther's writings in this regard by Farley in *Just Love*, 258.

18 By "gender" I mean culturally and socially constructed definitions of masculinity and femininity and their physical and mental traits, attitudes, and behaviors.

19 Karl Barth, *Church Dogmatics* III:2, 286; see Farley, *Just Love*, 133.

20 John Paul II, *Mulieris dignitatem*, August 15, 1988, para. 7; Farley, *Just Love*, 133–34.

21 These are "Conspicuous Descriptors of Gender Attributions" from Don Welch, *Macho Isn't Enough! Family Man in a Liberated World* (Atlanta: John Knox, 1985), 16.

22 Margaret A. Farley, "New Patterns of Relationship: Beginnings of a Moral Revolution," *Theological Studies* 36, no. 4 (1975): 637.

23 I borrow this distinction from James B. Nelson, *Body Theology* (Louisville, Ky.: Westminster John Knox, 1992), 21. The difference between theology of sexuality and "sexual theology" is that the former implies theologizing about sex and the latter applying experience of sex to theology.

24 Nelson, *Body Theology*, 22–24.

25 To be sure, not all objective understandings about the body have to be rigid or problematic. One can conceptualize, e.g., certain objectively shared bodily needs and capacities (i.e., basic caloric needs, physical need for rest, sexual capacities, etc.) and demand that these capacities must be supported. See Martha C. Nussbaum, *Women and Human Development: The Capacities Approach* (Cambridge: Cambridge University Press, 2000).

26 Farley, "New Patterns of Relationship," 634; according to Barbara F. Reskin, regardless of the group or society, dominant groups have a tendency to remain privileged because they have underwritten the rules. See the sociological concept called "differentiation" through which the dominant group maintains the status quo over the subordinates in Reskin, "Bringing the Men Back In: Sex Differentiation and the Devaluation of Women's Work," *Gender and Society* 2, no. 1 (1988): 58–81, esp. 60; Monique Wittig finds this differentiation to be especially oppressive to women, gays, and lesbians in "The Point of View: Universal or Particular?" *Feminist Issues* 3, no. 2 (1983) as quoted in Judith Butler, *Gender Trouble: Feminism and the Subversion of Identity* (New York: Routledge, 1990), 44. Cf. Cynthia F. Epstein, "Ideal Roles and Real Roles or the Fallacy of

the Misplaced Dichotomy," *Research in Social Stratification and Mobility* 4 (1985): 4, 36; Alison M. Jaggar, *Feminist Politics and Human Nature* (Totowa, N.J.: Rowman & Allanheld, 1983), 109–10; Catherine MacKinnon, *Feminism Unmodified* (Cambridge, Mass.: Harvard University Press, 1987), 38; and Candace West and Don H. Zimmerman, "Doing Gender," *Gender and Society* 1, no. 2 (1987): 137.

27 Lisa Sowle Cahill, "Gender and Christian Ethics," in *The Cambridge Companion to Christian Ethics*, ed. Robin Gill (Cambridge: Cambridge University Press, 2001), 113.

28 Farley, "New Patterns of Relationship," 634.

29 The culpability for supporting such traits does not lie solely on religious institutions, of course. These traits are also socially supported.

30 Margaret A. Farley, "The Church and the Family: An Ethical Task," *Horizons* 10, no. 1 (1983), 66. Joanne Carlson Brown and Rebecca Parker, "For God So Loved the World?" in *Violence against Women and Children: A Christian Theological Sourcebook*, ed. Carol J. Adams and Marie Fortune, 36–59 (New York: Continuum, 1995), 37. I do not agree with Brown and Parker's overarching and assertive claims that "Christianity is an abusive theology that glorifies suffering (56)," and that if such is not condemned, women have no reason to stay in it (38). There is not a monolithic "Christianity" to allow making such a generalizing statement *and* there may be many other reasons to stay in, one of which is to ameliorate it. Also, sacrifice *is* "essential in the furthering of the kingdom," so long as it is "always aimed at the establishment of mutual love." Christine E. Gudorf, "Parenting, Mutual Love, and Sacrifice," in *Women's Consciousness, Women's Conscience: A Reader in Feminist Ethics*, ed. Barbara Hilkert Andolsen, Christine E. Gudorf, and Mary D. Pellauer (San Francisco: Harper & Row, 1985), 190. Nevertheless, I find Brown and Parker's article helpful insofar as it points to the dangers of romanticizing and accepting abuse.

31 I want to be very clear that I am not claiming that agape is problematic per se. It only becomes a problem in a society of inequality where it is more specifically applied to, or stressed for, one group, especially the socially disadvantaged, more than the other. The idea of "forgiveness" or "love your enemy" would carry similar problems for the same reason. See Karen Lebacqz, "Love your Enemy: Sex, Power, and Christian Ethics," in *Feminist Theological Ethics: A Reader*, ed. Lois K. Daly (Louisville, Ky.: Westminster John Knox, 1994). My point is that there are limitations of agape as a norm. See Barbara Hilkert Andolsen, "Agape in Feminist Ethics," in idem, 146–59.

32 Andolsen, "Agape in Feminist Ethics," 150–53; Valerie Saiving Goldstein, "The Human Situation: a Feminine View," in *Womanspirit Rising*, ed. Carol P. Christ and Judith Plaskow, 25–42 (San Francisco: Harper & Row, 1992); Farley, "New Patterns of Relationship," 627–46; Mary Daly, *Beyond God the Father: Toward a Philosophy of Women's Liberation* (Boston: Beacon, 1973), 100; and Rosemary Radford Ruether and Eugene Bianchi, *From Machismo to Mutuality—Man Liberation* (New York: Paulist, 1976), 49–50.

33 During the recent economic downturn in the United States, many men became "stay-at-home dads" and women "breadwinning moms." Even excluding men who had been "forced to" stay home with kids, stay-at-home dads jumped 38 percent in the last three years, according to 2009 census estimates. See Kim

Janssen, "More Dads at Home Playing Mr. Mom: A Choice for Some But Men Lost Most Jobs in Recession," *Chicago Sun-Times*, September 30, 2010, http://www.suntimes.com/news/metro/2755976,CST-NWS-dads29.article; cf. Jeremy Adam Smith, *The Daddy Shift: How Stay-at-Home Dads, Breadwinning Moms, and Shared Parenting are Transforming the American Family* (Boston: Beacon, 2009). My point is that an inflexible complementary model based on a person's sex, vis-à-vis such a reality today, would result in negative consequences stemming from feelings that one is doing something that they are not supposed to be doing. My contestation is that the complementary model makes one feel "less manly" and "less womanly," which could have unfortunate consequences in one's life.

34 Farley, "New Patterns of Relationship," 637.

35 Farley, "New Patterns of Relationship," 638.

36 Pontifical Council for the Family, *Family, Marriage, and "De Facto" Unions* (Montreal, Quebec: Médiaspaul, 2000), 23. Until the Second Vatican Council, the Roman Catholic tradition (e.g., St. Augustine, The Council of Trent, Alphonsus Liguori, *Casti Connubii*) regarded the marital sexual act as a remedy for sin or for procreation, with the superiority of celibacy acknowledged. However, see Farley, *Just Love*, 47–49 for modern Roman Catholic developments and how love (unitive aspects) became equally important as the procreative.

37 Farley, *Just Love*, 47–48.

38 Patricia Beattie Jung and Ralph F. Smith, "Evaluating Heterosexism," chap. 2 in *Heterosexism: An Ethical Challenge* (Albany: State University of New York Press, 1993).

39 James P. Hanigan, "Unitive and Procreative Meaning: The Inseparable Link," in *Sexual Diversity and Catholicism: Toward the Development of Moral Theology*, ed. Patricia Beattie Jung with Joseph A. Coray (Collegeville, Minn.: Liturgical, 2001), 22–38, esp. 33. This attitude was more problematic prior to some adjustments made during and since The Second Vatican Council.

40 Cahill, "Gender and Christian Ethics," 114. Some argue that because David Hume had already concluded that the virtues of chastity and modesty, so prized in women, were artificial rather than natural virtues, that these norms were not considered "natural" or "given" by the eighteenth century. Others argued, however, that his moral framework provided the grounds for a justification of sexist discrimination. Ann Levey, "Under Constraint: Chastity and Modesty in Hume," *Hume Studies* 23, no. 2 (1997): 213, 225n2.

41 Christine E. Gudorf, "The Erosion of Sexual Dimorphism: Challenges to Religion and Religious Ethics," *Journal of the American Academy of Religion* 69, no. 4 (2001): 863, 866–67; Natalie Kertes Weaver, "Made in the Image of God: Intersex and the Decentering of Theological Anthropology" (paper presented at the annual convention of the Catholic Theological Society of America, Cleveland, Ohio, June 12, 2010), 8–9; Karen Lebacqz, "Difference or Defect? Intersexuality and the Politics of Difference," *The Annual of the Society of Christian Ethics*, 17 (1997): 213–14; and Patricia Beattie Jung and Aana Marie Vigen, eds., *God, Science, Sex, Gender: An Interdisciplinary Approach to Christian Ethics* (Urbana: University of Illinois Press, 2010). Some even went as far as to claim that it is not solely gender that is socially constructed. Judith Butler, e.g., does

not believe in an a priori reality and hence maintains that not only is gender socially constructed but also "sex and the naturalized institution of heterosexuality are *constructs*, socially instituted and socially regulated fantasies or 'fetishes' not *natural* categories. . . ." Butler, *Gender Trouble*, 161. For the purpose of this chapter, however, I only make the argument that gender norms are not "given."

42 For a womanist theology, see Emilie M. Townes, *In a Blaze of Glory: Womanist Spirituality as Social Witness* (Nashville: Abingdon, 1995); for a mujerista theology, see Ada María Isasi-Díaz, *En La Lucha: A Hispanic Women's Liberation Theology* (Minneapolis: Fortress, 1993); for Asian theology, see Kwok Pui-lan, "The Future of Feminist Theology: An Asian Perspective," in *Feminist Theology from the Third World: A Reader*, ed. Ursula King (Maryknoll, N.Y.: Orbis, 1994); for gender-queer LGBTIQ theology, see Mary Elise Lowe, "Gay, Lesbian, and Queer Theologies: Origins, Contributions, and Challenges," *Dialogue: A Journal of Theology* 48, no. 1 (2009): 49–61.

43 Kwok, "Future of Feminist Theology," in King, *Feminist Theology*, 67.

44 Included among the list of groups are Chinese, Japanese, Korean, Vietnamese, Thai, Filipino, Malaysian, Indonesian, Singaporean, Burmese, Hmong, Pacific Islander, Indian, Pakistani, and Sri Lankan. Taking into consideration only the ethno-religious diversity among them points to the problem of lumping them into a singular category. Again, this begs the questions concerning the purpose of such categorization and differentiation.

45 Rather than dismissing a wrongdoing as idiosyncratic or isolated, structural sin points to a "larger, social dimension of sin beyond individual wrongdoing." The implication is that we have "corporate responsibility for sinful actions that originate from social system." Miguel A. De La Torre, ed., *Ethics: A Liberative Approach* (Minneapolis: Fortress, 2013), 73.

46 Rosalind S. Chou, *Asian American Sexual Politics: The Construction of Race, Gender, and Sexuality* (Lanham, Md.: Rowman & Littlefield, 2012), 2; cf. Sharon M. Tan, "Composing Integrity: An Approach to Moral Agency for Asian Americans," *Journal of Race, Ethnicity, and Religion* 3, no. 2.10 (2012): 7.

47 Eduardo Bonilla-Silva, *Racism without Racists: Color-Blind Racism and the Persistence of Racial Inequality in the United States* (Lanham, Md.: Rowman & Littlefield, 2003).

48 Jonathan Y. Tan, *Asian American Theologies* (Maryknoll, N.Y.: Orbis, 2008), 24.

49 J. Tan, *Theologies*, 37–40; S. Tan, "Composing Integrity," 6–7; Andrew Sung Park, *Racial Conflict and Healing: An Asian-American Theological Perspective* (Maryknoll, N.Y.: Orbis, 1996), 22–23; cf. note that such racial differentiation is a similar concept as "Orientalism" as described by Edward W. Said, *Orientalism* (New York: Vintage, 1978).

50 Chou, *Sexual Politics*, 11–17; see also Ronald Takaki, *Strangers from a Different Shore* (Boston: Back Bay, 1998).

51 Chou, *Sexual Politics*, 10, 105; see also Yen Le Espiritu, *Asian American Women and Men: Labor, Laws, and Love* (Lanham, Md.: Rowman & Littlefield, 2008).

52 Chou, *Sexual Politics*, 17. This phenomenon is also referred to as "Racial Castration." See David L. Eng, *Racial Castration: Managing Masculinity in America* (Durham, N.C.: Duke University Press, 2001).

53 Hegemonic masculinity is "the configuration of gender practice which embodies the currently accepted answer to the problem of the legitimacy of patriarchy, which guarantees (or is taken to guarantee) the dominant position of men,
and the subordination of women." See R. W. Connell, *Masculinities* (Berkeley:
University of California Press, 2005), 77; see also Connell and James W. Mess-
erschmidt, "Hegemonic Masculinity: Rethinking the Concept," *Gender and
Society* 19, no. 6 (2005).

54 Chou, *Sexual Politics*, 106; see also Eng, "Introduction," *Racial Castration*.

55 Emphasized femininity, or "hegemonic femininity," is "oriented to accommo-
dating the interests and desires of men," and it "exaggerates gender difference
as strategy of 'adaptation to men's power' stressing empathy and nurturance;
'real' womanhood is described as 'fascinating.' . . ." Michael S. Kimmel with
Amy Aronson, *The Gendered Society Reader*, 5th ed. (Oxford: Oxford University
Press, 2013), 4; see also R. W. Connell, *Gender and Power* (Stanford: Stanford
University Press, 1987).

56 Fumitaka Matsuoka, *Out of Silence: Emerging Themes in Asian American Churches*
(Cleveland, Ohio: United Church, 1995), 73–77.

57 Chou, *Sexual Politics*, 90.

58 Chou, *Sexual Politics*, 97.

59 While I do not have the space to discuss it here, there is a similar phenomenon
within the gender-based associations of the human brain. Men were associated
with whatever hemisphere was considered superior at the time. That is, when it
was considered superior, men were identified with the right hemisphere, which
is associated with visual, spatial, artistic, musical, and mathematical talents,
which dominates the left hemisphere. Yet, when the left side was considered to
control reason and intellect, men were considered overwhelmingly more left-
brained. Jo Durden-Smith and Diane deSimone, *Sex and the Brain* (New York:
Warner, 1983), 171; G. W. Harris, "Sex Hormones, Brain Development and
Brain Function," *Endocrinology* 75 (1965); and Ruth Bleier, *Science and Gender: A
Critique of Biology and Its Theory on Women* (New York: Pantheon, 1984).

60 Hoon Choi, "Brothers in Arms and Brothers in Christ? The Military and the
Catholic Church as Sources for Modern Korean Masculinity," *Journal of the Society of Christian Ethics* 32, no. 2 (2012): 83–84.

61 Choi, "Brothers in Arms," 83.

62 Choi, "Brothers in Arms," 83.

63 See Christine E. Gudorf, "Western Religion and the Patriarchal Family," in
Religion and Sexual Health, ed. Ronald M. Green, 99–117 (Dordrecht, Nether-
lands: Kluwer, 1992); Del Martin, *Battered Wives* (San Francisco: Glide, 1976),
11; Diana E. H. Russell, *Rape in Marriage* (New York: Macmillan, 1983), 21–22,
57, 64; Russell, *Sexual Exploitation: Child Sexual Abuse and Work Place Harass-
ment* (Beverly Hills: Sage Publications, 1984); Russell, *The Secret Trauma: Incest
in the Lives of Girls and Women* (New York: Basic Books, 1986), 10; Joseph Pleck,
The Myth of Masculinity (Cambridge, Mass.: MIT Press, 1981), 20–25; Nancy
Chodorow, *The Reproduction of Mothering: Psychoanalysis and the Sociology of Gender* (Berkeley: University of California Press, 1978), 50.

64 Chou, *Sexual Politics*, 79.

65 Kristen Harrison, "The Body Electric: Thin-Ideal Media and Eating Disorders in Adolescents," *Journal of Communication* 50, no. 3 (2000): 119–43.

66 Chou, *Sexual Politics*, 81; Hernan Vera and Andrew M Gordon, *Screen Saviors: Hollywood Fictions of Whiteness* (Lanham, Md.: Rowman & Littlefield, 2003); Linda Bacon et al., "Size Acceptance and Intuitive Eating Improve Health for Obese, Female Chronic Dieters," *Journal of the American Diet Association* 105, no. 6 (2005): 929–36.

67 Chou, *Sexual Politics*, 82–83; Rosalind S. Chou and Joe R. Feagin, *The Myth of the Model Minority: Asian Americans Facing Racism* (Boulder, Colo.: Paradigm, 2008).

68 Chou, *Sexual Politics*, 95; on a related topic of self-image and self-hatred, see Jonathan Tran in this volume. He discusses the phenomenon of plastic surgery.

69 Chou, *Sexual Politics*, 98.

70 Chou, *Sexual Politics*, 107

71 Chou, *Sexual Politics*, 113.

72 Eng, *Racial Castration*, in Chou, *Sexual Politics*, 113.

73 Chou, *Sexual Politics*, 115; Jackson Katz and Jeremy Earp, *Tough Guise: Violence, Media and the Crisis in Masculinity*, directed by Sut Jhally (Media Education Foundation, 1999), DVD.

74 Chou, *Sexual Politics*, 116–17.

75 Gabrielle Bluestone, "Fraternity Brothers Googled Head Injury Symptoms as Pledge Lay Dying," *Gawker*, February 18, 2014, http://gaw.kr/zagISdC; see also Nicholas L. Syrett, *Company He Keeps: A History of White College Fraternities* (Chapel Hill: University of North Carolina Press, 2011).

76 Chou, *Sexual Politics*, 118–24; see also note 92.

77 Melinda Smith and Jeanne Segal, "Domestic Violence and Abuse: Signs of Abuse and Abusive Relationships," Helpguide.org, last updated February 2014, http://www .helpguide.org/mental/domestic_violence_abuse_types_signs_causes_effects. htm in Chou, *Sexual Politics*, 132.

78 See Thomas LaVeist, *Minority Populations and Health: An Introduction to Health Disparities in the United States* (San Francisco: Jossey-Bass, 2005); and Joe R. Feagin and Karyn D. McKinney, *The Many Costs of Racism* (Lanham, Md.: Rowman & Littlefield, 2003); and others quoted on pp. 107 and 134.

79 This research is often called "The Life Course Perspective," referring to the consequences of the cumulative impact of racism in a course of one's life. See Tracy Heather Strain, Randall MacLowry, and Eric Stange, "When the Bough Breaks," *Unnatural Causes*, episode 2, directed by Tracy Heather Strain, http:// www.unnaturalcauses.org/episode_descriptions.php?page=2.

80 See, e.g., "Resources Database," Asian and Pacific Islander American Health Forum, http://www.apiahf.org/resources/resources-database.

81 Elaine Kim, "Patriarchy and Asian American Community," in Matsuoka, *Out of Silence*, 74.

82 E. Kim, "Patriarchy," 74–75.

83 Hee-Kyu Heidi Park, "The Silver Dagger: Cultural Hybridity and Premarital Sexuality in Evangelical Korean American Women," *The Journal of Pastoral Theology* 22, no. 1 (2012): 5.8–5.9.

84 H. Park, "Silver Dagger," 5.7–5.8.

85 Sang Hyun Lee, *From a Liminal Place: An Asian American Theology* (Minneapolis: Fortress, 2010), 104–8; A. Park, *Racial Conflict*, 41–47.

86 Lee, *Liminal Place*, 107–8.

87 Again, I do not have the space to discuss here, but there is a similar phenomenon in our society at large. Most men do not feel that they have this power. Men, only insofar as social power is socially maintained and controlled by men, indirectly reap benefits from it. Hence, men struggle to maintain a self-image that is powerful because most do not have much power. In the process of maintaining a powerful image—whether it be restricting emotionality, trying to be successful, being physically and financially powerful—men tend to hurt themselves and others physically and emotionally. See Andreas Philaretou and Katherine Allen, "Reconstructing Masculinity and Sexuality," *The Journal of Men's Studies* 9, no. 3 (2001): 308–9; cf. Lucia Albino Gilbert, *Two Careers, One Family: The Promise of Gender Equality* (Newbury Park, Calif.: Sage, 1993); cf. Michael S. Kimmel, *The Gendered Society*, 2nd ed. (Oxford: Oxford University Press, 2004), 184; cf. Svend Aage Madsen, "Men's Mental Health: Fatherhood and Psychotherapy," *Journal of Men's Studies* 17, no. 1 (2009): 15–30.

88 Sharon Kim, *A Faith of Our Own: Second-Generation Spirituality in Korean American Churches* (New Brunswick, N.J.: Rutgers University Press, 2010), 22–26. Reclaiming their social standing and status is one of the four traditional functions of the Korean immigrant churches (24–25). In this book Kim recognizes the second-generation Korean formulation of their own "hybrid third space" that is less hierarchical than their parents' churches. However, she does not provide a gender analysis. That is, theses churches in the hybrid third space still retain the model of mostly male leadership. I owe this insight to Grace Kao.

89 Patrick S. Cheng, "Gay Asian Masculinities and Christian Theologies," *Cross-Currents* 61, no. 4 (2011): 542; Indie Harper, "No Asians, Blacks, Fats, or Femmes," in *For Colored Boys Who Have Considered Suicide When the Rainbow Is Still Not Enough: Coming of Age, Coming Out, and Coming Home*, ed. Keith Boykin (New York: Magnus), 129–35. Even when they seemed to be accepted by other gay men, they are often accepted by the "rice queens" who become predators by fetishizing and objectifying Asian men. See Cheng, "Multiplicity and Judges 19: Constructing a Queer Asian Pacific American Biblical Hermeneutics," *Semeia* 90/91 (2002): 126.

90 Patrick S. Cheng, *Rainbow Theology: Bridging Race, Sexuality, and Spirit* (New York: Seabury, 2013), 35–49. Predictably, LGBTIQ women suffer no less exclusion from the community. Kwok Pui-lan, "Gay Activism in Asian and Asian-American Churches," *The Witness* 87, no. 20 (2004).

91 Cheng, *Rainbow Theology*, 40; Leng Leroy Lim, "Webs of Betrayal, Webs of Blessings," in *Our Families, Our Voices: Snapshots of Queer Kinship*, ed. Robert E. Goss and Amy Adams Squire Strongheart (Binghamton, N.Y.: Harrington Park, 1997), 227–41; and Lim, " 'The Bible Tells Me to Hate Myself': The Crisis in Asian American Spiritual Leadership," *Semeia* 90/91 (2002): 320.

92 Cheng, *Rainbow Theology*, 41; Michael Kim, "Out and About: Coming of Age in a Straight White World," in *Asian American X: An Intersection of 21st Century*

Asian American Voices, ed. Arar Han and John Hsu (Ann Arbor: University of Michigan Press, 2004), 147. Antigay bias is of a different type than the racist or sexist stuff, hence my separate category for the "third bind." Unlike racism, to which Christian churches are technically opposed, and sexism, which at least in the gender complementarity model there is an affirmation of women as women, the "gay" case, however, does not have the same kind of affirmation. Christians are still wrestling with this question, but phenomenologically, the *experience* of the triple bind is still real and as damaging as the case of the other two. Incidentally, personally knowing some AA Christian communities, I am willing to wager on a "quadruple bind" if they also belong to a lower economic bracket.

93 S. Kim, *Faith of Our Own*, 127.

94 S. Kim, *Faith of Our Own*, 128.

95 S. Kim, *Faith of Our Own*, 127–28.

96 I am aware that many (Asian) Christian churches that do not recognize same-sex activity as compatible with faithful witness do so out of their genuine belief and often not out of spite. Particularly in these types of churches, I believe there are more possibilities for a conversation about discouraging discriminatory treatments and seeing all as moral agents and children of God. To that end, I endorse the documentary, *In God's House: Asian American Lesbian and Gay Families in the Church*, directed by Lina Hoshino (PANA Institute: Institute for Leadership Development and Study of Pacific Asian North American Religion at Pacific School of Religion, Berkeley), http://www.ingodshouse.com. The culturally sensitive approach of the documentary may be helpful in generating an open, non-threatening discussion.

97 Christine E. Gudorf, "Power to Create: Sacraments and Men's Need to Birth," *Horizons* 14, no. 2 (1987): 296–97.

98 Gudorf, "Power to Create," 287.

99 James B. Nelson, "Embracing Masculinity," in *Sexuality and the Sacred: Sources for Theological Reflection*, ed. James B. Nelson and Sandra P. Longfellow (Louisville, Ky.: Westminster John Knox, 1994), 211; see his discussion of Karl Barth's gender complementarity as in "fellow-humanity," 202. Cf. Karl Barth, *Church Dogmatics*, vol. 3, part 4 (Edinburgh: T&T Clark, 1961), esp. 166.

100 Russell Jeung, *Faithful Generations: Race and New Asian American Churches* (New Brunswick, N.J.: Rutgers University Press, 2005), 15.

101 Yen Le Espiritu, *Asian American Panethnicity: Bridging Institutions and Identities* (Philadelphia: Temple University Press, 1992), 259, quoted in Jeung, *Faithful Generations*, 9, 82–83; "racialized" this way has consequences, of course. Vincent Chin, a Chinese American, was killed because his attackers thought he was Japanese. See Frank H. Wu, "Why Vincent Chin Matters," *New York Times*, June 22, 2012, http://www.nytimes.com/2012/06/23/opinion/why-vincent-chin-matters.html?_r=0.

102 Jeung, *Faithful Generations*, 14–15.

103 Jeung, *Faithful Generations*, 15.

104 Jeung, *Faithful Generations*, 15.

105 S. Tan, "Composing Integrity," 8–14.

106 I am thinking of a Christian version of MANAA (Media Action Network for Asian Americans) or the social-media blog "Angry Asian Man," which documents (alongside accomplishments by Asian Americans) racism in social media, including outbursts of racial slurs after an Indian American won the Miss America Pageant. "Indian American Woman Crowned 2014 Miss America: And Racist Twitter Users Predictably Lose Their Minds," Angry Asian Man (blog), September 16, 2013, http://blog.angryasianman.com/2013/09/indian -american-woman-crowned-2014-miss.html.

107 See the comments on Connell Cowan and Melvyn Kinder, "Men Who Make Women Want to Scream," in *Perspectives on Marriage: A Reader*, ed. Kieran Scott and Michael Warren, 2nd ed. (London: Oxford University Press, 2001), 305.

108 While not having directly to do with this discussion, I am borrowing a similar approach as that found in Ronald F. Thiemann, *Religion in Public Life: A Dilemma for Democracy* (Washington, D.C.: Georgetown University Press, 1996). Thiemann argues for a kind of "revised liberalism" where the religious voice is not completely separated from public affairs. One of the ways to achieve this task is to refer to religious claims using more public language (instead of using strictly religious language that may alienate people). Similarly, I am advocating using a kind of language that is at least more effective, perhaps more just, in an attempt to convey the message to a wider audience.

109 I do, however, understand and sympathize with the fact that such an anger resulting from racio-sexist experiences is very difficult to channel. Hence, I do concede that expressions and outbursts of anger can be at times inevitable, powerful, and necessary.

110 Miguel A. De La Torre, *Reading the Bible from the Margins* (Maryknoll, N.Y.: Orbis, 2002), 92–96.

111 Kwok Pui-lan, "Touching the Taboo: On the Sexuality of Jesus," in *Sexuality and the Sacred: Sources for Theological Reflection*, ed. Marvin Mahan Ellison and Kelly Brown Douglas, 2nd ed. (Louisville, Ky.: Westminster John Knox, 2010), 122–23.

112 Kwok, "Touching the Taboo," 122.

113 Kwok, "Touching the Taboo," 132.

Chapter 3: Marriage, Family, and Parenting

1 Robin W. Lovin, *Christian Ethics: An Essential Guide* (Nashville: Abingdon, 2000).

2 Don Browning, "Biology, Ethics, and Narrative in Christian Family Theory," in *Promises to Keep: Decline and Renewal of Marriage in America*, ed. David Popenoe, Jean Bethke Elshtain, and David Blankenhorn (Lanham, Md.: Rowman & Littlefield, 1996) 131–32.

3 Willemien Otten, "Augustine on Marriage, Monasticism, and the Community of the Church," *Theological Studies* 59, no. 3 (1998): 398.

4 Otten, "Augustine on Marriage," 399.

5 Lisa Cahill, *Family: A Christian Social Perspective* (Minneapolis: Augsburg Fortress, 2000), 52.

6 Martin Luther, "A Sermon on the Estate of Marriage," in *Martin Luther's Basic Theological Writings*, ed. Timothy F. Lull (Minneapolis: Augsburg Fortress, 1989), 632.

7 Luther, "Estate of Marriage," in Lull, *Basic Theological Writings*, 631.

8 Luther, "Estate of Marriage," in Lull, *Basic Theological Writings*, 631.

9 Cahill, *Family*, 62–64.

10 Don S. Browning and Bonnie J. Miller-McLemore, eds., *Children and Childhood in American Religions* (New Brunswick, N.J.: Rutgers University Press, 2009), 130–35; Cahill, *Family*, 62.

11 Luther, "Estate of Marriage," in Lull, *Basic Theological Writings*, 637.

12 Luther, "Estate of Marriage," in Lull, *Basic Theological Writings*, 635.

13 Luther, "Estate of Marriage," in Lull, *Basic Theological Writings*, 637.

14 Elisabeth Schüssler Fiorenza, *In Memory of Her: A Feminist Theological Reconstruction of Christian Origins* (New York: Crossroad, 1994), 269. Please see parts II and III in particular in Fiorenza's *In Memory of Her*, and also Lisa Cahill, *Sex, Gender, and Christian Ethics* (Cambridge: Cambridge University Press, 1996) for a full analysis and extended discussion of church and household patriarchy in the Christian tradition.

15 See Barbara Hilkert Andolsen, "Agape in Feminist Ethics," *Journal of Religious Ethics* 9, no. 1 (1981): 69–83.

16 Stanley Hauerwas, *The Hauerwas Reader*, ed. John Berkman and Michael Cartwright (Durham, N.C.: Duke University Press, 2001), 512.

17 Hauerwas, *Hauerwas Reader*, 513.

18 Gilbert Meilaender, "Time for Love: The Place of Marriage and Children in the Thought of Stanley Hauerwas," *Journal of Religious Ethics* 40, no. 2 (2012): 252.

19 Stanley Hauerwas, *Disrupting Time: Sermons, Prayers, and Sundries* (Eugene, Ore.: Cascade, 2004), 111.

20 Stanley Hauerwas, *Truthfulness and Tragedy: Further Investigations in Christian Ethics* (South Bend, Ind.: University of Notre Dame Press, 1977), 151.

21 Meilaender, "Time for Love," 257. These three theologies of marriage (Augustine, Luther, Hauerwas) by no means exhaust the diversity and breadth of Christian theologies of marriage. An exhaustive survey on this topic is beyond the scope of this article. For extended reading and analysis of Christian theologies of marriage, please see the following: J. Gordon Melton and Nicholas Piediscalzi, eds., *The Churches Speak On: Sex and Family Life; Official Statements from Religious Bodies and Ecumenical Organizations* (Detroit: Gale Research, 1991); Glenn W. Olsen, ed., *Christian Marriage: A Historical Study* (New York: Crossroad, 2001); Adrian Thatcher, *Celebrating Christian Marriage* (Edinburgh: T&T Clark, 2001); Charles E. Curran and Julie Hanlon Rubio, eds., *Readings in Moral Theology, no. 15: Marriage* (New York: Paulist, 2009); Thatcher, *Marriage after Modernity: Christian Marriage in Postmodern Times* (New York: New York University Press, 1999); and Hans J. Hillerbrand, ed., *The Oxford Encyclopedia of the Reformation* (New York: Oxford University Press, 1996), 3.

22 Meilaender, "Time for Love," 257.

23 Stanley Hauerwas, *A Community of Character: Toward a Constructive Christian Social Ethic* (South Bend, Ind.: University of Notre Dame Press, 1981), 165.

24 Meilaender, "Time for Love," 258.

25 Masako Ishii-Kuntz, "Asian American Families," in *Handbook of Contemporary Families: Considering the Past, Contemplating the Future*, ed. Marilyn Coleman and Lawrence H. Ganong (Thousand Oaks, Calif.: Sage, 2004), 378–80.

26 To be sure, Buddhism, Taoism, lesser known folk religions, and even Christianity have also sculpted conceptions of family for Asian Americans. Yet the fact remains that Confucian values are embedded within the Asian American psychological and social structures of individual and family to a far greater extent than any of the aforementioned traditions. Walter H. Slote, "Psychocultural Dynamics within the Confucian Family," in *Confucianism and the Family*, ed. Walter H. Slote and George A. De Vos (Albany: State University of New York Press, 1998), 37–38; and Jeffrey Meyer, "Asian American Confucianism and Children," in Browning and Miller-McLemore, *Children and Childhood*, 180.

27 Matthew R. Mock, "Clinical Reflections on Refugee Families," in *Revisioning Family Therapy: Race, Culture, and Gender in Clinical Practice*, ed. Monica McGoldrick (New York: Guilford, 1998), 363.

28 "Asian and Pacific Presence: Harmony in Faith," United States Conference of Catholic Bishops, 2001, http://www.usccb.org/issues-and-action/cultural-diversity/asian-pacific-islander/resources/harmony-in-faith-additional-information.cfm.

29 Bob Suzuki, "The Asian-American Family," in *Parenting in a Multicultural Society: Practice and Policy*, ed. Mario D. Fantini and Rene Cardenas (New York: Longman, 1980), 78–81.

30 Slote, "Psychocultural Dynamics," in Slote and De Vos, *Confucianism and the Family*, 43–44.

31 Meyer, "Asian American Confucianism," in Browning and Miller-McLemore, *Children and Childhood*, 182.

32 Ross D. Parke and Raymond Buriel, "Socialization Concerns in African American, American Indian, Asian American and Latino Families," in *Contemporary Ethnic Families in the United States: Characteristics, Variations, and Dynamics*, ed. Nijole V. Benokraitis (Upper Saddle River, N.J.: Prentice Hall, 2002), 23.

33 One example is that of Guoju: "In the Han Dynasty there was a man named Guoju whose family was destitute. His mother would often eat less of her own food so that she could give it to Guoju's three-year-old son. Guoju said to his wife: 'We are so poor that we cannot give to mother the food she deserves. She has to share with our son. Should we not bury him?' When he had dug the grave about three feet deep, he uncovered a lump of gold, on which was inscribed: 'No government official nor ordinary person can take it away.' " Meyer, "Asian American Confucianism," in Browning and Miller-McLemore, *Children and Childhood*, 180.

34 Meyer, "Asian American Confucianism," in Browning and Miller-McLemore, *Children and Childhood*, 182–83. There are two other main sources of Confucian influence. The *Classic of Filial Piety*, which dates back to the Han Dynasty (206 B.C.E.–220 C.E.), purports to be a discussion between Confucius and one of his disciples. Its purpose "was to teach boys the overwhelming importance of filial piety and to urge them toward filial practice." The book *Family Rituals* by

the twelfth-century author Zhuxi is a codification of ritual practice and specific instructions for particular rites of passage for males and females.

35 Ronald E. Dolan, ed., *Philippines: A Country Study* (Washington, D.C.: Federal Research Division, 1991).

36 Luz Lopez Rodriguez, "Patriarchy and Women's Subordination in the Philippines," *Review of Women's Studies* 1, no. 1 (1990): 18.

37 Stephen T. Russell, Lisa J. Crockett, and Ruth K. Chao, eds., *Asian American Parenting and Parent-Adolescent Relationships* (New York: Springer 2010), 8–9.

38 Slote, "Psychocultural Dynamics," in Slote and De Vos, *Confucianism and the Family*, 38.

39 Suzuki, "Asian-American Family," in Fantini and Cardenas, *Parenting in a Multicultural Society*, 88–89.

40 Suzuki, "Asian-American Family," in Fantini and Cardenas, *Parenting in a Multicultural Society*, 90–91; Slote, "Psychocultural Dynamics," in Slote and De Vos, *Confucianism and the Family*, 49.

41 JoAnn M. Farver et al., "Ethnic Identity, Acculturation, Parenting Beliefs, and Adolescent Adjustment," *Merrill-Palmer Quarterly* 53, no. 2 (2007): 189.

42 Suzuki, "Asian-American Family," in Fantini and Cardenas, *Parenting in a Multicultural Society*, 96; see also K. S. Van Campen and S. T. Russell, "Cultural Differences in Parenting Practices: What Asian American Families Can Teach Us," *Frances McClelland Institute for Children, Youth, and Families Research Link* 2, no. 1 (2010).

43 There are similarities between the Asian American community and the black community with an average of 53 percent. Algea O. Harrison et al., "Family Ecologies of Ethnic Minority Children," *Child Development* 61, no. 2 (1990): 351.

44 Paul Taylor, ed., *The Rise of Asian Americans: Updated Edition* (Washington, D.C.: Pew Research Center, 2013), http://www.pewsocialtrends.org/2012/06/19/the-rise-of-asian-americans/.

45 Pauline Agbayani-Siewart, "Filipino American Culture and Family Values," in Benokraitis, *Contemporary Ethnic Families*, 37.

46 Russell et al., *Asian American Parenting*, 8–9.

47 Roger R. Wong, "Divorce Mediation among Asian Americans," in Benokraitis, *Contemporary Ethnic Families*, 336.

48 George A. De Vos, "Confucian Family Socialization: The Religion, Morality, and Aesthetics of Propriety," in Slote and De Vos, *Confucianism and the Family*, 370, 375.

49 Wong, "Divorce Mediation," in Benokraitis, *Contemporary Ethnic Families*, 336.

50 Slote, "Psychocultural Dynamics," in Slote and De Vos, *Confucianism and the Family*, 45.

51 Ruth K. Chao and Kevin F. Kaeochinda, "The Meanings of Parent-Adolescent Relationship Quality among Chinese American and Filipino American Adolescents," in Russell et al., *Asian American Parenting*, 82.

52 Chao and Kaeochinda, "Meanings of Parent-Adolescent Relationship," in Russell et al., *Asian American Parenting*.

53 Parke and Buriel, "Socialization Concerns," in Benokraitis, *Contemporary Ethnic Families*, 24.

54 See the editors' "Introduction," in Russell et al., *Asian American Parenting*, 5.

55 De Vos, "Confucian Family Socialization," in Slote and De Vos, *Confucianism and the Family*, 347.

56 See also Campen and Russell, "Cultural Differences."

57 While Asian Americans have many similarities with other minorities in America, such as extended family systems and familial obligation/loyalty, parental formality appears to be a uniquely Confucian influence. There have been studies comparing Asian American and African American emotional expressions in parenting (Fang Wu and Sen Qi, "Parenting within Cultural Context: Comparisons between African-American and Asian-American Parents" [lecture, Montreal, Quebec, April 15, 2005]), along with studies comparing Asian American and Western emotional expressions in parenting (Elizabeth A. Lee, "Expressive Suppression of Negative Emotion: A Comparison of Asian American and European American Norms for Emotional Regulation" [Ph.D. diss., Penn State University, 2011]) that implicitly back up this claim. One major mitigating factor in research is the apparent lack of methodological agreement on how emotional behavior display is to be measured.

58 Min Zhou, "Social Capital in Chinatown: The Role of Community-Based Organizations and Families in the Adaptation of the Younger Generation," in *Contemporary Asian America: A Multidisciplinary Reader*, ed. Min Zhou and James V. Gatewood, 315–35 (New York: New York University Press, 2000), 326.

59 Please see Campen and Russell, "Cultural Differences."

60 Farver et al., "Ethnic Identity," 190, 191, 197, 206; see also Campen and Russell, "Cultural Differences."

61 Farver et al., "Ethnic Identity," 201–5.

62 Amy Chua, *Battle Hymn of the Tiger Mother* (New York: Penguin, 2011).

63 Zhou, "Social Capital," in Zhou and Gatewood, *Contemporary Asian America*, 326.

64 Zhou, "Social Capital," in Zhou and Gatewood, *Contemporary Asian America*, 331.

65 One major issue that will not be able to be spoken to in any comprehensive way in this article is the issue of suicide among Asian Americans, particularly teens. Please see "Mental Health and Asian Americans," U.S. Department of Health and Human Services Office of Minority Health, last modified September 18, 2013, http://minorityhealth.hhs.gov/omh/browse.aspx?lvl=4&lvlid=54; Asian American Psychological Leadership Fellows Program, "Suicide among Asian Americans," American Psychological Association, May 2012, http://www.apa.org/pi/oema/resources/ethnicity-health/asian-american/suicide.aspx; National Alliance on Mental Illness, "Mental Health Issues among Asian American and Pacific Islander Communities," 2011, https://www2.nami.org/Template.cfm?Section=Fact_Sheets1&Template=/ContentManagement/ContentDisplay.cfm&ContentID=123209; Jeremy Kisch, E. Victor Leino, and Morton M. Silverman, "Aspects of Suicidal Behavior, Depression, and Treatment in College Students: Results from the Spring 2000 National College Health

Assessment Survey," *Suicide and Life-Threatening Behavior* 35, no. 1 (2005): 3–13; and Centers for Disease Control and Prevention, *National Center for Health Statistics* (Hyattsville, Md.: U.S. Public Health Service, 2001), for further reading. It is widely noted that cultural values regarding the stigmas of mental disease, family honor, and health care all constrain Asian Americans from accessing mental health care for depression and suicidal tendencies.

66 Zhou, "Social Capital," in Zhou and Gatewood, *Contemporary Asian America*, 326–27.

67 Zhou, "Social Capital," in Zhou and Gatewood, *Contemporary Asian America*, 328–29.

68 Yoonsun Choi, "Diversity Within: Subgroup Differences of Youth Problem Behaviors among Asian Pacific Islander American Adolescents," *Journal of Community Psychology* 36, no. 3 (2008): 353.

69 Won Kim Cook, Corina Chung, and Winston Tseng, "Demographic and Socioeconomic Profiles of Asian Americans, Native Hawaiians, and Pacific Islanders in the United States" (presentation, 25th Asian and Pacific Islander American Health Forum, July 2011).

70 Amy Chua, *The Triple Package: How Three Unlikely Traits Explain the Rise and Fall of Cultural Groups in America* (New York: Penguin, 2014).

71 Yoshinori Kamo, "Variations in Asian Grandparenting," in Benokraitis, *Contemporary Ethnic Families*, 386; Slote, "Psychocultural Dynamics," in Slote and De Vos, *Confucianism and the Family*, 40–41.

72 Kamo, "Variations in Asian Grandparenting," in Benokraitis, *Contemporary Ethnic Families*, 386.

73 Kamo, "Variations in Asian Grandparenting," in Benokraitis, *Contemporary Ethnic Families*, 387.

74 See Farver et al., "Ethnic Identity," 189.

75 Kamo, "Variations in Asian Grandparenting," in Benokraitis, *Contemporary Ethnic Families*, 390.

76 Kamo, "Variations in Asian Grandparenting," in Benokraitis, *Contemporary Ethnic Families*, 390–93.

77 Taylor, *Rise of Asian Americans*.

78 Audrey Singer and Jill H. Wilson, "Refugee Resettlement in Metropolitan America," *Migration Policy Institute*, March 1, 2007, http://www.migration policy.org/article/refugee-resettlement-metropolitan-america.

79 American Immigration Council, "Refugees: A Fact Sheet," *Immigration Policy Center*, 2010, http://www.immigrationpolicy.org/just-facts/refugees-fact-sheet.

80 Ishii-Kuntz, "Asian American Families," in Coleman and Ganong, *Handbook of Contemporary Families*, 373.

81 Rhacel Salazar Parrenas, "New Household Forms, Old Family Values: The Formation and Reproduction of the Filipino Transnational Family in Los Angeles," in Zhou and Gatewood, *Contemporary Asian America*, 338–39.

82 Parrenas, "New Household Forms," in Zhou and Gatewood, *Contemporary Asian America*, 336–51.

83 Parrenas, "New Household Forms," in Zhou and Gatewood, *Contemporary Asian America*, 341.

84 See Ishii-Kuntz, "Asian American Families," in Coleman and Ganong, *Handbook of Contemporary Families*, 354–55, and Farver et al., "Ethnic Identity," 187–88; Ishii-Kuntz and Farver both suggest that biculturality is the best adaptation for immigrants and refugees.

85 Farver et al., "Ethnic Identity," 186–88.

86 Please see Bernard S. Jackson, "The 'Institutions' of Marriage and Divorce in the Hebrew Bible," *Journal of Semitic Studies* 56, no. 2 (2011): 221–50; and G. P. Hugenberger, *Marriage as a Covenant: A Study of Biblical Law and Ethics Governing Marriage, Developed from the Perspective of Malachi* (Leiden: E. J. Brill, 1994), for further reading.

87 See David H. Jensen, *Parenting* (Minneapolis: Fortress, 2011), 50–58.

88 Farver et al., "Ethnic Identity," 191.

89 Shame causes fear, dependence, and hostility. Fear is the reaction of one to authoritarianism in highly patriarchal cultures. Dependence is intrinsic to the functioning of a patriarchal and hierarchal system, as one always must account to one's superior. Finally, hostility occurs because one is dependent on whom one fears. Slote, "Psychocultural Dynamics," in Slote and De Vos, *Confucianism and the Family*, 49.

90 Farver et al., "Ethnic Identity," 197.

91 Farver et al., "Ethnic Identity," 208.

92 Farver et al., "Ethnic Identity," 186.

93 Teresa W. Julian, Patrick C. McKenry, and Mary W. McKelvey, "Cultural Variations in Parenting: Perceptions of Caucasian, African-American, Hispanic, and Asian-American Parents," *Family Relations* 43, no. 1 (1994): 30–37; and Zhou, "Social Capital," in Zhou and Gatewood, *Contemporary Asian America*, 325.

94 Mock, "Clinical Reflections," in McGoldrick, *Revisioning Family Therapy*, 368.

95 Marsha Pravda Mirkin, "The Impact of Multiple Contexts on Recent Immigrant Families," in McGoldrick, *Revisioning Family Therapy*, 375.

96 Mirkin, "Impact of Multiple Contexts," in McGoldrick, *Revisioning Family Therapy*, 381.

97 Parrenas, "New Household Forms," in Zhou and Gatewood, *Contemporary Asian America*, 341–43.

98 Meilaender, "Time for Love," 258.

Chapter 4: Virtue Ethics

1 Edward P. Antonio, "Aristotle on Politics," in *Beyond the Pale: Reading Ethics from the Margins*, ed. Miguel A. De La Torre and Stacey M. Floyd-Thomas, 15–23 (Louisville, Ky.: Westminster John Knox, 2011), 20.

2 Jean Porter, "Virtue Ethics," in *The Cambridge Companion to Christian Ethics*, 2nd ed., ed. Robin Gill, 87–102 (Cambridge: Cambridge University Press, 2012), 88.

3 Augustine, *The City of God*, trans. John O'Meara (London: Penguin, 1984), 891.

4 Augustine, *City of God*, 891.

5 Cited in J. Philip Wogaman and Douglas M. Strong, eds., *Readings in Christian Ethics: A Historical Sourcebook* (Louisville, Ky.: Westminster John Knox, 1996), 62.

6 Porter, "Virtue Ethics," in Gill, *Cambridge Companion*, 91.

7 Thomas Aquinas, *Summa Theologiae* I–II, Q 55, art. 4.

8 J. Philip Wogaman, *Christian Ethics: A Historical Introduction* (Louisville, Ky.: Westminster John Knox, 1993), 86.

9 Thomas Aquinas, *Summa Theologiae* I–II, Q 63, art. 2, 3, 4.

10 Aquinas, *Summa Theologiae* I–II, Q 62, art. 4.

11 H. Richard Niebuhr, *Christ and Culture* (New York: Harper & Row, 1975), 129, 191.

12 Reinhold Niebuhr, *The Nature and Destiny of Man: A Christian Interpretation* (New York: Scribner, 1964), 1:268–85.

13 Jonathan Edwards' book *The Nature of True Virtue* is an important text in which he argues that "true virtue must chiefly consist in *love to God*; the Being of beings, infinitely the greatest and best" (14). The significance of this book lies in his recognition of the heart as the key moral faculty to realize the true virtue. He interconnects the life of true virtue with the exercising of the heart. "Therefore I suppose I shall not depart from the common opinion when I say, that virtue is the beauty of the qualities and exercises of the heart, or those actions which proceed from them" (2). Edwards, however, does not investigate the nature of the heart as a separate moral subject in his text. See Edwards, *The Nature of True Virtue* (Ann Arbor: University of Michigan Press, 1960).

14 Porter, "Virtue Ethics," in Gill, *Cambridge Companion*, 97.

15 Alasdair MacIntyre, *After Virtue: A Study in Moral Theory*, 2nd ed. (1981; Notre Dame, Ind.: University of Notre Dame Press, 1984), 150.

16 See, e.g., Martha Nussbaum, "Non-Relative Virtues: An Aristotelian Approach," in *The Quality of Life*, ed. Martha Nussbaum and Amartya Sen (Oxford: Oxford University Press, 1993), 242–70; and Nussbaum, "Virtue Ethics: A Misleading Category?" *The Journal of Ethics* 3, no. 3 (1999), 163–201. Her most recent book, *Political Emotions: Why Love Matters for Justice* (Cambridge, Mass.: Harvard University Press, 2013), discusses the important public role of emotions to sustain a "decent" liberal society. As for Stanley Hauerwas, see his *The Peaceable Kingdom: A Primer in Christian Ethics* (Notre Dame, Ind.: University of Notre Dame Press, 1983); and Hauerwas, *A Community of Character* (Notre Dame, Ind.: University of Notre Dame Press, 1991).

17 Hauerwas, *Peaceable Kingdom*, 68.

18 Jennifer A. Herdt, "Hauerwas among the Virtues," *Journal of Religious Ethics* 40, no. 2 (2012): 223.

19 Hauerwas, *Peaceable Kingdom*, 99.

20 Herdt, "Hauerwas among the Virtues," 222.

21 Miguel A. De La Torre, "Stanley Hauerwas on Church," in De La Torre and Floyd-Thomas, *Beyond the Pale*, 218.

22 De La Torre, "Stanley Hauerwas on Church," in De La Torre and Floyd-Thomas, *Beyond the Pale*, 221.

23 Jonathan Tran, "Time for Hauerwas's Racism," in *Unsettling Arguments: A Festschrift on the Occasion of Stanley Hauerwas's 70th Birthday*, ed. Charles R. Pinches, Kelly S. Johnson, and Charles M. Collier (Eugene, Ore.: Cascade, 2010), 256.

24 Julia Kristeva, *Powers of Horror: An Essay on Abjection* (New York: Columbia University Press, 1982), 6.

25 Kristeva, *Powers of Horror*, 68.

26 Derek Hook, "Racism as Abjection: A Psychoanalytic Conceptualisation for a Post-Apartheid South Africa," *South African Journal of Psychology* 34, no. 4 (2004): 672.

27 See Leonard Dinnerstein, Roger L. Nichols, and David M. Reimers, *Natives and Strangers: A Multicultural History of Americans* (Oxford: Oxford University Press, 2003), 193.

28 Wonhee Anne Joh, "Violence and Asian American Experience: From Abjection to *Jeong*," in *Off the Menu: Asian and Asian North American Women's Religion and Theology*, ed. Rita Nakashima Brock et al., 145–62 (Louisville, Ky.: Westminster John Knox, 2007), 152.

29 Joh, "Violence," in Brock et al., *Off the Menu*, 153.

30 This moral suspicion renders such non-European Christian ethicists as womanist ethicists critical of the cultural environment and circumstances that can influence individual and communal ethical perspectives with oppressive values. Based on this critical awareness, for instance, Melanie L. Harris develops seven virtues which include generosity, graciousness, compassion, spiritual wisdom, audacious courage, justice, and good community. Stacey M. Floyd-Thomas enumerates different "tenets of womanist virtue": radical subjectivity, traditional communalism, redemptive love, and critical engagement. For Harris' list, see chap. 5 in her *Gifts of Virtue, Alice Walker, and Womanist Ethics* (New York: Palgrave Macmillan, 2010), and for Floyd-Thomas, see her chapter " 'I Am Black and Beautiful, O Ye Daughters of Jerusalem . . .': African American Virtue Ethics and a Womanist Hermeneutics of Redemption," in *African American Religious Life and the Story of Nimrod*, ed. Anthony B. Pinn and Allen Dwight Callahan (New York: Palgrave Macmillan, 2008).

31 Huang Yong, "The Self-Centeredness Objection to Virtue Ethics: Zhu Xi's Neo-Confucian Response," *American Catholic Philosophical Quarterly* 84, no. 4 (2010): 651.

32 Yong, "Self-Centeredness Objection," 653.

33 Of course not all Western moral philosophers or ethicists regard practical reason as the key moral faculty. The Scottish Enlightenment thinkers such as David Hume and Adam Smith would argue that moral sentiment, not moral reason, should lead our moral lives. Modern feminist scholars of "ethics of care" would also argue that moral reason is not the central moral faculty. Still, it is not too much to say that the Aristotelian influence in Western moral thought and its tradition, which champions practical reason, is widespread and dominant.

34 Eunkang Koh, "Gender Issues and Confucian Scriptures: Is Confucianism Incompatible with Gender Equality in South Korea?" *Bulletin of the School of Oriental and African Studies* 71, no. 2 (2008): 345.

35 Namsoon Kang, "Confucian Familism and Its Social/Religious Embodiment in Christianity: Reconsidering the Family Discourse from a Feminist Perspective," *Asia Journal of Theology* 18, no. 1 (2004): 185.

36 Wai-ying Wong, "The Moral and Non-Moral Virtues in Confucian Ethics," *Asian Philosophy* 21, no. 1 (2011): 72.

37 Kwong-loi Shun, "Conception of the Person in Confucian Thought," in *Confucian Ethics: A Comparative Study of Self, Autonomy, and Community*, ed. Kwong-loi Shun and David B. Wong, 183–99 (New York: Cambridge University Press, 2004), 185.

38 John Berthrong, "*Xin (Hsin)*: Heart and Mind," in *Encyclopedia of Chinese Philosophy*, ed. Antonio S. Cua, 795–97 (New York: Routledge, 2002), 796.

39 Berthrong, "*Xin (Hsin)*," in Cua, *Encyclopedia of Chinese Philosophy*, 796.

40 Dennis Arjo, "*Ren Xing* and What It Is to Be Truly Human," *Journal of Chinese Philosophy* 38, no. 3 (2011): 457.

41 E.g., Jiyuan Yu compares Aristotle and Mencius by discussing their different understandings on the dynamic feature of the natural basis of human goodness. He writes, "Whereas Aristotle underscores the exercise of rationality, Mencius stresses the natural growth of the four seeds [of the heart]." See Yu, "The Moral Self and the Perfect Self in Aristotle and Mencius," *Journal of Chinese Philosophy* 28, no. 3 (2001): 238. In a similar way, Xiusheng Liu divides Mencius and Aristotle into two different schools, saying while Mencius and Hume can be grouped together as original thinkers who developed "sensibility theory," Aristotle is known to uphold the rationalist position. See Liu, "Mencius, Hume, and Sensibility Theory," *Philosophy East and West* 52, no. 1 (2002): 75–97.

42 Søren Kierkegaard, *Purity of Heart Is to Will One Thing* (Radford, Va.: Wilder Publications, 2008). He writes in this book, "Only the individual can truthfully will the Good. . . . For he is in touch with the demand that calls for purity of heart by willing only one thing" (118).

43 Jürgen Moltmann, *Theology of Hope: On the Ground and the Implications of a Christian Eschatology* (New York: Harper & Row, 1965), 35.

Chapter 5: Peace and War

1 "Ohio State and County QuickFacts," U.S. Census Bureau, last modified February 5, 2015, http://quickfacts.census.gov/qfd/states/39000.html.

2 Rosemary Radford Ruether, *America, Amerikkka: Elect Nation and Imperial Violence* (Oakville, Conn.: Equinox, 2007), 101.

3 Jodi Kim, *Ends of Empire: Asian American Critique and the Cold War* (Minneapolis: University of Minnesota Press, 2010), 1–2.

4 Stanley Hauerwas, *War and the American Difference: Theological Reflections on Violence and National Identity* (Grand Rapids: Baker Academic, 2011), 38.

5 Hauerwas, *War and the American Difference*, 39–40.

6 Hauerwas, *War and the American Difference*, 88.

7 Hauerwas, *War and the American Difference*, 87.

8 Thich Nhat Hanh, *For a Future to Be Possible: Buddhist Ethics for Everyday Life* (San Francisco: Parallax, 2007), 13–14.

9 Mark Allman, *Who Would Jesus Kill? War, Peace, and the Christian Tradition* (Winona, Minn.: Anselm Academic, 2008), 121.

10 Allman, *Who Would Jesus Kill?* 122–23.

11 Reinhold Niebuhr, *The Irony of American History* (New York: Charles Scribner's Sons, 1952; repr., Chicago: University of Chicago Press, 2008), 25. Citation is to the 2008 edition.

12 Jasbir Puar, "Feminists and Queers in the Service of Empire," in *Feminism and War: Confronting U.S. Imperialism*, ed. Robin L. Riley et al. (New York: Zed, 2008), 52.

13 Allman, *Who Would Jesus Kill?* 166.

14 St. Augustine, *The City of God*, trans. Henry Bettenson (New York: Penguin, 2003), 12–14.

15 St. Augustine, *City of God*, 13–14.

16 Allman, *Who Would Jesus Kill?* 167.

17 Allman, *Who Would Jesus Kill?* 199.

18 Allman, *Who Would Jesus Kill?* 200–4.

19 Daniel Philpott, *Just and Unjust Peace: An Ethic of Political Reconciliation* (New York: Oxford University Press, 2012), 31–32.

20 Philpott, *Just and Unjust Peace*, 174.

21 Susan Brooks Thistlethwaite, "Introduction," in *Interfaith Just Peacemaking: Jewish, Christian, and Muslim Perspectives on the New Paradigm of Peace and War*, ed. Susan Brooks Thistlethwaite (New York: Palgrave Macmillan, 2012), 1.

22 Allman, *Who Would Jesus Kill?* 239.

23 The actions of just peacemaking include: (1) supporting nonviolent direct action; (2) taking independent initiatives to reduce threat; (3) using cooperative conflict resolution; (4) acknowledging responsibility for conflict and justice, and seeking repentance and forgiveness; (5) advancing democracy, human rights, and interdependence; (6) fostering just and sustainable economic development; (7) working with emerging cooperative forces in the international system; (8) strengthening the United Nations and international efforts for cooperation and human rights; (9) reducing offensive weapons and the weapon trade; and (10) encouraging grassroots peacemaking groups. Allman, *Who Would Jesus Kill?* 241–50.

24 Niebuhr, *Irony of American History*, 40–41, 141.

25 Reinhold Niebuhr, *The Children of Light and the Children of Darkness: A Vindication of Democracy and a Critique of Its Traditional Defense* (New York: Scribner's, 1960), x. Niebuhr regarded the equilibrium of power between the communist bloc and that of free market democracies as desirable for global security, For this, according to Niebuhr, the United States should allow its allies to watch its usage of military power but the allies needed to cooperate with U.S. leadership because they faced the greater evil of communism. See Niebuhr, *Irony of American History*, 134.

26 Niebuhr, *Irony of American History*, 89–90.

27 Niebuhr, *Irony of American History*, 112.

28 Niebuhr, *Irony of American History*, 119.

29 Niebuhr, *Irony of American History*, 137.

30 Kim, *Ends of Empire*, 2–3.

31 Kim, *Ends of Empire*, 3.

32 Kim, *Ends of Empire*.

33 "Harry Holt's 'Dear Friends' Letter, 1955," *The Adoption History Project*, University of Oregon, http://darkwing.uoregon.edu/~adoption/archive/Holt DearFriendsltr.htm.

34 Kim, *Ends of Empire*, 168–69.

35 Kim, *Ends of Empire*, 208. Many Vietnamese mothers of mixed-racial children were prostitutes. The fathers of these children often did not know of the existence of their children or simply abandoned them.

36 Kim, *Ends of Empire*, 203.

37 Kim, *Ends of Empire*.

38 Kim, *Ends of Empire*, 18.

39 Harry Truman, "A Declaration of National Emergency, December 16, 1950," in *Almanac of American Military History*, ed. Spencer Tucker, vol. 3 (Santa Barbara, Calif.: ABC-CLIO, 2012), 1938.

40 Kim, *Ends of Empire*, 119.

41 Kim, *Ends of Empire*. Guerilla warfare and terrorism can hardly be justified. Before making a moral judgment on these tactics, however, we must carefully examine the larger sociopolitical structure that feeds upon guerilla warfare and terrorism. Otherwise, we may unintentionally support a large-scale military operation in retaliation for guerilla attacks and make a quick judgment on the moral character of those who choose guerilla attacks. According to Naim Stifan Ateek, a Palestinian liberation theologian, in the Palestinian context, young people were not born "terrorists" but became terrorists because of their experience of humiliation by the Israeli Army, desire for revenge for the killing or injury of a relative or a friend, desperation and frustration from the oppressive Israeli occupation, unemployment and confinement, imprisonment and torture, hopelessness, racism, and discrimination. Ateek emphasizes that we should attempt to understand the underlying causes of terrorism but not to justify. See Ateek, *A Palestinian Christian Cry for Reconciliation* (Maryknoll, N.Y.: Orbis, 2008), 116–17.

Similar to what Ateek argues, we should attempt to understand why North Vietnamese chose to use guerilla attacks rather than morally condemning the people. Furthermore, America's use of napalm, Agent Orange, and excessive bombings, which indifferently killed soldiers and civilians, could not be justified although America chose to use these weapons in order to retaliate against guerillas and terrorists.

42 Lisa Lowe, *Immigrant Acts: On Asian American Cultural Politics* (Durham, N.C.: Duke University Press, 1996), 8.

43 Gale Yee, " 'She Stood in Tears amid the Alien Corn': Ruth, the Perpetual Foreigner and Model Minority," in *Off the Menu: Asian and Asian North American Women's Religion and Theology*, ed. Rita Nakashima Brock et al. (Louisville, Ky.: Westminster John Knox, 2007), 46–48, 51–52.

44 Lowe, *Immigrant Acts*, 16.

45 Lowe, *Immigrant Acts*, 17.

46 Janet R. Jakobsen and Ann Pellegrini, *Love the Sin: Sexual Regulation and the Limits of Religious Tolerance* (Boston: Beacon, 2004), 49–50.

47 Many feminist scholars, such as Cynthia Enloe, Cynthia Cockburn, and M. Jacqui Alexander, offer sophisticated analyses of heteronormativity and the inseparable connection between the military and patriarchal masculinity in the process of nation-building and nation-maintaining.

48 Setsu Shigematsu with Anuradha Kristina Bhagwati and Eli Paintedcrow, "Women-of-Color Veterans on War, Militarism, and Feminism," in *Feminism and War: Confronting U.S. Imperialism*, ed. Robin L. Riley, Chandra Talpade Mohanty, and Minnie Bruce Pratt (New York: Zed, 2008), 95–96.

49 After five years in the marines and leaving as a captain, Bhagwati reflected that "the organization [the military or the marine corps] transforms a person's essence into something terribly destructive and self-destructive, regardless of who that person once was. . . . There's huge difference in a fighting organization that learns to fight because it has no other choice, and one that trains people to love killing, regardless of the context, time, place, or cause." See Shigematsu, "Women-of-Color," in Riley, Mohanty, and Pratt, *Feminism and War*, 95.

Bhagwati's reflection shows her feelings about "reflexive fire training" that conditions soldiers to shoot before thinking. Reflexive fire training would later inflict severe psychological suffering on the soldiers who killed another human beings. See Lt. Col. Dave Grossman, *On Killing: The Psychological Cost of Learning to Kill in War and Society*, rev. ed. (New York: Open Road Integrated Media, 2009), Kindle edition.

50 Deepti Hajela, "Asian American Soldier's Suicide Called a 'Wake-Up Call' for the Military," *Washington Post*, February 21, 2012, http://www.washingtonpost .com/politics/asian-american-soldiers-suicide-called-a-wake-up-call-for-the -military/2012/02/19/gIQA7Ke4QR_story.html?wpisrc.

51 Examining the U.S. overseas military bases, Seungsook Moon and Maria Hohn analyze how the U.S. military empire is interwoven with race, class, gender, and sexuality systems. Racial hierarchies within the U.S. military influence soldiers' interactions with local populations where U.S. bases are stationed. E.g., until 1967 when the U.S. Supreme Court ruled Jim Crow laws unconstitutional, the U.S. military maintained racial segregation and condoned racially segregated entertainments around the U.S. military bases (e.g., white-only clubs). Unfortunately, racial segregation in military entertainments still exists, e.g., in South Korea. In the 1970s racial conflicts in the U.S. military bases erupted violently in West Germany and in South Korea. See Hohn and Moon, "Introduction: The Politics of Gender, Sexuality, Race, and Class in the U.S. Military Empire," in *Over There: Living with the U.S. Military Empire from World War II to the Present*, ed. Hohn and Moon (Durham, N.C.: Duke University Press, 2010), 21–23.

52 Hal Taussig, *In the Beginning Was the Meal: Social Experimentation and Early Christian Identity* (Minneapolis: Fortress, 2009), 115.

53 Taussig, *In the Beginning*, 125–26.

54 Like Okinawa and Taiwan, Jeju also experienced "Red Hunting" during the U.S. military occupation in the northeastern Pacific Islands. With the help of

local elites, the U.S. military, as the successor of imperial Japan in the region, brutally hunted socialists and communists who were perceived as threats to the U.S. hegemony in the region. See Keun-Joo Christine Pae, "Feminist Activism as Interfaith Dialogue: A Lesson from Gangjeong Village of Jeju, Korea," *Journal of Korean Religion* 5, no. 1 (2014): 55–69.

55 See my previous argument in the "Holy War" section.

56 Jonathan Tran, *The Vietnamese War and Theologies of Memory: Time and Eternity in the Far Country* (Oxford: Wiley-Blackwell), 221–26.

57 Tran, *Vietnamese War*, 263–64.

58 Tran, *Vietnamese War*, 206.

59 Emilie M. Townes, *Womanist Ethics and the Cultural Production of Evil* (New York: Palgrave Macmillan, 2006), 22–23.

60 Grace M. Cho, *Haunting the Korean Diaspora: Shame, Secrecy, and the Forgotten War* (Minneapolis: University of Minnesota Press, 2008), 15–17.

61 Cho, *Haunting the Korean Diaspora*, 29.

62 Cho, *Haunting the Korean Diaspora*, 29.

63 Cho, *Haunting the Korean Diaspora*, 15, 29.

64 Rita Nakashima Brock and Rebecca Parker, *Saving Paradise: How Christianity Traded Love of This World for Crucifixion and Empire* (Boston: Beacon, 2008), 69–72.

65 Susan Brooks Thistlethwaite, "Militarism in North American Perspective," in *Women Resisting Violence: Spirituality for Life*, ed. Mary John Mananzan et al. (Eugene, Ore.: Wipf and Stock, 2001), 121. Reflective fire training was developed based on L. S. A. Marshall's study that 75 percent of combat soldiers in World War II did not directly fire at the enemy. The training that enabled soldiers to fire at any moving objects without thinking (i.e., muscle memory) raised shooting rates to 50 to 60 percent in Korea, and 85 to 90 percent in Vietnam. See Grossman, *On Killing*.

66 Brock and Parker, *Saving Paradise*, 144.

67 Thistlethwaite, "Militarism," in Mananzan et al., *Women Resisting Violence*, 124–25. Thistlethwaite further accentuates that in the world where violence and death are ubiquitous, the church must lead her people to the unity between body and spirit and between "sacredness and sensuality."

68 Rita Nakashima Brock and Gabriella Lettini, *Soul Repair: Recovering from Moral Injury after War* (Boston: Beacon, 2012), Kindle edition.

69 Brock and Lettini, *Soul Repair*.

70 Brock and Lettini, *Soul Repair*.

71 Brock and Lettini, *Soul Repair*.

72 Kwok, *Postcolonial Imagination*, 37.

73 Kwok, *Postcolonial Imagination*, 38.

74 Cynthia Cockburn, *From Where We Stand: War, Women's Activism, and Feminist Analysis* (New York: Zed, 2007), 258.

75 Dorothee Soelle, *The Silent Cry: Mysticism and Resistance*, trans. Barbara Rumscheidt and Martin Rumscheidt (Minneapolis: Fortress, 2001), 87 (bracketed text added).

Chapter 6: Wealth and Prosperity

1 Daniel K. Finn, "Preface," in *The True Wealth of Nations: Catholic Social Thought and Economic Life*, ed. Daniel K. Finn (Oxford: Oxford University Press, 2010), v.

2 The entire first part of the chapter is based on Sondra Ely Wheeler, *Wealth as Peril and Obligation: The New Testament on Possessions* (Grand Rapids: Eerdmans, 1995), 127–34. Only when a section is directly quoted is a reference cited; otherwise, the rest of the text is based on the aforementioned pages.

3 For a different interpretation of the Sermon on the Mount, see Walter Wink, *Jesus and Nonviolence: A Third Way* (Minneapolis: Fortress, 2003).

4 Wheeler, *Wealth as Peril*, 130–31.

5 Wheeler, *Wealth as Peril*, 132.

6 As Andrew Yuengert acknowledges, "in economics, income is assumed to be a comprehensive measure of command over everything that could possibly matter in life because everything that matters is assumed to be for sale in markets" (45). See Yuengert, "What Is 'Sustainable Prosperity for All' in the Catholic Social Tradition?" in Finn, *True Wealth of Nations*, 37–62.

7 Aristotle, *Nicomachean Ethics*, 1.5.

8 See Amartya Sen, *Development as Freedom* (New York: Anchor, 1999); and Martha Craven Nussbaum, *Creating Capabilities: The Human Development Approach* (Cambridge, Mass.: Belknap Press of Harvard University Press, 2011).

9 Andrew Yuengert, "The Common Good for Economists," *Faith and Economics* 38 (Fall 2001): 1–9.

10 John Paul II, *Sollicitudo Rei Socialis*, December 30, 1987, para. 28.2.

11 John Paul II, *Sollicitudo Rei Socialis*, para. 28.3

12 Pontifical Council for Justice and Peace, *Compendium of the Social Doctrine of the Church* (Rome: Libreria Editrice Vaticana, 2004), para. 338.

13 John Paul II, *Centesimus Annus*, May 1, 1991, para. 43.a.

14 Pontifical Council, *Compendium*, para. 329.

15 National Conference of Catholic Bishops, *Economic Justice for All: Pastoral Letter on Catholic Social Teaching and the U.S. Economy* (Washington, D.C.: Office of Publishing and Promotion Services, U.S. Catholic Conference), chap. 1, no. 24.

16 Yuengert, "Sustainable Prosperity for All?" in Finn, *True Wealth of Nations*, 47.

17 Mahbub ul Haq, "The Birth of the Human Development Index," in *Readings in Human Development: Concepts, Measures, and Policies for a Development Paradigm*, ed. Sakiko Fukuda-Parr and A. K. Shiva Kumar, 2nd ed., 127–37 (New Delhi, India: Oxford University Press, 2005).

18 Albino Barrera, "What Does Catholic Social Thought Recommend for the Economy?" in Finn, *True Wealth of Nations*, 14.

19 John XXIII, *Mater et Magistra*, no. 65.

20 David Hollenbach, *The Common Good and Christian Ethics* (Cambridge: Cambridge University Press, 2002), 81.

21 Pontifical Council, *Compendium*, para. 106.

22 *Catechism of the Catholic Church*, para. 1883.

23 Latin American Bishops, "Poverty of the Church" (Medellín, Columbia, September 6, 1968), no. 10.

24 Stephen J. Pope, "Proper and Improper Partiality and the Preferential Option for the Poor," *Theological Studies* 54, no. 2 (1993): 268.

25 As John Paul II observed, "given the worldwide dimension which the social question has assumed, this love of preference for the poor, and the decisions which it inspires in us, cannot but embrace the immense multitudes of the hungry, the needy, the homeless, those without medical care, and above all, those without hope of a better future. It is impossible not to take account of the existence of these realities. To ignore them would mean becoming like the 'rich man' who pretended not to know the beggar Lazarus lying at his gate (cf. Luke 16:19-31)." John Paul II, *Sollicitudo Rei Socialis*, para. 42.

26 Catholic Bishops, *Economic Justice for All*, chap. 1, no. 24.

27 Donal Dorr, *Option for the Poor and for the Earth: Catholic Social Teaching* (Maryknoll, N.Y.: Orbis, 2012), 7–8.

28 James P. Bailey, *Rethinking Poverty: Income, Assets, and the Catholic Social Justice Tradition* (Notre Dame, Ind.: University of Notre Dame Press, 2010), 47.

29 Barrera, "Catholic Social Thought," 24.

30 Barrera, "Catholic Social Thought," 25.

31 Barrera, "Catholic Social Thought," 25.

32 See Jennifer L. Hochschild, *Facing Up to the American Dream: Race, Class, and the Soul of the Nation* (Princeton, N.J.: Princeton University Press, 1995), 18.

33 Mara A. Cohen-Marks and Christopher Stout, "Can The American Dream Survive the New Multiethnic America? Evidence from Los Angeles," *Sociological Forum* 26, no. 4 (2011): 824.

34 Hochschild, *Facing Up*, xi.

35 Cohen-Marks and Stout, "Can the American Dream Survive?" 828, 841.

36 Cohen-Marks and Stout, "Can the American Dream Survive?"

37 Paul Taylor, ed., *The Rise of Asian Americans: Updated Edition* (Washington, D.C.: Pew Research Center, 2013), 1–2, http://www.pewsocialtrends.org/2012/06/19/the-rise-of-asian-americans.

38 Taylor, *Rise of Asian Americans*, 4.

39 Taylor, *Rise of Asian Americans*, 2

40 Taylor, *Rise of Asian Americans*, 2

41 Taylor, *Rise of Asian Americans*, 2

42 Jonathan Y. Tan, *Introducing Asian American Theologies* (Maryknoll, N.Y.: Orbis, 2008), 37.

43 Isao Takei and Arthur Sakamoto, "Poverty among Asian Americans in the 21st Century," *Sociological Perspectives* 54, no. 2 (2011): 251.

44 Tan, *Introducing Asian American Theologies*, 38.

45 See Won Moo Hurh and Kwang Chung Kim, "The 'Success' Image of Asian Americans: Its Validity, and Its Practical and Theoretical Implications," *Ethnic and Racial Studies* 12, no. 4 (1989): 512–38.

46 Tan, *Introducing Asian American Theologies*, 39. See also Frieda Wong and Richard Halgin, "The 'Model Minority': Bane or Blessing for Asian Americans?" *Journal of Multicultural Counseling and Development* 34, no. 1 (2006): 38–48.

47 Andrew Sung Park, *Racial Conflict and Healing: An Asian-American Theological Perspective* (Maryknoll, N.Y.: Orbis, 1996), 22–23.

48 Tan, *Introducing Asian American Theologies*, 40.

49 See the discussion in Hubert M. Blalock Jr., *Toward a Theory of Minority-Group Relations* (New York: Wiley, 1975); Jonathan H. Turner and Edna Bonacich, "Toward a Composite Theory of Middleman Minorities," *Ethnicity* 7, no. 2 (1980): 144–58; and Richard J. Jensen and Cara J. Abeyta, "The Minority in the Middle: Asian-American Dissent in the 1960s and 1970s," *Western Journal of Speech Communication* 51, no. 4 (1987): 404–16.

50 Tan, *Introducing Asian American Theologies*, 54.

51 Kenneth J. Guest, "Religion and Transnational Migration in the New China-town," in *Immigrant Faiths: Transforming Religious Life in America*, ed. Karen I. Leonard et al. (Lanham, Md.: AltaMira, 2005), 159.

52 Kenneth J. Guest, *God in Chinatown: Religion and Survival in New York's Evolving Immigrant Community* (New York: New York University Press, 2003), 201–6. For a theological consideration of how evangelical Christians in particular should regard Fuzhounese immigrants in Chinatown, see Amos Yong, "The Spirit of Jubilee: An Asian American Immigrant Consideration," chap. 6 in *The Future of Evangelical Theology: Soundings from the Asian American Diaspora* (Downers Grove, Ill.: InterVarsity, 2014).

53 See Fenggang Yang, "Chinese Christian Transnationalism: Diverse Networks of a Houston Church," in *Religion across Borders: Transnational Immigrant Networks*, ed. Helen Rose Ebaugh and Jane Saltzman Chafetz, 129–48 (Walnut Creek, Calif.: AltaMira, 2002).

54 Thao Ha, "The Evolution of Remittances from Family to Faith: The Vietnamese Case," in Ebaugh and Chafetz, *Religion across Borders*, 111–28.

55 Sharon Kim, *A Faith of Our Own: Second-Generation Spirituality in Korean American Churches* (New Brunswick, N.J.: Rutgers University Press, 2010), 57–58.

56 Soong-Chan Rah, *The Next Evangelicalism: Freeing the Church from Western Cultural Captivity* (Downers Grove, Ill.: InterVarsity, 2009), 61, 60.

57 The literature on the shamanistic influences in Korean Christianity is vast. For a sampling of the literature, particularly on the fusion between Pentecostalism, prosperity gospel, and shamanism, see Hwa Yung, "Mission and Evangelism: Evangelical and Pentecostal Theologies in Asia," in *Christian Theology in Asia*, ed. Sebastian C. H. Kim, 250–70 (New York: Cambridge University Press, 2008), 263.

58 Sang Hyun Lee, *From a Liminal Place: An Asian American Theology* (Minneapolis: Fortress, 2010), 121–22.

59 Park, *Racial Conflict*, 45–47.

60 Park, *Racial Conflict*, 46.

61 For a sampling of press about Forever 21, see Eva Wiseman, "The Gospel According to Forever 21," *Guardian*, July 16, 2011, http://www.theguardian.com/lifeandstyle/2011/jul/17/forever-21-fast-fashion-america.

Chapter 7: Racial Identity and Solidarity

1 In referring to racial solidarity and cooperation as a kind of disposition, I am taking cues from a baseline definition of solidarity in the Catholic social tradition wherein solidarity is understood as the moral and social virtue of interdependence: the "firm and persevering determination to commit oneself . . . to the good of all and of each individual, because we are all really responsible for all." See John Paul II, *Sollicitudo Rei Socialis*, December 30, 1987, para. 38.

2 In this essay I refer primarily to race or ethno-racial rather than race *and* ethnicity. In doing so I am affirming the notion that race and ethnicity are synonymous terms insofar as the category ethnicity has been deployed as a strategy to undermine race in the face of its descriptive complexity. But this strategy simply reinscribes the conceptual and descriptive problems of race to a more "localized" way of talking about identity. See J. Kameron Carter, *Race: A Theological Account* (New York: Oxford University Press, 2008), 44n14.

3 Bryan N. Massingale, *Racial Justice and the Catholic Church* (Maryknoll, N.Y.: Orbis, 2010); and Jennifer Harvey, *Whiteness and Morality: Pursuing Racial Justice through Reparations and Sovereignty* (New York: Palgrave Macmillan, 2012). See also Laurie M. Cassidy and Alex Mikulich, eds., *Interrupting White Privilege: Catholic Theologians Break the Silence* (Maryknoll, N.Y.: Orbis, 2007).

4 See Katie G. Cannon, *Black Womanist Ethics* (Eugene, Ore.: Wipf & Stock, 2006); M. Shawn Copeland, "Body, Representation, and Black Religious Discourse," in *Postcolonialism, Feminism, and Religious Discourse*, ed. Laura E. Donaldson and Kwok Pui-lan, 180–98 (New York: Routledge, 2002); and Emilie M. Townes, *Breaking the Fine Rain of Death: African American Health Issues and a Womanist Ethic of Care* (New York: Continuum, 1998).

5 Michele Alexander, *The New Jim Crow: Mass Incarceration in the Age of Colorblindness*, rev. ed. (New York: New Press, 2012).

6 James Cone, *A Black Theology of Liberation* (Maryknoll, N.Y.: Orbis, 1994), 5, 1.

7 Cone, *Black Theology*, 7.

8 Cone, *Black Theology*, 13, 101.

9 Cornel West, "On Black-Brown Relations," chap. 44 in *The Cornel West Reader* (New York: Basic Civitas, 1999), 504.

10 West, "On Black-Brown Relations," in *The Cornel West Reader*, 502.

11 For race as a form of social perception, see also Iris Marion Young, "Difference as a Resource for Democratic Communication," in *Deliberative Democracy: Essays on Reason and Politics*, ed. James Bohman and William Rehg, 383–406 (Cambridge, Mass.: MIT Press, 1997). See also Ki Joo (KC) Choi, "Should Race Matter? A Constructive Ethical Assessment of the Postracial Ideal," *Journal of the Society of Christian Ethics* 31, no. 1 (2011): 79–102.

12 On social novels, see D. M. Yeager, " 'Art for Humanity's Sake': The Social Novel as a Mode of Moral Discourse," *Journal of Religious Ethics* 33, no. 3 (2005): 474.

13 Sang Hyun Lee, *From a Liminal Place: An Asian American Theology* (Minneapolis: Fortress, 2010), 55.

14 Peter C. Phan, "Betwixt and Between: Doing Theology with Memory and Imagination," in *Journeys at the Margin: Toward an Autobiographical Theology in*

American-Asian Perspective, ed. Peter C. Phan and Jung Young Lee (Collegeville, Minn.: Liturgical, 1999), 113.

15 Lee, *From a Liminal Place*, 5.

16 Lee, *From a Liminal Place*, x.

17 Lee, *From a Liminal Place*, 55.

18 Lee, *From a Liminal Place*, 111–12.

19 Lee, *From a Liminal Place*, 112.

20 Lee, *From a Liminal Place*, 113.

21 Lee, *From a Liminal Place*, 113.

22 Thus Lee's conception of Asian American identity is congruous with Kathryn Tanner's postmodern account of culture as involving "complex and ad hoc relational processes as resistance, appropriation, subversion, and compromise." She concludes, "Creoles and exiles, . . . ethnic or racial minorities who revel in their own mixed heritage, become models for this interrelational notion of identity." See Tanner, *Theories of Culture: A New Agenda for Theology* (Minneapolis: Fortress, 1998), 58.

23 Lee, *From a Liminal Place*, 113. In this respect, Lee's account of hybridity can find common ground with Catholic theologian Rubén Rosario Rodríguez's advocacy of an account of *mestizaje* (fusion of cultures) as a form of Latino/a political solidarity in the struggle against Euro-American racism and racial paradigms. See Rodríguez, "The Public Relevance of Theology," chap. 3 in *Racism and God-Talk: A Latino/a Perspective* (New York: New York University Press, 2008).

24 Lee, *From a Liminal Place*, 15, 113–14.

25 Susan Saulny, "Black? White? Asian? More Young Americans Choose All of the Above," *New York Times*, January 29, 2011, http://www.nytimes .com/2011/01/30/us/30mixed.html.

26 "Who Is Marrying Whom," *New York Times*, January 29, 2011, http://www .nytimes.com/interactive/2011/01/29/us/20110130mixedrace.html.

27 "2010 Census Shows Asians Are Fastest-Growing Race Group," U.S. Census Bureau, March 21, 2012, http://www.census.gov/newsroom/releases/archives/ 2010_census/cb12-cn22.html.

28 "2010 Census Shows Asians."

29 Choe Sang-Hun, "Foreign Brides Challenge South Korean Prejudices," *New York Times*, June 24, 2005, http://www.nytimes.com/2005/06/23/world/ asia/23iht-brides.html.

30 Choe Sang-Hun, "South Koreans Struggle with Race," *New York Times*, November 1, 2009, http://www.nytimes.com/2009/11/02/world/asia/02race .html?scp=1&sq=South%20Koreans%20Struggle%20with%20Race&st=cse.

31 Amy Chua, *Battle Hymn of the Tiger Mother* (New York: Penguin, 2011).

32 Tamar Lewin, "Report Takes Aim at 'Model Minority' Stereotype of Asian-American Students," *New York Times*, June 10, 2008, http://www.nytimes.com/ 2008/06/10/education/10asians.html.

33 Thus one of the virtues of reconceiving Asian American identity as hybrid is that it mitigates attitudes that exclude multiracial Asians from counting as Asian simply because they are not "fully" Asian. As the historian Paul R. Spickard has observed, "For multiracial Asians, . . . one task is to defend themselves . . .

[a]gainst the subdominant discourse imposed by Asian Americans. Throughout their history, Asian Americans have also defined people of part-Asian descent, without regard to their actual life-situations or wishes. In thus specifying identities for mixed people of Asian ancestry, some Asian Americans have been guilty of stereotyping and oppressing, of mythologizing and dominating, as have Whites." Spickard, "What Must I Be? Asian Americans and the Question of Multiethnic Identity," in *Contemporary Asian America: A Multidisciplinary Reader*, ed. Min Zhou and James V. Gatewood, 2nd ed. (New York: New York University Press, 2007), 395.

34 Kwok Pui-lan, "The Conversation That Is Chinese Christianity," *Boston College Magazine*, Fall 2011, 46.

35 Kwok, "Conversation," 46.

36 Kwok, "Conversation," 46.

37 Kwok, "Conversation," 47. This is not unlike what took place in Asian Catholicism when, according to Peter C. Phan, the synod of Asian bishops called on the Asian Catholic Church to "discover their own identity" in response to the promulgation of *Gaudium et Spes* in 1965. See Phan, " 'Reception' or 'Subversion' of Vatican II by the Asian Churches? A New Way of Being Church in Asia," in *Vatican II Forty Years Later*, ed. William Madges (Maryknoll, N.Y.: Orbis, 2005), 48.

38 The more complicated legacy of intercultural encounters in Asian and Asian American religious experience is discussed further in Kwok Pui-lan, *Postcolonial Imagination and Feminist Theology* (Louisville, Ky.: Westminster John Knox, 2005). See also her discussion of the encounter between Western missionaries and mainland Chinese in Kwok, "Unbinding Our Feet: Saving Brown Women and Feminist Religious Discourse," in Donaldson and Kwok, *Postcolonialism*, 62–81.

39 See Soong-Chan Rah, *The Next Evangelicalism: Freeing the Church from Western Cultural Captivity* (Downers Grove, Ill.: InterVarsity, 2009). On Asian American evangelicals and mainline Protestant congregations, see Russell Jeung, *Faithful Generations: Race and New Asian American Churches* (New Brunswick, N.J.: Rutgers University Press, 2004). For second-generation Korean American churches, see Sharon Kim, *A Faith of Our Own: Second-Generation Spirituality in Korean American Churches* (New Brunswick, N.J.: Rutgers University Press, 2010).

40 Kirk Semple, "In New Jersey, Memorial for 'Comfort Women' Deepens Old Animosity," *New York Times*, May 18, 2012, http://www.nytimes.com/2012/05/19/nyregion/monument-in-palisades-park-nj-irritates-japanese-officials.html.

41 See also Norimitsu Onishi, "Ugly Images of Asian Rivals Becomes Best Sellers in Japan," *New York Times*, November 19, 2005, http://www.nytimes.com/2005/11/19/international/asia/19comics.html.

42 "South Korea and Japan Clash Over Sea's Name in Virginia Textbooks," BBC.com, last modified February 7, 2014, http://www.bbc.com/news/world-asia-26087123.

43 Sam Roberts, "A Debate in New York over the Name of a Sea between Japan and the Koreas," *New York Times*, February 11, 2014, http://www.nytimes

.com/2014/02/12/nyregion/a-debate-in-new-york-over-the-name-of-a-sea
-between-japan-and-the-koreas.html.

44 Paul Taylor, ed., *The Rise of Asian Americans: Updated Edition* (Washington, D.C.:
    Pew Research Center, 2013), 99, The full report can be accessed at www.pewsocial
    trends.org/2012/06/19/the-rise-of-asian-americans.

45 At least thirty South Koreans commit suicide a day. "The rate . . . doubled in the
    decade between 1999 and 2009." Mark McDonald, "Stressed and Depressed,
    Koreans Avoid Therapy," *New York Times*, July 6, 2011, http://www.nytimes
    .com/2011/07/07/world/asia/07iht-psych07.html. In Japan, 2003 saw a 7.1 per-
    cent increase in suicides, 2,284 more Japanese men and women than 2002. That
    comes to about 1 suicide every day. See J. Sean Curtin, "Suicide Also Rises in
    Land of Rising Sun," *AsiaTimesOnline*, July 28, 2004, http://www.atimes.com/
    atimes/Japan/FG28Dh01.html. There are equally jaw-dropping statistics from
    the World Health Organization for China and India. See "Suicide Statistics
    in Asians: Why Do People Kill Themselves?" AsianOffbeat.com, October 3,
    2007, http://www.asianoffbeat.com/default.asp?Display=935.

46 Dean Irvine, "The Cultural Contributors to Suicide in Asia," CNN.com,
    May 27, 2009, http://edition.cnn.com/2009/HEALTH/05/26/asia.suicide/.

47 Kirk Semple, "Suicides Soar among New York Koreans," *New York Times*, Decem-
    ber 31, 2009, http://www.nytimes.com/2009/12/31/nyregion/31suicides
    .html. According to the Department of Health and Human Services, sui-
    cide is the second-leading cause of death of Asian American women ages
    15 to 24. See Elizabeth Cohen, "Push to Achieve Tied to Suicide in Asian-
    American Women," CNN.com, May 16, 2007, http://www.cnn.com/2007/
    HEALTH/05/16/asian.suicides/index.html.

48 Carolyn Chen, "Asians: Too Smart for Their Own Good?" *New York Times*,
    December 19, 2012, http://www.nytimes.com/2012/12/20/opinion/asians-too
    -smart-for-their-own-good.html.

49 "Asian/Pacific American Heritage Month: May 2013," U.S. Census Bureau,
    http://www.census.gov/newsroom/releases/pdf/cb13ff-09_asian.pdf.

50 Wendy Wang, "The Rise of Intermarriage: Rates, Characteristics Vary by Race
    and Gender," *Pew Research Center*, February 16, 2012, http://www.pewsocialtrends
    .org/2012/02/16/the-rise-of-intermarriage/.

51 Tanzina Vega, "Colorblind Notion Aside, Colleges Grapple with Racial Tension,"
    New York Times, February 24, 2014, http://www.nytimes.com/2014/02/25/us/
    colorblind-notion-aside-colleges-grapple-with-racial-tension.html.

52 Kate Taylor and Jeffrey E. Singer, "In Queens, Immigrants Clash with Residents
    of New Homeless Shelter," *New York Times*, July 25, 2014, http://www.nytimes
    .com/2014/07/26/nyregion/homeless-shelters-opening-in-queens-stirs-ugly
    -exchanges.html.

53 As the sociologist Min Zhou points out, "Most Asian Americans seem to accept
    that 'white' is mainstream, average, and normal, and look to whites as their
    frame of reference for attaining higher social positions." See Zhou, "Are Asian
    Americans Becoming White?" in Zhou and Gatewood, *Contemporary Asian
    America*, 358. Given such attitudes, that Asian Americans may participate in

patterns of white racism and privilege should not be entirely unreasonable or unexpected.

54 "Intergroup Relations," chap. 3 in *The Rise of Asian Americans*, ed. Paul Taylor (Washington, D.C.: Pew Research Center, 2012), http://www.pewsocialtrends .org/2012/06/19/chapter-3-intergroup-relations/.

55 Claire Jean Kim and Taeku Lee, "Interracial Politics: Asian Americans and Other Communities of Color," in Zhou and Gatewood, *Contemporary Asian America*, 545.

56 Cf. Ronald Takaki, *Strangers from a Different Shore: A History of Asian Americans* (Boston: Little Brown, 1998).

57 Lee, *From a Liminal Place*, 117–22.

58 Cited from Chen, "Asians: Too Smart." Cf. Thomas J. Espenshade and Alexandria Walton Radford, *No Longer Separate, Not Yet Equal: Race and Class in Elite College Admission and Campus Life* (Princeton, N.J.: Princeton University Press, 2011).

59 Scott Jaschik, "Meritocracy or Bias?" *Inside Higher Ed*, August 13, 2013, http:// www.insidehighered.com/news/2013/08/13/white-definitions-merit-and -admissions-change-when-they-think-about-asian-americans.

60 Mia Tuan, *Forever Foreigners or Honorary Whites: The Asian Ethnic Experience Today* (New Brunswick, N.J.: Rutgers University Press, 1999). See also Rosalind S. Chou and Joe R. Feagin, *The Myth of the Model Minority: Asian Americans Facing Racism* (Boulder, Colo.: Paradigm, 2008).

61 Consider, for instance, Julie Chen, now a media personality for CBS. When starting her career in news broadcasting, she was told by her news director that she would be less relatable to the Dayton, Ohio community because she looked Asian and, therefore, too foreign. In response, she admits to having double eyelid surgery to make her look less Chinese in order to advance her news career. See Kat Chow, "Why Do We Describe Asian Eyes as 'Almond-Shaped'?" NPR.org, September 16, 2013, http://www.npr.org/blogs/codeswitch/2013/09/16/2194 02847/-almond-shaped-eyes-remarkably-exotic-yet-too-foreign. In addition to the prevalence of eyelid surgery among Asian Americans, skin whiteners are also popular among many Asian Americans, as well as other minorities. See Arun Venugopal, "The Dark Side of Fair Skin," WNYC.org, April 7, 2014, http:// www.wnyc.org/story/dark-side-fair-skin-quest-whiteness/. (Many thanks to the students in my spring 2014 class, Race, Politics, and Theology, for drawing my attention to the phenomenon of cosmetic whitening.) According to Zhou, accounts from many second-generation Asian Americans "[suggest] that whitening has more to do with the beliefs of white America than with the actual situation of Asian Americans. Speaking perfect English, effortlessly adopting mainstream cultural values and even intermarrying members of the dominant group may help reduce this 'otherness' at the individual level but have little effect on the group as a whole" (Zhou, "Becoming White," in Zhou and Gatewood, *Contemporary Asian America*, 359). It is worth noting, however, others wonder whether such cosmetic whitening is simply a function of aesthetic taste that has little to do with race. See Maureen O'Connor, "Is Race Plastic: My Trip into the 'Ethnic Plastic Surgery' Minefield," *New York Magazine*, July 27, 2014, http://nymag.com/thecut/2014/07/ethnic-plastic-surgery.html.

62 See Kim and Lee, "Interracial Politics," in Zhou and Gatewood, *Contemporary Asian America*. They write, "Group perceptions of discrimination and identity also shape the prospects for conflict and cooperation between Asian Americans and other groups of color. Studies show that . . . [w]hile roughly 40 percent of Asian Americans report having personally experienced discrimination, few Americans (Asian Americans included) believe that Asian Americans as a group face special obstacles. This data suggests that Asian Americans, on the one hand, and Blacks and Latinos, on the other, may not readily identify with each other or perceive common interests, *despite their shared experience of racial discrimination in the United States*" (545, emphasis added).

63 See also K. Christine Pae and James W. McCarty III, "The Hybridized Public Sphere: Asian American Christian Ethics, Social Justice, and Public Discourse," *Journal of the Society of Christian Ethics* 32, no. 1 (2012): 93–114; and Sharon M. Tan, "Composing Integrity: An Approach to Moral Agency for Asian Americans," *Journal of Race, Ethnicity, and Religion* 3, no. 2.10 (2012): 1–31.

64 Brian Bantum, "Neither Fish nor Fowl: Presence as Politics," chap. 2 in *Redeeming Mulatto: A Theology of Race and Christian Hybridity* (Waco, Tex.: Baylor University Press, 2010).

65 See, for instance, K. Anthony Appiah, "Race, Culture, Identity: Misunderstood Connections," in *Color Conscious: The Political Morality of Race*, ed. K. Anthony Appiah and Amy Gutmann, 92–105 (Princeton, N.J.: Princeton University Press, 1996).

66 Such comments are increasingly included in the category of less overt forms of discrimination called racist microaggressions. See, for instance, Tanzina Vega, "Students See Many Slights as Racial 'Microaggressions,' " *New York Times*, March 21, 2014, http://www.nytimes.com/2014/03/22/us/as-diversity-increases-slights -get-subtler-but-still-sting.html. For more examples, see the "Asian Archives" of National Public Radio's *The Race Card Project*, http://theracecardproject .com/tag/asian/.

Chapter 8: Health Care

1 Anemona Hartocollis, "Changing Her Mind, a Queens Woman Decides to Remain on Life Support," *New York Times*, October 6, 2012, http://www .nytimes.com/2012/10/07/nyregion/sungeun-grace-lee-changes-her-mind -and-decides-to-stay-on-life-support.html.

2 Anemona Hartocollis, "In SungEun Grace Lee Case, Right to Die Is Weighed against a Family's Wishes," *New York Times*, October 4, 2012, http://www .nytimes.com/2012/10/05/nyregion/in-sungeun-grace-lee-case-right-to-die -is-weighed-against-a-familys-wishes.html.

3 Vivian Yee, "For Pastor Trying to Keep Daughter Alive, Party Is Grim," *New York Times*, October 7, 2012, http://www.nytimes.com/2012/10/08/nyregion/ grim-birthday-for-rev-man-ho-lee-fighting-to-keep-daughter-alive.html.

4 Giorgio Agamben, *Homo Sacer: Sovereign Power and Bare Life*, trans. Daniel Heller-Roazen (Stanford: Stanford University Press, 1998). Agamben moves from "natural life," (or zoē), common to all life-forms, to "bare life" with some ambiguity but implies some kind of equivalence between the two: "The

fundamental categorical pair of Western politics is not that of friend/enemy but that of bare life/political existence, zoē/bios, exclusion/inclusion" (8). However, while "natural life" may have the nuance of a fresh or initial state, Leland de la Durantaye writes that in speaking of "bare life," Agamben relies on Walter Benjamin's understanding of *das blosse Leben*, making it clear that "bare life" "is not an initial state so much as what becomes visible through a stripping away of predicates and attributes . . . 'naked or bare (and bared) life is not a prior substance, but instead what remains after the withdrawal of all forms.'" De la Durantaye, *Giorgio Agamben: A Critical Introduction* (Stanford: Stanford University Press, 2009), 203.

5 M. Therese Lysaught and Joseph J. Kotva, eds., *On Moral Medicine: Theological Perspectives in Medical Ethics*, 3rd ed. (Grand Rapids: Eerdmans, 2012), 3.

6 For the sake of clarity, this chapter distinguishes between health care and bioethics in the following way: health care focuses on the implications of social interactions and environments for health, whereas bioethics focuses on the implications of technological procedures and research.

7 This chapter also makes a subtle but important distinction between health care and medicine. Health care is inclusive of medicine; the latter focuses on the actual techniques and therapies administered to an individual.

8 See "Health-Related Quality of Life," Centers for Disease Control and Prevention, last updated November 1, 2012, http://www.cdc.gov/hrqol/, for a discussion of the variable factors involved in determining quality of life.

9 See Amy Laura Hall, *Conceiving Parenthood: American Protestantism and the Spirit of Reproduction* (Grand Rapids: Eerdmans, 2008).

10 See Grace Yia-Hei Kao, "Prospects for Developing Asian American Christian Ethics," *Society of Asian North American Christian Studies* 3 (2011), 96–98.

11 See, e.g., Wonhee Anne Joh's construction of a postcolonial Christology, where the cross demonstrates both pain and suffering and is a subversive gesture of love. Joh, *Heart of the Cross: A Postcolonial Christology* (Louisville, Ky.: Westminster John Knox, 2006).

12 E.g., Gary B. Ferngren most strongly contends that Christians *primarily* sought out naturalistic cures over against supernatural healing; in reviews of Ferngren's book, both Andrew Daunton-Fear and Hector Avalos dispute this. See Ferngren, *Medicine and Health Care in Early Christianity* (Baltimore: Johns Hopkins University Press, 2009), 93; Andrew Daunton-Fear, review of *Medicine and Health Care*, by Ferngren, *Journal of Theological Studies* 61, no. 2 (2010): 757–60; and Hector Avalos, review of *Medicine and Health Care*, by Ferngren, *Church History* 79, no. 1 (2010): 182–84.

13 Ferngren, *Medicine and Health Care*, 87.

14 Ferngren, *Medicine and Health Care*, 93.

15 Ferngren, *Medicine and Health Care*, 96.

16 Ferngren, *Medicine and Health Care*, 98.

17 Ferngren, *Medicine and Health Care*, 114n4.

18 Ferngren, *Medicine and Health Care*, 118.

19 Ferngren, *Medicine and Health Care*, 121.

20 Citing Andrew Crislip, Ferngren states the three characteristics of hospitals as inpatient facilities, professional medical care, and charitable care. Again, given the underlying philosophies of Greco-Roman society, prior to Christianity there were no organizations that were comparable to what we understand as a hospital; any institutions organized to care for the sick were for economic or military rather than charitable reasons. Ferngren, *Medicine and Health Care*, 124.

21 While beyond the scope of this chapter, the history of medical missions provides an important look into the intersection between ideas of physical and spiritual health. Scholars have critically highlighted colonialism's influence on medical missions; at the same time, Christian doctors and nurses also often worked against colonial bureaucracy, acculturated to new environments, and provided much-needed medical services and supplies. For a brief overview of medical missions, see Alex McKay, "Towards a History of Medical Missions," *Medical History* 51, no. 4 (2007): 547–51; and David Hardiman, *Healing Bodies, Saving Souls: Medical Missions in Asia and Africa* (Amsterdam: Editions Rodopi BV, 2006). Hardiman also provides an excellent overview of Christian medical missions as well as scholarship in that area in the introduction to that volume.

22 See United States Conference of Catholic Bishops, *Ethical and Religious Directives for Catholic Health Care Services*, 5th ed., November 17, 2009, http://www.usccb .org/issues-and-action/human-life-and-dignity/health-care/upload/Ethical -Religious-Directives-Catholic-Health-Care-Services-fifth-edition-2009.pdf.

23 K. D. O'Rourke, T. Kopfen-Steiner, and R. Hamel, "A Brief History: A Summary of the Development of the *Ethical and Religious Directives for Catholic Health Care Services*," *Health Progress* 82, no. 6 (2001), http://www.chausa.org/docs/ default-source/health-progress/a-brief-history-pdf.pdf?sfvrsn=0.

24 Michel Foucault, *The History of Sexuality*, Vintage ed. (New York: Vintage, 1980), 142.

25 Rey Chow, *The Protestant Ethnic and the Spirit of Capitalism* (New York: Columbia University Press, 2002), 7.

26 Nayan Shah, *Contagious Divides: Epidemics and Race in San Francisco's Chinatown* (Berkeley: University of California Press, 2001), 46.

27 John Wesley, "Sermon 88: On Dress," General Board of Global Ministries, http://www.umcmission.org/Find-Resources/John-Wesley-Sermons/Sermon -88-On-Dress.

28 Megan Vaughan, *Curing Their Ills: Colonial Power and African Illness* (Stanford: Stanford University Press, 1991), 74, as cited in Hardiman, *Healing Bodies, Saving Souls*, 6.

29 "By a practice I am going to mean any coherent and complex form of socially established cooperative human activity through which goods internal to that form of activity are realized in the course of trying to achieve those standards of excellence which are appropriate to, and partially definitive of, that form of activity, with the result that human powers to achieve excellence, and human conceptions of the ends and goods involved, are systematically extended." Alasdair MacIntyre, *After Virtue: A Study in Moral Theory*, 3rd ed. (South Bend, Ind.: Notre Dame University Press, 2007), 205.

30 Allen Verhey, "The Doctor's Oath—and a Christian Swearing It," in *Theological Ethics in Medical Ethics*, ed. M. Therese Lysaught and Joseph J. Kotva, Jr., 3rd ed. (Grand Rapids: Eerdmans, 2012), 225.

31 Stanley Hauerwas, "Salvation and Health: Why Medicine Needs the Church," in Lysaught and Kotva, *On Moral Medicine*, 50.

32 Margaret A. Farley, *Compassionate Respect: A Feminist Approach to Medical Ethics and Other Questions* (New York: Paulist, 2003).

33 Shah, *Contagious Divides*, 45.

34 "Naturalization Laws 1790–1795," accessed June 1, 2014, http://www.indiana .edu/~kdhist/H105-documents-web/week08/naturalization1790.html.

35 Matthew Frye Jacobson, *Whiteness of a Different Color: European Immigrants and the Alchemy of Race* (Cambridge, Mass.: Harvard University Press, 1999), 68.

36 Jacobson, *Whiteness of a Different Color*, 74.

37 Jacobson, *Whiteness of a Different Color*, 82.

38 Jacobson, *Whiteness of a Different Color*, 73.

39 See Gwen Sharp, "Old 'Yellow Peril' Anti-Chinese Propaganda," *Sociological Images*, June 20, 2014, http://thesocietypages.org/socimages/2008/07/08/old -yellow-peril-anti-chinese-posters/, for examples of public campaign posters from the late nineteenth century.

40 Alexandra M. Stern, review of *Contagious Divides*, by Shah, *H-Net* (2001), http://www.h-net.org/reviews/showrev.php?id=5650.

41 Shah, *Contagious Divides*, 210.

42 Shah, *Contagious Divides*, 44.

43 Shah, *Contagious Divides*, 249. Bonnie Tsui's article "Chinatown Revisited" highlights the variety of U.S. Chinatowns today, from historic urban ones (e.g., Philadelphia, San Francisco) to newer suburban communities (e.g., Houston, Monterey Park). Tsui, "Chinatown Revisited," *New York Times*, January 24, 2014, http://www.nytimes.com/2014/01/26/travel/chinatown-revisited.html.

44 J. S. Lin-Fu, "Population Characteristics and Health Care Needs of Asian Pacific Americans," *Public Health Reports* 103, no. 1 (1988): 18–27.

45 Anne Fadiman, *The Spirit Catches You and You Fall Down: A Hmong Child, Her American Doctors, and the Collision of Two Cultures* (New York: Farrar, Straus & Giroux, 2012).

46 Chau Trinh-Shevrin, Nadia Shilpi Islam, and Mariano Jose Rey, eds., *Asian American Communities and Health: Context, Research, Policy, and Action* (San Francisco: Jossey-Bass, 2009), 8.

47 "Profile: Asian Americans," U.S. Department of Health and Human Services Office of Minority Health, accessed April 10, 2015, http://minorityhealth.hhs .gov/omh/browse.aspx?lvl=3&lvlid=63.

48 Tracy Seipel, "Obamacare: Asian-Americans Sign Up in Droves; Latinos Disproportionately Stay Away," *San Jose Mercury News*, accessed March 25, 2014, http:// www.mercurynews.com/health/ci_25404950/obamacare-asian-americans -sign-up-droves-latinos-disproportionately.

49 See Lisa A. Cooper and Neil R. Powe, *Disparities in Patient Experiences, Health Care Processes, and Outcomes: The Role of Patient-Provider Racial, Ethnic, and Language Concordance*, Commonwealth Fund, July 2004, http://www

.commonwealthfund.org/programs/minority/cooper_raceconcordance_753. pdf, for a review of literature on the need for racial-ethnic physician-patient concordance. A more recent study highlights, however, that such concordance is part of a matrix of factors needed for successful physician-patient relationships; perceived similarities in values and beliefs along with communication style also strongly influence a patient's perception of a physician. See Richard L. Street Jr. et al., "Understanding Concordance in Patient-Physician Relationships: Personal and Ethnic Dimensions of Shared Identity," *Annals of Family Medicine* 6, no. 3 (2008): 198–205, doi:10.1370/afm.821.

50 However, I note that this study did not have sufficiently granular data to determine the breakdown of Asian American ethnic subgroups.

51 See Ji Hyun Lim, "Doctors, The APA Dream Profession," *AsianWeek Magazine*, October 12, 2001, http://www.asian-nation.org/doctors.shtml.

52 Renae Waneka and Joanne Spetz, *The Diversity of California's Registered Nursing Workforce*, California Board of Registered Nursing, May 2012, http://www .rn.ca.gov/pdfs/schools/diversity.pdf.

53 Yen Le Espiritu, "Gender, Migration, and Work," *Revue Européenne Des Migrations Internationales* 21, no. 1 (2005): 55–75, doi:10.4000/remi.2343.

54 Trinh-Shevrin, Islam, and Rey, *Asian American Communities and Health*, 287.

55 "Cervical Cancer," WomensHealth.gov, accessed June 9, 2014, http://women shealth.gov/minority-health/asian-americans/cervical-cancer.html.

56 "Asian American Populations," Centers for Disease Control and Prevention, last updated July 2, 2013, http://www.cdc.gov/minorityhealth/populations/ REMP/asian.html.

57 "Profile: Asian Americans."

58 *State of Lung Disease in Diverse Communities 2010*, American Lung Association, 2010, http://www.lung.org/assets/documents/publications/lung-disease-data/ solddc_2010.pdf, 103.

59 Trinh-Shevrin, Islam, and Rey, *Asian American Communities and Health*, 188.

60 "HIV and Asian and Pacific Islander Women: Fact Sheet," Banyan Tree Project, n.d., http://www.banyantreeproject.org/extras/factsheets/women_fs_FINAL. pdf.

61 Trinh-Shevrin, Islam, and Rey, *Asian American Communities and Health*, 242.

62 "HIV/AIDS and Asian Americans," U.S. Department of Health and Human Services Office of Minority Health, accessed April 9, 2015, http://minorit yhealth.hhs.gov/omh/browse.aspx?lvl=4&lvlid=51. I could not locate data about whether men who transmitted HIV to their female partners were in fact infected by male partners; however, this possibility warrants further exploration.

63 Trinh-Shevrin, Islam, and Rey, *Asian American Communities and Health*, 414.

64 See "Asian-American Women More Likely to Attempt Suicide," by Michael Martin, NPR.org, September 23, 2009, http://www.npr.org/templates/story/ story.php?storyId=113114107.

65 Laurie Meyers, "Asian-American Mental Health," *Monitor on Psychology* (a publication of the American Psychological Association) 37, no. 2 (2006): 44, http:// www.apa.org/monitor/feb06/health.aspx.

66 Tanzina Vega, "As Parents Age, Asian-Americans Struggle to Obey a Cultural Code," *New York Times*, January 14, 2014, http://www.nytimes.com/2014/01/15/us/as-asian-americans-age-their-children-face-cultural-hurdles.html.

67 A related area of research is the way in which Christian ideas about responding to pain intersect with cultural ones; do various Asian American cultures encourage a stoicity in pain, or even see it as necessary?

68 In 1985, under Secretary Margaret M. Heckler, the U.S. Department of Health and Human Services (DHHS) released the seminal *Report of the Secretary's Task Force on Black and Minority Health*. The report was a public health landmark; not only was it the first time the DHHS conducted a cross-sectional analysis of minority health issues (African Americans, Hispanics, Asian American/Pacific Islanders, and Native Americans), but as a direct result the Office of Minority Health (OMH) was created. It also mobilized Asian American constituencies to organize for increased awareness of Asian American health issues that relied on more disaggregated data. See Trinh-Shevrin, Islam, and Rey, *Asian American Communities and Health*, 424.

69 Here, I am thankful for Emilie M. Townes' work, *Breaking the Fine Rain of Death: African American Health Issues and a Womanist Ethic of Care* (New York: Continuum, 1998). While she focuses on issues that are particularly relevant to the African American community, she does so within the context of communal lament. Such lament is ethical insofar as it names our suffering and gives rise to hope and the possibility of healing for *all*, not just the community in which one is located (24).

70 There is no explicit data on Asian American Christian perspectives on health care; nevertheless, some tentative trends can be extrapolated from polls conducted on political and social perspectives. Recent surveys seem to suggest that Asians Americans are continuing to shift politically liberal. While a majority of Asian Americans are unaffiliated with any religion, the second-largest majority are Christians, almost evenly divided between Catholics (19 percent) and Protestants (22 percent). Among Protestants, 13 percent identify themselves as Evangelical. "Chapter 1: Religious Affiliation," in *Asian Americans: A Mosaic of Faiths* (Washington, D.C.: The Pew Forum on Religion and Public Life, 2012), http://www.pewforum.org/2012/07/19/asian-americans-a-mosaic-of-faiths-religious-affiliation/. While Asian American Protestants do lean politically conservative compared to the overall Asian American population, they favor a larger role for government compared to their white counterparts (51 percent and 29 percent, respectively). At the same time, Asian American Evangelicals hold similar views on same-sex relations and abortions as white Evangelicals, with a majority against both (65 percent and 64 percent, respectively). Napp Nazworth, "Pew Report: Asian-American Evangelicals Less Republican than White Evangelicals," *Christian Post*, July 20, 2012, http://www.christianpost.com/news/pew-report-asian-american-evangelicals-less-republican-than-white-evangelicals-78579/.

71 Ann-Marie Yamada, Karen Kyeunghae Lee, and Min Ah Kim, "Community Mental Health Allies: Referral Behavior among Asian American Immigrant

Christian Clergy," *Community Mental Health Journal* 48, no. 1 (2012): 107–13, doi:10.1007/s10597–011–9386–9.

72 Esther Oh, a psychiatrist at the UCLA Neuropsychiatric Institute, recently launched a research project that ultimately aims to help Korean families to better understand the mental health issues that Korean American youth face. The project's focus is on collecting data from pastors who work with Korean youth, and it hopefully will reveal more clearly the various barriers to mental health treatment as well as raise new possibilities for collaborations between families, pastors, and physicians. Esther Oh, "Dr. Esther Oh on Partnering with Pastors," *KoreAm*, December 10, 2014, http://iamkoream.com/dr-esther-oh-on-partnering-with-pastors/.

73 Farley, *Compassionate Respect*, 42.

74 John Updike, "Seven Stanzas at Easter," in *Telephone Poles and Other Poems* (New York: Random House, 2012).

Chapter 9: Immigration

1 In 2000, 60 percent of new legal immigrants to the United States were Hispanic, while 20 percent were Asians. However, in 2010, 37 percent were Asians while 31 percent were Hispanic. Paul Taylor, ed., *The Rise of Asian Americans: Updated Edition* (Washington, D.C.: Pew Research Center, 2013), http://www.pewsocialtrends.org/2012/06/19/the-rise-of-asian-americans/2/.

2 Jan Lin, "Globalization and the Revalorizing of Ethnic Places in Immigration Gateway Cities," in *Migration, Globalization, and Ethnic Relations: An Interdisciplinary Approach*, ed. Mohsen M. Mobasher and Mahmoud Sadri (Upper Saddle River, N.J.: Pearson Prentice Hall, 2004), 183.

3 One prominent example is the frequent immigration of people from former or current colonies to their colonial powers through historical and cultural connections (e.g., Algerians, Moroccans, and Tunisians to France; Filipinos and Puerto Ricans to the United States).

4 M. Daniel Carroll R., *Christians at the Border: Immigration, the Church, and the Bible* (Grand Rapids: Baker Academic, 2008), 103.

5 Dana Wilbanks, *Re-Creating America: The Ethics of U.S. Immigration and Refugee Policy in a Christian Perspective* (Nashville: Abingdon, 2008), 102.

6 Wilbanks, *Re-Creating America*, 13–14.

7 This trope of the promised land is closely associated with that of covenant in Scripture, which is another example that discloses how the idea of covenant influenced the mindset of early colonists in New England. Conceiving themselves as the New Israel, namely the covenanted people, early colonists depicted "Old Europe" as "Egypt," George Washington as an American "Moses," and Native Americans as Canaanites with a decimating impact on the latter.

8 Cited in Studs Terkel, *American Dreams: Lost and Found* (New York: Pantheon, 1980), 10.

9 Wilbanks says, "Race remains at the heart of the immigration debates even when it is not explicitly mentioned" (*Re-Creating America*, 16).

10 Wilbanks, *Re-Creating America*, 15.

11 The 1943 Magnuson Act repealed the Chinese Exclusion Act, allowing the naturalization of the Chinese already here but only with a small quota (one hundred or so). On June 18, 2012, the United States issued a formal apology about the wrongs done to people of Chinese descent, acknowledging the racist nature of its past legislations. Grace Kao, "Government 'Apologies' for Historical Injustices: Why They Matter," *Dr. Grace Kao* (blog), June 22, 2012, http://www.drgracekao.com/2012/06/22/government-apologies-for-historical-injustices-why-they-matter/.

12 The internment of Japanese Americans during World War II and the scapegoating of Korean Americans in the L.A. Riots of 1992 are such examples.

13 Bryan S. K. Kim et al., "Cultural Value Similarities and Differences among Asian American Ethnic Groups," *Cultural Diversity and Ethnic Minority Psychology* 7, no. 4 (2001): 343–61. These characteristics reflect mostly the cultural traditions of Chinese, Filipino, Indian, Vietnamese, Korean, and Japanese (in the order of population size) who constitute the six largest groups of Asian Americans making up 83 percent of its population (Taylor, *Rise of Asian Americans*).

14 Various researches show that Asian immigrants put high values on marriage, family, parenthood, the wisdom and authority of parents and the elderly, hard work, and career success. According to Pew Research, about 67 percent of Asian Americans surveyed reported that family is "one of the most important things in their lives" compared to the general public, 50 percent of whom said so. Similarly, successful marriage counts as a high priority in their value system, which is reflected in their lower divorce rates and the higher percentage of the children of Asian immigrants who live in households with two married parents. And the parents exercise considerable moral influence on the children in the choice of their professions and spouses. Asian Americans also hold a stronger belief in the rewards of hard work (Taylor, *Rise of Asian Americans*). The Pew research does not distinguish between Asian immigrants and Asian Americans because the foreign born are still by far the dominant group among Asian Americans, constituting about 74 percent of its population.

15 Mark Landler, "S. Korean State Visit Highlights Bond between 2 Leaders," *New York Times*, October 12, 2011, http://www.nytimes.com/2011/10/13/world/asia/south-korean-state-visit-highlights-bond-between-obama-and-lee-myung-bak.html.

16 Christy Chiang-Hom, "Transnational Cultural Practices of Chinese Immigrant Youth and Parachute Kids," in *Asian American Youth: Culture, Identity, and Ethnicity*, ed. Jennifer Lee and Min Zhou, 143–58 (New York: Routledge, 2004).

17 Taylor, *Rise of Asian Americans*. One should be very careful not to make any blanket characterization of the economic success of Asian Americans. Many Southeast Asians and Koreans are financially suffering. In addition, despite their high education achievements, many Asian Americans cannot find positions that are compatible to their achievements; they find difficulty in translating educational achievement into corresponding occupational and financial standings.

18 Michael Hoefer, Nancy Rytina, and Bryan Baker, *Estimates of the Unauthorized Immigrant Population Residing in the United States: January 2011*, Office of Immigration Statistics, March 2012, http://www.dhs.gov/xlibrary/assets/statistics/publications/ois_ill_pe_2011.pdf.

19 "The Facts on Immigration Today," Center for American Progress, October 23, 2014, https://www.americanprogress.org/issues/immigration/report/2014/10/23/59040/the-facts-on-immigration-today-3/.

20 Alejandro Portes and Rubén G. Rumbaut, *Immigrant America: A Portrait*, 3rd ed. (Berkeley: University of California Press, 2006), 63–64.

21 As discussed elsewhere in this volume, the classic myth of the model minority stereotypes Asian Americans as hardworking, highly educated, family-oriented, law-abiding, obedient, economically self-sufficient, and overall successful. This prima facie "compliment" to Asian Americans, of course, comes as an implicit critique to the alleged cultural deficiencies and nonmodel behavior of other racial-ethnic minorities (e.g., African Americans and Latinos/as) as being poor, uneducated, promiscuous, economically dependent, and lawbreaking. The myth not only inaccurately characterizes all Asian Americans as successful (when in fact there is notable heterogeneity within the group) but is also dangerous to Asian Americans for isolating them from other minority groups. Asian Americans thus face double marginalization as model minorities and perpetual foreigners: the former stereotype makes them suspect as white proxies to other racial-ethnic groups, while the latter stereotype does not allow them to be treated equally by whites.

22 Daniel J. Elazar, "Federal Models of (Civil) Authority," *Journal of Church and State* 33, no. 2 (1991): 244.

23 Carroll R., *Christians at the Border*, 104.

24 Not only misunderstanding but also competition for limited resources and deteriorating economic conditions escalate the tensions and conflicts between minority groups, including the African American and Latino relationship, because many feel desperate, frustrated, and fearful that their survival is at stake.

25 Dae Sil Kim's film "Sa-I-Gu," a story of the L.A. Riots, convincingly shows the necessity of coalition building and community relationship among racial minorities to avoid violent conflicts. "Sa I Gu (Official Version)," YouTube video, 41:30, posted by KAFFNYDigital, March 19, 2012, https://www.youtube.com/watch?v=G_UyYj-pR8U.

26 I did not include Native Americans here because my focus is the urban contexts of the United States (e.g., New York, Los Angeles) where the known conflicts and interactions have been between Asian Americans and African Americans and Latinos/as.

27 Edward Chang, "Myths and Realities of Korean-Black American Relations," in *Black-Korean Encounter: Toward Understanding and Alliance: Dialogue between Black and Korean Americans in the Aftermath of the 1992 Los Angeles Riots: A Two-Day Symposium, May 22–23, 1992*, ed. Eui-Young Yu (Los Angeles: AAPAS, California State University, 1994), 86.

28 In comparison, substantial proportions of Latin American and Caribbean immigrants work in agriculture, manufacturing, industry, and construction, thus more directly competing with African Americans and blue-collar whites.

29 Lin, "Globalization," 198.

30 Alex Norman, "Comments from the Panelists (in response to audience questions)," in Yu, *Black-Korean Encounter*, 37.

31 One recent example of this fear is found in Samuel P. Huntington, "The Hispanic Challenge," *Foreign Policy*, October 28, 2009, http://www.foreignpolicy.com/articles/2004/03/01/the_hispanic_challenge.

32 Orlando O. Espín, *Idol and Grace: On Traditioning and Subversive Hope* (Maryknoll, N.Y.: Orbis, 2014), 64.

33 Cf. Carroll R., *Christians at the Border*, 108.

34 See Soong-Chan Rah, *The Next Evangelicalism: Freeing the Church from Western Cultural Captivity* (Downers Grove, Ill.: InterVarsity, 2009), esp. chaps. 3 and 6.

35 Asian Americans' voter turnout rate (47 percent) was considerably lower than that of non-Hispanic whites (64 percent) and African Americans (67 percent) in 2012 (Taylor, *Rise of Asian Americans*).

36 Espín, *Idol and Grace*, 69.

37 Wilbanks, *Re-Creating America*, 121.

38 Frank H. Wu, *Yellow: Race in America beyond Black and White* (New York: Basic Books, 2002), 315.

39 One sees in these practices the operation of the Asian communal tradition; ultimately both parents and children mutually benefit through a short-term financial and emotional sacrifice of the family.

40 Espín, *Idol and Grace*, 86.

41 These tasks can be done more effectively when Asian immigrants nurture English-speaking congregations within their own or work closely with existing Asian American churches in their communities.

Chapter 10: The Environment

1 Grace Yia-Hei Kao, "A Feminist Eulogy? By Grace Yia-Hei Kao," *Feminism and Religion*, November 15, 2013, http://feminismandreligion.com/2013/11/15/a-feminist-eulogy-by-grace-yia-hei-kao/.

2 Kwok Pui-lan, *Postcolonial Imagination and Feminist Theology* (Louisville, Ky.: Westminster John Knox, 2005), 146–49.

3 Lynn White Jr., "The Historical Roots of Our Ecologic Crisis," *Science* 155, no. 3767 (1967): 1203–7. During the Middle Ages, the technological and scientific advancement in Europe coincided with the Medieval view of humanity and nature. European nations spread themselves around the world, "conquering, looting, and colonizing" (1204–5). White maintains that "Christianity . . . not only established a dualism of man and nature but also insisted that it is God's will that man exploit nature for his proper ends" (1205). Based on this historical analysis of Europe during the Middle Ages, he claims "Christianity bears a huge burden of guilt" for "the Christian dogma of man's transcendence of, and rightful mastery over, nature" (1206). As an alternative Christian view, White proposes that Christian tradition should look back to St. Francis of Assisi, who "tried to depose man from his monarchy over creation and set up a democracy of all God's creatures" (1206). See also Christopher Hamlin and David M. Lodge, "Beyond Lynn White: Religion, the Contexts of Ecology, and the Flux of Nature," in *Religion and the New Ecology: Environmental Responsibility in a World in Flux*, ed. Christopher Hamlin and David M. Lodge, 1–25 (Notre Dame, Ind.: University of Notre Dame Press, 2006).

4 John Passmore, *Man's Responsibility for Nature: Ecological Problems and Western Traditions* (New York: Scribner, 1974). Cited in John F. Haught, "Theology and Ecology in an Unfinished Universe," in Hamlin and Lodge, *Religion and the New Ecology*, 227–28.

5 Rosemary Radford Ruether argues that White exaggerates the extent to which Christianity is responsible; Willis Jenkins argues that there should be plural ways of responding to and engaging in environmental issues beyond the scope of the Christian tradition. Ruether, "Ecological Theology: Roots in Tradition, Liturgical and Ethical Practice for Today," in *Dialog: A Journal of Theology* 42, no. 3 (2003): 226–34; and Jenkins, "After Lynn White: Religious Ethics and Environmental Problems," in *Journal of Religious Ethics* 37, no. 2 (2009): 283–309.

6 Hamlin and Lodge, "Beyond Lynn White," in Hamlin and Lodge, *Religion and the New Ecology*, 3–4. Originally from Peter W. Bakken, Joan Gibb Engel, and J. Ronald Engel, *Ecology, Justice, and Christian Faith: A Critical Guide to the Literature* (Westport, Conn.: Greenwood, 1995).

7 Haught, "Theology and Ecology," in Hamlin and Lodge, *Religion and the New Ecology*, 226–45.

8 Haught, "Theology and Ecology," in Hamlin and Lodge, *Religion and the New Ecology*, 229.

9 Elizabeth DeLoughrey and George B. Handley, "Introduction: Toward an Aesthetics of the Earth," in *Postcolonial Ecologies: Literatures of the Environment*, ed. Elizabeth DeLoughrey and George B. Handley (New York: Oxford University Press, 2011), 9–10.

10 Haught, "Theology and Ecology," in Hamlin and Lodge, *Religion and the New Ecology*, 229–31.

11 Haught, "Theology and Ecology," in Hamlin and Lodge, *Religion and the New Ecology*, 233.

12 Haught, "Theology and Ecology," in Hamlin and Lodge, *Religion and the New Ecology*, 233–36.

13 John Hart, *Sacramental Commons: Christian Ecological Ethics* (Lanham, Md.: Rowman & Littlefield, 2006), 17–18, 31, 56, and 120.

14 Haught, "Theology and Ecology," in Hamlin and Lodge, *Religion and the New Ecology*, 237.

15 Haught, "Theology and Ecology," in Hamlin and Lodge, *Religion and the New Ecology*, 243.

16 Willis Jenkins, *Ecologies of Grace: Environmental Ethics and Christian Theology* (Oxford: Oxford University Press, 2008), 1–31.

17 Jürgen Moltmann, *The Source of Life: The Holy Spirit and the Theology of Life*, trans. Margaret Kohl (Minneapolis: Fortress, 1997), 111–24.

18 Sallie McFague, *The Body of God: An Ecological Theology* (Minneapolis: Fortress, 1993), vii, 14–16, 19–20, and 35. McFague recapitulates early Christianity's emphasis upon embodiment expressed in "the incarnation (the Word made flesh) and Christology (Christ was fully human) to the Eucharist (this is my body, this is my blood), the resurrection of the body, and the church (the body of Christ who is its head)" (14). It is through "the bodies of all other life-forms

on the planet" that "each of us is recognized, responded to, loved, touched, and cared for—as well as oppressed, beaten, raped, mutilated, discarded, and killed" (16).

19 Kwok Pui-lan addresses the issue of environmental degradation in her *Postcolonial Imagination*. Chung Hyun Kyung draws from her Korean culture to suggest a Korean ecofeminist identity, "salimist," in *The Letter from the Future: Goddess-spell According to Hyun Kyung* (Seoul: Yolimwon, 2001).

20 McFague, *Body of God*, 38–47.

21 McFague, *Body of God*, 65–97. By critically engaging with Christian creation spirituality, McFague integrates a deep appreciation of all life and urges transformative actions toward a new salvation.

22 McFague, *Body of God*, 99–107. Features of the common creation story include: humans' place in the scheme of things dwindles as God relates to a long evolutionary history of the universe and all other planetary life-forms; it is an ongoing "historical narrative," always changing, living, and evolving in an unfinished and dynamic universe; "the radical interrelatedness and interdependence of all aspects" of the common story is highlighted; there is "the multileveled character of the universe, from the flow of energy in subatomic reality to the incredibly complex set of levels that comprise a human being"; it is a public story, "available to all" (104–7).

23 McFague, *Body of God*, 179–91. Quotations are from pp. 188–89.

24 McFague, *Body of God*, 199–201.

25 McFague, *Body of God*, 204.

26 Grace Y. Kao, "Exploring the Korean First Birthday Celebration as a Site for Comparative Religious Ethics and Chinese Thought," in *Religious Ethics in a Time of Globalism: Shaping a Third Wave of Comparative Analysis*, ed. Elizabeth M. Bucar and Aaron Stalnaker (New York: Palgrave Macmillan, 2012), 152.

27 Sangamithra Iyer, "Tasty Worship at Flushing Temple," *Open City*, June 11, 2012, http://opencitymag.com/tasty-worship/.

28 Vandana Shiva, "War against Nature and the People of the South," in *Views from the South: The Effects of Globalization and the WTO on Third World Countries*, ed. Sarah Anderson (Oakland, Calif.: Food First; Chicago: International Forum on Globalization, 2000), 93; Jeffrey M. Humphreys, *The Multicultural Economy 2013*, University of Georgia Terry College of Business Selig Center for Economic Growth, http://www.latinocollaborative.com/wp-content/uploads/2013/10/Multicultural-Economy-2013-SELIG-Center.pdf; The Nielsen Company, *State of Asian American Consumer: Growing market, growing impact*, Quarter 3, 2012, http://www.nielsen.com/content/dam/corporate/us/en/reports-down loads/2012-Reports/State-of-the-Asian-American-Consumer-Report.pdf; and *Overconsumption? Our Use of the World's Natural Resources*, Friends of the Earth Europe, Global 2000, and Sustainable Europe Research Institute, September 2009, http://www.foe.co.uk/sites/default/files/downloads/overcon sumption.pdf. Despite the tendency of making an internal distinction between the first generation and the second and following generations, as well as among different Asian ethnic groups, "Asian" in the above research refers to persons with origins in all parts of Asia. Regardless of their diverse racial/ethnic origins,

Asians in the United States are often categorized as a singular group, especially for the purpose of analyzing their consumption patterns in the consumer market. An average North American consumes about 90 kilograms of natural resources daily, compared to an average Asian consumption of 14 kilograms of natural resources per day. Despite this reality of an overconsuming North American culture, Asian Americans cannot be simply excused from their own overconsumption.

29 Shiva, "War against Nature," in Anderson, *Views from the South*, 93–95.

30 "Shark Finning PSA by Ang Lee for WildAid," YouTube video, 1:42, posted by benthiccanada, October 25, 2007, http://www.youtube.com/watch?v=fkxoRPv4ugE; Te-Ping Chen, "Off the Menu: Hong Kong Government Bans Shark's Fin," *Wall Street Journal*, September 16, 2013, http://blogs.wsj.com/chinarealtime/2013/09/16/off-the-menu-hong-kong-government-bans-sharks-fin/; Russell McClendon, "China Bans Shark-Fin Soup at State Banquets," *Huffington Post*, last updated January 25, 2014, http://www.huffingtonpost.com/2013/12/16/china-shark-fin-soup_n_4452897.html; and "Losing the Taste for Shark Fins: Our Campaign to Save a Mighty Animal," Humane Society of the United States, May 1, 2013, http://www.humanesociety.org/issues/shark_finning/timelines/shark_fins.html.

31 Kwok, *Postcolonial Imagination*, 145.

32 Kwok, *Postcolonial Imagination*, 144–49.

33 Chung, *Letter from the Future*, 236.

34 Chung, *Letter from the Future*, 236–40.

35 McFague, *Body of God*, 5 and 106. McFague includes other aspects of the earth on which humans are heavily dependent, such as "clean air and water."

36 McFague, *Body of God*, 20. McFague integrates transcendence and immanence as well as spirit and body by arguing that God's transcendence is not "external to or apart from" the universe, but "the source, power, and goal—the spirit—that enlivens (and loves) the entire process and its material forms." For her the transcendence of God is the spirit of the universe, while all of us in the universe are "inspirited bodies" of God whose images reflect the divine image. Evidenced in McFague's focus on embodiment is a trait of white feminist ethicists', namely Sara Ruddick's and Alison M. Jaggar's binary integrations of justice and care by deconstructing a hierarchical binary between reason and emotion, mind and body, as well as the abstract and the concrete. Likewise, McFague underlines the equal importance of the physical, the body, and immanence to the metaphysical, mind, and transcendence in her organic model of the universe. Although her focus on the embodiment of transcendence in an immanent way is drawn from early Christianity's focus on embodiment, her emphasis upon the significance of the body echoes that of contemporary secular feminists both in its strengths and limitations.

37 Jane Bennett, *Vibrant Matter: A Political Ecology of Things* (Durham, N.C.: Duke University Press, 2010), 2–18, and 111–19. There is another way of avoiding this anthropocentric scope by invoking political theorist Jane Bennett's concept of "thing-power." In *Vibrant Matter* Bennett highlights "the vitality of materiality" in her discussion of "thing-power" and recapitulates some of these terms used to

describe a source of actions: Baruch Spinoza's "conatus" as "active impulsion" or tendency to persist; Bruno Latour's "actant" for a source of action; Theodor Adorno's "nonidentity" for "a presence that acts upon us;" and vital materialists' "materiality" evenly applicable to "humans and non-humans." While her move beyond the narrow anthropocentric scope on nonhuman bodies was successful in challenging the current pattern that "assigns activity to people and passivity to things," her adoption of "actant" was nonetheless intended to underline the active role or "generativity" of "things."

Bennett thus modifies the concept of agency and broadens its narrow anthropocentric scope to include vibrant nonhuman matters by highlighting the agential capacity that others have to make an impact on human life on ontological grounds before they enter into human *episteme*. I would press a little further than Bennett in arguing that agential capacity also exists beyond human and others' *episteme*, thus rendering humans more vulnerable than those who do not possess epistemological and moral agency. Thus, I suggest that the nonhuman existents have greater agential—organic, biological, physiological, and life-giving—capacities that existentially sustain our shared planetary life beyond and outside human moral agency, making us ontologically more vulnerable to those who do not own the same epistemological and moral agential capacity as we humans do.

Both Bennett and I emphasize the ontological or existential importance of nonhuman materials or existents, respectively. Yet we differ in that Bennett develops her political ecology of things by breaking down what I would later call "an existent" into smaller vibrant matters to highlight "the common materiality of all that is" and the functional roles these materials play, whereas I construct my Asian American environmental ethic by emphasizing the importance of existence of the wholeness of each in constituting our indebted life together.

38 McFague, *Body of God*, 105–8.

39 Tu Weiming, "The Ecological Turn in New Confucian Humanism: Implications for China and the World," in *Daedalus* 130, no. 4 (2001): 243–64, part of an issue entitled "Religion and Ecology: Can the Climate Change?" Acknowledging a recent movement toward "a retrieval and reappropriation of Confucian ideas" for environmental ethics, Tu proposes "an anthropocosmic worldview," reflecting the Confucian idea of "the 'unity of Heaven and Humanity' . . . that embraces Earth" (243–44).

40 Herbert Fingarette, *Confucius: The Secular as Sacred* (Long Grove, Ill.: Waveland, 1998), 16–17 and 73–74. Although Confucius' metaphor inscribes human relationship both in Confucius' use and in Fingarette's interpretation, I would like to expand this organic relationship among human persons to that of all existents in the universe.

41 Although Confucius' metaphor of the holy rite is directed to human relationship, I would like to expand this organic relationship among human persons to that of all existents in the universe.

42 Hannah Ka, "Respectful Grace and Graceful Respect: A Korean Feminist Ethic" (Ph.D. diss., Claremont Graduate University, 2011), 157–64; and Fingarette, *Confucius*, 73–74.

43 Ilsup Ahn, "Economy of 'Invisible Debt' and Ethics of 'Radical Hospitality':
Toward a Paradigm Change of Hospitality from 'Gift' to 'Forgiveness,' " in *Journal of Religious Ethics* 38, no. 2 (2010): 243–67. Despite a different origination
in, development of, and context to which the term indebtedness is applied, I
want to recognize Asian American Christian ethicist Ilsup Ahn's use of indebtedness. Ahn employs the term indebtedness in conjunction with forgiveness
in his Christian ethics of radical hospitality to address the immigration issue.
Distinguishing his notion of Christian radical hospitality from other forms of
"soft hospitality," which is based on a reciprocal or equal exchange of gifts, he
states, "a Christian theology of radical hospitality should transcend law, duty,
and debt" (258). By engaging in a discussion with Jacques Derrida and Friedrich
Nietzsche, as well as in a theological reflection on biblical texts, Ahn highlights the importance of "the creditors' intentional remembrance of their own
indebtedness" to the original Creditor, God, for radical hospitality in human
relationships (259) in order not to reduce God's forgiveness "to a form of gift
in the economy of debt" (260). He further elaborates this sense of indebtedness
by turning to the story in Matt 18:23-35 where "the original debtor's remembrance of his own being forgiven is critically connected with his duty to forgive
his sub-debtor" without reducing it to the economy of debt (260). The outcome
of this sense of indebtedness appears in embracing "the otherness of strangers" by reducing the creditors' or the host citizens' "political, economic, and
cultural privileges" (261–62). Although Ahn applies this indebtedness rather
unilaterally when he positions the hosting citizens as creditors while "refugees,
strangers, and migrants" are considered to be "indebted others," his implication of indebtedness bears a resemblance to my notion of indebtedness for two
reasons. Indebtedness is used outside the conventional financial context, and the
indebtedness is viewed as "a source of grace" (264). Despite the differences, this
shared use of the term indebtedness still exemplifies the import of this sense of
indebtedness for Asian and Asian Americans; Ka, "Respectful Grace," 92 and
102–21. Drawing from my experience in a Korean American immigrant Christian community, I present a notion of indebtedness in my doctoral dissertation
in order to capture the unequal support endlessly being provided to indefinite
others in a variety of ways at different times within the life of a particular
immigrant community. Their contribution or support, with few exceptions,
was neither unilateral nor reciprocal between the giver and the recipient, but
multidimensional and multidirectional among the unspecified recipient/givers
in a flux of time, instigating a deep sense of indebtedness (*shin-sae*: 신세: 身
世: entrusting one's body to the world) to each other within the community.
This sense of indebtedness can be paraphrased as "grateful and thankful feelings" in a positive sense (114). This notion of indebtedness is, then, expanded
beyond the financial terms of "debtor" and "creditor" to capture my intended
meaning of the Korean notion that describes "various ways of being indebted
to each other within our community" (114). For the purpose of formulating an
Asian American Christian environmental ethic, I expand the application of this
notion beyond its original conception to include all forms of life on this planet
Earth.

44 Ka, "Respectful Grace," 113–15 and 237–44.

45 Ka, "Respectful Grace," 115, 126, and 134.

46 Anthony Weston, *The Incompleat Eco-Philosopher: Essays from the Edges of Environmental Ethics* (Albany: State University of New York Press, 2009), 89–107.

47 McFague, *Body of God*, 106.

48 Laozi, *Tao Te Ching: A New English Version*, ed. Stephen Mitchell (New York: Harper & Row, 1988), 1 and 41; and Edward Slingerland, "Effortless Action: The Chinese Spiritual Ideal of *Wu-wei*," *Journal of the American Academy of Religion* 68, no. 2 (2000): 293–328. Among various contextual and philosophical interpretations of the Chinese concept of *wu-wei*, my adaptation of *wu-wei* (literally meaning "in the absence of/without doing," commonly translated as "nonaction" or "nondoing") is close to Laozi's Taoist concept. See chapter 37 in *Tao Te Ching*.

49 McFague, *Body of God*, 5, 106–9, and 128–29. McFague's ecological theology is geared toward an action-oriented Christian environmental ethic energized by her partiality toward justice and care. Even though McFague and I have similar understandings about human dependency on other forms of life, she takes it in another direction by claiming that ecological issues are "a people issue" and "a justice issue" (5). Finding theological and biblical grounds for human responsibility to care for the earth, she sanctions an anthropocentric action-oriented ethics. Her advocacy for just, liberating, healing, and caring actions, once again, echoes white feminists' integration of justice and care that relies heavily on the actions of moral agents who are endowed with more capability and are able to assume heavier responsibility than the objective and receptive beneficiary of these actions. Recall that both McFague and I admitted that humans are more vulnerable and dependent upon others. In her Christian environmental ethics derived from her ecological theology, however, it is indeed humans who take the initiative in active roles as clearly reflected in her use of action verbs: liberate, heal, and care (106–9 and 128–29). The vocabulary she chooses when speaking of human responsibility in her ecological theology signals active human capacities.

50 Ahn, "Economy of Invisible Debt," 258, 260, and 264. Although used in a different context, Ahn's call for a Christian theology of radical hospitality highlights the notion of "the invisible debt" in humans' sacred relationship to God. Although the applied context of his argument is the immigration crisis, I hope to expand his radical hospitality to include all existents situated in horizontal indebted relationships among themselves. Then one may be able to apply this deep sense of indebtedness as "a source of grace."

51 "An Inquiry on the Great Learning," in *A Source Book in Chinese Philosophy*, trans. and comp. by Wing-Tsit Chan (Princeton, N.J.: Princeton University Press, 1963), 659–60.

52 Laozi, *Tao Te Ching*, 42.

53 Laozi, *Tao Te Ching*, 42–43.

Chapter 11: Education and Labor

1 T. M. Moore, "Some Observations Concerning the Educational Philosophy of John Calvin," *Westminster Theological Journal* 46, no. 1 (1984): 140–55.

2 Pope Paul VI, *Declaration on Christian Education: Gravissimum Educationis*, October 28, 1968, para. 2, http://www.vatican.va/archive/hist_councils/ii_vatican_council/documents/vat-ii_decl_19651028_gravissimum-educationis_en.html.

3 "Fast Facts: Public School Choice Programs," U.S. Department of Education, accessed February 19, 2014, https://nces.ed.gov/fastfacts/display.asp?id=6.

4 *Epperson v. Arkansas*, 393 U.S. 97 (1968).

5 Amy Gutmann, "Education," in *A Companion to Applied Ethics*, ed. R. G. Frey and Christopher Heath Wellman (Malden, Mass.: Blackwell, 2005), 499.

6 Gutmann, "Education," in Frey and Wellman, *Companion to Applied Ethics*, 498.

7 Pope Paul VI, *Gravissimum Educationis*, para. 1.

8 United States Conference of Catholic Bishops, "Catholic Education," http://www.usccb.org/beliefs-and-teachings/how-we-teach/catholic-education/, accessed March 20, 2015.

9 Pope Leo XIII, *Rerum Novarum: Encyclical of Pope Leo XIII on Capital and Labor*, May 15, 1891, para. 3, http://www.vatican.va/holy_father/leo_xiii/encyclicals/documents/hf_l-xiii_enc_15051891_rerum-novarum_en.html.

10 Pope Leo XIII, *Rerum Novarum*, para. 41.

11 Max Weber, *The Protestant Ethic and the Spirit of Capitalism*, trans. Talcott Parsons (Tacoma, Wash.: Angelico Press), 2014.

12 "Social Creed of the Churches 1908," United Church of Christ, http://www.ucc.org/justice/social-creed-of-the-churches.html.

13 "A Social Creed for the 21st Century," National Council of Churches, http://nationalcouncilofchurches.us/common-witness/2007/social-creed.php, accessed March 20, 2015.

14 Cathleen Falsani, "The Worst Ideas of the Decade: The Prosperity Gospel," *Washington Post*, n.d., http://www.washingtonpost.com/wp-srv/special/opinions/outlook/worst-ideas/prosperity-gospel.html.

15 Paul Taylor, ed., *The Rise of Asian Americans: Updated Edition* (Washington, D.C.: Pew Research Center, 2013), http://www.pewsocialtrends.org/2012/06/19/the-rise-of-asian-americans/.

16 Taylor, *Rise of Asian Americans*.

17 Taylor, *Rise of Asian Americans*.

18 Taylor, *Rise of Asian Americans*.

19 Amy Chua, *Battle Hymn of the Tiger Mother* (New York: Penguin, 2011).

20 National Education Association, *Beyond Black and White: API Students and School Desegregation* (Washington, D.C.: National Education Association, 2008).

21 Lydia Lum, "Report: Asian American Academic Achievement in California Lags Heavily within Certain Subgroups," *Diverse: Issues in Higher Education*, December 30, 2010, http://diverseeducation.com/article/14485/.

22 Taylor, *Rise of Asian Americans*.

23 "Critical Issues Facing Asian Americans and Pacific Islanders," White House Initiative on Asian Americans and Pacific Islanders, accessed February 5, 2014, http://www.whitehouse.gov/administration/eop/aapi/data/critical-issues.

24 "The Asian-American Labor Force in the Recovery," Department of Labor, July 22, 2011, http://www.dol.gov/_sec/media/reports/asianlaborforce/.

25 "Asian-American Labor Force," Department of Labor.

26 Marcus T. Smith, "Fact Sheet: The State of Asian American Women in the United States," Center for American Progress, November 7, 2013, http://www.americanprogress.org/issues/race/report/2013/11/07/79182/fact-sheet-the-state-of-asian-american-women-in-the-united-states/.

27 Smith, "Fact Sheet."

28 Hye Jin Rho et al., *Diversity and Change: Asian American and Pacific Islander Workers* (Washington, D.C.: Center for Economic and Policy Research, 2011).

29 "Asian-American Labor Force," Department of Labor.

30 Mary Dorinda Allard, "Asians in the U.S. Labor Force: Profile of a Diverse Population," *Monthly Labor Review* 134, no. 11 (2011).

31 Hao Li, "Asian Americans Increasingly Defying the STEM Stereotype," *International Business Times*, August 6, 2010, http://www.ibtimes.com/asian-americans-increasingly-defying-stem-stereotype-246578.

32 Allard, "Asians in the U.S. Labor Force," 22.

33 Laws dealing with immigration and education (most recently, *Schuette v. BAMN* 572 U.S. Ct., No. 12–682, April 22, 2014) come to mind.

34 Susan Berfield, "Forever 21's Fast (and Loose) Fashion Empire," *Bloomberg Businessweek*, January 20, 2011, http://www.businessweek.com/magazine/content/11_05/b4213090559511.htm; and "U.S. Labor Department Seeks Enforcement of Subpoena Issued to Forever 21: Recent Investigation Reveals Evidence of Wage Violations among Forever 21 Apparel Contractors and Manufacturer," United States Department of Labor, October 25, 2012, http://www.dol.gov/opa/media/press/whd/WHD20121989.htm.

35 Rita Nakashima Brock et al., *Off the Menu: Asian and Asian North American Women's Religion and Theology* (Louisville, Ky.: Westminster John Knox, 2007), xx.

36 Peter C. Phan, *Christianity with an Asian Face: Asian American Theology in the Making* (Maryknoll, N.Y.: Orbis, 2003), 245.

37 Phan, *Christianity with an Asian Face*, 245.

38 Phan, *Christianity with an Asian Face*, 247.

39 Phan, *Christianity with an Asian Face*, 247.

40 Phan, *Christianity with an Asian Face*, 247.

41 Anselm Kyongsuk Min, "From Autobiography to Fellowship of Others: Reflections on Doing Ethnic Theology Today," in *Journeys at the Margin: Toward an Autobiographical Theology in American-Asian Perspective*, ed. Peter C. Phan and Jung Young Lee, 135–59 (Collegeville, Minn.: Liturgical, 1999), 155.

42 Min, "From Autobiography to Fellowship," in Phan and Lee, *Journeys at the Margin*, 155.

43 Min, "From Autobiography to Fellowship," in Phan and Lee, *Journeys at the Margin*, 155.

Chapter 12: Cosmetic Surgery

1 In writing this essay, I have been greatly served by comments and suggestions from Grace Yia-Hei Kao, Ilsup Ahn, and Brandon Morgan.

2 Plastic Surgery Institute, description of "Valentine Mouth Rejuvenation," http://www.ceydeli.com/face-procedures-panama-city/valentine-mouth -rejuvenation.

3 Jeyup S. Kwaak, "Surgeons in Korea Defend 'Smile Surgery,'" *Wall Street Journal*, August 27, 2013, http://blogs.wsj.com/scene/2013/08/27/surgeons-in -korea-defend-smile-surgery/.

4 "Daily Chart: A Cut Above," *Economist Online*, April 23, 2012, http://www .economist.com/blogs/graphicdetail/2012/04/daily-chart-13.

5 On this point, see Carl Elliott, "Pursued by Happiness and Beaten Senseless: Prozac and the American Dream," *Hastings Center Report* 30, no. 2 (2000): 3–12. Also see his larger treatment of these issues in Elliott, *Better than Well: American Medicine Meets the American Dream* (New York: W. W. Norton, 2004).

6 Jeyup S. Kwaak, "Surgeons Defend 'Smile Surgery,'" *Wall Street Journal*, August 27, 2013, http://blogs.wsj.com/korearealtime/2013/08/27/surgeons -defend-smile-surgery/.

7 For a troubling video of these images, see "Candidates of Miss Korean in One Gif," http://imgur.com/0MMzzLQ.

8 Steve Nolan, "Has Plastic Surgery Made These Beauty Queens All Look the Same? Koreans Complain about Pageant 'Clones,'" *Daily Mail*, April 25, 2013, http:// www.dailymail.co.uk/news/article-2314647/Has-plastic-surgery-20-Korean -beauty-pageant-contestants-look-Pictures-contest-hopefuls-goes-viral.html.

9 Anthony Youn, "Asia's Ideal Beauty: Looking Caucasian," CNN.com, last updated June 26, 2013, http://www.cnn.com/2013/06/25/health/asian -beauty/. Youn begins his article with a troubling story of a mother bringing her teenage daughter, Jane, in for cosmetic surgery. He concludes with the fol- lowing comments, which we might call the rudimentary considerations with which a Christian plastic surgeon should assess these issues: "a string of events caused me to reconsider whether I should continue to perform these opera- tions. Are these surgeries really the right thing for patients? For society? First, I encountered Jane and her mother. Then, I received a request from a mom to perform an Asian eyelid surgery on her son. 'He really wants the surgery done,' the mother said. 'He wants to look handsome.' Then I found out her son was only 8. And I had a daughter. The most beautiful girl I've ever seen—perfect in every way. She looks just like her mother, except for one feature that she's inherited from her daddy. She has no fold of her upper eyelids. And I hope she never feels the need to change that." See also Youn's book *In Stitches: A Memoir* (New York: Gallery, 2011).

10 Eugenia Kaw, "Medicalization of Racial Features: Asian American Women and Cosmetic Surgery," *Medical Anthropology Quarterly* 7, no. 1 (1993): 74–89; see also Kaw quoted in Alicia Ouellette, "Eyes Wide Open: Surgery to Westernize the Eyes of the Asian Child," *The Hastings Center Report* 39, no. 1 (2009): 17. Thanks to Grace Yia-Hei Kao for directing me to these texts.

11 Eugenia Kaw, "Opening Faces: The Politics of Cosmetic Surgery and Asian American Women," in *In Our Own Words: Readings on the Psychology of Women and Gender*, ed. Mary Crawford and Rhoda Kesler Unger, 55–73 (New York:

McGraw-Hill, 1997), 56. In this article Kaw expands on her earlier work in "Medicalization of Racial Features."

12 Kaw, "Medicalization of Racial Features," 75.

13 Kaw, "Medicalization of Racial Features," 75.

14 Michelle Man, "Cosmetic and Plastic Surgery," Asian-Nation.org, http://www .asian-nation.org/cosmetic-surgery.shtml; and American Society of Plastic Surgeons, *2012 Plastic Surgery Statistics Report* (2013), http://www.plasticsurgery .org/Documents/news-resources/statistics/2012-Plastic-Surgery-Statistics/ full-plastic-surgery-statistics-report.pdf.

15 American Society of Plastic Surgeons, *2012 Plastic Surgery Statistics*.

16 American Society of Plastic Surgeons, *2012 Plastic Surgery Statistics*.

17 Andrew Lam, "Body Language," *The Nation*, March 30, 2007, http://www .thenation.com/article/body-language.

18 Calum MacLeod, "Medical Tourists Flock to Seoul for Cosmetic Surgery," *USA Today*, last updated December 27, 2011, http://usatoday30.usatoday.com/ news/world/story/2011–12–26/south-korea-plastic-surgery/52236372/1.

19 See also Joanne L. Rondilla, "Racial Features and Cosmetic Surgery," in *Encyclopedia of Asian American Issues Today*, ed. Edith Wen-Chu Chen and Grace J. Yoo, 451–55 (Columbus: Gracewood, 2009), 454.

20 See Haruka Sakaguchi, "Cosmetic Surgery: An Asian American Perspective," *Verily*, October 25, 2013, http://verilymag.com/cosmetic-surgery-an-asian-american -perspective/; and Jennifer Kung, "Mochi Survey: Attitudes toward Asian American Cosmetic Surgery," *Mochi*, Winter 2010, http://www.mochimag .com/article/mochi-survey-attitudes-toward-asian-american-cosmetic-surgery.

21 Deborah Netburn, " 'Gangnam Style' Sets World Record: Gallops to 1 Billion Video Views," *Los Angeles Times*, December 21, 2012, http://articles.latimes .com/2012/dec/21/business/la-fi-tn-gangnam-style-one-billion-20121221.

22 Sarah Bon, "Billion Dollar Industry to Be: Plastic Surgery in South Korea," TheRichest.com, January 16, 2014, http://www.therichest.com/expensive -lifestyle/billion-dollar-industry-to-be-plastic-surgery-in-south-korea/; and MacLeod, "Medical Tourists."

23 Zara Stone, "The K-Pop Plastic Surgery Obsession," *Atlantic*, May 24, 2013, http:// www.theatlantic.com/health/archive/2013/05/the-k-pop-plastic-surgery -obsession/276215/. Also see Heesu Lee, "Gangnam-Style Nip and Tuck Draws Tourists to Seoul's Beauty Belt," Bloomberg.com, September 29, 2013, http://www.bloomberg.com/news/articles/2013-09-29/gangnam-style -nip-and-tuck-draws-tourists-to-seoul-s-beauty-belt; and Kanga Kong, "Chinese Overtake Americans as Top Medical Tourists in Korea," *Wall Street Journal*, February 19, 2014, http://blogs.wsj.com/korearealtime/2014/02/19/chinese -overtake-americans-as-top-medical-tourists-in-korea/.

24 "Cosmetic/Plastic Surgery Is Driving South Korea's Emergence as a Top Medical Tourism Destination," MyMEDHoliday.com, June 12, 2013, http://www .mymedholiday.com/blog/2013/06/345/cosmeticplastic-surgery-is-driving -south-koreas-emergence-as-a-top-medical-tourism-destination/.

25 Heesu Lee, "Perfecting the Face-Lift, Gangnam Style," Bloomberg.com, October 10, 2013, http://www.businessweek.com/articles/2013-10-10/

plastic-surgery-lifts-south-korean-tourism; and Kong, "Chinese Overtake Americans."

26 Lee, "Perfecting the Face-Lift."

27 E.g., "31 Crazy Before and After Photos of Korean Plastic Surgery," BuzzFeed.com, April 4, 2013, http://www.buzzfeed.com/kierawrr/31-crazy-before-and-after -photos-of-korean-plastic-4gx1. Mathew Crawford directed me to this post.

28 Sakaguchi, "Cosmetic Surgery." Regarding Julie Chen, see Allison Takeda, "Julie Chen Reveals She Got Plastic Surgery to Look Less Chinese: See the Before and After Pictures," Us Weekly, September 12, 2013, http://www .usmagazine.com/celebrity-news/news/julie-chen-reveals-she-got-plastic -surgery-to-look-less-chinese-see-the-before-and-after-pictures-2013129.

29 Consider Gena Corea's likening artificial reproductive technologies to the cattle industry and prostitution, an argument that has the unfortunate effect of liken- ing women to cows and prostitutes. Corea, The Mother Machine: Reproductive Technologies from Artificial Insemination to Artificial Wombs (New York: Harper & Row, 1985).

30 Consider "Why Are Asians Obsessed with Fairness? The 'Snow-White Complex' vs Tanorexia," The Jade Lotus (blog), December 4, 2011, http://thejadelotusbeauty .blogspot.com/2011/12/why-are-asians-obsessed-with-fairness.html.

31 Stone, "K-Pop Plastic Surgery."

32 Kaw, "Opening Faces," in Crawford and Unger, In Our Own Words, 70.

33 Gerald P. McKenny, To Relieve the Human Condition: Bioethics, Technology, and the Body (Albany: State University of New York Press, 1997), 7–38.

34 Here I have in mind Christian appropriations of Alasdair MacIntyre's tradition- alism and the Christian restatement of Christendom in John Milbank's Theology and Social Theory: Beyond Secular Reason (Oxford: Blackwell, 1992).

35 Kaw, "Medicalization of Racial Features," 81.

36 See Anne Fadiman's now-classic text on the authority of modern medical cul- ture. Fadiman, The Spirit Catches You and You Fall Down: A Hmong Child, Her American Doctors, and the Collision of Two Cultures (New York: Farrar, Straus, & Giroux, 1997).

37 On bioethics and autonomy, see Catriona MacKenzie, "Conceptions of Auton- omy and Conceptions of the Body in Bioethics," in Feminist Bioethics: At the Center, on the Margins, ed. Jackie Leach Scully, Laurel E. Baldwin-Ragaven, and Petya Fitzpatrick, 71–90 (Baltimore: Johns Hopkins University Press, 2010).

38 On this point, see Stanley Hauerwas, "Rational Suicide and Reasons for Liv- ing," in Suffering Presence: Theological Reflections on Medicine, the Mentally Handi- capped, and the Church (Notre Dame: University of Notre Dame Press, 1986), 100–113.

39 On the deficiencies of much contemporary moral reasoning, see Cora Dia- mond, The Realistic Spirit: Wittgenstein, Philosophy, and the Mind (Cambridge: MIT Press), 309–82; and Diamond, "The Importance of Being Human," in Human Beings, ed. David Cockburn, 32–62 (Cambridge: Cambridge University Press, 1991).

40 See Judith Jarvis Thomson's seminal articulation of these matters in her splendidly argued "A Defense of Abortion," in *Bioethics*, ed. John Harris, 25–41 (Oxford: Oxford University Press, 2001).

41 Nancy Press, "Genetic Testing and Screening," in *From Birth to Death and Bench to Clinic: The Hastings Center Bioethics Briefing Book for Journalists, Policymakers, and Campaigns*, ed. Mary Crowley, 73–78 (Garrison, N.Y.: The Hastings Center, 2008), http://www.thehastingscenter.org/Publications/BriefingBook/Detail.aspx?id=2176. For possible positive uses, see Hessel Bouma III, "The Search for Shalom," in *On Moral Medicine: Theological Perspectives in Medical Ethics*, ed. Stephen E. Lammers and Allen Verhey, 2nd ed., 569–75 (Grand Rapids: Eerdmans, 1998).

42 For a powerful story about parents who choose not to abort and the ways that choice carries racial freight, see Mitchell Zuckoff, *Choosing Naia: A Family's Journey* (New York: Beacon, 2003). Zuckoff's work puts in bold relief the point here regarding the complexity of abortion as both a theological and political issue.

43 Julian Savulescu, "Genetic Selection to Determine How Our Children Look, Think and Act Isn't Recklessly Playing God. It's a Gift to Future Generations," *Reader's Digest*, August 2012.

44 Savulescu, "Genetic Selection."

45 I am of course rehearsing Wittgenstein's caricature of skeptical argument. See §246 of Ludwig Wittgenstein, *Philosophical Investigations*, trans. G. E. M. Anscombe, P. M. S. Hacker, and Joachim Schulte, rev. 4th ed. (Oxford: Wiley-Blackwell, 2009).

46 One might consider what Giorgio Agamben calls the double exclusion and double capture of late modern culture in *Homo Sacer: Sovereign Power and Bare Life* (Stanford: Stanford University Press, 1999), 82. Nathaniel Lee helped me make this connection.

47 Toni Morrison, *The Bluest Eye: A Novel* (New York: Holt, Rinehart, and Winston, 1970). On the politics of racial color, see Matthew Frye Jacobson, *Whiteness of a Different Color: European Immigrants and the Alchemy of Race* (Cambridge, Mass.: Harvard University Press, 1999); and Patricia Hill Collins, *Black Sexual Politics: African Americans, Gender, and the New Racism* (New York: Routledge, 2005).

48 Anne Anlin Cheng, *The Melancholy of Race: Psychoanalysis, Assimilation, and Hidden Grief* (New York: Oxford University Press, 2001). Cheng draws specifically from Judith Butler, *Bodies That Matter: On the Discursive Limits of "Sex"* (New York: Routledge, 1993), 12–13, but I find Butler most helpful on these issues when she theorizes Hegel's pragmatism over against Kant's transcendental critique in "Restaging the Universal: Hegemony and the Limits of Formalism," in *Contingency, Hegemony, Universality: Contemporary Dialogues on the Left*, ed. Judith Butler, Ernesto Leclau, and Slavoj Žižek, 11–43 (New York: Verso, 2000). Also see Butler, *Subjects of Desire: Hegelian Reflections in Twentieth-Century France* (New York: Columbia University Press, 1987), along with her classic *Gender Trouble: Feminism and the Subversion of Identity* (New York: Routledge, 1990).

49 The conception is itself agnostic as to whether selfhood can be gained in non-circumscribed ways or if the pretension is itself confined to the mythical freedom Foucault parodies as the "repressive hypothesis" in the first volume of his sex series. Michel Foucault, *The History of Sexuality: Volume 1: An Introduction* (New York: Vintage, 2012), 15–50. Regarding female agency within traditioned social contexts, see Saba Mamood, *Politics of Piety: The Islamic Revival and the Feminine Subject* (Princeton, N.J.: Princeton University Press, 2005).

50 Cheng, *Melancholy of Race*, 59. Cheng references Kaja Silverman's *The Threshold of the Visible World* (New York: Routledge, 1996), and one might also visit Silverman's *Flesh of My Flesh* (Stanford: Stanford University Press, 2009). Natalie Carnes directed me to Silverman's *Flesh of My Flesh*.

51 Stanley Cavell, *The Claim of Reason: Wittgenstein, Skepticism, Morality, and Tragedy* (Oxford: Oxford University Press, 1999), 23. Emphasis original.

52 Stanley Cavell, *Must We Mean What We Say? A Book of Essays* (Cambridge: Cambridge University Press, 1976), 25.

53 For an account of what this "with me" might look like, consider Wendell Berry, *Sex, Economy, Freedom, and Community: Eight Essays* (New York: Pantheon, 1994); Sarah Coakley, *Powers and Submissions: Spirituality, Philosophy, and Gender* (Oxford: Blackwell, 2012); and Coakley, *God, Sexuality, and the Self: An Essay "On the Trinity"* (Cambridge: Cambridge University Press, 2013).

54 One can point to any number of Pauline texts, but specifically I have in mind 2 Cor 5, Gal 3, and all those passages wherein St. Paul presents the church in terms of what John Howard Yoder would later describe as "The Politics of Jesus." Yoder, *The Politics of Jesus: Vicit Agnus Noster* (Grand Rapids: Eerdmans, 1994).

55 Amy Laura Hall begins *Conceiving Parenthood* with this troubling scenario. In the following, I try to reimagine it. Hall, *Conceiving Parenthood: American Protestantism and the Spirit of Reproduction* (Grand Rapids: Eerdmans, 2007), 6.

56 Walter Brueggemann and William Bellinger make the case that much of Psalms takes place in a juridical context where accusations fly against those associated with YHWH. The seeming departure from the "inspiring" affirmations of self—the "I" in the I-Thou language that dominates Ps 139 according to Brueggemann and Bellinger—in verses 1-18 to the petitions against enemies in verses 19-24 should be read together: those who make accusations against God's people insult the way God has created them. Walter Brueggemann and William H. Bellinger Jr., *Psalms: New Cambridge Bible Commentary* (Cambridge: Cambridge University Press, 2014), 580–84.

List of Contributors

Ilsup Ahn: Carl I. Lindberg Professor of Philosophy, North Park University (Ph.D.: University of Chicago)

A first-generation Korean American and ordained elder in the United Methodist Church, Ahn's scholarly interests include religion and politics, migration studies, environmental ethics, Asian American studies, and contemporary social theories. He is the author of two books, *Position and Responsibility* (2009) and *Religious Ethics and Migration* (2013). The founder and original convener of the Asian and Asian American Working Group of the Society of Christian Ethics, he is currently serving on the International Scholarly Relations Committee at the Society of Christian Ethics and the steering committee for Religion and Migration Group at the American Academy of Religion.

Christina A. Astorga: Professor, University of Portland (Ph.D.: Loyola School of Theology)

A Catholic laywoman and first-generation immigrant from the Philippines, Astorga was the former chairperson of the Theology Department of the Ateneo de Manila University and founding director of the Center for the Study of Catholic Social Thought of Duquesne University. She is currently Professor and Chair of the Theology Department of the University of Portland. Her research interests are in the areas of fundamental moral theology, social ethics, and feminist ethics, with particular reference to Asian/Filipino social issues. She is the author of two books: *Catholic Moral Theology and Social Ethics: A New Method* (2013), which won the College Theology Society 2014 Book of the Year award, and *The Beast, the Harlot, and the Lamb: Faith Confronts Systemic Evil* (2000), which won the National Book Award in the Philippines.

Hoon Choi: Assistant Professor, Bellarmine University (Ph.D.: Loyola University Chicago)

Hoon Choi is a 1.5-generation Korean American and Roman Catholic who served for three years as the director of Religious Education at the 103 Korean Martyr's Roman Catholic Church in Chicago. His previous military service in the Korean army and embodied life as a racial-ethnic minority in the United States is reflected in Choi's scholarly interests in (de)constructing norms of masculinities and the state of Korean and Korean American Christianity. He has presented his work on these and other topics at the Society of Christian Ethics and the American Academy of Religion and is working on a book on Roman Catholic masculinities.

Ki Joo (KC) Choi: Associate Professor, Seton Hall University (Ph.D.: Boston College)

A first-generation Korean American who immigrated to the United States at the age of four and is denominationally unaffiliated, Choi's research and teaching areas are in ecumenical ethics (Catholic and Reformed), war and peace, evolutionary studies and ethics, aesthetics, and the political morality of race and ethnicity. He is the coeditor of an undergraduate reader in the Catholic intellectual tradition entitled *Christianity and Culture* (2010). He is a faculty administrator in Seton Hall's Department of the University Core, currently serves as interim chair of the Department of Religion, and is a past member of the Editorial Board of the *Journal of the Society of Christian Ethics*. He is currently working on a monograph exploring the moral relevance of racial identity from an Asian American perspective.

Hannah Ka: Assistant Pastor of Discipleship, Korean United Methodist Church of San Diego (Ph.D.: Claremont Graduate University)

A first-generation Korean American and active member of Pacific, Asian, and North American Asian Women in Theology and Ministry (PANAAWTM), Ka's recently defended dissertation constructs a Korean feminist notion of the self as "an indebted entity" in multiple indebted relationships by highlighting how one is both existentially and functionally indebted to others. Her current research focuses on expanding the extent of indebted relations to include both human and nature—both living and nonliving—existents.

Grace Y. Kao: Associate Professor and Co-Director of the Center for Sexuality, Gender, and Religion, Claremont School of Theology (Ph.D.: Harvard University)

A second-generation Taiwanese American and evangelical-Presbyterian (PCUSA) church-hopper, Kao's research and teaching interests include rights (human and nonhuman animal), ecofeminism, and Asian American Christianity. She serves on the Board of Directors of the Society of Christian Ethics (SCE), the Board of Advisors for the Pacific, Asian, and North American Asian Women in Theology and Ministry (PANAAWTM), the Editorial Board of the Journal of Race, Ethnicity, and Religion (JRER), and the steering committees for the Animals and Religion Group and the Women of Color Scholarship, Teaching, and Activism Group at the American Academy of Religion (AAR). She is the author of *Grounding Human Rights in a Pluralist World* (2011) and is working on a second book that applies restorative justice principles to several cases of injustice against Asian Americans for which the U.S. government has apologized. She holds the honor of being the first Asian American woman to have earned tenure at her institution.

SueJeanne Koh: Affiliate Faculty, Loyola University Maryland (Th.D. candidate in Theology and Ethics, Duke Divinity School)

SueJeanne Koh is a second-generation Korean American Presbyterian (PCUSA) who worked as a nonprofit editor and grant writer before finding her passion for theological studies. As a Forum for Theological Exploration (FTE) Dissertation Fellow, she explores in her dissertation the relationship between the ethics of self-sacrifice and generational memory, particularly as it intersects with Asian American experiences. She is the theological ethics editor of *Syndicate*, an online journal. Her other research interests include systematic theologies, feminist and womanist thought, and intersections between secularism and Christianity.

Hak Joon Lee: Professor, Fuller Theological Seminary (Ph.D.: Princeton Theological Seminary)

Lee is a first-generation Korean American and an ordained Minister of Word and Sacrament in the Presbyterian Church (U.S.A.) whose current research interests include covenant, Trinitarian ethics, public theology in the global era, and the ethics and spirituality of Dr. Martin Luther King Jr. He is the author of three books in English (*Covenant and Communication: A Christian Moral Conversation with Jürgen Habermas* [2006], *We Will Get to the Promised Land: Martin Luther King Jr.'s Communal-Political Spirituality* [2006], *The Great World House: Martin Luther King Jr. and Global Ethics* [2011]) and two books in Korean (*A Paradigm Shift in Korean Churches* [2011] and *Bridge Builders* [2007]). In 2007 Lee founded G2G Christian Education Center, a research institute on Asian American Christianity and culture and published the first systematic curriculum for Korean American youth entitled *Identity: A Curriculum for Korean American Christian Youth.*

Irene Oh: Associate Professor and Director of Peace Studies, The George Washington University (Ph.D.: University of Virginia)

A fourth-generation Korean American, child of Presbyterian and Buddhist parents, and scholar of religion, Oh specializes in comparative ethics. She has served on the Board of Directors of the Society of Christian Ethics, cofounded the Society for the Study of Muslim Ethics, cochaired the Comparative Religious Ethics Group for the American Academy of Religion, and currently sits on the editorial board of the *Journal of Religious Ethics.* The author of *The Rights of God: Islam, Human Rights, and Comparative Ethics* (2007), she is working on a second book about the ethics of motherhood while parenting her own "hapa" (half-Asian, half-white) children.

Keun-Joo Christine Pae: Associate Professor, Denison University (Ph.D.: Union Theological Seminary in the City of New York)

The first Korean female national to be ordained an Episcopal priest, Pae has research interests in feminist peacemaking and interfaith spiritual activism, transnationalized militarism with focus on the intersection between gender and race, transnational feminist ethics, and Asian/Asian American perspectives on postcolonial racial relations. She serves on the steering committee of the Pacific, Asian, and North American Asian Women in

Theology and Ministry (PANAAWTM) and is completing her first book, *Sex and War: A Christian Feminist Ethic of War and Peace.*

Sharon M. Tan: McVay Professor of Christian Ethics and Vice President for Academic Affairs/Dean of the Seminary, United Theological Seminary of the Twin Cities (Ph.D. and J.D.: Emory University)

A first-generation Malaysian Chinese American whose Christian identity has been shaped by Pentecostal, Episcopalian, and Presbyterian traditions, Tan has researched and taught on the work of justice, reconciliation, virtue ethics, and the interrelationship between religion and politics. She is the author of *The Reconciliation of Classes and Races: How Religion Contributes to Politics and Law* (2009) and is completing a book on moral agency among Asian Americans.

Jonathan Tran: Associate Professor, Baylor University (Ph.D.: Duke University)

Tran immigrated, at an early age, to America at the end of the Vietnam War and became, in his late teens, a Christian through a Chinese Baptist church. He is the author of *Foucault and Theology* (2011), *The Vietnam War and Theologies of Memory: Time, Eternity, and Redemption in the Far Country* (2010), and the coeditor, with Myles Werntz, of *Corners in the City of God: "The Wire" and Theology* (2013). He also serves on the Board of Directors of the Society of Christian Ethics and the Editorial Board of the Encounter Traditions series of Stanford University Press. He serves as Faculty Master of Baylor's Honors Residential College.

Scripture Index

Author Index

Subject Index